CCSP Self-Study

CCSP Cisco Secure PIX Firewall Advanced Exam Certification Guide

Cisco Press

Cisco Press
201 West 103rd Street
Indianapolis, IN 46290 USA

CCSP Self-Study

CCSP Cisco Secure PIX Firewall Advanced Exam Certification Guide

Greg Bastien, Christian Degu

Copyright© 2003 Cisco Systems, Inc.

Published by:
Cisco Press
201 West 103rd Street
Indianapolis, IN 46290 USA

Printed in the United States of America 1 2 3 4 5 6 7 8 9 0

First Printing March 2003

Library of Congress Cataloging-in-Publication Number: 2002107269

ISBN: 1-58720-067-8

Warning and Disclaimer

This book is designed to provide information about the Cisco Secure PIX Firewall Advanced Exam (CSPFA 9E0-111 and 642-521) for the Cisco Certified Security Professional. Every effort has been made to make this book as complete and accurate as possible, but no warranty or fitness is implied.

The information is provided on an "as is" basis. The authors, Cisco Press, and Cisco Systems, Inc. shall have neither liability nor responsibility to any person or entity with respect to any loss or damages arising from the information contained in this book or from the use of the discs or programs that may accompany it.

The opinions expressed in this book belong to the authors and are not necessarily those of Cisco Systems, Inc.

Feedback Information

At Cisco Press, our goal is to create in-depth technical books of the highest quality and value. Each book is crafted with care and precision, undergoing rigorous development that involves the unique expertise of members of the professional technical community.

Reader feedback is a natural continuation of this process. If you have any comments regarding how we could improve the quality of this book, or otherwise alter it to better suit your needs, you can contact us through e-mail at feedback@ciscopress.com. Please be sure to include the book title and ISBN in your message.

We greatly appreciate your assistance.

Publisher	John Wait
Editor-In-Chief	John Kane
Cisco Representative	Anthony Wolfenden
Cisco Press Program Manager	Sonia Torres Chavez
Cisco Marketing Communications Manager	Scott Miller
Cisco Marketing Program Manager	Edie Quiroz
Executive Editor	Brett Bartow
Acquisitions Editor	Michelle Grandin
Production Manager	Patrick Kanouse
Senior Development Editor	Christopher Cleveland
Project Editor	Marc Fowler
Copy Editor	Gayle Johnson
Technical Editors	Will Aranha
	Mesfin Goshu
	Jonathan Limbo
	Gilles Piché
CD Content	Jonathan Limbo
Team Coordinator	Tammi Ross
Book Designer	Gina Rexrode
Cover Designer	Louisa Adair
Compositor	Mark Shirar
Indexer	Larry Sweazy

CISCO SYSTEMS

Corporate Headquarters
Cisco Systems, Inc.
170 West Tasman Drive
San Jose, CA 95134-1706
USA
http://www.cisco.com
Tel: 408 526-4000
      800 553-NETS (6387)
Fax: 408 526-4100

European Headquarters
Cisco Systems Europe
11 Rue Camille Desmoulins
92782 Issy-les-Moulineaux
Cedex 9
France
http://www-europe.cisco.com
Tel: 33 1 58 04 60 00
Fax: 33 1 58 04 61 00

Americas Headquarters
Cisco Systems, Inc.
170 West Tasman Drive
San Jose, CA 95134-1706
USA
http://www.cisco.com
Tel: 408 526-7660
Fax: 408 527-0883

Asia Pacific Headquarters
Cisco Systems Australia,
Pty., Ltd
Level 17, 99 Walker Street
North Sydney
NSW 2059 Australia
http://www.cisco.com
Tel: +61 2 8448 7100
Fax: +61 2 9957 4350

Cisco Systems has more than 200 offices in the following countries. Addresses, phone numbers, and fax numbers are listed on the Cisco Web site at www.cisco.com/go/offices

Argentina • Australia • Austria • Belgium • Brazil • Bulgaria • Canada • Chile • China • Colombia • Costa Rica • Croatia • Czech Republic • Denmark • Dubai, UAE • Finland • France • Germany • Greece • Hong Kong Hungary • India • Indonesia • Ireland • Israel • Italy • Japan • Korea • Luxembourg • Malaysia • Mexico The Netherlands • New Zealand • Norway • Peru • Philippines • Poland • Portugal • Puerto Rico • Romania Russia • Saudi Arabia • Scotland • Singapore • Slovakia • Slovenia • South Africa • Spain • Sweden Switzerland • Taiwan • Thailand • Turkey • Ukraine • United Kingdom • United States • Venezuela • Vietnam Zimbabwe

Trademark Acknowledgments

All terms mentioned in this book that are known to be trademarks or service marks have been appropriately capitalized. Cisco Press or Cisco Systems, Inc. cannot attest to the accuracy of this information. Use of a term in this book should not be regarded as affecting the validity of any trademark or service mark.

About the Authors

Greg Bastien, CCNP, CCSP, CISSP, currently works as a senior network security engineer for True North Solutions, Inc. as a consultant to the U.S. Department of State. He is an adjunct professor at Strayer University, teaching networking and network security classes. He completed his undergraduate and graduate degrees at Embry-Riddle Aeronautical University while on active duty as a helicopter flight instructor in the U.S. Army. He lives with his wife, two sons, and two dogs in Monrovia, Maryland.

Christian Degu, CCNP, CCDP, CCSP, currently works as a consulting engineer to the Federal Energy Regulatory Commission. He is an adjunct professor at Strayer University, teaching computer information systems classes. He has a master's degree in computer information systems. He resides in Alexandria, Virginia.

About the Technical Reviewers

Will Aranha is currently a principal security engineer with Symantec Corp. His primary job is as a technical product manager, which includes determining new product support, baselining, and providing technical training to the security engineering staff. Aranha is well-versed in many information security products and practices. Along with numerous firewall/VPN and IDS deployments, both domestic and international, he provides third-tier technical support to a 24/7 Security Operations Center, serving as a subject matter expert for all Managed Services supported products. Aranha has also contributed to the growth and success of the start-up company Riptech, Inc., which was acquired by Symantec Corp. It is now the premier security solutions provider in the market. In his free time, he has completed many industry-leading security certifications.

Mesfin Goshu, CCIE No. 8350, is a system engineer for Metrocall Wireless Inc., the second-biggest wireless company in the U.S. He is responsible for designing, maintaining, troubleshooting, and securing Metrocall's backbone. He has been with Metrocall for almost six years. He has an extensive background in OSPF, BGP, MPLS, and network security. He has a BSc in computer and information science and civil engineering. He currently is working toward an MSc in telecommunications. As a senior network engineer, he has worked for INS and the Pentagon as a contractor. He has been in the networking field for more than nine years.

Jonathan Limbo, CCIE Security No. 10508, is currently working as a Security and VPN support engineer acting as escalation for PIX issues as well as for other security and VPN products. Jonathan has worked in the IT industry for 5 years, most of which as a Network Engineer.

Gilles Piché is a security consultant who has been working in the Network Security field in Canada for over 6 years. Prior to that, he did contract work with the Canadian government in a network engineering capacity. Gilles is also a Cisco Certified Security Instructor and has been teaching Cisco Security courses for Global Knowledge Network (Canada) for the last 2 years.

Dedications

To Ingrid, Joshua, and Lukas. Thank you for putting up with me while I was locked in the office.—Greg

To my father, Aberra Degu, and my mother, Tifsehit Hailegiorgise. Thank you for inspiring me and loving me as you have. To my brother, Petros, and sisters, Hiwote and Lula, I love you guys. —Christian

Acknowledgments

Writing this book has been a difficult and time-consuming yet extremely rewarding project. Many have contributed in some form or fashion to the publishing of this book. We would especially like to thank the Cisco Press team, including Michelle Grandin, Acquisitions Editor, and Christopher Cleveland, Senior Development Editor, for their guidance and encouragement throughout the entire writing process. We would also like to thank the technical reviewers, who had to endure our draft manuscripts and who helped us remain on track throughout the process.

Contents at a Glance

Contents

Icons Used in This Book

Throughout this book, you will see the following icons used for networking devices:

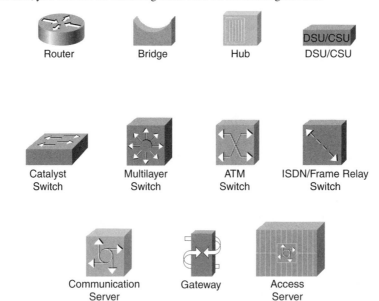

The following icons are used for peripherals and other devices:

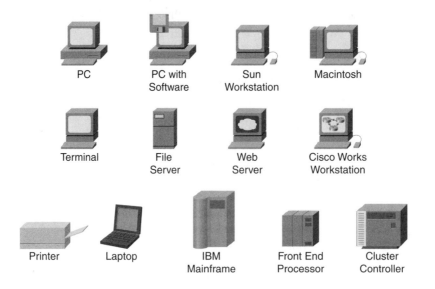

The following icons are used for networks and network connections:

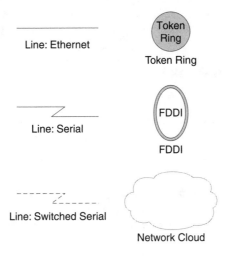

Introduction

The primary goal of this book is to help you prepare to pass either the 9E0-111 or 642-521 Cisco Secure PIX Firewall Advanced (CSPFA) exams as you strive to attain the CCSP certification, or a focused PIX certification.

Who Should Read This Book?

Network security is a very complex business. The Cisco PIX Firewall performs some very specific functions as part of the security process. It is very important to be familiar with many networking and network security concepts before you undertake the CSPFA certification. This book is designed for security professionals or networking professionals who are interested in beginning the security certification process.

How to Use This Book

This book consists of 15 chapters. Each one builds on the preceding chapter. The chapters that cover specific commands and configurations include case studies or practice configurations. Appendix B includes an additional "master" case study that combines many different topics. It also has a section with configuration examples that might or might not work. It is up to you to determine if the configurations fulfill the requirements and why.

The chapters cover the following topics:

- **Chapter 1, "Network Security"**—This chapter provides an overview of network security—the process and potential threats. It also discusses how network security has become increasingly important to businesses as companies continue to become more intertwined and their network perimeters continue to fade. Chapter 1 discusses the network security policy and two Cisco programs that can help companies design and implement sound security policies, processes, and architecture.

- **Chapter 2, "Firewall Technologies and the Cisco PIX Firewall"**—This chapter covers the different firewall technologies and the Cisco PIX Firewall. It examines the design of the PIX Firewall and discusses some of that design's security advantages.

- **Chapter 3, "The Cisco Secure PIX Firewall"**—Chapter 3 deals with the design of the Cisco PIX Firewall in greater detail. It lists the different PIX models and their intended applications and discusses the various features available with each model and how each model should be implemented.

- **Chapter 4, "System Maintenance"**—Chapter 4 discusses the installation and configuration of the Cisco PIX Firewall OS. It covers the different configuration options that allow for remote management of the PIX.

- **Chapter 5, "Understanding Cisco PIX Firewall Translation and Connections"**—This chapter covers the different transport protocols and how the PIX Firewall handles them. It also discusses network addressing and how the PIX can alter node or network addresses to secure those elements.

- **Chapter 6, "Getting Started with the Cisco PIX Firewall"**—This is where we really begin to get to the "meat" of the PIX. This chapter covers the basic commands required to make the PIX operational. It discusses the methods of connecting to the PIX Firewall and some of the many configuration options available with the PIX.

- **Chapter 7, "Configuring Access"**—This chapter covers the different configurations that allow you to control access to your network(s) using the PIX Firewall. It also covers some of the specific configurations required to allow certain protocols to pass through the firewall.

- **Chapter 8, "Syslog"**—Chapter 8 covers the PIX Firewall's logging functions and the configuration required to allow the PIX Firewall to log in to a syslog server.

- **Chapter 9, "Cisco PIX Firewall Failover"**—This chapter discusses the advantages of a redundant firewall configuration and the steps required to configure two PIX firewalls in failover mode.

- **Chapter 10, "Virtual Private Networks"**—Many businesses have multiple locations that need to be interconnected. Chapter 10 explains the different types of secure connections of virtual private networks that can be configured between the PIX Firewall and other VPN endpoints. It covers the technologies and protocols used to create and maintain VPNs across public networks.

- **Chapter 11, "PIX Device Manager"**—The Cisco PIX Firewall can be managed using a variety of tools. Chapter 11 discusses the PIX Device Manager, a web-based graphical user interface (GUI) that can be used to manage the PIX.

- **Chapter 12, "Content Filtering with the Cisco PIX Firewall"**—It is a common practice for hackers to embed attacks into the content of a web page. Certain types of program code are especially conducive to this type of attack due to their interactive nature. This chapter discusses these types of code and identifies their dangers. It also covers the different PIX configurations for filtering potentially malicious traffic passing through the firewall.

- **Chapter 13, "Overview of AAA and the Cisco PIX Firewall"**—It is extremely important to ensure that only authorized users access your network. Chapter 13 discusses the different methods of configuring the PIX Firewall to interact with authentication, authorization, and accounting (AAA) services. This chapter also introduces the Cisco Secure Access Control Server (CSACS), which is Cisco's AAA server package.

- **Chapter 14, "Configuration of AAA on the Cisco PIX Firewall"**—This chapter discusses the specific configuration on the PIX Firewall for communication with the AAA server, including the CSACS. It covers the implementation, functionality, and troubleshooting of AAA on the PIX Firewall.

- **Chapter 15, "Attack Guards and Multimedia Support"**—Many different attacks can be launched against a network and its perimeter security devices. This chapter explains some of the most common attacks and how the PIX Firewall can be configured to repel them.

Each chapter follows the same format and incorporates the following features to assist you by assessing your current knowledge and emphasizing specific areas of interest within the chapter:

- **"Do I Know This Already?" Quiz**—Each chapter begins with a quiz to help you assess your current knowledge of the subject. The quiz is broken into specific areas of emphasis that allow you to determine where to focus your efforts when working through the chapter.

- **Foundation Topics**—This is the core section of each chapter. It focuses on the specific protocol, concept, or skills you must master to successfully prepare for the examination.

- **Foundation Summary**—Near the end of each chapter, the foundation topics are summarized into important highlights from the chapter. In many cases, the foundation summaries include tables, but in some cases the important portions of each chapter are simply restated to emphasize their importance within the subject matter. Remember that the foundation portions are in the book to assist you with your exam preparation. It is very unlikely that you will be able to successfully complete the certification exam by just studying the foundation topics and foundation summaries, although they are a good tool for last-minute preparation just before taking the exam.

- **Q&A**—Each chapter ends with a series of review questions to test your understanding of the material covered. These questions are a great way to ensure that you not only understand the material but also exercise your ability to recall facts.

- **Case Studies/Scenarios**—The chapters that deal more with configuring the Cisco PIX Firewall have brief scenarios. These scenarios help you understand the different configuration options and how each component can affect another component within the firewall configuration. Two case studies near the end of the book allow you to practice configuring the firewall to perform specific functions. There is also a section that includes configurations that might or might not work. You are asked to determine if the configuration will work correctly, and why or why not. Because the certification exam asks specific questions about configuring the Cisco PIX Firewall, it is very important to become intimately familiar with the different commands and components of the PIX configuration.

- **CD-based practice exam**—On the CD included with this book, you'll find a practice test with more than 200 questions that cover the information central to the CSPFA exam. With our customizable testing engine, you can take a sample exam, either focusing on particular topic areas or randomizing the questions. Each test question includes a link that points to a related section in an electronic PDF copy of the book, also included on the CD.

The Certification Exam and This Preparation Guide

The questions for each certification exam are a closely guarded secret. But even if you obtained the questions and passed the exam, you would be in for quite an embarrassment as soon as you arrived at your first job that required PIX skills. The point is to *know* the material, not just to successfully pass the exam. We know what topics you must understand to pass the exam. Coincidentally, these are the same topics required for you to be proficient with the PIX Firewall. We have broken these into "foundation topics" and cover them throughout this book. Table I-1 describes each foundation topic.

Table I-1 *CSPFA Foundation Topics*

Reference Number	Exam Topic	Description
1	Firewalls	Firewalls process network traffic in three different ways. Chapter 2 discusses these technologies and their advantages.
2	PIX Firewall overview	Chapter 2 explains the PIX Firewall's design and its advantages compared to other firewall products.
3	PIX Firewall models	Currently, the PIX Firewall has six different models. Chapter 3 discusses each model, its specifications, and how and when it is applied.
4	PIX Firewall licensing	Chapter 3 discusses the different licensing options available for the PIX Firewall and how each license applies.
5	User interface	The CLI is one of the methods used to configure the PIX Firewall. Chapter 6 covers the CLI and many of the commands used to configure the firewall.
6	Configuring the PIX Firewall	Many different commands are used to configure the PIX Firewall. These commands are discussed in Chapters 6 through 15.
7	Examining the PIX Firewall status	Verifying the configuration of the PIX Firewall helps you troubleshoot connectivity issues.

Table I-1 *CSPFA Foundation Topics (Continued)*

Reference Number	Exam Topic	Description
8	Time setting and NTP support	It is important to ensure that your firewall time is synchronized with your network. Chapter 6 covers the commands for configuring time on the PIX Firewall.
9	ASA security levels	The Adaptive Security Algorithm is a key component of the PIX Firewall. It is discussed in great detail in Chapters 2, 3, 5, and 6.
10	Basic PIX Firewall configuration	The basic configuration of the PIX Firewall is discussed in Chapter 6.
11	Syslog configuration	The logging features of the PIX Firewall are covered in Chapter 8.
12	Routing configuration	Because the firewall operates at multiple layers of the OSI model, it can route traffic as well as filter it. The route commands for the PIX Firewall are discussed in Chapter 6.
13	DHCP server configuration	The PIX Firewall can function as both a DHCP server and a DHCP client. These configurations are covered in Chapters 3 and 6.
14	Transport Protocols	The transport layer protocols and how they are handled by the PIX Firewall are discussed in Chapter 5.
15	Network Address Translation	Network Address Translation is used by many different firewalls to secure network segments. This is discussed in Chapters 5 and 6.
16	Port Address Translations	Port Address Translation is a method used by the PIX Firewall to NAT multiple internal sources to a single external address. This configuration is covered in Chapters 5 and 6.
17	Configuring DNS support	As a perimeter device, the PIX Firewall must support the Domain Name Service. Configuring DNS on the PIX is discussed in Chapter 5.
18	ACLs	Access control lists are used to allow or deny traffic between different network segments that attach via the PIX Firewall. Configuring ACLs is discussed in Chapter 7.
19	Using ACLs	Configuring ACLs is discussed in Chapter 7.
20	URL filtering	The PIX Firewall can be configured to work with other products to perform URL content filtering. This is done to ensure that users use company assets in accordance with company policies. Configuring the PIX for content filtering is discussed in Chapter 12.
21	Overview of object grouping	Service, host, and network objects can be grouped to make processing by the firewall more efficient. Object grouping is discussed in Chapter 7.
22	Getting started with group objects	Object grouping is discussed in Chapter 7.
23	Configuring group objects	Object grouping is discussed in Chapter 7.

Table I-1   *CSPFA Foundation Topics (Continued)*

Reference Number	Exam Topic	Description
24	Nested object groups	Object groups can be nested into other object groups. Object grouping is discussed in Chapter 7.
25	Advanced protocols	Many advanced protocols require special handling by the firewall. Some protocols require multiple inbound and outbound connections. The handling of advanced protocols by the PIX Firewall is discussed in Chapter 7.
26	Multimedia support	Multimedia protocols are considered advanced protocols. The handling of advanced protocols by the PIX Firewall is discussed in Chapter 7.
27	Attack guards	The PIX Firewall can be configured to recognize an attack and react to it. This is covered in Chapter 15.
28	Intrusion detection	The PIX Firewall can be configured to perform as an Intrusion Detection System as well as a firewall. It also can be configured to work with external IDSs. These issues are covered in Chapter 15.
29	Overview of AAA	AAA is a method of ensuring that you can verify who is accessing your network resources, restrict their access to specific resources, and keep track of what actions they take on the network. Configuring the PIX Firewall to support AAA is discussed in Chapters 13 and 14.
30	Installation of CSACS for Windows NT/2000	CSACS is a Cisco AAA server product. Installing and configuring CSACS is covered in Chapter 13.
31	Authentication configuration	Configuring CSACS is discussed in Chapters 13 and 14.
32	Downloadable ACLs	Configuring CSACS is discussed in Chapters 13 and 14.
33	Understanding failover	Mission-critical systems require high-availability solutions to minimize any chance of network outages. Two PIX firewalls can be configured as a high-availability solution. This configuration is covered in Chapter 9.
34	Failover configuration	PIX failover configuration is discussed in Chapter 9.
35	LAN-based failover configuration	PIX failover configuration is discussed in Chapter 9.
36	PIX Firewall enables a secure VPN	Dedicated circuits between different locations can be cost-prohibitive. It is much less expensive and just as secure to create an encrypted connection between those locations across public network space. Configuring virtual private networks is discussed in Chapter 10.
37	IPSec configuration tasks	Configuring virtual private networks is discussed in Chapter 10.
38	Prepare to configure VPN support	Both ends of a virtual private network must have a termination point. The PIX Firewall can be configured as a VPN termination point. Configuring virtual private networks is discussed in Chapter 10.

Table I-1 *CSPFA Foundation Topics (Continued)*

Reference Number	Exam Topic	Description
39	Configure IKE parameters	IKE is a key exchange method used to ensure that the encrypted connection is not easily compromised.
		Configuring virtual private networks is discussed in Chapter 10.
40	Configure IPSec parameters	IP Security (IPSec) is a standard for creating an encrypted VPN connection. Configuring virtual private networks is discussed in Chapter 10.
41	Test and verify VPN configuration	Configuration and troubleshooting of Virtual Private Networks is discussed in Chapter 10.
42	Cisco VPN Client	Remote users can create a VPN from their computers to the company network using VPN client software. Configuring virtual private networks and VPN client software is discussed in Chapter 10.
43	Scale PIX Firewall VPNs	Configuring virtual private networks is discussed in Chapter 10.
44	PPPoE and the PIX Firewall	PPPoE is used to connect multiple hosts via a single dialup or broadband connection. Some PIX Firewall models support PPPoE. This topic is covered in Chapter 10.
45	Remote access	The PIX Firewall can be managed either locally or remotely. Configuring the PIX to allow remote access is discussed in Chapter 4.
46	Command-level authorization	Remote management of the PIX Firewall is discussed in Chapter 4.
47	PDM overview	The PIX Device Manager (PDM) is a web-enabled tool for remote management of the PIX Firewall. Remote management of the PIX using the PDM is discussed in Chapter 11.
48	PDM operating requirements	The PIX Device Manager (PDM) is a web-enabled tool for remote management of the PIX Firewall. Remote management of the PIX using the PDM is discussed in Chapter 11.
49	Prepare for PDM	The PIX Device Manager (PDM) is a web-enabled tool for remote management of the PIX Firewall. Remote management of the PIX using the PDM is discussed in Chapter 11.
50	Using PDM to configure the PIX Firewall	The PIX Device Manager (PDM) is a web-enabled tool for remote management of the PIX Firewall. Remote management of the PIX using the PDM is discussed in Chapter 11.
51	Using PDM to create a site-to-site VPN	The PIX Device Manager (PDM) is a web-enabled tool for remote management of the PIX Firewall. Remote management of the PIX using the PDM is discussed in Chapter 11.
52	Using PDM to create a remote access VPN	The PIX Device Manager (PDM) is a web-enabled tool for remote management of the PIX Firewall. Remote management of the PIX using the PDM is discussed in Chapter 11.

Overview of the Cisco Certification Process

The network security market is currently in a position where the demand for qualified engineers vastly exceeds the supply. For this reason, many engineers consider migrating from routing/networking to network security. Remember that *network security* is simply *security* applied to *networks*. This sounds like an obvious concept, but it is a very important one if you are pursuing your security certification. You must be very familiar with networking *before* you can begin applying security concepts. All CCSP candidates must first pass the Cisco Certified Networking Associate (CCNA) exam. The skills required to complete the CCNA give you a solid foundation that you can expand into the Network Security field.

Table 1-2 contains a list of the exams in the CCSP certification series. Because all exam information is managed by Cisco Systems and is therefore subject to change, candidates should continually monitor the Cisco Systems site for course and exam updates at www.cisco.com/go/training.

Table I-2   *CCSP Certification Exams*

Exam Number	Exam Name	Comments on Upcoming Exam Changes
640-100	MCNS 3.0, Managing Cisco Network Security	In Summer 2003, a new exam, SECUR 642-501, will become available. This exam will eventually replace the 640-100 exam. If recertification candidates pass this exam, they will be considered recertified at the CCNA or CCDA level.
9E0-111	CSPFA 3.0, Cisco Secure PIX Firewall Advanced Exam	By Summer 2003, a new exam will be available to certification candidates taking the PIX exam: 642-521. Note that the renumbering signifies that those passing this exam will be considered recertified at the CCNA or CCDA level. There are no significant changes between the 9E0-111 exam and the 642-521 exam.
9E0-100	CSIDS 3.0, Cisco Secure Intrusion Detection Systems	There are no anticipated changes to this exam as of the time that this book was printed. Be sure to refer to the Cisco Systems website for current information regarding exam numbers and content.
9E0-121	CSVPN 3.0, Cisco Secure Virtual Private Networks	By Summer 2003, a new exam will be available to certification candidates taking the VPN exam: 642-511. Note that the renumbering signifies that those passing this exam will be considered recertified at the CCNA or CCDA level. There are no significant changes between the 9E0-121 exam and the 642-511 exam.
9E0-131	CSI 1.0, Cisco SAFE Implementation	There are no anticipated changes to this exam as of the time that this book was printed. Be sure to refer to the Cisco Systems website for current information regarding exam numbers and content.

Taking the CSPFA Certification Exam

As with any Cisco certification exam, it is best to be thoroughly prepared before taking the exam. There is no way to determine exactly what questions are on the exam, so the best way to prepare is to have a good working knowledge of all subjects covered on the exam. Schedule yourself for the exam, and be sure to be rested and ready to focus before taking the exam.

The best place to find the latest available Cisco training and certifications is www.cisco.com/go/training.

Tracking CCSP Status

You can track your certification progress by checking the Certification Tracking System at https://www.certmanager.net/~cisco_s/login.html. You must create an account, using information found on your score report, the first time you log on to this site. Exam results take up to 10 days to be updated.

How to Prepare for the Exam

The best way to prepare for any certification exam is to use a combination of the preparation resources, labs, and practice tests. This book integrates some practice questions and labs to help you better prepare. If possible, you should get some hands-on time with the Cisco PIX Firewall. There is no substitute for experience, and it is much easier to understand the commands and concepts when you can actually see the PIX in action. If you do not have access to a PIX, a variety of simulation packages are available for a reasonable price. Last, but certainly not least, Cisco.com provides a wealth of information about the PIX and all the products it interacts with. No single source can adequately prepare you for the CSPFA exam unless you already have extensive experience with Cisco products and a background in networking or netowrk security. At a minimum, you will want to use this book combined with www.cisco.com/public/support/tac/home.shtml to prepare for the exam.

Assessing Your Exam Readiness

After completing a number of certification exams, I have found that you don't really know if you're adequately prepared for the exam until you have completed about 30% of the questions. At this point, if you aren't prepared, it's too late. First, always be sure that you are preparing for the correct exam. This book helps you assess your readiness for either of the following two CSPFA exams: 9E0-111 and 642-521. The best way to determine your readiness is to work through the "Do I Know This Already?" quizzes, the Q&A questions at the end of each chapter, and the case studies and scenarios. It is best to work your way through the entire book unless you can complete each subject without having to do any research or look up any answers.

Cisco Security Specialists in the Real World

Cisco has one of the most recognized names on the Internet. You cannot go into a data center or server room without seeing some Cisco equipment. Cisco certified security specialists can bring quite a bit of knowledge to the table due to their deep understanding of the relationship between networking and network security. This is why the Cisco certification carries such clout. Cisco certifications demonstrate to potential employers and contract holders a certain professionalism and the dedication required to complete a goal. Face it: If these certifications were easy to acquire, everyone would have them.

PIX and Cisco IOS Software Commands

A firewall or router is not normally something you fiddle with. After you have it properly configured, you tend to leave it alone until there is a problem or until you need to make some other configuration change. This is why the question mark (**?**) is probably the most widely used Cisco IOS Software command. Unless you have constant exposure to this equipment, it can be difficult to remember the numerous commands required to configure devices and troubleshoot problems. Most engineers remember enough to go in the right direction and use the **?** to recall the correct syntax. This is life in the real world. However, the **?** is unavailable in the testing environment. Many questions on the exam require you to select the best command to perform a certain function. It is extremely important to become familiar with the different commands and their respective functions.

Conventions Used in This Book

This book uses the following Cisco Systems, Inc. syntax conventions:

- **Bold** indicates a command or keyword that the user enters literally as shown.

- *Italic* indicates a command argument or option for which the user supplies a value.

- The vertical bar/pipe symbol (|) separates alternative, mutually exclusive command options. That is, the user can enter one and only one of the options divided by the pipe symbol.

- Square brackets ([ ]) indicate an optional element for the command.

- Braces ({ }) indicate a required option for the command. The user must enter this option.

- Braces within brackets ([{ }]) indicate a required choice if the user implements the command's optional element.

Rules of the Road

We have always found it confusing when different addresses are used in the examples throughout a technical publication. For this reason, we use the address space shown in Figure I-1 when assigning network segments in this book. Note that the address space we have selected is all reserved space per RFC 1918. We understand that these addresses are not routable across the Internet and are not normally used on outside interfaces. Even with the millions of IP addresses available on the Internet, there is a slight chance that we could have chosen to use an address that the owner did not want published in this book.

Figure I-1   *Addressing for Examples*

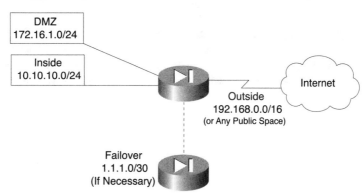

It is our hope that this will help you understand the examples and the syntax of the many commands required to configure and administer the Cisco PIX Firewall.

Rather than jumping directly into what you need to know for the CSPFA 9E0-111 or 642-521 examinations, we felt it more important for you to understand some background information about network security and why it is an integral part of business today. After all, passing the exam is nice, but understanding what the position of network security professional entails is critical.

CHAPTER 1

Network Security

In the past, *information security* was a term used to describe the physical security measures used to keep vital government or business information from being accessed by the public and to protect it against alteration or destruction. This was done by storing valuable documents in locked filing cabinets or safes and restricting physical access to areas where those documents were kept. With the proliferation of computers and electronic media, the old way of accessing data changed. As technology continued to advance, computer systems were interconnected to form computer networks, allowing systems to share resources, including data. The ultimate computer network, which interconnects almost every publicly accessible computer network, is the Internet. Although the methods of securing data have changed dramatically, the concept of network security remains the same as that of information security.

Because computers can warehouse, retrieve, and process tremendous amounts of data, they are used in nearly every facet of our lives. Computers, networks, and the Internet are an integral part of many businesses. Our dependence on computers continues to increase as businesses and individuals become more comfortable with technology and as technology advances make systems more user-friendly and easier to interconnect.

A single computer system requires automated tools to protect data on that system from users who have local system access. A computer system that is on a network (a *distributed system*) requires that the data on that system be protected not only from local access but also from unauthorized remote access and from interception or alteration of data during transmission between systems.

Vulnerabilities

To understand cyber-attacks, you must remember that computers, no matter how advanced, are still just machines that operate based on predetermined instruction sets. Operating systems and other software packages are simply compiled instruction sets that the computer uses to transform input into output. A computer cannot determine the difference between authorized input and unauthorized input unless this information is written into the instruction sets. Any point in a software package at which a user can alter the software or gain access to a system (that was not specifically designed into the software) is called a *vulnerability*. In most cases, a hacker gains access to a network or computer by exploiting a vulnerability. It is possible to remotely connect to a computer on any of 65,535 ports. As hardware and software technology continue to advance, the "other side" continues to search for and discover new vulnerabilities. For this reason, most software manufacturers continue to produce *patches* for their products as vulnerabilities are discovered.

Threats

Potential threats are broken into the following two categories:

- **Structured threats**—Threats that are preplanned and focus on a specific target. A structured threat is an organized effort to breach a specific network or organization.

- **Unstructured threats**—This threat is the most common because it is random and tends to be the result of hackers looking for a target of opportunity. An abundance of script files are available on the Internet to users who want to scan unprotected networks for vulnerabilities. Because the scripts are free and run with minimal input from the user, they are widely used across the Internet. Many unstructured threats are not of a malicious nature or for any specific purpose. The people who carry them out are usually just novice hackers looking to see what they can do.

Types of Attacks

The motivations for cyber-attackers are too numerous and varied to list. They range from the novice hacker who is attracted by the challenge to the highly skilled professional who targets an organization for a specific purpose (such as organized crime, industrial espionage, or state-sponsored intelligence gathering). Threats can originate from outside the organization or from inside. *External threats* originate outside an organization and attempt to breach a network either from the Internet or via dialup access. *Internal threats* originate from within an organization and are usually the result of employees or other personnel who have some authorized access to internal network resources. Studies indicate that internal threats perpetrated by disgruntled employees or former employees are responsible for the majority of network security incidents within most organizations.

There are three major types of network attacks, each with its own specific goal:

- **Reconnaissance attacks**—An attack designed not to gain access to a system or network, but only to search for and track vulnerabilities that can be exploited later.

- **Access attacks**—An attack designed to exploit a vulnerability and to gain access to a system on a network. After gaining access, the user can

  — Retrieve, alter, or destroy data

  — Add, remove, or change network resources, including user access

  — Install other exploits that can be used later to gain access to the network

- **Denial of service (DoS) attacks**—An attack designed solely to cause an interruption on a computer or network.

Reconnaissance Attacks

The goal of this type of attack is to perform reconnaissance on a computer or network. The goal of this reconnaissance is to determine the makeup of the targeted computer or network and to search for and map any vulnerabilities. A reconnaissance attack can indicate the potential for other, more-invasive attacks. Many reconnaissance attacks are written into scripts that allow novice hackers or script kiddies to launch attacks on networks with a few mouse clicks. Here are some of the more common reconnaissance attacks:

- **Domain Name Service (DNS) queries**—A DNS query provides the unauthorized user with such information as what address space is assigned to a particular domain and who owns that domain.

- **Ping sweeps**—A ping sweep tells the unauthorized user how many hosts are active on the network. It is possible to drop ICMP at the perimeter devices, but this occurs at the expense of network troubleshooting.

- **Vertical scans**—This involves scanning the service ports of a single host and requesting different services at each port. This method allows the unauthorized user to determine what type of operating system and services are running on the computer.

- **Horizontal scans**—This involves scanning an address range for a specific port or service. A very common horizontal scan is the FTP sweep. This is done by scanning a network segment, looking for replies to connection attempts on port 21.

- **Block scans**—This is a combination of the vertical scan and the horizontal scan. In other words, it scans a network segment and attempts connections on multiple ports of each host on that segment.

Access Attacks

As the name implies, the goal of an access attack is to gain access to a computer or network. Having gained access, the user can perform many different functions. These functions can be broken into three distinct categories:

- **Interception**—Gaining unauthorized access to a resource. This could be access to confidential data such as personnel records, payroll, or research and development projects. As soon as the user gains access, he might be able to read, write to, copy, or move this data. If an intruder gains access, the only way to protect your sensitive data is to save it in an encrypted format (beforehand). This prevents the intruder from being able to read the data.

- **Modification**—Having gained access, the unauthorized user can alter the resource. This includes not only altering file content, but also altering system configurations, unauthorized system access, and unauthorized privilege escalation. Unauthorized system access is achieved by exploiting a vulnerability in either the operating system or a software package running on that system. Unauthorized privilege escalation is when a user who has a low-level but authorized account attempts to gain higher-level or more-privileged user account information or increase his privilege level. This gives him greater control over the target system or network.

- **Fabrication**—With access to the target system or network, the unauthorized user can create false objects and introduce them into the environment. This can include altering data or inserting packaged exploits such as a virus, worm, or Trojan horse, which can continue attacking the network from within.

  - **Virus**—Computer viruses range from annoying to destructive. They consist of computer code that attaches itself to other software running on the computer. This way, each time the attached software opens, the virus reproduces and can continue growing until it wreaks havoc on the infected computer.

  - **Worm**—A worm is a virus that exploits vulnerabilities on networked systems to replicate itself. A worm scans a network, looking for a computer with a specific vulnerability. When it finds a host, it copies itself to that system and begins scanning from there as well.

  - **Trojan horse**—A Trojan horse is a program that usually claims to perform one function (such as a game) but does something completely different (such as corrupting data on your hard disk). Many different types of Trojan horses get attached to systems. The effects of these programs range from minor user irritation to total destruction of the computer's file system. Trojan horses are sometimes used to exploit systems by creating user accounts on systems so that an unauthorized user can gain access or upgrade his privilege level.

Denial of Service (DoS) Attacks

A DoS attack is designed to deny user access to computers or networks. These attacks usually target specific services and attempt to overwhelm them by making numerous requests concurrently. If a system is not protected and cannot react to a DoS attack, it can be very easy to overwhelm that system by running scripts that generate multiple requests. It is possible to greatly increase a DoS attack's magnitude by launching it from multiple systems against a single target. This practice is called a distributed denial of service attack (DDoS). A common practice by hackers is to use a Trojan horse to take control of other systems and enlist them in a DDoS attack.

Network Security Policy

The network security policy is the core of the network security process. Every company should have a written network security policy. At a minimum, that policy should fulfill the following objectives:

- Analyze the threat based on the type of business performed and type of network exposure.

- Determine the organization's security requirements.

- Document the network infrastructure and identify potential security breach points.

- Identify specific resources that require protection and develop an implementation plan.

NOTE   An effective network security policy must include physical security to prevent unauthorized users from gaining local access to equipment.

The *security process* is the implementation of the security policy. It is broken into four steps that run continuously, as shown in Figure 1-1.

Figure 1-1   *Security Process*

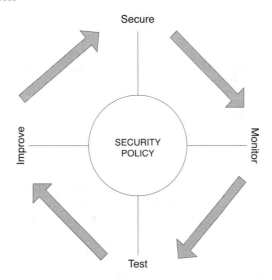

Step 1: Secure

Step 1 is implementing your network security design. This includes hardening your network systems by installing security devices such as firewalls, intrusion detection sensors, and AAA (authentication, authorization, and accounting) servers. Firewalls on the network perimeter prevent unwanted traffic from entering the network. Firewalls within the network verify that only authorized traffic moves from one network segment to another. Restrict access to resources to only authorized users, and implement a strong password convention. Implement data encryption to protect data passing from one network to another across an unsecured connection (via the Internet) or to protect sensitive data within your network. The Cisco PIX Firewall and Cisco Secure IDS are both industry-leading network security devices. The purpose of this step is to prevent unauthorized access to the network and to protect network resources.

Step 2: Monitor

Step 2 is monitoring the network. By installing the Cisco Secure IDS at key points of the network, you can monitor both internal and external traffic. It is important to monitor both internal and external traffic, because you can check for violations of your network security policy from internal sources and attacks from external sources and determine if any external attacks have breached your network. All your perimeter devices, including firewalls and perimeter routers, can provide log data. This log data can and should be filtered to look for specific incidents.

Step 3: Test

Step 3 involves testing the effectiveness of your security design. Verify that the security equipment is properly configured and functioning correctly. The Cisco Secure Scanner is an excellent tool for verifying the capabilities of your design and determining how effective your security devices will be as they are currently configured.

Step 4: Improve

Step 4 involves the data from your intrusion detection sensors and your test data to improve the design. An effective security policy is always a work in progress. It continues to improve with every cycle of the process. This does not necessarily mean implementing new hardware with every cycle. It could be changing certain company procedures or documenting new potential threats and vulnerabilities.

It is very important to remember that security is an ongoing process that is based on the security policy.

AVVID and SAFE

Cisco has two programs in place—AVVID and SAFE—to help network architects design secure network solutions. Both of these programs are based on proven solutions that have been tested for full functionality and interoperability.

What Is AVVID?

AVVID is the Cisco Architecture for Voice, Video, and Integrated Data. AVVID is an open architecture that is used by Cisco partners to develop various solutions. Every Cisco partner solution is rigorously tested for interoperability with Cisco products. AVVID is designed for large enterprise networks requiring an infrastructure that can support emerging applications such as IP telephone, content delivery, and storage. This *network of networks* concept allows the use of a single network infrastructure to support the concurrent operation of multiple solutions. The Cisco Enterprise Solutions Engineering team creates design guides for use when planning enterprise network infrastructure using Cisco products, software, and features. These solutions provide the following benefits:

- **Network performance**, measured by the following three metrics rather than just throughput:

  - **Application response time**—This metric measures how well an application responds to changes on a network and how well it responds to network congestion and changes its link speed.

  - **Device performance**—This metric measures the limitations in performance of individual network devices such as switches or routers. A poorly performing device can become a bottleneck to the network, so it is important that devices are not overtaxed. Device performance measures errors, drops, and CPU usage as well as packet-per-second throughput.

  - **Protocol performance**—This metric measures the ability of devices to operate dynamically by verifying that devices and the network can handle the use of routing protocols and the Spanning-Tree Protocol (STP).

- **Scalability** must allow a network to grow into the future. The network must be designed to allow growth in the following areas:

  - **Topology**—A topology must be selected so that changes do not require major reconfiguration of the entire network.

  - **Addressing**—The addressing scheme should allow for changes with a minimum impact on the addressing scheme and should allow for route summarization.

  - **Routing protocols**—The design should be such that changes in the network are easily handled by the routing protocols.

- **Availability** is always a major concern to network managers. A network's ability to overcome outages and adapt to changes is paramount. Three availability issues are incorporated into the AVVID design model:

> — **Equipment and link redundancy**—This includes not only redundant components and high-availability configurations, but also redundancy within the equipment, such as dual power supplies and other features designed into the modular products.
>
> — **Protocol resiliency**—The focus here is to use the most resilient protocol. Multiple redundant protocols do not necessarily provide the best solution.
>
> — **Network capacity design**—A network design that allows for significant expansion in the event of a redundant link failure.

The AVVID network infrastructure design incorporates many different topologies and technologies to provide optimum efficiency and stability.

What Is SAFE?

Cisco's Secure Blueprint for Enterprise Networks (SAFE) is a guide for network designers focusing on the implementation of secure enterprise networks. It is based on Cisco AVVID. SAFE uses best practices and the interoperability of various Cisco and Cisco Partner products. It uses the following design fundamentals (from the Cisco Systems SAFE white paper, copyright 2000):

- Security and attack mitigation based on policy
- Security implementation throughout the infrastructure (not just specialized security devices)
- Secure management and reporting
- Authentication and authorization of users and administrators to critical network resources
- Intrusion detection for critical resources and subnets
- Support for emerging networked applications

The SAFE Network Security Blueprint is composed of the critical areas of network security:

- **Perimeter security**—Protects access to the network by controlling access on the network's entry and exit points
- **Secure connectivity**—Provides secure communications via virtual private networks (VPNs)
- **Application security**—Ensures that critical servers and applications are protected
- **Identity**—Solutions that provide secure authentication and authorization
- **Security management and monitoring**—Allows for centralized management of security resources and the detection of unauthorized activity on the network

---

NOTE   Cisco SAFE Implementation 1.0 (exam 9E0-131) was released on December 31, 2002, and is a requirement for the CCSP Certification. For more information, refer to www.cisco.com/go/certifications

---

Q&A

The questions in this section are designed to ensure your understanding of the concepts discussed in this chapter.

The answers to these questions can be found in Appendix A.

1 True or false: Network security means locking your computer in a filing cabinet.

2 What is the goal of a reconnaissance attack?

3 True or false: A horizontal scan affects more hosts on a network than a vertical scan.

4 True or false: To secure your network, you only need to install a firewall.

5 What is the difference between a security policy and a security process?

This chapter covers the following exam topics for the Cisco Secure PIX Firewall Advanced Exam:

1. Firewalls
2. PIX Firewall Overview

CHAPTER 2

Firewall Technologies and the Cisco PIX Firewall

The Cisco PIX Firewall is one of many firewalls on the market today. Different manufacturers employ different technologies in their designs. This chapter discusses the different technologies and how they are applied on the Cisco PIX Firewall.

How to Best Use This Chapter

This chapter is straightforward. It covers a few basic concepts and discusses how they are applied to the Cisco PIX Firewall. There are few questions in the "Do I Know This Already?" section, few review questions, and no scenarios. The fact that this topic is easy does not make it any less important. On the contrary, the concepts in this chapter are the foundation of much of what you need to understand to pass the CSPFA Certification Exam. Unless you do exceptionally well on the "Do I Know This Already?" pretest and are 110% confident in your knowledge of this area, I recommend that you read through the entire chapter.

"Do I Know This Already?" Quiz

The purpose of this quiz is to help you determine your current understanding of the topics covered in this chapter. Write down your answers and compare them to the answers in Appendix A. If you have to look at any references to correctly answer these questions, you should definitely read the entire chapter.

1 What are the three basic firewall technologies?

2 Of the three firewall technologies, which one generates a separate connection on behalf of the requestor and usually operates at the upper layers of the OSI model?

3 Which firewall technology is commonly implemented on a router?

4 What items does a packet filter look at to determine whether to allow the traffic?

5 What firewall technology does the Cisco PIX Firewall use?

  A Proxy filtering

  B Packet filtering

  C Stateful inspection

  D Proxy inspection

6 What are the advantages of the Cisco PIX Firewall over competing firewall products?

7 How many PIX firewalls can you operate in a high-availability cluster?

8 What is the ASA, and how does the Cisco PIX Firewall use it?

9 Why is cut-through proxy more efficient than traditional proxy?

Check your answers with Appendix A. Remember that this section is not called "How Much Am I Familiar With?". If you did not do extremely well in this section, you should read this chapter.

Foundation Topics

Firewall Technologies

Firewalls are the key equipment used for network perimeter security. The function of a firewall is to permit or deny traffic that attempts to pass through it based on specific pre-defined rules. All firewalls perform the function of examining network traffic and affecting this traffic based on the rule set, however the methods they employ can be different. There are three different types of firewall technologies:

- Packet filtering
- Proxy
- Stateful inspection

Packet Filtering

A packet-filtering firewall simply inspects incoming traffic at the transport layer of the Open System Interconnection (OSI) reference model. The packet-filtering firewall analyzes TCP or UDP packets and compares them to a set of established rules called an *access control list (ACL)*. Packet filtering inspects the packet for only the following elements:

- Source IP address
- Source port
- Destination IP address
- Destination port
- Protocol

NOTE   In addition to the elements just listed, some packet-filtering firewalls check for header information to determine if the packet is from a new connection or an existing connection.

These elements are compared to the ACL (rule set) to determine if the packets are permitted or denied. Some of the disadvantages of packet filtering are as follows:

- ACLs can be very complex and difficult to manage.
- A packet-filtering firewall can be tricked into permitting access to an unauthorized user falsely representing himself (*spoofing*) with an IP address that is authorized by the ACL.

- Many new applications (such as multimedia applications) create multiple connections on random ports with no way to determine which ports will be used until the connection is established. Because access lists are manually configured, it is very difficult to provide support for these applications.

Packet filtering is a feature that is commonly used on routers. Chapter 7, "Configuring Access," discusses ACLs as applied to the Cisco PIX Firewall in greater detail.

Proxy

proxy, *n,* the agency of a person who acts as a substitute for another person; authority to act for another. (New Webster's Dictionary of the English Language)

Although this definition does not define a proxy firewall, the function is very similar. A proxy firewall, commonly called a *proxy server,* acts on behalf of hosts on the protected network segments. The protected hosts never make any connections with the outside world. Hosts on the protected network send their requests to the proxy server, where they are authenticated and authorized. At this point, the proxy server sends a request on behalf of the requesting host to the external host and forwards the reply to the requesting host. Proxies run at the upper layers of the OSI reference model. Most proxy firewalls are designed to cache commonly used information to expedite the response time to the requesting host. The processing workload required to perform proxy services is significant and increases with the number of requesting hosts. Large networks usually implement several proxy servers to avoid problems with throughput. The number of applications that a requesting host can access via a proxy is limited. By design, proxy firewalls support only specific applications and protocols. The major disadvantage of proxy servers is that they are applications that run on top of operating systems. A device can be only as secure as the operating system it is running on. If the operating system is compromised, the unauthorized user can take control of the proxy firewall and gains access to the entire protected network.

Stateful Inspection

Stateful inspection, also called *stateful packet filtering,* is a combination of packet filtering and proxy services. This technology is the most secure and provides the most functionality because connections are not only applied to an ACL, but are logged into a *state table*. After a connection is established, all session data is compared to the state table. If the session data does not match the state table information for that connection, the connection is dropped. Chapter 3, "The Cisco Secure PIX Firewall," covers stateful inspection in further detail.

Stateful packet filtering is the method used by the Cisco PIX Firewall.

Cisco PIX Firewall

Four major characteristics of the Cisco Secure PIX Firewall's design make it a leading-edge, high-performance security solution:

- Secure real-time embedded system
- Adaptive Security Algorithm
- Cut-through proxy
- Redundancy

Secure Real-Time Embedded System

Unlike most firewalls, the Cisco PIX Firewall runs on a single proprietary embedded system. Whereas most firewalls run a firewall application over a general-purpose operating system, the PIX has a single system that is responsible for operating the device. This single system is beneficial for the following reasons:

- **Better security**—The PIX operating environment is a single system that was designed with functionality and security in mind. Because there is no separation between the operating system and the firewall application, there are no known vulnerabilities to exploit.

- **Better functionality**—The combined operating environment requires fewer steps when you configure the system. For example, if multiple IP addresses are bound to the external interface of an application firewall that runs over a general operating system, you must configure the networking portions (that is, Address Resolution Protocol [ARP] entries and routing) on the operating system and then apply the ACLs or rules in the firewall application. On the Cisco PIX Firewall, all these functions are combined into a single system. As soon as an IP address is bound to an interface, the PIX automatically replies to ARP requests for that address without its having to be specifically configured.

- **Better performance**—Because the operating environment is a single unit, it allows for streamlined processing and much greater performance. The Cisco PIX 535 Firewall can handle 500,000 concurrent connections while maintaining stateful inspection of all connections.

Adaptive Security Algorithm (ASA)

The *Adaptive Security Algorithm* is the key to stateful connection control on the Cisco PIX Firewall. It creates a stateful session flow table (also called the *state table*). Source and destination addresses and other connection information are logged into the state table. By using the ASA, the Cisco PIX Firewall can perform stateful filtering on the connections in addition to filtering packets.

Cut-Through Proxy

Cut-through proxy is a method of transparently performing authentication and authorization of inbound and outbound connections at the firewall. Cut-through proxy requires very little overhead and provides a significant performance advantage over application proxy firewalls.

Redundancy

The Cisco Secure PIX 515 series and above can be configured in pairs with a primary system and a hot standby. This redundancy and stateful failover make the PIX a high-availability solution for use in protecting critical network segments. If the primary firewall fails, the secondary automatically assumes the load, dramatically reducing the chances of a network outage. Failover is discussed in greater detail in Chapter 9, "Cisco PIX Firewall Failover."

Foundation Summary

The three firewall technologies are packet filtering, proxy, and stateful inspection. The Cisco PIX Firewall utilizes stateful inspection and further increases security with the Adaptive Security Algorithm. The PIX is more secure and more efficient than competing firewalls because it is a single operating environment rather than a firewall application running on another operating system. The Cisco PIX Firewall can be configured in pairs to reduce the possibility of an outage due to system failure.

Q&A

As mentioned in the Introduction, the questions in this book are written to be more difficult than what you should experience on the exam. The questions are designed to ensure your understanding of the concepts discussed in this chapter and to adequately prepare you to complete the exam. Use the simulated exams on the CD to practice for the exam.

The answers to these questions can be found in Appendix A.

1 True or false: Packet filtering can be configured on Cisco routers.

2 What design feature allows the Cisco Secure PIX Firewall to outperform conventional application firewalls?

   A   The Packet Selectivity Algorithm

   B   Super-packet filtering

   C   A single embedded operating environment

   D   Hot standby proxy processing

3 True or false: Cut-through proxy technology allows users to do anything they want after authenticating at the firewall.

4 What steps are required to add an ARP entry to a Cisco PIX Firewall?

   A   Edit the /etc/interfaces/outside/arp.conf file.

   B   You don't need to add an ARP entry on a PIX Firewall.

   C   Add the ARP entry using the GUI interface.

   D   Use the **set arp** command in interface config mode.

5 True or false: There is no limit on the number of connections an application proxy firewall can handle.

6 True or false: The Adaptive Security Algorithm requires a tremendous amount of processing by the firewall. Even though it is not very efficient, the PIX can handle it.

7 True or false: Redundancy allows you to configure two or more PIX firewalls in a cluster to protect critical systems.

This chapter covers the following exam topics for the Cisco Secure PIX Firewall Advanced Exam:

2. PIX Firewall Overview
3. PIX Firewall Models
4. PIX Firewall Licensing

CHAPTER 3

The Cisco Secure PIX Firewall

This chapter discusses the Cisco PIX Firewall in greater detail. It covers the many different models available, including their design and specifications.

How to Best Use This Chapter

Chapter 2, "Firewall Technologies and the Cisco PIX Firewall," gave you insight into the different firewall technologies and the functionality designed into the Cisco PIX Firewall. This chapter gives you more-specific information about this functionality and how this makes the PIX a truly high-performance solution. This chapter also covers all the PIX models available today and the possible configurations of each model. It is very important for you to understand the technology that powers the Cisco PIX Firewall in great detail. Test yourself with the "Do I Know This Already?" quiz and see how familiar you are with the PIX in general and with the specifics of each available model.

"Do I Know This Already?" Quiz

The purpose of this quiz is to help you determine your current understanding of the topics covered in this chapter. Write down your answers and compare them to the answers in Appendix A. If you have to look at any references to correctly answer the questions about the PIX functionality, you should read that portion and double-check your thinking by reviewing the Foundation Summary. It is a good idea to be familiar with the different PIX models, their purpose, and their available options. The concepts in this chapter are the foundation of much of what you need to understand to pass the CSPFA Certification Exam. Unless you do exceptionally well on the "Do I Know This Already?" pretest and are 100% confident in your knowledge of this area, you should read through the entire chapter.

1 What is the ASA, and how does the Cisco PIX Firewall use it?

2 What three authentication methods can the PIX Firewall use when performing cut-through proxy?

3 Why does the ASA generate random TCP sequence numbers?

4 If a user has successfully authenticated but cannot establish a connection to the server, what is most likely the problem?

5 What is the best way to remove the ASA from a PIX Firewall?

6 What components of a TCP session does the ASA write to the state table?

7 What can cause a session object to be deleted from the state table?

8 What are the three ways to initiate a cut-through proxy session?

9 What happens to a reply that does not have the correct TCP sequence number?

10 How many interfaces does a PIX 501 have, and how many network segments does it support?

11 What X509 certificates do all PIX firewalls support?

12 What is the maximum throughput of the PIX 535?

13 How many interfaces can you install in a PIX 515?

14 What is the lowest model number of the PIX Firewall family to support failover?

15 What are three methods of managing a Cisco PIX Firewall?

Foundation Topics

Overview of the Cisco PIX Firewall

As discussed in Chapter 2, the design of the Cisco PIX Firewall provides some significant advantages over application-based firewalls. Having a single operating environment allows the device to operate more efficiently, and because it was designed with security in mind, it is not vulnerable to any known exploits.

Adaptive Security Algorithm (ASA)

A key part of the operating environment is the Adaptive Security Algorithm (ASA). The ASA is more secure and efficient than packet filtering and provides better performance than application-type proxy firewalls. The ASA segregates the network segments connected to the firewall, maintains secure perimeters, and can control traffic between those segments. The firewall's interfaces are assigned *security levels*. The PIX can allow outbound traffic to pass from an interface with a higher security level (inside) to an interface with a lower security level (outside) without an explicit rule for each resource on the higher-level segment. Traffic that is coming from an interface with a lower security level destined for an interface with a higher security level must meet the following two requirements: A static translation must exist for the destination, and an access list or conduit must be in place to allow the traffic.

The ASA is designed to function as a stateful, connection-oriented process that maintains session information in a *state table*. Applying the security policy to the state table controls all traffic passing through the firewall. The ASA writes the connection information to the state table as an outbound connection is initiated. If the connection is allowed by the security policy, the request goes out. Return traffic is compared to the existing state information. If the information does not match, the firewall drops the connection. The security emphasis on the connection rather than on the packets makes it nearly impossible to gain access by hijacking a TCP session.

Figure 3-1 and the following list explain the mechanics of how ASA and stateful filtering work on the PIX:

Figure 3-1 *How the Adaptive Security Algorithm Works*

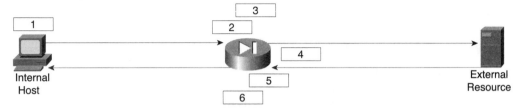

The following list explains the mechanics of how ASA and stateful filtering work on the PIX:

1 The internal host initiates a connection to an external resource.

2 The PIX writes the following information about this connection into the state table:

— Source IP

— Source port

— Destination IP

— Destination port

— TCP sequencing information

— Additional TCP/UDP flags

— A randomly generated TCP sequence number is applied

This entry in the state table is called the session object.

3 The connection object is compared to the security policy. If the connection is *not* allowed, the session object is deleted, and the connection is dropped.

4 If the connection is approved by the security policy, the request continues to the external resource.

5 The external resource replies to the request.

6 The response arrives at the firewall and is compared to the session object. If the response matches the session object, the traffic passes to the internal host. If it does *not* match, the connection is dropped.

Cut-Through Proxy

The cut-through proxy feature on the Cisco PIX Firewall provides significantly better performance than application proxy firewalls, because it completes user authentication at the application layer, verifies authorization against the security policy, and then opens the connection as authorized by the security policy. Subsequent traffic for this connection is no longer handled at the application layer but is statefully inspected, providing significant performance benefits over proxy-based firewalls.

Figure 3-2 and the following list explain the mechanics of cut-through proxy:

1 A connection to the firewall is initiated via HTTP, FTP, or Telnet, and the user is prompted by the PIX Firewall for a user ID and password.

2 The Cisco PIX Firewall uses either Remote Authentication Dial-In User Service (RADIUS) or Terminal Access Controller Access Control System (TACACS+) protocols to forward the user information to an external authentication server, where it is validated.

NOTE   Users can authenticate to a user database on the PIX, but it is more efficient to use an external authentication server with RADIUS or TACACS+, because the processing required by the PIX Firewall to maintain and query an internal database increases the firewall's workload.

---

3 After successful authentication, the connection is opened at the network layer, the session information is written to the connection table, and the ASA process shown in Figure 3-1 begins.

Figure 3-2   *How Cut-Through Proxy Works*

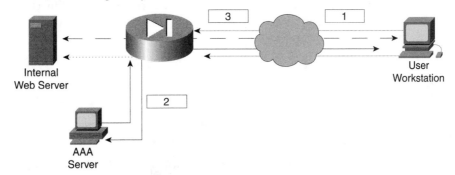

Internal
Web Server

User
Workstation

AAA
Server

Cisco PIX Firewall Models and Features

Currently, six models of the Cisco PIX Firewall are available. These models provide services that range from the small office/home office (SOHO) to the enterprise network and Internet service provider (ISP):

• **Cisco Secure PIX 501**—This firewall is intended for SOHO use and incorporates an integrated 10/100 Ethernet switch.

• **Cisco Secure PIX 506**—This model is intended for remote office/branch office (ROBO) use and comes with two 10BASE-T Ethernet interfaces.

- **Cisco Secure PIX 515**—This model is designed for small-to-medium businesses and branch office installations.
- **Cisco Secure PIX 520**—This model is intended for enterprise networks. It is no longer being manufactured and is nearing end of product life.
- **Cisco Secure PIX 525**—This model is intended for large enterprise networks and ISPs.
- **Cisco Secure PIX 535**—This model is the most robust of the PIX Firewall series. It is intended for very large enterprise networks and ISPs.

All the PIX firewalls have the functionality described in the following sections incorporated into their design:

Intrusion Protection

PIX firewalls were designed to detect a variety of attacks. They can be integrated with the Cisco Secure Intrusion Detection Sensor to dynamically react to different threats.

AAA Support

PIX firewalls work with RADIUS or TACACS+ and the Cisco Access Control Server (ACS) to provide authentication, authorization, and accounting (AAA) functionality. It is also possible to configure a local user database on the PIX rather than integrate with an external authentication server.

X.509 Certificate Support

Digital certificates are your digital identification that verify you are who you claim to be and validate the integrity of your data. Digital certificates are most commonly combined with encryption to secure data in the following four ways:

- **Authentication**—Digital certificates are used to verify the identity of a user or server.
- **Integrity**—If data has been digitally signed and it is altered, the digital certificate becomes invalid, indicating to the recipient that the data is no longer valid.
- **Token verification**—Digital tokens can be used to replace passwords, because it can be very simple to guess a password. A digital certificate is an encrypted file that resides on your computer and can only be decrypted by your password. To compromise your certificate, a user would have to have *both* the encrypted file and your password.
- **Encryption**—Digital certificates verify the identity of both ends of an encrypted connection and dynamically negotiate the parameters of that connection. Using digital certificates to negotiate virtual private networks (VPNs) is discussed in detail in Chapter 10, "Virtual Private Networks."

PIX firewalls support the Simple Certificate Enrollment Protocol (SCEP) and can be integrated with the X.509 digital identification solutions:

- Entrust Technologies, Inc.—Entrust/PKI 4.0
- Microsoft Corporation—Windows 2000 Certificate Server 5.0
- VeriSign—Onsite 4.5
- Baltimore Technologies—UniCERT 3.05

Network Address Translation/Port Address Translation

PIX firewalls can statically or dynamically translate internal private (RFC 1918) addresses to public addresses. They can also hide multiple hosts on the internal network behind a single public address.

Firewall Management

PIX firewalls can be managed using one of three methods:

- **Cisco command-line interface (CLI)**—The CLI uses commands consistent with other Cisco products. The PIX can be configured to allow access to the CLI via console, Telnet, and SSH. All system configurations can be saved as a text file for archive and recovery purposes.
- **PIX Device Manager (PDM)**—The PDM is a graphical user interface (GUI) that can be used to manage a single firewall or multiple perimeter firewalls in an enterprise network. The GUI connects to each device via a secure connection and provides a simplified method of managing each device. The PDM also provides real-time log data that can be used to track events and do limited troubleshooting.
- **Cisco Secure Policy Manager (CSPM)**—The CSPM is a GUI that can manage up to 500 security devices, including PIX firewalls, Cisco VPN routers, and Cisco Secure Intrusion Detection Sensors. The CSPM is a scalable solution designed to allow enterprise network security managers to consolidate security policies and manage devices from a single source.

Simple Network Management Protocol (SNMP)

PIX firewalls allow limited SNMP support. Because SNMP was designed as a network management protocol and not a security protocol, it can be used to exploit a device. For this reason, the PIX Firewall allows only *read-only* access to remote connections. This allows the manager to remotely connect to the device and monitor SNMP traps but does not allow him to change any SNMP settings.

Syslog Support

PIX firewalls log four different types of events onto Syslog:

- Security
- Resource
- System
- Accounting

The PIX can be configured to react differently to any of eight severity levels for each event type. Logs are stored in system memory and can be forwarded to a syslog server. It is a recommended practice to select the appropriate log level that generates the syslog details required to track session-specific data.

Virtual Private Networks (VPNs)

All PIX firewalls are designed to function as a termination point or *VPN gateway* for virtual private networks. This functionality allows administrators to create encrypted connections with other networks over the Internet.

NOTE   The USB port on PIX firewalls is not currently being used.

The following sections describe the characteristics and connection capabilities of each of the six PIX models.

Cisco Secure PIX 501

The Cisco PIX 501 Firewall was designed for the small office/home office (SOHO). It has a 133-MHz processor, 16 MB of RAM, and 8 MB of Flash memory. It has an external Ethernet interface and an integrated four-port Ethernet hub on the internal side. It has a 9600-baud console port that is used for local device management. The 501 does not support failover.

Connection capabilities for the PIX 501 are as follows:

- Maximum clear-text throughput—10 Mbps
- Maximum throughput (DES)—6 Mbps
- Maximum throughput (3DES)—3 Mbps
- Maximum concurrent connections—3500
- Maximum concurrent VPN peers—5

As shown in Figure 3-3, the front panel of the PIX 501 has a power indicator and two rows of LEDs for link and network activity. These indicators are divided into two groups:

- The outside Ethernet interface
- The four inside Ethernet interfaces (hub)

Figure 3-3   *PIX 501 Front Panel*

Cisco Secure PIX 506

The Cisco PIX 506 Firewall was designed for the remote office/branch office (ROBO) environment. It has a 200-MHz processor, 32 MB of RAM, and 8 MB of Flash memory. It has a fixed outside Ethernet interface and a fixed inside Ethernet interface. It has a 9600-baud console port that is used for local device management. The 506 does not support failover.

Connection capabilities for the PIX 506 are as follows:

- Maximum clear-text throughput—20 Mbps
- Maximum throughput (DES)—20 Mbps
- Maximum throughput (3DES)—10 Mbps
- Maximum concurrent connections—3500
- Maximum concurrent VPN peers—25

As shown in Figure 3-4, the PIX 506 has three status LEDs on the front panel that indicate power to the system, that the system is active (the OS is fully loaded), and that there is network activity on any interface.

Figure 3-4 *PIX 506 Front Panel*

As shown in Figure 3-5, the rear of the PIX 506 contains the Ethernet ports and the console port.

Figure 3-5 *PIX 506 Rear Panel*

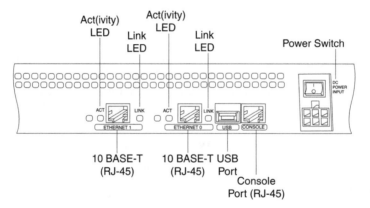

Using a DB-9 or DB-25 null-modem cable or a rollover cable with a DB-9 or DB-25 serial port adapter completes the console connection, as shown in Figure 3-6.

Figure 3-6   *PIX 506 Console Connection*

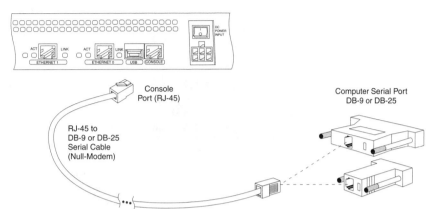

Cisco Secure PIX 515

The Cisco PIX 515 Firewall was designed for small-to-medium-sized businesses. The PIX 515 is the smallest firewall of the PIX family that is designed to be rack-mountable and that fits a standard 1U (1.75-inch) configuration. It has a 433-MHz processor, 32 MB or 64 MB of RAM, and 16 MB of Flash memory. It has two fixed 10/100 Ethernet interfaces that have a default configuration of outside (Ethernet 0) and inside (Ethernet 1) and contains two PCI slots for the installation of up to four additional Ethernet interfaces. It has a 9600-baud console port that is used for local device management. The 515 can be configured for failover using a failover cable connected to the 115-kbps serial connection. The PIX Firewall OS version 6.2 provides the functionality for long-distance failover. This is discussed in greater detail in Chapter 9, "Cisco PIX Firewall Failover."

Connection capabilities for the PIX 515 are as follows:

- Maximum clear-text throughput—188 Mbps
- Maximum throughput (DES)—100 Mbps
- Maximum throughput (3DES)—63 Mbps
- Maximum concurrent connections—125,000
- Maximum concurrent VPN peers—2000

As shown in Figure 3-7, the PIX 515 has three status LEDs on the front panel that indicate power to the system, that the system is active (the OS is fully loaded), and that there is network activity on any interface.

Figure 3-7 *PIX 515 Front Panel*

The rear of the PIX 515 contains the Ethernet ports and the console port. The PIX 515 can handle up to four additional Ethernet interfaces. This could be a single four-port Ethernet card (see Figure 3-8) or two single-port cards (see Figure 3-9). The PIX 515 automatically recognizes and numbers any additional interfaces that are installed. The PIX 515 can also be configured with a VPN accelerator card (VAC). The VAC handles much of the VPN traffic processing (encryption and decryption), thus improving the firewall's performance. The VAC is recommended for firewalls that will connect multiple high-traffic VPNs.

Figure 3-8 *PIX 515 with an Additional Four-Port Interface*

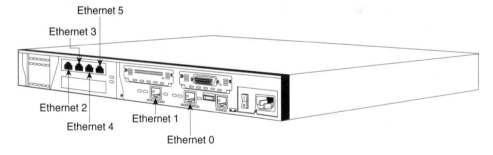

Figure 3-9 *PIX 515 with Two Additional Interfaces*

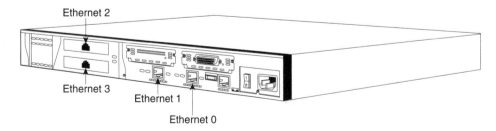

NOTE   The installation of additional interfaces and failover requires that the software license be upgraded from the basic license (515-R) to the 515-UR (unrestricted) license. A maximum of three interfaces can be installed using the restricted license.

The console connection for the PIX 515 is the same as for the 506.

Cisco Secure PIX 520

The Cisco PIX 520 Firewall is an older design that was originally built for enterprise networks. It is rack-mountable, has a 3.5-inch floppy drive, has all the interfaces accessing the front of the device, and fits the 3U (5.25-inch) configuration. It has a 350-MHz processor, up to 128 MB of RAM, and 16 MB of Flash memory. It has four PCI slots for the installation of Ethernet interfaces and can handle up to ten interfaces. It has a 9600-baud console port that is used for local device management. The 515 can be configured for failover using a failover cable connected to the 115-kbps serial connection.

Connection capabilities for the PIX 520 are as follows:

- Maximum clear-text throughput—370 Mbps
- Maximum throughput (DES)—100 Mbps
- Maximum throughput (3DES)—63 Mbps
- Maximum concurrent connections—250,000
- Maximum concurrent VPN peers—2000

The position of the network interface cards (NICs) is very important, because Ethernet 0 and Ethernet 1 are assigned as the outside and inside interfaces by default. The PIX 520 automatically recognizes and numbers any additional interfaces that are installed. A maximum of six interfaces can be installed in the PIX 520 using a restricted license.

Figures 3-10 through 3-12 show different configurations for NICs in the PIX 520.

Figure 3-10 *PIX 520 with Four Single-Interface Cards*

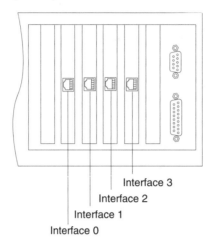

Figure 3-11 *PIX 520 with Two Single Cards and a Four-Port Card*

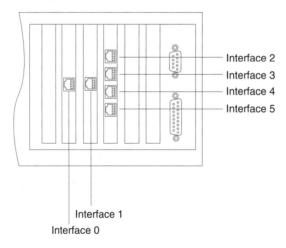

Figure 3-12   *PIX 520 with a Single Card and a Four-Port Card*

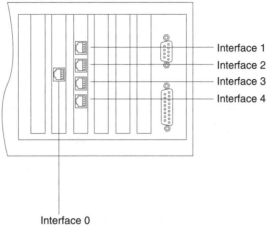

Interface 1
Interface 2
Interface 3
Interface 4

Interface 0

The console connection for the PIX 520 is on the front of the device. It requires either a DB-9-to-DB-25 null-modem cable or a rollover cable with adapters at each end, as shown in Figure 3-13. Refer to www.cisco.com for the pinout of the DB-9-to-DB-25 null modem cable.

Figure 3-13   *PIX 520 Console Connection*

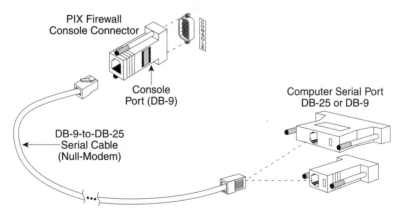

PIX Firewall
Console Connector

Console
Port (DB-9)

Computer Serial Port
DB-25 or DB-9

DB-9-to-DB-25
Serial Cable
(Null-Modem)

NOTE	The installation of additional interfaces and failover requires that the software license be upgraded from the Restricted Bundle.

Cisco Secure PIX 525

The Cisco PIX 525 Firewall is an enterprise firewall. It provides perimeter security for large enterprise networks. The 525 is rack-mountable in a 2U (3.5-inch) configuration. It has a 600-MHz processor, up to 256 MB of RAM, and 16 MB of Flash memory. It has two fixed 10/100 Ethernet interfaces. The two fixed interfaces are Ethernet 0, which is the outside interface by default, and Ethernet 1, which is the inside interface by default. The 525 also includes three PCI slots for the installation of up to six additional Ethernet interfaces. It has a 9600-baud console port that is used for local device management. The 525 can be configured for failover using a failover cable connected to the 115-kbps serial connection. The PIX 525 can also be configured with a VAC. The VAC handles much of the processing of VPN traffic (encryption and decryption), thus improving the firewall's performance. The VAC is recommended for firewalls that will connect multiple high-traffic VPNs.

Connection capabilities for the PIX 525 are as follows:

- Maximum clear-text throughput—370 Mbps
- Maximum throughput (DES)—100 Mbps
- Maximum throughput (3DES)—100 Mbps
- Maximum concurrent connections—280,000
- Maximum concurrent VPN peers—2000

As shown in Figure 3-14, the PIX 525 has two LEDs on the front. These LEDs indicate that the firewall has power and that the system is active (the OS is loaded).

Figure 3-14 *PIX 525 Front Panel*

The rear of the 525, shown in Figure 3-15, is similar in design to the 515, with fixed interfaces and additional PCI slots. The PIX 525 can support 10/100 Mbps and Gbps Ethernet interface cards.

Figure 3-15   *PIX 525 Rear Panel*

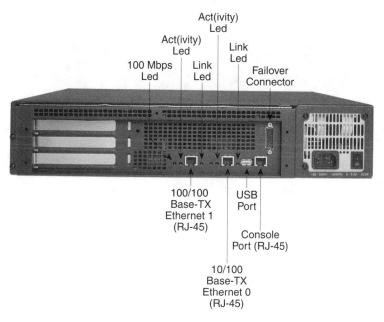

The console connection for the PIX 525 is the same as for the 506.

NOTE   The installation of additional interfaces and failover requires that the software license be upgraded from the Restricted Bundle.

Cisco Secure PIX 535

The Cisco PIX 535 Firewall is the ultimate enterprise firewall designed for enterprise networks and service providers. The 535 is rack-mountable and fits a 3U configuration. It has a 1-GHz processor, up to 1 GB of RAM, and 16 MB of Flash memory. It has nine PCI slots for the installation of up to ten Ethernet interfaces. It has a 9600-baud console port that is used for local device management, as shown in Figure 3-16.

Figure 3-16 *PIX 535 Rear Panel*

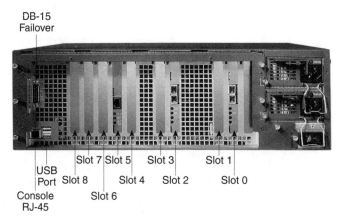

The 535 can be configured for failover using a failover cable connected to the 115-kbps serial connection. The PIX 535 is also available with redundant hot-swappable power supplies. The PIX 535 can also be configured with a VAC. The VAC handles much of the VPN traffic processing (encryption and decryption), thus improving the firewall's performance. The VAC is recommended for firewalls that will connect multiple high-traffic VPNs.

Connection capabilities for the PIX 535 are as follows:

- Maximum clear-text throughput—1 GBps
- Maximum throughput (DES)—100 Mbps
- Maximum throughput (3DES)—100 Mbps
- Maximum concurrent connections—500,000
- Maximum concurrent VPN peers—2000

As shown in Figure 3-17, the PIX 535 has two LEDs on the front. These LEDs indicate that the firewall has power and that the system is active (the IOS is loaded).

Figure 3-17   *PIX 535 Front Panel*

The PCI slots are divided into different bus speeds. The slots are numbered from right to left, and slots 0 through 3 run at 64-bit/66 MHz and can support Gigabit Ethernet interface cards (PIX-1GE-66). Slots 4 through 8 run at 32-bit/33 MHz and can support Fast Ethernet interface cards (PIX-1FE and PIX-4FE).

NOTE	Do not mix 33-MHz and 66-MHz cards on the same bus. This causes the overall speed of the 66-MHz bus to be reduced to 33 MHz.

The PIX 535 also supports a VPN accelerator card (PIX-VPN-ACCEL). It should be installed only on the 32-bit/33-MHz bus.

The console connection for the PIX 535 is the same as for the 506.

NOTE	The installation of additional interfaces and failover requires that the software license be upgraded from the Restricted Bundle.

Foundation Summary

The Cisco PIX Firewall uses the Adaptive Security Algorithm to perform stateful inspection. It performs cut-through proxy by authenticating a user against a AAA server and comparing the user request against the security policy. Currently, six PIX Firewall models are available. Table 3-1 lists their features.

Table 3-1   *PIX Models and Features*

Firewall Model	501	506	515	520	525	535
Intended Application	Small office/home office	Remote office/ branch office	Small/ medium business	Enterprise	Enterprise	Enterprise/ ISP
Intrusion Protection	Yes	Yes	Yes	Yes	Yes	Yes
AAA Support	Yes	Yes	Yes	Yes	Yes	Yes
X.509 Certificate Support	Yes	Yes	Yes	Yes	Yes	Yes
AVVID Partner Support	Yes	Yes	Yes	Yes	Yes	Yes
Maximum Installed Interfaces	One plus a four-port hub	Two	Six	Six	Eight	Ten
Supports DHCP	Yes	Yes	Yes	Yes	Yes	Yes
Net Address Translation	Yes	Yes	Yes	Yes	Yes	Yes
Port Address Translation	Yes	Yes	Yes	Yes	Yes	Yes
PPP Over Ethernet	Yes	Yes	Yes	Yes	Yes	Yes
Cisco PIX Command Line	Yes	Yes	Yes	Yes	Yes	Yes
PIX Device Manager	Yes	Yes	Yes	Yes	Yes	Yes

Table 3-1   *PIX Models and Features (Continued)*

Firewall Model	501	506	515	520	525	535
Cisco Secure Policy Manager	Yes	Yes	Yes	Yes	Yes	Yes
SNMP and Syslog Support	Yes	Yes	Yes	Yes	Yes	Yes
Failover Support	No	No	Yes	Yes	Yes	Yes
Maximum Throughput	10 Mbps	20 Mbps	188 Mbps	370 Mbps	370 Mbps	1 GBps
Maximum Throughput (DES)	6 Mbps	20 Mbps	100 Mbps	100 Mbps	100 Mbps	100 Mbps
Maximum Throughput (3DES)	3 Mbps	10 Mbps	63 Mbps	100 Mbps	100 Mbps	100 Mbps
Maximum Concurrent Connections	3500	3500	125,000	250,000	280,000	500,000
Maximum Concurrent VPN Peers	5	25	2000	2000	2000	2000
Processor	133 MHz	200 MHz	433 MHz	350 MHz	600 MHz	1.0 GHz
RAM	16 MB	32 MB	32/64 MB	Up to 128 MB	Up to 256 MB	Up to 1 GB
Flash Memory	8 MB	8 MB	16 MB	16 MB	16 MB	16 MB

Q&A

As mentioned in the Introduction, the questions in this book are written to be more difficult than what you should experience on the exam. The questions are designed to ensure your understanding of the concepts discussed in this chapter and adequately prepare you to complete the exam. You should take the simulated exams on the CD to practice for the exam.

The answers to these questions can be found in Appendix A.

1 List four advantages of ASA.

2 What are the three firewall technologies?

  A   Packet filtering, proxy, connection dropping

  B   Stateful inspection, packet filtering, proxy

  C   Stateful proxy, stateful filtering, packet inspection

  D   Cut-through proxy, ASA, proxy

3 How does cut-through proxy work in a PIX Firewall?

4 What happens to the session object after a connection ends?

5 True or false: A PIX 501 is designed to support five network segments.

6 How many interfaces can the PIX 525 handle?

7 How many PCI slots does the PIX 506 have?

8 True or false: If the ACT LED on the front of a PIX 525 is lit, it means that everything is working correctly.

9 True or false: The interfaces on a PIX 520 are numbered top to bottom and left to right.

10 True or false: You don't need a license for any Cisco PIX Firewall. If you own the appliance, you can do anything you want with it.

This chapter covers the following exam topics for the Cisco Secure PIX Firewall Advanced Exam:

45. Remote Access

CHAPTER 4

System Maintenance

In addition to the posted exam topic of "Remote Access," this chapter also covers these important system maintenance topics for the PIX:

- Activation key upgrade
- Installing a new OS on the Cisco PIX Firewall
- Upgrading the Cisco PIX Firewall operating system
- Creating a boot helper diskette using a Windows PC
- Password recovery

How to Best Use This Chapter

Chapter 3, "The Cisco Secure PIX Firewall," gave you insight into the different models of the Cisco PIX Firewall as well as the features and available configurations. This chapter provides information about how to configure access for the PIX, access the PIX, and maintain the PIX's integrity through upgrades. In addition, you will learn about password recovery and how to create a boot helper diskette. It is very important for you to understand the technology that powers the Cisco PIX Firewall in great detail. Test yourself with the "Do I Know This Already?" quiz and see how familiar you are with these aspects of the PIX.

"Do I Know This Already?" Quiz

The purpose of this quiz is to help you determine your current understanding of the topics covered in this chapter. Write down your answers and compare them to the answers in Appendix A. If you have to look at any references to correctly answer the questions about PIX functionality, (re)read that portion of the material. The concepts in this chapter are the foundation of much of what you need to understand to pass the CSPFA Certification Exam. Unless you do exceptionally well on the "Do I Know This Already?" pretest and are 100% confident in your knowledge of this area, you should read through the entire chapter.

1 How many ways can you access the PIX Firewall?

2 What is the command to change the Telnet password?

3 Which version of SSH does PIX support?

4 What is the activation key?

5 Give one reason why you would need to change the activation key on your PIX Firewall.

Foundation Topics

Accessing the Cisco PIX Firewall

The PIX Firewall can be accessed via the console port or remotely through the following methods:

- Telnet
- Secure Shell (SSH)
- A browser using PIX Device Manger (PDM)

Console port access lets a single user configure the Cisco PIX Firewall. A user connects a PC or laptop to the PIX through the console access port using a rollover cable.

The following sections describe how to access the PIX remotely via Telnet and SSH. Chapter 11, "PIX Device Manager," covers access via the PDM as well as other aspects of the PDM in greater detail.

Accessing the Cisco PIX Firewall with Telnet

You can manage the PIX via Telnet from hosts on any internal interface. With IPSec configured, you can use Telnet to remotely administer the console of a Cisco PIX Firewall from lower-security interfaces.

To access the PIX Firewall via a Telnet connection, you have to first configure the PIX for Telnet access:

Step 1   Enter the PIX Firewall **telnet** command:

```
telnet local_ip [mask] [if_name]
```

You can identify a single host or a subnet that can have Telnet access to the PIX Firewall. For example, to let a host on the internal interface with an address of 10.1.1.1 access the PIX Firewall, enter the following:

```
telnet 10.1.1.24 255.255.255.255 inside
```

Step 2   Configure the Telnet password using the **passwd** command:

```
passwd telnetpassword
```

If you do not set a password, the default Telnet password is **cisco**.

Step 3   If required, set the duration for how long a Telnet session can be idle before the PIX disconnects the session. The default duration is 5 minutes. To configure the timeout for 15 minutes, you would enter

```
telnet timeout 15
```

Step 4 To protect access to the console with an authentication server, use the **aaa authentication telnet console** command. (AAA authentication is optional.)

This requires that you have a username and password on the authentication server. When you access the console, the PIX prompts you for these login credentials. If the authentication server is offline, you can still access the console by using the username **pix** and the password set with the **enable password** command.

Step 5 Save the commands in the configuration using the **write memory** command.

As soon as you have Telnet configured on the Cisco PIX Firewall, you are ready to access the PIX via a Telnet session. You can start a Telnet session to the PIX from the Windows command-line interface (CLI).

Accessing the Cisco PIX Firewall with Secure Shell (SSH)

SSH is an application running on top of a reliable transport layer, such as TCP/IP, that provides strong authentication and encryption capabilities. The Cisco PIX Firewall supports the SSH remote shell functionality provided in SSH version 1. SSH version 1 also works with Cisco IOS Software devices. Up to five SSH clients are allowed simultaneous access to the PIX console.

NOTE SSH v1.*x* and v2 are entirely different protocols and are incompatible. Make sure that you download a client that supports SSH v1.*x*.

Like Telnet, SSH also first has to be configured on the PIX Firewall. To configure the SSH, follow these steps:

Step 1 Identify a host/network to be used to access the PIX Firewall console using SSH. The syntax for the **ssh** command is

```
ssh ip_address [netmask] [interface_name]
```

For example, to let a host on the internal interface with an address of 10.1.1.1 access the PIX via SSH, enter the following:

```
ssh 10.1.1.25 255.255.255.255 inside
```

Step 2 The password used to perform local authentication is the same as the one used for Telnet access. It is set using the **passwd** command:

```
passwd password
```

Step 3   Specify how long in minutes a session can be idle before being
disconnected. The default duration is 5 minutes, although you can set this
duration anywhere between 1 and 60 minutes. The command to
configure this setting is as follows:

```
ssh timeout number
```

To gain access to the Cisco PIX Firewall console using SSH, you have to install an SSH
client. After installing the SSH client, enter the username **pix** (the default), and then enter
the password.

When you start an SSH session, a dot (.) appears on the Cisco PIX Firewall console before
the SSH user authentication prompt appears:

```
pix(config)# .
```

The display of the dot does not affect SSH's functionality. The dot appears at the console
when you generate a server key or decrypt a message using private keys during SSH key
exchange before user authentication occurs. These tasks can take up to 2 minutes or longer.
The dot is a progress indicator that verifies that the PIX is busy and has not hung.

Installing a New Operating System

Installing a new operating system (OS) on a Cisco PIX Firewall is similar in some respects
to installing a new OS on your PC. You must consider fundamental questions such as
whether you have enough memory and disk space (Flash size for PIX) when deciding
whether to upgrade the operating system. Table 4-1 shows the RAM and Flash memory
requirements for the different versions and releases of the Cisco PIX Firewall OS.

Table 4-1   *PIX Software RAM/Flash Memory Requirements*

PIX Software Version	Memory
PIX Software version 4.4(*x*)	2 MB Flash, 16 MB RAM
PIX Software version 5.0(*x*)	2 MB Flash, 32 MB RAM
PIX Software version 5.1(*x*)	2 MB Flash, 32 MB RAM
PIX Software version 5.2(*x*)	8 MB Flash, 32 MB RAM
PIX Software version 5.3(*x*)	8 MB Flash, 32 MB RAM
PIX Software version 6.0(*x*)	8 MB Flash, 32 MB RAM
PIX Software version 6.1(*x*)	8 MB Flash, 32 MB RAM
PIX Software version 6.2(*x*)	8 MB Flash, 32 MB RAM

In addition to the memory and Flash requirements, you should consider the model of Cisco
PIX Firewall before installing an OS. For example, the OS required for the Cisco PIX
Firewall model 506 is 5.1*x* or greater, the Cisco PIX Firewall model 525 needs 5.2*x* or
greater, and the Cisco PIX Firewall model 535 needs 5.3*x* or greater.

To determine the RAM memory and Flash memory you have running on your Cisco PIX Firewall, use the **show version** command. The output from this command also tells you which PIX OS you are currently running, as shown in Example 4-1.

Example 4-1 *Sample Output from the **show version** Command*

```
PIX520# show version

Cisco Secure PIX Firewall Version 5.1(1)
Compiled on Wed 23-Feb-00 10:22 by hyen

Finesse Bios V3.3

PIX520 up 7 days 13 hours

Hardware:   SE440BX2, 32 MB RAM, CPU Pentium II 349 MHz
Flash AT29C040A @ 0x300, 2MB
BIOS Flash AM28F256 @ 0xfffd8000, 32KB

Encryption hardware device: PIX PL2
0: ethernet0: address is 0090.2742.ff45, irq 11
1: ethernet1: address is 0090.2742.fdb6, irq 10
2: ethernet2: address is 0090.2743.0275, irq 15

Licensed Features:
Failover: Enabled
VPN-DES: Enabled
VPN-3DES: Disabled
Maximum Interfaces: 6

Serial Number: 18014702 (0x112e1ee)
<--- More --->

Activation Key: 0x8cb9bdcb 0x863a858b 0x2ae0c93b 0x3a46651a
```

As you can see, the OS version is 5.1(1), and the Flash memory size is 2 MB.

Notice the last line of Example 4-1, which starts with **Activation Key**. The activation key is the license key for the PIX OS. It is important to save your configuration and write down your activation key before upgrading to a newer version of the PIX OS.

Upgrading Your Activation Key

Three important reasons might prompt you to upgrade or change your activation key:

- Your Cisco PIX Firewall does not have failover activated.
- Your PIX does not currently have VPN-DES or VPN-3DES encryption enabled.
- You are upgrading from a connection-based license to a feature-based license.

Before the release of PIX 6.2, the activation keys were changed in monitor mode. Cisco PIX Firewall version 6.2 introduces a method of upgrading or changing the license for your Cisco PIX Firewall remotely without entering monitor mode and without replacing the software image. With this new feature, you can enter a new activation key for a different PIX license from the CLI. To enter an activation key, use the following command:

```
activation-key license#
```

You replace *license#* with the key you get with your new license. For example:

```
activation-key 0x14355378 0xabcdef01 0x2645678ab 0xcdef01274
```

After changing the activation key, you must reboot the PIX Firewall to enable the new license. If you are upgrading to a newer version and you are changing the activation key, you must reboot the Cisco PIX Firewall twice—once after the new image is installed, and again after the new activation key has been configured.

If you are downgrading to a lower Cisco PIX Firewall software version, it is important to ensure that the activation key running on your system is not intended for a higher version before you install the lower-version software image. If this is the case, you must first change the activation key to one that is compatible with the lower version before installing and rebooting. Otherwise, your system might refuse to reload after you install the new software image.

The **show activation-key** command output indicates the status of the activation key:

- If the activation key in the PIX Flash memory is the same as the activation key running on the PIX, the **show activation-key** output reads as follows:

    ```
    The flash activation key is the SAME as the running key.
    ```

- If the activation key in the PIX Flash memory is different from the activation key running on the PIX, the **show activation-key** output reads as follows:

    ```
    The flash activation key is DIFFERENT from the running key.
    The flash activation key takes effect after the next reload.
    ```

- If the PIX Flash memory software image version is not the same as the running PIX software image, the **show activation-key** output reads as follows:

    ```
    The flash image is DIFFERENT from the running image.
    The two images must be the same in order to examine the flash activation
    key.
    ```

Example 4-2 shows sample output from the **show activation-key** command.

Example 4-2   **show activation-key** *Command Output*

```
Pix(config)# show activation-key

Serial Number: 480221353 (0x1c9f98a9)
 Running Activation Key: 0x66df4255 0x36dc5fc 0x28d2ec4d 0x09f6287f
Licensed Features:
Failover:          Enabled
VPN-DES:           Enabled
VPN-3DES:          Enabled
```

Example 4-2 **show activation-key** *Command Output (Continued)*

```
Maximum Interfaces: 6
Cut-through Proxy:  Enabled
Guards:             Enabled
URL-filtering:      Enabled
Inside Hosts:       Unlimited
Throughput:         Unlimited
IKE peers:          Unlimited

The flash activation key is the SAME as the running key.
pix(config)#
```

Upgrading the Cisco PIX OS

There are three procedures for upgrading a PIX OS. The use of these procedures is determined by which PIX OS is currently running on the PIX device and the model of the Cisco PIX Firewall.

- You can use the **copy tftp flash** command (you must be in privileged mode to do this) with any Cisco PIX Firewall model running PIX Software version 5.1.1 or later.

- You can use this command from monitor mode. This is the same procedure as **copy tftp flash**, but as the name indicates, you are in a different mode (monitor mode instead of enable mode) when you copy from the TFTP server. PIX devices that do not have an internal floppy drive (501, 506, 515, 525, and 535) come with a ROM boot monitor program that is used to upgrade the Cisco PIX Firewall's image. For PIX devices that are running 5.0 and earlier OS versions, a boothelper disk is required to create boothelper mode, similar to ROM monitor mode.

- PIX Firewall version 6.2 introduces an HTTP client that lets you use the **copy** command to retrieve PIX configurations, software images, or Cisco PDM software from any HTTP server.

Upgrading the OS Using the copy tftp flash Command

Step 1 Download the binary software image file pix*nnx*.bin, where *nn* is the version number and *x* is the release number (which you can find at Cisco.com in the document "Cisco PIX Firewall Upgrading Feature Licenses and System Software"). Place the image file in the root of your TFTP server.

Step 2 Enter the **copy tftp flash** command.

Step 3 Enter the IP address of the TFTP server.

Step 4 Enter the source filename (the image file you downloaded—*.bin).

Step 5 Enter **Yes** to continue.

Example 4-3 shows a sample upgrade.

Example 4-3   *Upgrading the OS Using* **copy tftp flash** *Command*

```
PIX# copy tftp flash
Address or name of remote host [127.0.0.1]? 192.168.1.14
Source file name [cdisk]? pix611.bin
copying tftp://192.168.1.14/pix611.bin to flash
[yes¦no¦again]? yes
!!!!!!!!!!!!!!!!!!!!!!!!!!!!!!!!!!!!!!!!!!!!!!!!!!!!!!!!!!!!!!!!!!!!!!!!!!!!!!!!!!!!!!!
!!
Received 2562048 bytes
Erasing current image
Writing 2469944 bytes of image
!!!!!!!!!!!!!!!!!!!!!!!!!!!!!!!!!!!!!!!!!!!!!!!!!!!!!!!!!!!!!!!!!!!!!!!!!!!!!!!!!!!!!!!
!!
Image installed.
PIX#
```

NOTE   Under no circumstances must you ever download a Cisco PIX Firewall image earlier than version 4.4 with TFTP. Doing so corrupts the Cisco PIX Firewall Flash memory unit and requires special recovery methods that must be obtained from the Cisco TAC.

Upgrading the OS Using Monitor Mode

If you are upgrading your Cisco PIX Firewall from version 5.0.*x* or earlier to version 5.1.*x* or later, you need to use the boothelper or monitor mode method for the upgrade. This is because before version 5.1, the PIX Firewall Software did not provide a way to TFTP an image directly into Flash. Starting with PIX Firewall Software version 5.1, the **copy tftp flash** command was introduced to copy a new image directly into the PIX's Flash.

The following steps describe how to upgrade the PIX Firewall using monitor mode:

Step 1   Download the binary software image file pix*nnx*.bin, where *nn* is the version number and *x* is the release number (which you can find at Cisco.com in the document "Cisco PIX Firewall Upgrading Feature Licenses and System Software"). Place the image file in the root of your TFTP server.

Step 2   Reload the PIX, and press the Esc key (or enter a BREAK character) to enter monitor mode. For PIX devices running 5.0 and earlier OS versions, a boothelper disk is required. (See the section "Creating a Boothelper Diskette Using a Windows PC" later in this chapter.)

Step 3   Use the **interface** command to specify which PIX interface the TFTP server is connected out of. The default is **interface 1** (inside).

NOTE   The Cisco PIX Firewall cannot initialize a Gigabit Ethernet interface from monitor or boothelper mode. Use a Fast Ethernet or Token Ring interface instead.

Step 4   Use the **address** command followed by an IP address to specify the PIX interface IP address.

Step 5   Use the **server** command followed by an IP address to specify the TFTP server's IP address.

Step 6   Use the **file** command followed by the filename of the image on the TFTP server to specify the filename of the Cisco PIX Firewall image.

Step 7   Use the **ping** command followed by the IP address of the TFTP server to verify connectivity. (This is an optional but recommended command to test connectivity.)

Step 8   If needed, enter the **gateway** command to specify the IP address of a router gateway through which the server is accessible. (This is also an optional command.)

Step 9   Enter **tftp** to start downloading the image from the TFTP server.

Step 10   After the image downloads, you are prompted to install the new image. Enter **y** to install the image to Flash.

Step 11   When prompted to enter a new activation key, enter **y** if you want to enter a new activation key or **n** to keep your existing activation key.

Example 4-4 shows sample output for upgrading using monitor mode.

Example 4-4   *PIX Upgrade: Monitor Mode Output*

```
Using 1: i82558 @ PCI(bus:0 dev:14 irq:10), MAC: 0060.2422.e0b1
Use ? for help.
Monitor> interface 1
monitor> address 10.1.1.1

address 10.1.1.1
monitor> server 10.1.1.12

server 10.1.1.12
monitor> file pix601.bin

file cdisk
monitor> ping 10.1.1.12

Sending 5, 100-byte 0x5b8d ICMP Echoes to 10.1.12, timeout is 4 seconds:
!!!!!
Success rate is 100 percent (5/5)
```

continues

Example 4-4 *PIX Upgrade: Monitor Mode Output (Continued)*

```
monitor> tftp

tftp pix601.bin@10.1.1.12...............................
Received 626688 bytes

PIX admin loader (3.0) #0: Mon Oct 17 10:43:02 PDT 2002
Flash=AT29C040A @ 0x300
Flash version 6.0.1, Install version 6.0.1

Installing to flash
```

Upgrading the OS Using an HTTP Client

You can also perform a PIX OS upgrade by connecting to an HTTP server where the image is stored. To retrieve a configuration from an HTTP server, enter the following command:

configure http[s]://[*user:password@*]*location*[:*port*]/*pathname*

SSL is used when you enter **https**. The *user* and *password* options are used for basic authentication when you log in to the server. The *location* option is the server's IP address (or a name that resolves to the IP address). The *port* option specifies the port to contact on the server. It defaults to 80 for HTTP and to 443 for HTTPS. The *pathname* option is the name of the resource that contains the configuration to retrieve.

Creating a Boothelper Diskette Using a Windows PC

The boothelper diskette, as described earlier in this chapter, provides assistance for Cisco PIX Firewall models 510 and 520 running PIX Software version 5.0(*x*) or 4.*x* to be upgraded to a newer version:

Step 1 Go to the Cisco website and download the rawrite.exe utility, which you use to write the PIX binary image to a floppy diskette (you must have a CCO account to do this).

Step 2 Download the PIX binary image (.bin file) that corresponds to the software version you are upgrading to.

Step 3 Download the corresponding boothelper binary file that matches the version you are upgrading to.

For example, if you are upgrading from PIX Software version 5.3 to 6.1(1), you need to download three files:

— rawrite.exe

— pix611.bin

— bh61.bin (boothelper file)

Step 4   Run the rawrite.exe program by entering **rawrite** at the DOS prompt.
When prompted, enter the name of the boothelper file you want written
to the floppy diskette, as shown in Example 4-5.

Example 4-5   *Creating a Bootable Diskette from Windows*

```
C:\rawrite
RaWrite 1.2 - Write disk file to raw floppy diskette
Enter source file name: bh61.bin
Enter destination drive: a:
Please insert a formatted diskette into drive A: and press -ENTER- :
Number of sectors per track for this disk is 18.
Writing image to drive A:. Press ^C to abort.
Track: 11 Head: 1 Sector: 16
Done.
C:\>0
```

Reboot the PIX with the disk you created. The PIX comes up in boothelper mode. Follow
the procedure beginning with Step 3 of the earlier section "Upgrading the OS Using
Monitor Mode" to continue with the upgrade process.

Auto Update Support

Auto Update is a protocol specification introduced with Cisco PIX Firewall version 6.2.
The Auto Update specification provides the infrastructure necessary for remote
management applications to download PIX configurations and software images and
perform basic monitoring from a centralized location.

The Auto Update specification allows the Auto Update Server to either push configuration
information or send requests for information to the PIX, or it causes the PIX to periodically
poll the Auto Update Server. The Auto Update Server can also send a command to the PIX
to send an immediate polling request at any time. Communication between the Auto Update
Server and the PIX requires a communications path and local CLI configuration on each
Cisco PIX Firewall.

To configure the Auto Update server on the PIX, use the **auto-update server** command:

```
auto-update server url [verify-certificate]
```

In place of the *url* parameter, use the following syntax:

```
[http[s]://][user:password@]location[:port]/pathname
```

SSL is used when **https** is specified. The *user* and *password* segment is used for basic
authentication when you log in to the server. The *location* parameter is the server's IP
address (or a DNS host name that resolves to the IP address). The *port* segment specifies
the port to contact on the server. The default is 80 for HTTP and 443 for HTTPS. The
pathname segment is the name of the resource.

The **verify-certificate** option specifies that the certificate returned by the server should be verified.

Password Recovery

If you ever find yourself in the unfortunate circumstance of forgetting or losing the console and Telnet password to your Cisco PIX Firewall, don't panic. Like most Cisco products, PIX devices have a procedure to recover lost passwords. Unlike the Cisco router password recovery process, which entails changing the configuration register number, PIX uses a different method. PIX uses a password lockout utility to regain access to the locked-out device. The password lockout utility is based on the PIX software release you are running. Table 4-2 shows the binary filename (that is included with the utility) and the corresponding PIX OS on which it is used. These files can be downloaded from the Cisco website.

Table 4-2   *PIX OS Filenames*

Filename	PIX Software Version
nppix.bin	4.3 and earlier releases
np44.bin	4.4 release
np50.bin	5.0 release
np51.bin	5.1 release
np52.bin	5.2 release
np60.bin	6.0 release
np61.bin	6.1 release
np62.bin	6.2 release

When you boot the Cisco PIX Firewall with one of these binary files, the console password is erased from Flash memory, the enable password is erased, and the Telnet password is reset to **cisco**.

Cisco PIX Firewall Password Recovery: Getting Started

The procedure for password recovery on the Cisco PIX Firewall with a floppy drive is slightly different than with a diskless Cisco PIX Firewall. The difference is in how the Cisco PIX Firewall boots with the binary files listed in Table 4-2. Firewall models that have a floppy drive boot from a disk, and diskless firewall models boot from a TFTP server.

In addition to the binary files, you need the following items:

- Laptop or PC
- Terminal-emulating software
- TFTP software (only for diskless PIX Firewall models)
- The rawrite.exe utility (needed only for firewall models that have floppy drives to create the boot disk)

Password Recovery Procedure for a PIX with a Floppy Drive (PIX 520)

Step 1   Create the boot disk by executing the rawrite.exe file on your laptop or PC and writing np*xxn*.bin to the bootable floppy.

Step 2   Make sure that your terminal-emulating software is running on your PC and that you connected the console cable to the Cisco PIX Firewall.

NOTE   Because you are locked out, you see only a password prompt.

Step 3   Insert the PIX Password Lockout Utility disk into the PIX's floppy drive. Push the Reset button on the front of the PIX.

Step 4   The PIX boots from the floppy, and you see a message that says "Erasing Flash Password. Please eject diskette and reboot."

Step 5   Eject the disk and press the Reset button. Now you can log in without a password.

Step 6   When you are prompted for a password, press Enter. The default Telnet password after this process is "cisco." The enable password is also erased, and you have to enter a new one.

Password Recovery Procedure for a Diskless PIX (PIX 501, 506, 515, 525, and 535)

Step 1   Start your terminal-emulation software and connect your laptop or PC to the PIX's console port.

Step 2   After you power on the Cisco PIX Firewall and the startup messages appear, send a BREAK character or press the Esc key. The **monitor>** prompt is displayed.

Step 3   At the **monitor>** prompt, use the **interface** command to specify which interface the ping traffic should use.

Step 4   Use the **address** command to specify the IP address of the PIX interface.

Step 5   Use the **server** command to specify the IP address of the remote TFTP server containing the PIX password recovery file.

Step 6   Use the **gateway** command to specify the IP address of a router gateway through which the server is accessible.

Step 7   Use the **file** command to specify the filename of the PIX password recovery file, such as np62.bin.

Step 8   Use the **tftp** command to start the download. As the password recovery file loads, the following message is displayed:

```
Do you wish to erase the passwords? [yn] y
Passwords have been erased.
```

Foundation Summary

- The PIX can be accessed for management purposes in several different ways. It can be accessed via the console port, remotely through Telnet, via SSH, and through the PIX Device Manager (PDM).

- Before upgrading the Cisco PIX Firewall OS, it is important to determine your current hardware settings—namely, the RAM and Flash memory size.

- The activation key is the license for the PIX OS. Before the release of PIX 6.2, the activation keys were changed in monitor mode. Cisco PIX Firewall version 6.2 introduces a method of upgrading or changing the license for your PIX remotely without entering monitor mode and without replacing the software image using the **activation-key** command.

- There are three ways to perform the PIX Firewall OS upgrade:

  — **copy tftp flash**

  — Using monitor mode with a boothelper diskette for PIX firewalls with an OS version earlier than 5.0

  — Using an HTTP client (available only with version 6.2)

- Auto Update is a protocol specification introduced with Cisco PIX Firewall version 6.2. The Auto Update specification provides the infrastructure necessary for remote management applications to download PIX configurations and software images and to perform basic monitoring from a centralized location.

- It is possible to recover from a lockout from the Cisco PIX Firewall due to forgotten or lost passwords. After determining the PIX's OS version, you can download the corresponding file and boot the PIX through monitor mode.

Q&A

As mentioned in the Introduction, the questions in this book are more difficult than what you should experience on the exam. The questions do not attempt to cover more breadth or depth than the exam; however, they are designed to make sure that you know the answer. Hopefully, these questions will help limit the number of exam questions on which you narrow your choices to two options and then guess. Be sure to use the CD and take the simulated exams.

The answers to these questions can be found in Appendix A.

1   What command upgrades a PIX 525 device running a 5.3 OS version to 6.11?

   A   install

   B   setup

   C   copy 6.11

   D   copy tftp flash

2   What binary file is required to perform a password recovery procedure on a PIX device running OS version 5.2?

   A   np52.bin

   B   pix52.bin

   C   bh52.bin

   D   pass52.bin

3   What circumstance(s) warrant(s) the use of a boothelper disk in the OS upgrade procedure?

   A   A corrupt binary image

   B   A PIX 520 device

   C   A PIX device running a 5.0 or earlier PIX OS

   D   No circumstance warrants the use of a boothelper disk.

4   What is the console password set to after a successful password recovery procedure?

   A   password

   B   cisco

   C   secret

   D   It is erased and set to blank.

5 What is the Telnet password set to after a successful password recovery procedure?

A password

B cisco

C secret

D It is erased and set to blank.

6 Which of the following could be reasons to change (upgrade) your activation key for the PIX?

A You are upgrading your memory.

B Your current PIX Firewall does not have failover activated.

C You are upgrading the processor on your PIX Firewall.

D Your current PIX Firewall does not have VPN-3DES enabled.

7 What command changes the SSH password for login?

A **change ssh password**

B **password**

C **passwd**

D **ssh pass**

8 What is the default amount of time a Telnet session can be idle?

A 2 minutes

B 15 minutes

C 5 minutes

D 12 minutes

9 What is the command to configure Auto Update on the Cisco PIX Firewall?

A **auto update**

B **auto-update server** *url*

C **config auto-update**

D **update server** *url*

10 Which version of SSH does the PIX support?

    A   2.1

    B   2.2

    C   3.1

    D   1

This chapter covers the following exam topics for the Cisco Secure PIX Firewall Advanced Exam:

9. ASA security levels
14. Transport Protocols
15. Network Address Translation
17. Port Address Translations
18. Configuring DNS support

CHAPTER 5

Understanding Cisco PIX Firewall Translation and Connections

This chapter presents an overview of the different network transport protocols and how they are processed by the PIX Firewall.

How to Best Use This Chapter

Reconsider the comment in the Introduction about how important it is to *know* the PIX commands, not just have an idea of what they are and what they do. It is very important to fully understand the concepts discussed in this chapter, because they are the basis for the topics discussed in Chapter 6, "Getting Started with the Cisco PIX Firewall." To completely understand how the many different PIX commands work, you must first have a good understanding of how the Cisco PIX Firewall processes network traffic.

"Do I Know This Already?" Quiz

The purpose of this quiz is to help you determine your current understanding of the topics covered in this chapter. Write down your answers and compare them to the answers in Appendix A. If you have to look at any references to correctly answer the questions about PIX functionality, you should read that portion and double-check your thinking by reviewing the Foundation Summary topics.

1 What is the difference between TCP and UDP?

2 On which transport protocol does PIX change the sequence number?

3 What is the default security for traffic origination on the inside network segment going to the outside network?

4 True or false: You can have multiple translations in a single connection.

5 What commands are required to complete NAT on a Cisco PIX Firewall?

6 How many external IP addresses must be used to configure PAT?

7 True or false: NAT requires that you configure subnets for the external IP addresses.

8 How many nodes can you hide behind a single IP address when configuring PAT?

9 How does PAT support multimedia protocols?

10 What is an embryonic connection?

11 What is the best type of translation to use to allow connections to web servers from the Internet?

12 How does the Cisco PIX Firewall handle outbound DNS requests?

Foundation Topics

How the PIX Firewall Handles Traffic

The term *network security* simply refers to the application of security principles to a computer network. To apply security to a network, you must first understand how networks function. It stands to reason that to secure how traffic flows across a network, you must first understand how that traffic flows. This chapter discusses end-to-end traffic flow and how that traffic is handled by the Cisco PIX Firewall.

Interface Security Levels and the Default Security Policy

By default, the Cisco PIX Firewall applies security levels to each interface. The more secure the network segment, the higher the security number. Security levels range from 0 to 100. By default, 0 is applied to Ethernet 0 and is given the default name *outside*. 100 is applied to Ethernet 1 and is given the default name *inside*. Any additional interfaces are configured using the **nameif** command. The security level can be from 1 to 99. The Adaptive Security Algorithm (ASA) allows traffic from a higher security level to pass to a lower security level without a specific rule in the security policy allowing the connection as long as a **nat/global** command is configured for those interfaces. Any traffic passing from a lower security level to a higher security level must be allowed by the security policy (that is, access lists or conduits). If two interfaces are assigned the same security level, traffic cannot pass between those interfaces (this configuration is not recommended).

Transport Protocols

Traffic that traverses a network always has a source and destination address. This communication is based on the seven layers of the OSI reference model. Layers 5 through 7 (the upper layers) handle the application data, and Layers 1 through 4 (lower layers) are responsible for moving the data from the source to the destination. The data is created at the application layer (Layer 7) on the source machine. Transport information is added to the upper-layer data, and then network information, followed by data link information. At this point the information is transmitted across the physical medium as electronic signals. The upper-layer data combined with the transport information is called a *segment*. As soon as the network information is added to the segment, it is called a *packet*. The packet is encapsulated at the data link layer (Layer 2) with the addition of the source and destination MAC address and is now called a *frame*. Figure 5-1 shows how the data is encapsulated at each layer of the OSI reference model.

Figure 5-1 *Encapsulation of Upper-Layer Data*

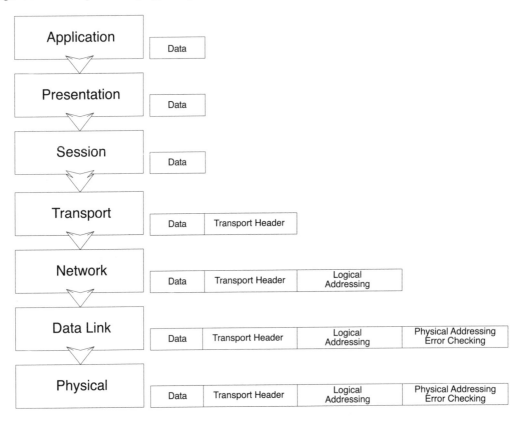

The two transport protocols used by TCP/IP are Transmission Control Protocol (TCP) and User Datagram Protocol (UDP). These protocols are very different. Each has its strengths and weaknesses. For this reason, they are used in different ways to play on their strengths:

- **TCP**—a connection-oriented transport protocol that is responsible for reliability and efficiency of communication between nodes. TCP completes these tasks by creating connections as *virtual circuits* that act as two-way communications between the source and destination. TCP is very reliable and guarantees the delivery of data between nodes. TCP also can dynamically modify a connection's transmission variables based on changing network conditions. TCP sequence numbers and TCP acknowledgment numbers are included in the TCP header. These features allow the source and destination to verify the correct, orderly delivery of data. Unfortunately, the overhead required for TCP can make it slow and keeps it from being the optimum transport protocol for some connections.

- **UDP**—a connectionless transport protocol that is used to get the data to the destination. UDP provides no error checking, no error correction, and no verification of delivery. UDP defers the reliability issues to the upper-layer protocols and simply resends the data rather than verifying delivery. UDP is a very simple and very fast protocol.

The upper layers determine which of the transport protocols is used when data is encapsulated at the source node.

Figure 5-2 illustrates the TCP communication between nodes that do not have a firewall between them. This connection requires four different transmissions to negotiate the connection:

1 The source sends a segment to the destination, asking to open a TCP session. A TCP flag is set to SYN, indicating that the source wants to initiate synchronization or a handshake. The source generates a TCP sequence number of 125.

2 The destination receives the request and sends back a reply with the TCP flags ACK and SYN set, indicating an acknowledgment of the SYN bit (receive flow) and initiation of the transmit flow. It replies to the original TCP sequence number by adding 1, sending back a sequence number of 126. It also generates and sends its own TCP sequence number, 388.

3 The source receives the SYN/ACK and sends back an ACK to indicate the acknowledgment of the SYN for the setup of the receive flow. It adds 1 to the value of the TCP sequence number generated by the destination and sends back the number 389.

4 The acknowledgment is received, and the handshake is complete.

Figure 5-2 *TCP Communication Between Nodes Without a PIX*

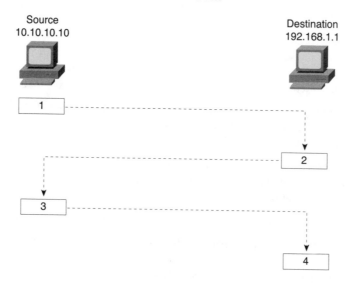

Now look at how this communication is handled by the Cisco PIX Firewall (see Figure 5-3). You first notice that the number of steps required for the same transaction has changed from four to eight, although everything appears to be the same to both the source and destination.

Figure 5-3   *TCP Communication Between Nodes with a PIX*

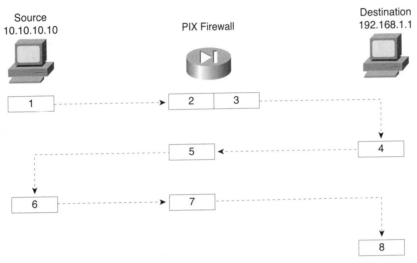

The following is a list of actions taken by the Cisco PIX Firewall when processing a TCP handshake and opening a TCP session (refer to Figure 5-3):

1 The source machine initiates the connection by sending SYN. It is received by the Cisco PIX Firewall en route to the destination. PIX verifies the connection against the running configuration to determine if translation is to be completed. The running configuration is stored in memory, so this process occurs very quickly. The firewall checks to see if the inside address, 10.10.10.10, is to be translated to an outside address—in this case, 192.168.1.10 s/b 192.168.1.1. If the translation is to be completed, the PIX creates a *translation slot* if one does not already exist for this connection.

2 All the session information is written to the state table, and the Cisco PIX Firewall randomly generates a new TCP sequence number. This connection slot is marked in the state table as an *embryonic* (half-open) connection.

3 After the connection is verified against the security policy, the PIX allows the connection outside using the translated source address and the newly generated TCP sequence number.

4 The destination receives the connection request (SYN) and replies with a SYN ACK.

5 The PIX verifies the SYN ACK from the destination and matches the acknowledgment number against the randomly generated sequence number. It verifies the connection slot and forwards the connection back to the source using the original source address and sequence number plus 1.

6 Any packets that do not match the session object exactly are dropped and logged.

7 The source completes the connection by responding with an ACK. The acknowledgment number is not randomized as it passes through the PIX, and the connection slot is marked as *active-established*.

8 The embryonic counter is reset, and data is transmitted between the nodes.

The process used by the PIX to handle UDP traffic is completely different from the process for TCP traffic. This is due to UDP's characteristics. UDP is a connectionless protocol that does not negotiate a connection. Without any setup or termination, it is very difficult to determine the state of a UDP session. Because of the inability to determine session state, it is very easy to spoof UDP packets and hijack a UDP session. Some applications use UDP rather than TCP for data transfer. Many of these are real-time applications or applications that have no reliability requirements. These applications include network video applications, Common Internet File System (CIFS), NetBIOS Domain Name System (DNS), and remote procedure call (RPC).

The default security policy allows UDP packets to pass from a higher security level to a lower security level. For UDP packets to pass in the other direction, they must be allowed by the security policy. It is very important to restrict inbound UDP access as much as possible. Due to UDP's limitations, many applications that operate over UDP are targets for exploitation by hackers.

The Cisco PIX Firewall handles UDP traffic in the following manner:

1 The source machine initiates the UDP connection. It is received by the PIX Firewall en route to the destination. The PIX applies the default rule and any necessary translation, creates a session object in the state table, and allows the connection to pass to the outside interface.

2 Any return traffic is matched with the session object, and the session timeout is applied. The session timeout is 2 minutes by default. If the response does not match the session object or is not within the timeout, the packet is dropped. If everything matches, the response is allowed through to the requesting source.

3 Any inbound UDP sessions from a lower security level to a higher security level must be allowed by the security policy, or the connection is dropped.

Address Translation

The current Internet Protocol standard being used is version 4 (IPv4). IPv4 consists of 32 bits, which represents approximately 4 billion individual IP addresses. This seems like a tremendous number of addresses, but the Internet continues to grow at an incredible rate, and with the current standard, we will run out of addresses. Two factors are being implemented to help deal with this issue. This first is Internet Protocol version 6 (IPv6). IPv6 is a total redesign of the Internet Protocol and is still in development. The second factor that is being used to conserve the public address space is RFC 1918, which defines address allocation for private internets. RFC 1918 sets aside network space to be used for private networks. This address space is not accessible via the public Internet. The Internet Assigned Numbers Authority (IANA) reserved the following address space for private networks:

10.0.0.0 through 10.255.255.255: 16,777,214 hosts
172.16.0.0 through 172.31.255.255: 1,048,574 hosts
192.168.0.0 through 192.168.255.255: 65,534 hosts

RFC 1918 has had a tremendous impact on Internet addressing and the design of public and private networks. The challenge to RFC 1918 addressing is that private addresses cannot be publicly routed. Hence, address translation is implemented. Not only does address translation provide a method of conserving public address space, it also provides an additional level of protection for internal nodes, because there is no way to route to a private address from the Internet.

Address translation is the method used by the Cisco PIX Firewall to give internal nodes with private IP addresses access to the Internet. The internal node addresses that are translated are called *local addresses,* and the addresses that are translated to are called *global addresses.* **nat** and **global** commands are applied to specific interfaces. Most commonly, Network Address Translation (NAT) takes place, translating internal addresses to external addresses, although the PIX is not limited to this configuration. It is possible to translate any address at one interface to another address at any other interface. Two types of NAT can be implemented on a Cisco PIX Firewall:

- **Dynamic address translation**—Translates multiple local addresses into a limited number of global public addresses or possibly a single global address. This is called *dynamic address translation* because the firewall selects the first available global address and assigns it when creating an outbound connection. The internal source retains the global address for the duration of the connection. Dynamic address translation is broken into two types:

  - **Network Address Translation (NAT)**—Translating multiple local addresses to a pool of global addresses.

  - **Port Address Translation (PAT)**—Translating multiple local addresses to a single global address. This method is called *Port Address Translation* because the firewall uses a single translated source address but changes the source port to allow multiple connections via a single global address. The limitation for PAT is approximately 64,000 hosts due to the limited number of available ports (65,535) and the number of ports already assigned to specific services. Some applications do not work through PAT because they require specific source and destination ports.

- **Static translation**—Allows for a one-to-one ratio of local to global addresses. Static translation is commonly used when the internal node must be accessed from the Internet. Web servers and mail servers must have static addresses so that users on the Internet can connect to them via their global address.

Translation Commands

Table 5-1 describes the commands and arguments used to configure NAT, PAT, and static translation on a Cisco PIX Firewall. All the PIX commands are covered in much greater detail in Chapter 6. This table helps you understand the syntax of the commands given in the following examples.

Table 5-1 *Translation Commands*

Command	Description
nat	Associates a network with a pool of global addresses.
global	Identifies the global addresses to be used for translation.
static	Maps the one-to-one relationship between local addresses and global addresses.
netmask	A reserved word that is required to identify the network mask.
dns	Specifies that DNS replies that match the xlate should be translated.
outside	Allows you to enable or disable address translation for the external addresses.
timeout	Sets the idle timeout for the translation slot.
id	Also called the *nat_id*. The number that matches the **nat** statement with the **global** statement. This is how the PIX determines which local addresses translate to which global address pool.
internal_if_name	The interface name for the network with the higher security level.
external_if_name	The interface name for the network with the lower security level.
local_ip	The IP addresses or network that are to be translated. This can be a specific network segment (10.10.10.0) or can include all addresses (0.0.0.0).
global_ip	The IP address or range of IP addresses that the local addresses translate to.
network_mask	The network mask for a specific network segment. This applies to both local and global addresses.
max_cons	The maximum number of concurrent connections allowed through a static translation.
em_limit	The maximum number of allowed embryonic connections. The default is 0, which allows unlimited connections. You can limit the number of embryonic connections to reduce an attack's effectiveness by flooding embryonic connections.
norandomseq	This option stops the ASA from randomizing the TCP sequence numbers. This normally is used if the firewall is located inside another firewall and data is being scrambled, with both firewalls randomizing the sequence number.

Network Address Translation

NAT allows you to translate a large number of local addresses behind a limited number of global addresses. This lets you keep your internal network addressing scheme hidden from external networks. To configure NAT on a Cisco PIX Firewall, you simply need to define the local and global addresses. In Figure 5-4, all nodes on the internal network are being translated to a pool of addresses on the external network.

Figure 5-4   *Network Address Translation*

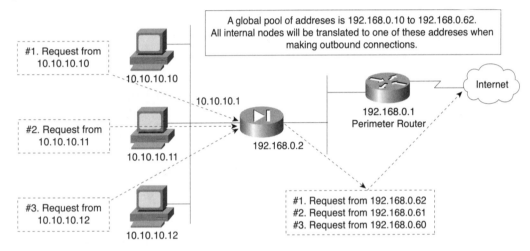

Two commands are required to complete this configuration:

- **nat**—Defines the addresses to be translated:

```
LabPIX(config)# [nat] [(internal_if_name)] [id] [local_ip] [network_mask]
```

Here's an example:

```
LabPIX(config)# nat (inside) 1 0.0.0.0 0.0.0.0
```

- **global**—Defines the pool of addresses to translate to:

```
LabPIX(config)# [global] [(external_if_name)] [id] [global_ip] [netmask]
   [network_mask]
```

Here's an example:

```
LabPIX(config)# global (outside) 1 192.168.0.10-192.168.0.62 netmask
   255.255.255.192
```

Notice the [*id*] in both the **nat** and **global** commands. It allows you to assign specific addresses to translate. The addresses in the **nat** command translate to the addresses in the global command that contains the same ID. The only ID that cannot be used here is 0. The command **nat 0** is used on the PIX to identify addresses that are *not* to be translated. The **nat 0** command is commonly called the "no nat" command.

Port Address Translation

PAT allows you to translate your local addresses behind a single global address. The commands required to perform PAT are exactly the same as NAT. The only difference in defining PAT is that you define a single global address rather than a range. Figure 5-5 shows all local nodes behind a single global address being translated.

Figure 5-5   *Port Address Translation*

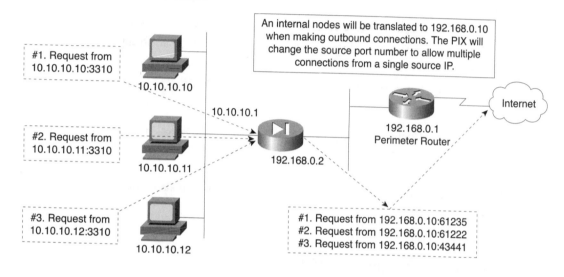

Here's the **nat** command syntax:

```
LabPIX(config)# [nat] [(internal_if_name)] [id] [local_ip] [network_mask]
```

Here's an example:

```
LabPIX(config)# nat (inside) 1 0.0.0.0 0.0.0.0
```

Here's the **global** command syntax:

```
LabPIX(config)# [global] [(external_if_name)] [id] [global_ip] [netmask]
   [network_mask]
```

Here's an example:

```
LabPIX(config)# global (outside) 1 192.168.0.10 netmask 255.255.255.255
```

Static Translation

Although static translation is not an exam topic, it is very important for you to understand how it works. Static translation maps a single local address to a single global address. It is most commonly used when the local node must be accessed from the public space (Internet). In the following command, the local node 10.10.10.9 is configured to have a global address of 192.168.0.9. Remember that the **static** command configures only the address translation. To allow access to the local node from a lower security level interface, you need to configure either a *conduit* or an *access list*:

```
LabPIX(config)# [static] [(internal_if_name, external_if_name)] [global_ip]
  [local_ip]
LabPIX(config)# static (inside, outside) 192.168.0.9 10.10.10.9
LabPIX(config)# conduit permit tcp host 192.168.0.9 eq www any
```

or

```
LabPIX(config)# access-list 101 permit tcp any host 192.168.0.9 eq www
```

If you are using an access list, you need to create an access group to apply the access list to the correct interface:

```
LabPIX(config)# access-group 101 in interface outside
```

NOTE   Chapter 7, "Configuring Access," discusses conduits and access lists in greater detail.

This is the configuration used in Figure 5-6. Note that the node is now accessible from the Internet.

Figure 5-6   *Static Translation*

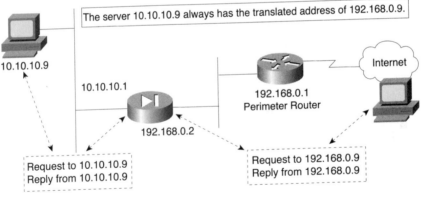

The server 10.10.10.9 always has the translated address of 192.168.0.9.

10.10.10.9

10.10.10.1

192.168.0.2

192.168.0.1
Perimeter Router

Internet

Request to 10.10.10.9
Reply from 10.10.10.9

Request to 192.168.0.9
Reply from 192.168.0.9

Using the static Command for Port Redirection

One of the improvements of PIX OS version 6.0 is that the **static** command can be used to redirect services to specific ports as well as translate the host's address. This command allows the outside user to connect to a specific address/port and have the PIX redirect the traffic to the appropriate inside/DMZ server. The syntax for this command is as follows:

```
LabPIX(config)# [static] [(internal_if_name, external_if_name)] {tcp | udp}
   [global_ip] [global_port] [local_ip] [local_port] [netmask mask]
   [max connections [emb_limit[noramdomseq]]]
```

For example:

```
LabPIX(config)# static (inside, outside) tcp 192.168.0.9 ftp 10.10.10.9 2100 netmask
   255.255.255.255 0 0
```

Configuring Multiple Translation Types on the Cisco PIX Firewall

It is a good practice to use a combination of NAT and PAT. If you have more internal hosts than external IP addresses, you can configure both NAT and PAT. Your first group of hosts translates to the global addresses that are listed, and the remaining hosts use PAT and translate to the single global address. If you do not configure NAT and PAT, the PIX automatically performs NAT starting at the highest IP of the global IP range and performs PAT with the lowest IP after all other addresses have been used. If the location has any servers that need to be accessed from the Internet (web servers, mail servers, and so on), they must be configured for static translation.

In the following syntax examples, the internal network consisting of 254 hosts translates to 52 external addresses (192.168.0.10 to 192.168.0.62). This means that the remaining 202 hosts translate to 192.168.0.63.

```
LabPIX(config)# [nat] [(internal_if_name)] [id] [local_ip] [network_mask]
LabPIX(config)# nat (inside) 1 10.10.10.0 255.255.255.0
LabPIX(config)# [global] [(external_if_name)] [id] [global_ip] [netmask]
   [network_mask]
LabPIX(config)# global (outside) 1 192.168.0.10-192.168.0.62 netmask
255.255.255.192
LabPIX(config)# [global] [(external_if_name)] [id] [global_ip] [netmask]
   [network_mask]
LabPIX(config)# global (outside) 1 192.168.0.63 netmask 255.255.255.255
```

NOTE   It is recommended that any devices that have a static translation and are accessed from the Internet be segregated from the rest of the internal network. These devices should be on a separate network segment that connects to an additional interface on the PIX Firewall. This is normally called a *demilitarized zone (DMZ) segment.*

The addresses assigned for static translation cannot be part of the global IP pool. This is a one-to-one relationship between the outside address and the address being translated.

Example 5-1 shows the commands for this type of configuration.

Example 5-1 *Configuring Multiple Translation Types*

```
LabPIX(config)# nat (inside) 1 0.0.0.0 0.0.0.0
LabPIX(config)# global (outside) 1 192.168.0.10-192.168.0.61 netmask
  255.255.255.192
LabPIX(config)# global (outside) 1 192.168.0.62 netmask 255.255.255.255
LabPIX(config)# static (DMZ, outside) 192.168.0.3 172.16.1.2
LabPIX(config)# static (DMZ, outside) 192.168.0.4 172.16.1.3
LabPIX(config)# static (DMZ, outside) 192.168.0.5 172.16.1.4
LabPIX(config)# access-list 101 permit tcp [specific source] host 192.168.0.3 eq
  smtp
LabPIX(config)# access-list 101 permit tcp any host 192.168.0.4 eq www
LabPIX(config)# access-list 101 permit udp [specific source] host 192.168.0.5 eq
  domain
LabPIX(config)# access-group 101 in interface outside
```

Figure 5-7 depicts the configuration shown in Example 5-1. Note that the traffic that is allowed inbound is routed to the DMZ rather than going to the internal network. Remember that static translation provides the mechanism for external hosts to connect to internal nodes, but because the connection is from a lower security level to a higher security level, there must be a rule in the security policy allowing the connection.

Figure 5-7 *Combined NAT, PAT, and Static Translation*

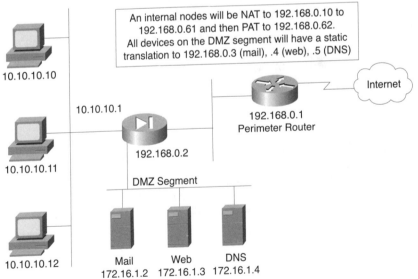

Bidirectional Network Address Translation

Cisco PIX Firewall software version 6.2 allows NAT of external source IP addresses for packets traveling from the outside interface to an inside interface. All the functionality available with traditional **nat**, **pat**, and **static** commands is available bidirectionally.

Translation Versus Connection

A single user on a workstation located on the internal network is connecting to his web-based e-mail, making an online stock purchase, researching a new software package that he intends to buy, and backing up a database at a remote branch office. How many connections does he have going from his workstation? It is difficult to tell, because many of these tasks require multiple connections between the source and destination. How many translated sessions does he have going? One.

Most configurations create a single translated session, and from that session the user can create multiple connections. It is possible to create multiple translated sessions. This normally occurs when the internal node is accessing resources via different network segments all attached to the firewall (such as outside, DMZ1, DMZ2, and so on).

Translation occurs at the network layer (Layer 3) of the OSI model and deals only with packets. Connections, however, deal with the transport layer (Layer 4). Therefore, connections can be considered a subset of a single translation. It is possible to troubleshoot both translation and connection issues. It is recommended that you verify translation before attempting to troubleshoot a connection problem, because the connection cannot be established if the translation has not occurred.

The command used to troubleshoot translations is **xlate**. You can see the translation table by using the command **show xlate**, or you can clear the table with **clear xlate**. Any time you make a change to the translation table, it is a good idea to **clear xlate**. This forces the translation slots to drop, and the Cisco PIX Firewall rebuilds the translation table. If you do not run the **clear xlate** command, the system does not drop the translation slots until they time out, which is 3 hours by default. The following commands can make a change to the translation table:

- **nat**
- **global**
- **static**
- **route**
- **alias**
- **conduit**

Table 5-2 documents the options and arguments that come into play with the **show xlate** and **clear xlate** commands.

Table 5-2   **show/clear xlate** *Command Options*

Command Option	Description
detail	If specified, displays the translation type and interface information.
[**global**	**local** *ip1*[-*ip2*] [**netmask** *mask*]	Displays active translations by global IP address or local IP address using the network mask to qualify the IP address.
interface *if1* [,*if2*] [,*ifn*]	Displays active translations by interface.
lport	**gport** *port* [-*port*]	Displays active translations by local and global ports.
state	Displays active translations by state (use the translation flags listed in Table 5-3).

Table 5-3   *Translation Flags*

Flag	Description
s	Static translation slot
d	Dumps the translation slot on the next cleaning cycle
r	Port map translation (PAT)
n	No randomization of TCP sequence number
o	Outside address translations
i	Inside address translations
D	DNS A RR rewrite
I	Identity translation from nat0

If you cannot clear **xlate**, it is possible (but not preferred) to clear the translation table by doing a reload, or by rebooting the PIX.

The command used to troubleshoot connections is **show conn**. This command displays the number and status of all active TCP connections for the specific options selected. Table 5-4 lists the many options for the **show conn** command.

Table 5-4   **show conn** *Command Options*

Command Option	Description
count	Displays the number of used connections (its accuracy depends on the volume and type of traffic).
detail	Displays the specified translation type and interface information.
foreign I **local** *ip* [*-ip2*] **netmask** *mask*	Displays active connections by foreign or local IP address and qualifies connections by network mask.
fport I **lport** *port1* [*-port2*]	Displays foreign or local active connections by port.
protocol tcp I **udp** I *protocol*	Displays active connections by protocol type.
state	Displays active connections by their current state (see Table 5-5).

Table 5-5   *Connection Flags*

Flag	Description
U	Up
f	Inside FIN
F	Outside FIN
r	Inside acknowledged FIN
R	Outside acknowledged FIN
s	Awaiting outside SYN
S	Awaiting inside SYN
M	SMTP data
T	TCP SIP connection
I	Inbound data
O	Outbound data
q	SQL*Net data
d	Dump
P	Inside back connection
E	Outside back connection
G	Group
a	Awaiting outside ACK to SYN
A	Awaiting inside ACK to SYN
B	Initial SYN from outside

continues

Table 5-5 *Connection Flags (Continued)*

Flag	Description
R	RPC
H	H.323
T	UDP SIP connection
m	SIP media connection
t	SIP transient connection
D	DNS

Configuring DNS Support

It is not necessary to configure DNS support on the Cisco PIX Firewall. By default, the PIX identifies each outbound DNS request and allows only a single response to that request. The internal host can query several DNS servers for a response, and the PIX allows the outbound queries. However, the PIX allows only the first response to pass through the firewall. All subsequent responses to the original query are dropped.

Foundation Summary

The Foundation Summary is a consolidation of the information covered in this chapter. It helps you continue to review the information in this chapter to prepare for the Certification Exam.

All interfaces on the Cisco PIX Firewall are assigned security levels. The higher the number, the more secure the interface. Traffic is allowed to pass from an interface with a higher security level to an interface with a lower security level without a specific rule in the security policy. By default, the outside interface (Ethernet 0) is assigned a security level of 0, and the inside interface (Ethernet 1) is assigned a security level of 100. All other interfaces must be manually assigned a security level using the **nameif** command. Traffic does not pass through two interfaces if they have the same security level.

The PIX Firewall handles the two transport protocols completely differently. Because TCP is connection-oriented and creates a session, it is relatively simple for the PIX to handle the traffic. TCP also generates a TCP sequence number, and the PIX randomizes that number as it passes through the firewall on its way to the destination. This way, it is very difficult to hijack a TCP session by selecting the next sequence number in the series. Figure 5-8 shows how the PIX Firewall handles a TCP handshake.

Figure 5-8 *PIX Handling TCP Traffic*

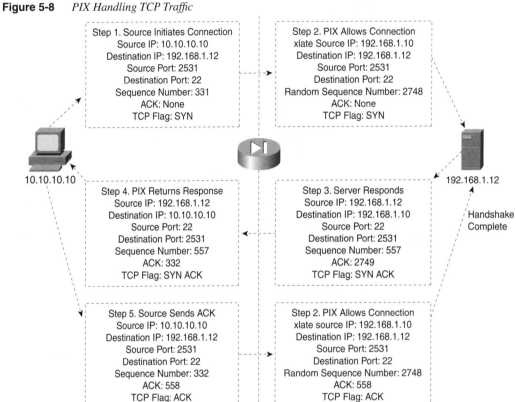

UDP is a connectionless protocol, so it is very difficult to determine a connection's state. When outbound UDP traffic is generated, the PIX completes the necessary address translation and saves the session object in the state. If the response does not arrive within the timeout period (the default is 2 minutes), the connection is closed. If the response arrives within the timeout, the PIX verifies the connection information. If it matches the session object in the state table, the PIX allows the traffic. Figure 5-9 shows how the PIX typically handles UDP traffic.

There are two types of address translation:

- **Dynamic address translation** is broken into two categories:
  - **Network Address Translation (NAT)**—Multiple local hosts translate to a pool of global addresses.
  - **Port Address Translation (PAT)**—Multiple local hosts translate to a single global address.

Figure 5-9   *PIX Handling UDP Traffic*

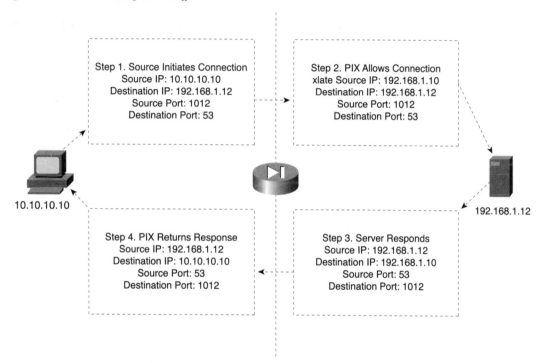

- **Static translation**—A single local address translates to a single global address. Static rules provide the translation to allow connection from a lower security level to a higher security level, but this connection must be allowed in the security policy. This connection can be allowed using either the **conduit** or **access-list** command. Access lists must be part of an access group and must be configured to a specific interface.

Multiple connections can take place through a single translation. Translations take place at the network layer, and connections occur at the transport layer. Therefore, connections are a subset of translations. Two specific commands are used to troubleshoot translation:

- **show xlate**—This command displays translation slot information. Many options are available to display specific information about the address translations.
- **clear xlate**—This command clears the translation table. Again, many options allow you to clear specific portions of the translation table.

A single command with numerous options is used to troubleshoot connections:

- **show conn**—Displays the number of and information about the active connections for the options specified.

Q&A

As mentioned in the Introduction, the questions in this book are written to be more difficult than what you should experience on the exam. The questions are designed to ensure your understanding of the concepts discussed in this chapter and adequately prepare you to complete the exam. You should use the simulated exams on the CD to practice for the exam.

The answers to these questions can be found in Appendix A.

1 When should you run the command **clear xlate**?

   A When updating a conduit on the firewall

   B When editing the NAT for the inside segment

   C When adding addresses to the global pool

   D All of the above

2 What happens if you configure two interfaces with the same security level?

3 True or false: The quickest way to clear the translation table is to reboot the PIX.

4 True or false: If you configure a static translation for your web server, everyone can connect to it.

5 Which of the following is not a method of address translation supported by the PIX?

   A Network Address Translation

   B Socket Address Translation

   C Port Address Translation

   D Static

6 True or false: It is easy t o hack into a PIX over UDP 53, because it accepts DNS resolves from anyone.

7 What the does the PIX normally change when allowing a TCP handshake between nodes on different interfaces and performing NAT?

8 What the does the PIX normally change when allowing a TCP handshake between nodes on different interfaces and performing PAT?

9 You have configured two additional DMZ interfaces on your PIX Firewall. How do you prevent nodes on DMZ1 from accessing nodes on DMZ2 without adding rules to the security policy?

   A Route all traffic for DMZ2 out the outside interface.

   B Dynamically NAT all DMZ2 nodes to a multicast address.

   C Assign a higher security level to DMZ2.

   D All of the above

10 True or false: It is possible to hide an entire Class C network behind a single IP using PAT.

11 True or false: TCP is a much better protocol than UDP, because it does handshakes and randomly generates TCP sequence numbers.

12 Which of the following **nat** commands is/are correct?

   A LabPIX(config)# **nat (inside) 1 0.0.0.0 0.0.0.0**

   B LabPIX(config)# **nat (inside) 1 0.0**

   C LabPIX(config)# **nat (inside) 1 0 0**

   D A and B

   E A and C

   F All of the above

13 When would you want to configure NAT and PAT for the same inside segment?

14 What is RFC 1918?

15 True or false: By default, an embryonic connection terminates after 2 minutes.

16 What command shows all active TCP connections on the PIX?

17 Why is there an *id* field in the **nat** command?

This chapter covers the following exam topics for the Cisco Secure PIX Firewall Advanced Exam:

    5. User interface
    6. Configuring the PIX Firewall
    8. Time setting and NTP support
    13. DHCP server configuration

CHAPTER 6

Getting Started with the Cisco PIX Firewall

This chapter describes the basic preparation and configuration required to use the network firewall features of the Cisco PIX Firewall. It focuses on how to establish basic connectivity from the internal network to the public Internet.

"Do I Know This Already?" Quiz

The purpose of this quiz is to help you determine your current understanding of the topics covered in this chapter. Write down your answers and compare them to the answers in Appendix A. The concepts in this chapter are the foundation of much of what you need to understand to pass the CSPFA Certification Exam. Unless you do exceptionally well on the "Do I Know This Already?" pretest and are 100% confident in your knowledge of this area, you should read through the entire chapter.

1 How do you access privileged mode?

2 What is the function of the **nameif** command?

3 What six commands produce a basic working configuration for a Cisco PIX Firewall?

4 Why is the **route** command important?

5 What is the command to flush out the ARP cache on a Cisco PIX Firewall?

6 True or false: It is possible to configure the outside interface on a Cisco PIX Firewall to accept DHCP requests.

7 What type of environment uses the PIX DHCP client feature?

8 What command releases and renews an IP address on the PIX?

9 Give at least one reason why it is beneficial to use NTP on the Cisco PIX Firewall.

10 Why would you want to secure the NTP messages between the Cisco PIX Firewall and the NTP server?

Foundation Topics

Access Modes

The Cisco PIX Firewall contains a command set based on Cisco IOS Software technologies that provides three administrative access modes:

- Unprivileged mode is available when you first access the PIX Firewall through console or Telnet. It displays the > prompt. This mode lets you view only restricted settings.

- You access privileged mode by entering the **enable** command and the enable password. The prompt then changes to # from >. In this mode you can change a few of the current settings and view the existing Cisco PIX Firewall configuration. Any unprivileged command also works in privileged mode. To exit privileged mode, enter the **disable**, **exit**, or **^z** command.

- You access configuration mode by entering the **configure terminal** command. This changes the prompt to (config)# from #. In this mode you can change system configurations. All privileged, unprivileged, and configuration commands work in this mode. Use the **exit** or **^z** command to exit configuration mode.

NOTE	PIX version 6.2 supports 16 privilege levels. This new feature allows Cisco PIX Firewall commands to be assigned to one of the 16 levels. These privilege levels can also be assigned to users. This is discussed in detail in Chapter 4, "System Maintenance."

Configuring the PIX Firewall

Six important commands are used to produce a basic working configuration for the PIX Firewall:

> **interface**
> **nameif**
> **ip address**
> **nat**
> **global**
> **route**

Before you use these commands, it can prove very useful to draw a diagram of your Cisco PIX Firewall with the different security levels, interfaces, and IP addresses. Figure 6-1 shows one such diagram that is used for the discussion in this chapter.

Figure 6-1 *Documenting Cisco PIX Firewall Security Levels, Interfaces, and IP Addresses*

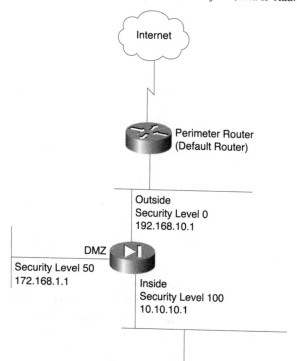

interface Command

The **interface** command identifies the interface hardware card, sets the speed of the interface, and enables the interface all in one command. All interfaces on a Cisco PIX Firewall are shut down by default and are explicitly enabled by the **interface** command. The basic syntax of the **interface** command is as follows:

```
interface hardware_id hardware_speed [shutdown]
```

Table 6-1 describes the command parameters for the **interface** command.

Table 6-1   **interface** *Command Parameters*

Command Parameter	Description
hardware_id	Indicates the interface's physical location on the Cisco PIX Firewall.
hardware_speed	Sets the connection speed, depending on which medium is being used. **1000auto** sets Ethernet speeds automatically. However, it is recommended that you configure the speed manually. **1000sxfull**—Sets full-duplex Gigabit Ethernet. **1000basesx**—Sets half-duplex Gigabit Ethernet. **1000auto**—Automatically detects and negotiates full-/half-duplex Gigabit Ethernet. **10baset**—Sets 10 Mbps half-duplex Ethernet (very rare these days). **10full**—Sets 10 Mbps full-duplex Ethernet. **100full**—Sets 100 Mbps full-duplex Ethernet. **100basetx**—Sets 100 Mbps half-duplex Ethernet. Make sure that the *hardware_speed* setting matches the port speed on the Catalyst switch the interface is connected to.
shutdown	The **shutdown** parameter administratively shuts down the interface. This parameter performs a very similar function in Cisco IOS Software. However, unlike with IOS, the command **no shutdown** cannot be used here. To place an interface in an administratively up mode, you reenter the **interface** command without the **shutdown** parameter.

Here are some examples of the **interface** command:

```
interface ethernet0 100full
interface ethernet1 100full
interface ethernet2 100full
```

nameif Command

As the name intuitively indicates, the **nameif** command is used to name an interface and assign a security value from 1 to 99. The outside and inside interfaces are named by default and have default security values of 0 and 100, respectively. By default, the interfaces have their hardware ID. Ethernet 0 is the outside interface, and Ethernet 1 is the inside interface. The names that are configured by the **nameif** command are user-friendly and are easier to use for advanced configuration later.

The syntax of the **nameif** command is

```
nameif hardware_id if_name security_level
```

Table 6-2 describes the command parameters for the **nameif** command.

Table 6-2   **nameif** *Command Parameters*

Command Parameter	Description
hardware_id	Indicates the interface's physical location on the Cisco PIX Firewall.
if_name	The name by which you refer to this interface. The name cannot have any spaces and must not exceed 48 characters.
security_level	A numerical value from 1 to 99 indicating the security level.

Here are some examples of the **nameif** command:

```
nameif ethernet0 outside security0
nameif ethernet1 inside security100
nameif ethernet2 dmz security20
```

The *security_level* value controls how hosts/devices on the different interfaces interact with each other. By default, hosts/devices connected to interfaces with higher security levels can access hosts/devices connected to interfaces with lower-security interfaces. Hosts/devices connected to interfaces with lower-security interfaces cannot access hosts/devices connected to interfaces with higher-security interfaces without the assistance of access lists or conduits.

You can verify your configuration by using the **show nameif** command.

ip address Command

All the interfaces on the Cisco PIX Firewall that will be used must be configured with an IP address. The IP address can be configured manually or through Dynamic Host Configuration Protocol (DHCP). The DHCP feature is usually used on Cisco PIX Firewall small office/home office (SOHO) models. DHCP is discussed later in this chapter.

The **ip address** command is used to configure IP addresses on the PIX interfaces. The **ip address** command binds a logical address (IP address) to the hardware ID. Table 6-3 describes the parameters for the **ip address** command, the syntax of which is as follows:

```
ip address if_name ip_address [netmask]
```

Table 6-3   **ip address** *Command Parameters*

Command Parameter	Description
if_name	The interface name that was configured using the **nameif** command.
ip_address	The interface's IP address.
netmask	The appropriate network mask. If the mask value is not entered, the PIX assigns a classful network mask.

Here's an example of the **ip address** command:

```
ip address inside 10.10.10.14 255.255.255.0
```

Use the **show ip** command to view the configured IP address on the PIX interface.

nat Command

The **nat** (Network Address Translation) command lets you translate a set of IP addresses to another set of IP addresses.

NOTE   PIX 6.2 supports bidirectional translation of inside network IP addresses to global IP addresses and translation of outside IP addresses to inside network IP addresses.

The **nat** command is always paired with a **global** command, with the exception of the **nat 0** command. Table 6-4 describes the command parameters for the **nat** command, the syntax of which is as follows:

```
nat (if_name) nat_id local_ip [netmask]
```

Table 6-4   nat *Command Parameters*

Command Parameter	Description
(if_name)	The internal network interface name.
nat_id	The ID number to match with the global address pool.
local_ip	The IP address that is translated. This is usually the inside network IP address. It is possible to assign all the inside network for the *local_ip* through **nat (inside) 1 0 0**.
netmask	Network mask for the local IP address.

Here are some examples of the **nat** command:

```
nat (inside) 1 10.10.10.0 255.255.255.0
nat (inside) 1 172.16.1.0 255.255.255.0
```

Chapter 5, "Understanding Cisco PIX Firewall Translation and Connections," discusses NAT in greater detail.

global Command

The **global** command is used to define the address or range of addresses that the addresses defined by the **nat** command are translated into. It is important that the *nat_id* be identical to the *nat_id* used in the **nat** command. The *nat_id* pairs the IP address defined by the **global** and **nat** commands so that network translation can take place. The syntax of the **global** command is

```
global (if_name) nat_id global_ip | global_ip-global_ip [netmask]
```

Table 6-5 describes the parameters and options for the **global** command.

Table 6-5   **global** *Command Parameters*

Command Parameter	Description
(if_name)	The external network where you use these global addresses.
nat_id	Identifies the global address and matches it with the **nat** command it is pairing with.
global_ip	A single IP address. When a single IP address is specified, the PIX automatically performs Port Address Translation (PAT). A warning message indicating that the PIX will PAT all addresses is displayed on the console.
global_ip-global_ip	Defines a range of global IP addresses to be used by the PIX to NAT.
netmask	The network mask for the global IP address(es).

There should be enough global IP addresses to match the local IP addresses specified by the **nat** command. If there aren't, you can leverage the shortage of global addresses by PAT entry, which permits up to 64,000 hosts to use a single IP address. PAT divides the available ports per global IP address into three ranges:

- 0 to 511
- 512 to 1023
- 1024 to 65535

PAT assigns a unique source port for each UDP or TCP session. It attempts to assign the same port value of the original request, but if the original source port has already been used, PAT starts scanning from the beginning of the particular port range to find the first available port and assigns it to the conversation. PAT has some restrictions in its use. For example, it cannot support H.323 or caching name server use. The following example shows a configuration using a range of global IP and single IP for PAT:

```
nat (inside) 1 10.0.0.0 255.0.0.0
global (outside) 1 192.168.10.15-192.168.1.62 netmask 255.255.255.0
global (outside) 1 192.168.10.65 netmask 255.255.255.0
```

When a host or device tries to start a connection, the PIX Firewall checks the translation table if there is an entry for that particular IP. If there is no existing translation, a new *translation slot* is created. The default time that a translated IP is kept in the translation table is 3 hours. You can change this with the **timeout xlate** *hh:mm:ss* command. To view the translated addresses, use the **show xlate** command.

route Command

The **route** command tells the Cisco PIX Firewall where to send information that is forwarded on a specific interface and that is destined for a particular network address. You add static routes to the PIX using the **route** command.

Table 6-6 describes the **route** command parameters, the syntax of which is as follows:

```
route if_name ip_address netmask gateway_ip [metric]
```

Table 6-6   **route** *Command Parameters*

Command Parameter	Description
if_name	The name of the interface where the data leaves from.
ip_address	The IP address to be routed.
netmask	The network mask of the IP address to be routed.
gateway_ip	The IP address of the next-hop address. Usually this is the IP address of the perimeter router.
metric	Specifies the number of hops to *gateway_ip*.

The following example shows a default route configuration on a Cisco PIX Firewall:

```
route outside 0.0.0.0 0.0.0.0 192.168.1.3 1
```

The **1** at the end indicates that the gateway router is only one hop away. If a metric is not specified in the **route** command, the default is 1. You can configure only one default route on the PIX Firewall. It is good practice to use the **clear arp** command to clear the PIX Firewall's ARP cache before testing your new route configuration.

RIP

The Routing Information Protocol (RIP) can be enabled to build the Cisco PIX Firewall routing table. RIP configuration specifies whether the PIX updates its routing tables by passively listening to RIP traffic and whether the interface broadcasts itself as a default route for network traffic on that interface. It is also important to configure the router providing the RIP updates with the network address of the PIX interface. The syntax to enable RIP is

```
rip if_name default | passive [version [1 | 2]] [authentication [text | md5
    key (key_id)]]
```

Table 6-7 describes the **rip** command parameters.

Table 6-7   **rip** *Command Parameters*

Command Parameter	Description
if_name	The interface name.
default	Broadcasts a default route on the interface.
passive	Enables passive RIP on the interface. The Cisco PIX Firewall listens for RIP routing broadcasts and uses that information to populate its routing tables.
version	The RIP version. Use **version 2** for RIP update encryption. Use **version 1** to provide backward compatibility with the older version.
authentication	Enables authentication for RIP version 2.
text	Sends RIP updates in clear text.
md5	Encrypts RIP updates using MD5 encryption.
key	The key to encrypt RIP updates. This value must be the same on the routers and on any other device that provides RIP version 2 updates. The *key* is a text string of up to 16 characters in length.
key_id	The key identification value. The key_id can be a number from 1 to 255. Use the same key_id that is in use on the routers and any other device that provides RIP version 2 updates.

Testing Your Configuration

Making sure that the configuration you entered works is an important part of the configuration process. At this point you would test basic connectivity from the inside interface out to the other interfaces. Use the **ping** and **debug** commands to test your connectivity.

The **ping** command sends an ICMP echo request message to the target IP and expects an ICMP echo reply. By default, the PIX denies all inbound traffic through the outside interface. Based on your network security policy, you should consider configuring the PIX to deny all ICMP traffic to the outside interface, or any other interface you deem necessary, by entering the **icmp** command. The **icmp** command controls ICMP traffic that terminates on the PIX. If no ICMP control list is configured, the PIX accepts all ICMP traffic that terminates at any interface (including the outside interface). For example, when you first configure the PIX, it is a good idea to be able to ping an interface and get a response. The following makes that possible for the outside interface:

```
icmp permit any any outside
```

icmp permit any any outside is used during the testing/debugging phase of your configuration process. Make sure that you change it to not responding to ping request after you complete testing. It is a security risk to leave it accepting and responding to ICMP packets.

After the **icmp permit** command has been configured, you can ping the outside interface on your Cisco PIX Firewall and ping from hosts on each firewall interface. For example:

```
ping outside 192.168.1.1
```

You can also monitor ping results by starting **debug icmp trace**.

Saving Your Configuration

Configuration changes that you have made stay in the PIX's RAM unless you save them to Flash memory. If for any reason the PIX must be rebooted, the configuration changes you made are lost. So when you finish entering commands in the configuration, save the changes to Flash memory with the **write memory** command, as follows:

```
Pix# write memory
```

NOTE There is one obvious advantage of not having configuration changes committed to Flash memory immediately. For example, if you make a configuration that you cannot back out of, you simply reboot and get back the settings you had before you made the changes.

You are now done configuring the Cisco PIX Firewall. This basic configuration lets protected network users start connections and prevents users on unprotected networks from accessing (or attacking) protected hosts.

Use the **write terminal** or **show running-config** command to view your current configuration.

Configuring DHCP on the Cisco PIX Firewall

The Cisco PIX Firewall has features that let it be configured as a:

- DHCP server
- DHCP client

Using the PIX Firewall DHCP Server

The DHCP server is usually used in SOHO environments with lower-end models of the Cisco PIX Firewall, such as the 501 and 506 units. Table 6-8 shows DHCP clients that are supported by PIX.

Table 6-8   *Cisco PIX Firewall DHCP Client Support*

PIX Firewall Version	Cisco PIX Firewall Platform	Maximum Number of DHCP Client Addresses (Active Hosts)
Version 5.2 and earlier	All platforms	10
Version 5.3 to version 6.0	PIX 506/506E	32
	All other platforms	256
Version 6.1 and higher	PIX 501	32
	PIX 501 with optional 50-user license	128
		256
	PIX 506/506E	256
	All other platforms	

The PIX DHCP server can be enabled only on the inside interface.

As with all other DHCP servers, you have to configure DNS, WINS, IP address lease time, and domain information on the PIX. Six steps are involved in enabling the DHCP server feature on the PIX:

Step 1   Enable the DHCP daemon on the Cisco PIX Firewall to listen to DHCP requests from clients:

```
dhcpd enable inside
```

Step 2   Specify the IP address range that the PIX DHCP server assigns:

```
dhcpd address 10.10.10.15-10.10.10.100 inside
```

Step 3   Specify the lease length to grant to the client. The default is 3600 seconds:

```
dhcpd lease 2700
```

Step 4   Specify a DNS server (optional):

```
dhcpd dns 192.168.10.68 192.168.10.73
```

Step 5   Specify WINS servers (optional):

```
dhcpd wins 192.168.10.66
```

Step 6   Configure the domain name the client uses (optional):

```
dhcpd domain axum.com
```

Configuring the PIX Firewall DHCP Client

DHCP client support on the Cisco PIX Firewall is designed for use by SOHO environments in which DSL and cable modems are used. The DHCP client can be enabled only on the PIX's outside interface. When the DHCP client is enabled, DHCP servers on the outside provide the outside interface with an IP address.

NOTE   The DHCP client does not support failover configuration.

The DHCP client feature on your firewall is enabled by the **ip address dhcp** command:

```
ip address outside dhcp [setroute] [retry retry_cnt]
```

The **setroute** option tells the Cisco PIX Firewall to set its default route using the default gateway parameter that the DHCP server returns. Do not configure a default route when using the **setroute** option.

NOTE   The same command, **ip address dhcp,** is used to release and renew the outside interface's IP address.

To view current information about the DHCP lease, enter the following command:

```
show ip address dhcp
```

Configuring Time Settings on the Cisco PIX Firewall

There are at least two ways in which the PIX gets its time setting information:

- NTP server
- System clock

Network Time Protocol (NTP)

The Network Time Protocol (NTP) is used to implement a hierarchical system of servers that provide a source for a precise synchronized time among network systems. It's important to maintain a consistent time throughout all network devices, such as servers, routers, and switches. When analyzing network events, logs are an important source of information. Analyzing and troubleshooting network events can be difficult is there is time inconsistency with network devices on the network. Furthermore, some time-sensitive operations, such as validating certificates and certificate revocation lists (CRLs), require precise time stamps.

NOTE	The latest Cisco PIX Firewall OS, version 6.2, lets you obtain the system time from NTP version 3 servers. This feature is available only on Cisco PIX Firewall version 6.2.

The syntax to enable an NTP client on the PIX is

```
ntp server ip_address [key number] source if_name [prefer]
```

Table 6-9 describes the parameters of the **ntp** command.

Table 6-9   **ntp** *Command Parameters*

Command Parameter	Description
ip_address	This is the time server's IP address with which the PIX synchronizes.
key	This option requires an authentication key when sending packets to the NTP server.
number	The authentication key. This number is useful when you use multiple keys and multiple servers for identification purposes.
source	If the **source** keyword is not specified, the routing table is used to determine the interface.
if_name	The interface name used to send packets to the NTP server.
prefer	Reduces switching back and forth between servers by making the specified server the preferred time server.

Communication of messages between the PIX and the NTP servers can be authenticated to prevent the PIX from synchronizing time with rogue NTP servers. The three commands used to enable NTP authentication are as follows:

```
ntp authenticate
ntp authentication-key number md5 value
ntp trusted-key number
```

The **ntp authenticate** command enables NTP authentication and refuses synchronization to an NTP server unless the server is configured with one of the authentication keys specified using the **ntp trusted-key** command.

The **ntp authentication-key** command is used to define authentication keys for use with other NTP commands to provide a higher degree of security. The *number* parameter is the key number (1 to 4294967295). **md5** is the encryption algorithm. The *value* parameter is the key value (an arbitrary string of up to 32 characters).

The **ntp trusted-key** command is used to define one or more key numbers corresponding to the keys defined with the **ntp authentication-key** command. The Cisco PIX Firewall requires the NTP server to provide this key number in its NTP packets. This provides protection against synchronizing the PIX system clock with an NTP server that is not trusted.

To get remove NTP configuration, use the **clear ntp** command.

PIX Firewall System Clock

The second method of configuring the time setting on the PIX Firewall is the system clock.
The system clock is usually set during the initial setup interview question when you're
configuring a new Cisco PIX Firewall. You can change it later using the **clock set**
command:

```
clock set hh:mm:ss month day year
```

Three characters are used for the *month* parameter. The *year* is a four-digit number. For
example, to set the time and date to 17:51 and 20 seconds on April 9, 2003, you would enter

```
clock set 17:51:20 apr 9 2003
```

NOTE   The system time, unlike NTP, is not synchronized with other network devices.

Cisco PIX Firewall version 6.2 has made some improvements to the **clock** command. The
clock command now supports daylight saving (summer) time and time zones. To configure
daylight saving time, enter the following command:

```
clock summer-time zone recurring [week day month hh:mm week day
   month hh:mm [offset]]
```

Table 6-10 describes the parameters for the **clock** command.

Table 6-10   **clock** *Command Parameters*

Command Parameter	Description
summer-time	Automatically switches to summer time (for display purposes only).
zone	The name of the time zone.
recurring	Indicates that summer time should start and end on the days specified by the values that follow this keyword. The summer time rule defaults to the United States rule.
week day	Sets the day of the week (Sunday, Monday).
month	The full name of the month, such as April.
hh:mm	The time in 24-hour military format.
offset	The number of minutes to add during summer. The default is 60 minutes.

Time zones are set just for the purpose of display. It does not change the internal PIX time,
which remains universal time clock (UTC). To set the time zone, use the **clock timezone**
command.

The following **clock summer-time** command specifies that summertime starts on the first
Sunday in April at 2 a.m. and ends on the last Sunday in October at 2 a.m.:

```
pix(config)# clock summer-time PDT recurring 1 Sunday April 2:00 last Sunday
   October 2:00
```

Sample PIX Configuration

Example 6-1 shows sample output for a PIX configuration. Can you identify some of the commands that have been discussed in this chapter?

Example 6-1 *Sample PIX Configuration*

```
pix# show config
: Saved
: Written by deguc at 11:29:39.859 EDT Fri Aug 8 2002
PIX Version 6.2(2)
nameif ethernet0 outside security0
nameif ethernet1 inside security100
nameif ethernet2 dmz security20
enable password GgtfiV2tiX5zk297 encrypted
passwd kP3Eex5gnkza7.w9 encrypted
hostname pixfirewall
domain-name axum.com
clock timezone EST -5
clock summer-time EDT recurring
fixup protocol ftp 21
fixup protocol http 80
fixup protocol h323 h225 1720
fixup protocol h323 ras 1718-1719
fixup protocol ils 389
fixup protocol rsh 514
fixup protocol rtsp 554
fixup protocol smtp 25
fixup protocol sqlnet 1521
fixup protocol sip 5060
fixup protocol skinny 2000
names
pager lines 24
no logging on
interface ethernet0 100full
interface ethernet1 100full
interface ethernet2 100full
mtu outside 1500
mtu inside 1500
mtu dmz 1500
ip address outside 192.168.1.10.1 255.255.255.224
ip address inside 10.10.10.1 255.255.0.0
ip address dmz 172.16.1.1 255.255.255.0
ip audit info action alarm
ip audit attack action alarm
no failover
pdm location 10.10.10.14 255.255.255.255 inside
arp timeout 14400
global (outside) 1 192.168.1.20-192.168.1.110 netmask 255.255.255.224
global (outside) 1 192.168.1.111
global (dmz) 1 172.16.1.10-172.16.1.20 netmask 255.255.255.224

nat (inside) 1 0.0.0.0 0.0.0.0 0 0
nat (dmz) 1 0.0.0.0 0.0.0.0 0 0
```

continues

Example 6-1 *Sample PIX Configuration (Continued)*

```
route outside 0.0.0.0 0.0.0.0 192.168.1.10.3 1
timeout xlate 3:00:00
timeout conn 1:00:00 half-closed 0:10:00 udp 0:02:00 rpc 0:10:00 h323 0:05:00
  sip 0:30:00 sip_media 0:02:00
timeout uauth 0:05:00 absolute
aaa-server TACACS+ protocol tacacs+
aaa-server RADIUS protocol radius
aaa-server LOCAL protocol local
 http server enable
http 10.10.10.14 255.255.255.255 inside
no snmp-server location
no snmp-server contact
snmp-server community public
no snmp-server enable traps
floodguard enable
no sysopt route dnat
telnet 10.10.10.14  255.255.255.255 inside
telnet timeout 5
 terminal width 80
Cryptochecksum:62a73076955b1060644fdba1da64b15f
```

Foundation Summary

Table 6-11 provides a quick reference to the commands needed to configure the Cisco PIX Firewall, time server and NTP support, and the DNS server.

Table 6-11   *Command Reference*

Command	Description
enable	Specifies to activate a process, mode, or privilege level.
interface	Identifies the speed and duplex settings of the network interface boards.
nameif	Lets you name interfaces and assign security levels.
ip address	Identifies addresses for network interfaces and lets you set how many times the PIX Firewall polls for DHCP information.
nat	Lets you associate a network with a pool of global IP addresses.
global	Defines a pool of global addresses. The global addresses in the pool provide an IP address for each outbound connection and for inbound connections resulting from outbound connections. Ensure that associated **nat** and **global** command statements have the same *nat_id*.
route	Used to enter a default or static route for an interface.
write terminal	Displays the current configuration on the terminal.
rip	Enables IP routing table updates from received RIP broadcasts.
dhcpd	Controls the DHCP server feature.
ntp server	Synchronizes the PIX Firewall with the network time server that is specified and authenticates according to the authentication options that are set.
clock	Lets you specify the time, month, day, and year for use with time-stamped syslog messages.

Q&A

The questions in this section are designed to ensure your understanding of the concepts discussed in this chapter and adequately prepare you to complete the exam. Use the simulated exams on the CD to practice for the exam.

The answers to these questions can be found in Appendix A.

1 What command tests connectivity?

   A   ping

   B   nameif

   C   ip address

   D   write terminal

2 What command saves the configuration you made on the Cisco PIX Firewall?

   A   write terminal

   B   show start-running config

   C   write memory

   D   save config

3 What command assigns security levels to interfaces on the PIX?

   A   ip address

   B   route

   C   nameif

   D   secureif

4 What command flushes the ARP cache on a PIX?

   A   flush arp cache

   B   no arp cache

   C   clear arp

   D   You cannot flush the ARP cache.

5 True or false: The DHCP client feature is primarily designed for large corporate enterprise networks and ISPs.

6 Why would you want authentication enabled between the PIX and the NTP server? (Select all that apply.)

   A   To ensure that the PIX does not synchronize with an unauthorized NTP server

   B   To maintain the integrity of the communication

   C   To increase the speed of communication

   D   To reduce latency

7 True or false: The DHCP client feature can be configured on the PIX's inside interface.

8 How do you access privileged mode?

   A   Enter the **enable** command and the enable password.

   B   Enter the **privilege** command and the privilege password.

   C   Enter the super-secret password.

   D   Enter the **privilege** command only.

9 How do you view the current configuration on your PIX? (Select all that apply.)

   A   **write terminal**

   B   **show current**

   C   **write memory**

   D   **save config**

10 In a DHCP client configuration, what is the command to release and renew the IP address on the outside interface?

   A   **ipconfig release**

   B   **ip address dhcp outside**

   C   **outside ip renew**

   D   **ip address renew outside**

This chapter covers the following exam topics for the Cisco Secure PIX Firewall Advanced Exam:

18. ACLs
19. Using ACLs
21. Overview of object grouping
22. Getting started with group objects
23. Configuring group objects
24. Nested object groups
25. Advanced protocols
26. Multimedia support

CHAPTER 7

Configuring Access

Managing controlled access to network resources from an untrusted (Internet) network is a very important function of the PIX Firewall. Access lists, static NATs, and authentication and authorization are ways to provide access through the PIX Firewall in a controlled fashion. In addition, PIX version 6.2 has new features such as object grouping and TurboACL. These new features make managing and implementing a complex security policy much easier and more scalable.

"Do I Know This Already?" Quiz

The purpose of this quiz is to help you determine your current understanding of topics covered in this chapter. Write down your answers and compare them to the answers in Appendix A. If you have to look at any references to correctly answer the questions about PIX functionality, you should read that portion and double-check your thinking by reviewing the Foundation Summary. The concepts in this chapter are the foundation of much of what you need to understand to pass the CSPFA Certification Exam. Unless you do exceptionally well on the "Do I Know This Already?" pretest and are 100% confident in your knowledge of this area, you should read through the entire chapter.

1. What do static NAT settings do?

2. True or false: Static NAT is the only configuration that lets inbound access in.

3. Can the **conduit** command be used in place of the **access-list** command?

4. About how many access list entries (ACEs) in one access list does TurboACL support?

5. What is the minimum memory required to run TurboACL?

6. What is the command to enable TurboACL globally on the PIX Firewall?

7. What is the minimum number of access list entries needed for TurboACL to compile?

8. What is the function of object groups?

9. What is the command to enable a network object group?

10. What are the four object type options when you're creating object groups?

Foundation Topics

Configuring Inbound Access Through the PIX Firewall

A two-step approach lets connections initiated from lower-security interfaces access higher-security interfaces:

Step 1   Static Network Address Translation

Step 2   Access lists/conduits

Static Network Address Translation

Static Network Address Translation (NAT) creates a permanent, one-to-one mapping between an address on an internal network (a higher security level interface) and an external network (a lower security level interface) in all PIX versions. For an external host to initiate traffic to an inside host, a static translation rule needs to exist for the inside host. This can also be done using a **nat 0 access-list** address translation rule. Without the persistent translation rule, the translation cannot occur.

NOTE   Unlike NAT and PAT, static NAT requires a dedicated address on the outside network for each host, so it does not save registered IP addresses.

The syntax for the **static** command is

```
static [(prenat_interface, postnat_interface)] {mapped_address|interface}
    real_address [dns] [netmask mask] [norandomseq] [max_conns [em_limit]]
```

Table 7-1 describes the **static** command parameters.

Table 7-1   static *Command Parameters*

Command Parameter	Description
prenat_interface	Usually the inside interface, in which case the translation is applied to the inside address.
postnat_interface	The outside interface when *prenat_interface* is the inside interface. However, if the outside interface is used for *prenat_interface*, the translation is applied to the outside address, and the *postnat_interface* is the inside interface.
mapped_address	The address that *real_address* is translated into.
interface	Specifies to overload the global address from **interface**.
real_address	The address to be mapped.

Table 7-1   **static** *Command Parameters (Continued)*

Command Parameter	Description
dns	Specifies that DNS replies that match the xlate are translated.
netmask	A reserved word that is required before you specify the network mask.
mask or *network_mask*	Pertains to both *global_ip* and *local_ip*. For host addresses, always use 255.255.255.255. For network addresses, use the appropriate class mask or subnet mask. For example, for Class A networks, use 255.0.0.0. A sample subnet mask is 255.255.255.224.
norandomseq	Does not randomize the TCP/IP packet's sequence number. Use this option only if another inline firewall is also randomizing sequence numbers and the result is scrambling the data. Using this option opens a security hole in the PIX Firewall.
max_conns	The maximum number of connections permitted through the static IP address at the same time.
em_limit	The embryonic connection limit. An embryonic connection is one that has started but has not yet completed. Set this limit to prevent an attack by a flood of embryonic connections. The default is 0, which means unlimited connections.

The following example maps a server with an internal IP address of 10.1.1.10 to the IP address 192.168.10.10:

```
PIXFIREWALL(conf)#static (inside, outside) 192.168.100.10 10.1.100.10 netmask
  255.255.255.255
```

The **static** command can also be used to translate an IP subnet:

```
PIXFIREWALL(conf)#static (inside, outside) 192.168.1.0 10.1.100.0 netmask
  255.255.255.0
```

In this example, the Class A subnet of 10.1.100.0 255.255.255.0 is to be translated to the Class C network of 192.168.10.0. This sample configuration gives the same IP address to the host on the 10.1.100.0 255.255.255.0 to be translated on the 192.168.10.0 255.255.255.0 network. A host with an IP address of 10.1.100.10 is mapped to 192.168.1.10.

Static Port Address Translation

In PIX 6.0, the port redirection feature was added to allow outside users to connect to a particular IP address/port and have the PIX redirect the traffic to the appropriate inside server; the **static** command was modified. The shared address can be a unique address or a shared outbound Port Address Translation (PAT) address, or it can be shared with the external interface. For example, static PAT lets you redirect inbound TCP and UDP services. Using the **static** command's **interface** option, you can use static PAT to permit external hosts to access TCP or UDP services residing on an internal host. (As always, though, an access list should also be in place to control access to the internal host.) The command to configure static PAT is as follows:

```
static [(internal_if_name, external_if_name)] {tcp | udp}{global_ip | interface}
    global_port local_ip local_port [netmask mask][max_conns [emb_limit
    [norandomseq]]]
```

Static PAT supports all applications that are supported by (regular) PAT, including the same application constraints. Like PAT, static PAT does not support H.323 or multimedia application traffic. The following example enables static port address translation (static PAT) for FTP service, interfaces, and hosts:

```
static (inside, outside) tcp 192.168.1.14 ftp 10.1.2.8 ftp
```

The next example shows the following:

- The PIX redirects external users' Telnet requests to IP address 192.168.1.24 to 10.1.2.19.

- The PIX redirects external users' HTTP port 8080 requests to PAT address 192.168.1.24 to 10.1.2.20 port 80.

```
static (inside,outside) tcp 192.168.1.24 telnet 10.1.2.19 telnet netmask
    255.255.255.255
static (inside,outside) tcp 192.168.1.24. 8080 10.1.2.20 www netmask
    255.255.255.255
access-list 101 permit tcp any host 192.168.1.24 eq 8080
access-list 101 permit tcp any host 172.18.124.99 eq telnet
```

Notice that the outside IP address 192.168.1.24 is the same for both mappings, but the internal IP address is different. Also notice that external users directed to 192.168.1.24:8080 are sent as HTTP requests to 10.1.2.20, which is listening on port 80.

TCP Intercept Feature

Before version 5.3, the Cisco PIX Firewall offered no mechanism to protect systems that could be reached via a static and TCP conduit from TCP SYN attacks. When the embryonic connection limit was configured in a **static** command statement, the earlier PIX version simply dropped new connection attempts as soon as the embryonic threshold was reached. A mild TCP SYN attack could potentially create service disruption to the server in question. For **static** command statements without an embryonic connection limit, PIX passes all traffic. If the affected system does not have TCP SYN attack protection (most operating systems do not offer sufficient protection), the affected system's embryonic connection table overloads, and all traffic stops.

With the new TCP intercept feature, as soon as the optional embryonic connection limit is reached, and until the embryonic connection count falls below this threshold, every SYN bound for the affected server is intercepted. For each SYN, the PIX responds on behalf of the server with an empty SYN/ACK segment. The PIX retains pertinent state information, drops the packet, and waits for the client's acknowledgment. If the ACK is received, a copy of the client's SYN segment is sent to the server, and a TCP three-way handshake is performed between the PIX and the server. If this three-way handshake completes, the connection resumes as normal. If the client does not respond during any part of the connection phase, PIX Firewall retransmits the necessary segment using exponential back-offs.

This feature requires no change to the Cisco PIX Firewall command set, only that the embryonic connection limit on the **static** command now has a new behavior.

nat 0 Command

If you have a public address on the inside network, and you want the inside hosts to go to the outside without translation, you can disable NAT. The **nat 0** command disables address translation so that inside IP addresses are visible to the outside. It is important to note that the **nat 0** command is used in combination with an access list to provide access to traffic originating *from* the inside host/network *to* the outside network *without translation*. The following example demonstrates the use of the **nat 0** command:

```
nat (inside) 0 192.168.1.10 255.255.255.255
access-list 121 permit 192.168.1.10 255.255.255.255 any
```

This can also be configured as follows:

```
access-list 121 permit 192.168.1.10 255.255.255.255 any
nat (inside) 0 access-list 121
```

Neither **static** nor **nat 0** allows a connection to be instantiated from the outside network. The **static** command simply identifies a host/network on the inside and permanently maps it to a global IP address. **nat 0** makes the IP address visible for the outside network. An access list is required to establish a connection to the identified host/network using **static** or **nat 0**, as shown in all the previous examples.

Access Lists

An access list typically consists of multiple access list entries (ACEs) organized internally by PIX Firewall as a linked list. When a packet is subjected to access list control, the Cisco PIX Firewall searches this linked list linearly to find a matching element. The matching element is then examined to determine if the packet is to be transmitted or dropped. Access lists work on a first-match basis, so for inbound access, you must deny first and then permit after.

The general syntax of the **access-list** command is

```
access-list ID action protocol source_address s_mask s_port destination_address
           d_mask d_port
```

Table 7-2 describes the parameters for the **access-list** command.

Table 7-2   **access-list** *Command Parameters*

Parameter	Description
ID	The name or number you create to identify a group of **access-list** command statements, such as 101.
action	**permit** or **deny**, depending on whether you want to permit or deny access to the server. By default, all inbound access is denied, so you must permit access to a specific protocol or port.
protocol	**tcp**, **udp**, **icmp**, and so on.
source_address	The host or network address of the source host or network that must access the *destination_address*. Use **any** or **0.0.0.0** to let any host access the *destination_address*. If you specify a single host, precede the address with **host**.
s_mask	Netmask bits (mask) to be applied to *source_address* if the source address is for a network mask.
s_port	Specifies the protocol port used by the source host to initiate the connection.
destination_address	The host or network global address that you specified with the **static** command. For a host address, precede the address with **host**; for networks, specify the network address and the appropriate network mask.
d_mask	Netmask bits (mask) to be applied to *destination_address* if the destination address is a network mask.
d_port	The *port* parameter with the exact port name or number for the destination server protocol. The port name or number is preceded by the **eq** (equal) parameter, such as **eq http**. **lt**, **gt**, and **neq** are also supported as qualifiers.

The **access-list** command creates the rule you want. The created rule is applied by using the **access-group** command to the desired PIX interface. It is also important to note that unlike Cisco IOS Software access lists, which use wildcards (that is, 0.0.0.255 for a Class C address) to identify their network masks, PIX software uses a regular subnet mask (that is, 255.255.255.0 for a Class C address) when defining the network mask.

NOTE   Specify only one **access-group** command for each interface.

The syntax for the **access-group** command is as follows:

```
access-group ID in interface interface_name
```

The *ID* is the same identifier that was specified in the **access-list** command The *interface_name* parameter is the interface's name.

Example 7-1 illustrates the use of the **static** and **access-list** commands to permit connections from lower-security interfaces to higher-security interfaces on the PIX.

Example 7-2 *Permitting Connections from Lower-Security Interfaces to Higher-Security Interfaces on the PIX*

```
Pixfirewall(config)# static (inside, outside) 192.168.1.10 10.1.100.10
  netmask 255.255.255.255
Pixfirewall(config)# access-list acl_out permit tcp any host 192.168.1.10 eq www
Pixfirewall (config)# access-group acl_out in interface outside
```

The **static** command statically translates 10.1.100.10 to 192.168.1.10. The **access-list** command permits HTTP access only to host 10.1.100.10 (translated into 192.168.1.10). The **access-group** command applies the access list acl_out to the outside interface.

Figure 7-1 illustrates the use of the **static** and **access-list** commands in this example.

Figure 7-1   *Use of Access Lists and Static Address Translation in a PIX Environment*

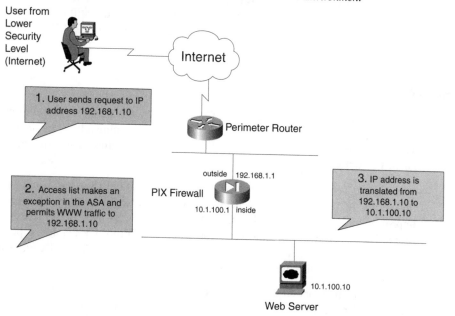

To view the created access list, use the **show access-list** *id* command, where *id* is the access list name or number.

Access lists can also be used to control outbound access on the PIX. An outbound access list restricts users from starting outbound connections or from accessing specific destination addresses or networks. By default, outbound access is permitted, so you use the **deny** action to restrict access when using an outbound access list. Due to this fact, for outbound access lists, you must deny first and permit after.

For example, if you wanted to restrict users on the inside interface from accessing a website at address 172.16.68.20 on the outside interface, you would use the commands shown in Example 7-2.

Example 7-3 *Restricting Inside Users' Access to an External Web Server on Port 80*

```
pixfirewall(config)# access-list acl_in deny tcp any host 172.16.68.20 eq www
pixfirewall(config)# access-list acl_in permit ip any any
pixfirewall(config)# access-group acl_in in interface inside
```

This access list configuration lets any user start WWW connections, with the exception of 172.16.68.20.

NOTE   Starting with Cisco PIX Firewall OS version 5.3, access lists are the preferred method of managing network access. The **conduit** command was used in earlier versions. Access lists provide improved flexibility. However, the **conduit** command is still supported to maintain backward compatibility with configurations written for previous PIX Firewall versions.

TurboACL

TurboACL is a feature introduced with Cisco PIX Firewall version 6.2 that improves the average search time for access control lists (ACLs) containing a large number of entries. The search time for long ACLs is improved because this feature causes the PIX to compile tables for ACLs.

The TurboACL feature can be enabled globally on the entire PIX Firewall and then disabled for specific ACLs. It can also be enabled for only specific ACLs. Search performance improvement is seen in ACLs that have more than 19 ACEs. For ACLs that contain few ACEs, TurboACL does not improve performance. The TurboACL feature is applied only to ACLs with 19 or more entries. The implementation of TurboACL in PIX Firewall version 6.2 supports access lists with up to 16,000 access list entries.

The minimum memory required for TurboACL is 2.1 MB. Approximately 1 MB of memory is required for every 2000 ACL elements. High-end PIX Firewall models, such as the PIX 525 and PIX 535, are the most appropriate for memory-demanding TurboACL.

NOTE   Because some models of Cisco PIX Firewall, such as the PIX 501, have limited memory, implementing the TurboACL feature might cause problems, such as not being able to load Cisco PIX Device Manager.

Configuring Individual TurboACL

The individual TurboACL command can be used to enable Turbo configuration for individual ACLs when TurboACL is not globally enabled. The syntax of this command is as follows:

```
[no] access-list acl_name compiled
```

This command is used to individually enable or disable TurboACL on a specific ACL. The *acl_name* parameter in the command must specify an existing ACL. This command causes the TurboACL process to mark the ACL specified by *acl_name* as Turbo-configured and Turbo-compiles the ACL if the ACL has 19 or more ACEs and has not yet been Turbo-compiled.

If you enter the **no** form of this command, the TurboACL process deletes the TurboACL structures associated with the ACL and marks the ACL as non-Turbo.

Globally Configuring TurboACL

The syntax for enabling TurboACL for the entire PIX is as follows:

```
[no] access-list compiled
```

This configures TurboACL on all ACLs having 19 or more entries. This command causes the TurboACL process to scan all existing ACLs. During the scan, it marks and Turbo-compiles any ACL that has 19 or more ACEs and has not yet been Turbo-compiled.

The command **no access-list compiled**, which is the default, causes the TurboACL process to scan all compiled ACLs and mark every one as non-Turbo. It also deletes all existing TurboACL structures.

Object Grouping

Another feature that is incorporated into the PIX 6.2 software is object grouping. This lets you group objects such as hosts (servers and clients), services, and networks and apply security policies and rules to the group. Object grouping lets you apply access rules to logical groups of objects. When you apply a Cisco PIX Firewall command to an object group, the command affects all network objects defined in the group. This can reduce a very large number of access rules to a manageable number. This in turn reduces the time spent configuring and troubleshooting access rules in large or complex networks.

The syntax for creating object groups is

```
[no] object-group object-type grp-id
```

Use the first parameter, *object-type*, to identify the type of object group you want to configure. There are four options:

- **network**
- **protocol**

- **service**
- **icmp-type**

Replace *grp-id* with a descriptive name for the group.

network *object-type*

The **network** object group is used to group hosts and subnets. Server and client hosts can be grouped by functions. For example, mail servers, web servers, or a group of client hosts that have special privileges on the network can be grouped accordingly.

Example 7-3 shows a web_servers object group.

Example 7-4 *Configuring an Object Group*

```
pixfirewall(config)# object-group network web_servers
pixfirewall(config-network)# description Public web servers
pixfirewall(config-network)# network-object host 192.168.1.12
pixfirewall(config-network)# network-object host 192.168.1.14
pixfirewall(config-network)# exit
pixfirewall(config)# access-list 102 permit tcp any object-group web_servers eq www
pixfirewall(config)# access-group 102 in interface outside
```

Notice that when you enter the **object-group** command, the system enters the appropriate subcommand mode for the type of object you are configuring. In this case, you see the config-network subcommand prompt. **network-object host** adds the host to the network object group. The description is optional, but it is helpful to have it in there.

| NOTE | It is also possible to use a name instead of an IP address when defining the network host. For example: |

```
(config)# object-group network mis_ftp_servers
(config-network)#network-object host mis.ftp.server01
(config-network)#network-object host mis.ftp.server02
(config-network)#network-object mis.ftp.server01
(config-network)#exit
```

To display the configured object group, use the **show object-group** command, as shown in Example 7-4.

Example 7-5 *Displaying Configured Object Groups*

```
pix(config)# show object-group
object-group network web_servers
  description: Public web servers
  network-object host 192.168.1.12
  network-object host 192.168.1.14
```

protocol *object-type*

The **protocol** *object-type* identifies a group of IP protocols using keywords such as **icmp**, **tcp**, **udp**, or an integer in the range of 1 to 254 representing an IP protocol number. The syntax for the command is **object-group protocol** *grp-id*. To add a single protocol to the current protocol object group, use the **protocol-object** *protocol* command. Example 7-5 shows how to use object-group protocol subcommand mode to create a new protocol object group.

Example 7-6   *Creating a New Protocol Object Group*

```
config)# object-group protocol_grp_citrix
(config-protocol)#protocol-object tcp
(config-protocol)#protocol-object citrix
(config-protocol)#exit
```

service *object-type*

The **service** *object-type* identifies port numbers that can be grouped. This is particularly useful when you're managing an application. The syntax for **service** *object-type* is

```
[no] object-group service obj_grp_id tcp | udp | tcp-udp
```

As soon as you are in the **service** subcommand, the command **port-object eq service** adds a single TCP or UDP port number to the service object group. **port-object range** *begin_service end_service* adds a range of TCP or UDP port numbers to the service object group. Example 7-6 shows how to use object-group service subcommand mode to create a new port (service) object group.

Example 7-7   *Creating a New Port (Service) Object Group*

```
config)# object-group service mis_service tcp
(config-service)#port-object eq ftp
(config-service)#port-object range 5200 6000
(config-service)#exit
```

icmp-type *object-type*

ICMP object groups can be created to group certain types of ICMP messages. For example, ICMP messages of echo-reply, echo, and unreachable with numerical values of 8, 0, and 3, respectively, can be grouped as shown in Example 7-7.

Example 7-8   *Grouping ICMP Messages*

```
pix(config)# object-group icmp-type icmp_test
pix(config-icmp-type)# icmp-object 0
pix(config-icmp-type)# icmp-object 3
pix(config-icmp-type)# icmp-object 8
```

Nesting Object Groups

You can add an object group within an object group. The **object-group** command allows logical grouping of the same type of objects and construction of hierarchical object groups for structured configuration. To nest an object group within another object group, use the **group-object** command. Example 7-8 illustrates the use of nested object groups.

Example 7-9 *Configuring Nested Object Groups*

```
pixfirewall(config)# object-group network Public_servers
pixfirewall(config-network)# description Public servers
pixfirewall(config-network)# network-object host 192.168.1.18
pixfirewall(config-network)# group-object web_servers

pixfirewall(config)# object-group network web_servers
pixfirewall(config-network)# description web servers
pixfirewall(config-network)# network-object host 192.168.1.12
pixfirewall(config-network)# network-object host 192.168.1.14
```

Using the fixup Command

The ports that are specified by the **fixup** command are the services that the PIX listens for. The **fixup** command can be used to change the default port assignments or to enable or disable application inspection for the following protocols and applications:

- FTP
- H.323
- HTTP
- Internet Locator Service (ILS)
- Remote Shell (RSH)
- Real-Time Streaming Protocol (RTSP)
- Session Initiation Protocol (SIP)
- Skinny (or Simple) Client Control Protocol (SCCP)
- Simple Mail Transfer Protocol (SMTP)
- SQL*Net

The basic syntax for the **fixup** command is as follows:

```
[no] fixup protocol [protocol] [port]
```

To change the default port assignment, identify the protocol and the new port number to assign. Use the **no fixup protocol** command to reset the application inspection entries to the default configuration. The **clear fixup** command removes **fixup** commands from the configuration you added. However, it does not remove the default **fixup protocol** commands.

The following example shows how to define multiple ports for HTTP by entering separate commands:

```
fixup protocol http 8080
fixup protocol http 8888
```

These commands do not change the standard HTTP port assignment (80). After you enter these commands, the PIX listens for HTTP traffic on ports 80, 8080, and 8888. You can view the explicit (configurable) **fixup protocol** settings with the **show fixup** command, as shown in Example 7-9.

Example 7-10 *Displaying Configurable* **fixup protocol** *Settings*

```
Pixfirewall(config)# show fixup
fixup protocol ftp 21
fixup protocol http 80
fixup protocol h323 h225
fixup protocol h323 ras 1
fixup protocol ils 389
fixup protocol rsh 514
fixup protocol rtsp 554
fixup protocol smtp 25
fixup protocol sqlnet 152
fixup protocol sip 5060
fixup protocol skinny 200
fixup protocol http 8080
fixup protocol http 8888
```

Advanced Protocol Handling

Some applications require special handling by the Cisco PIX Firewall application inspection function. These types of applications typically embed IP addressing information in the user data packet or open secondary channels on dynamically assigned ports. The application inspection function works with NAT to help identify the location of embedded addressing information.

In addition to identifying embedded addressing information, the application inspection function monitors sessions to determine the port numbers for secondary channels. Many protocols open secondary TCP or UDP ports to improve performance. The initial session on a well-known port is used to negotiate dynamically assigned port numbers. The application inspection function monitors these sessions, identifies the dynamic port assignments, and permits data exchange on these ports for the duration of the specific session. Multimedia applications and FTP applications exhibit this kind of behavior.

File Transfer Protocol (FTP)

The FTP application inspection inspects FTP sessions and performs four tasks:

- Prepares a dynamic secondary data connection
- Tracks the **ftp** command-response sequence

- Generates an audit trail
- NATs the embedded IP address

FTP application inspection prepares secondary channels for FTP data transfer. The channels are allocated in response to a file upload, a file download, or a directory listing event, and they must be prenegotiated. The port is negotiated through the PORT or PASV (227) commands.

You can use the **fixup** command to change the default port assignment for FTP. The command syntax is as follows:

```
[no] fixup protocol ftp [strict] [port]
```

The **port** option lets you configure the port at which the PIX listens for FTP traffic.

The **strict** option prevents web browsers from sending embedded commands in FTP requests. Each **ftp** command must be acknowledged before a new command is allowed. Connections sending embedded commands are dropped. The **strict** option only lets the server generate the PASV reply command (227) and only lets the client generate the PORT command. The PASV reply and PORT commands are checked to ensure that they do not appear in an error string.

If you disable FTP fixups with the **no fixup protocol ftp** command, outbound users can start connections only in passive mode, and all inbound FTP is disabled.

Multimedia Support

The PIX supports several popular multimedia applications. Its application inspection function dynamically opens and closes UDP ports for secure multimedia connections. Supported multimedia applications include the following:

- Microsoft Netshow
- Microsoft Netmeeting
- Intel Internet Video Phone
- VDOnet VDOLive
- RealNetworks RealAudio and RealVideo
- VocalTech
- White Pine Meeting Point
- White Pine CuSeeMe
- Xing StreamWorks
- VXtreme WebTheatre

Foundation Summary

Inbound traffic that initiates from the outside is automatically denied access by default on the PIX. Rules have to be put in place to permit traffic to initiate from the outside to servers and subnet on the Cisco PIX Firewall. The rules are usually made up of a **static nat** command and access list. The **static nat** command identifies the subnet or host where traffic will be permitted to go to from the outside. Access lists are then configured to identify and permit the type of traffic to the subnet or host identified by the **static** command. The following is an example of rule that permits http traffic to be intitated from the outside to a webserver 10.1.2.39 on the inside interface of the PIX:

```
static(inside, outside) 192.168.1.12 10.1.2.39 netmask 255.255.255.255
access-list 120 permit tcp any host 192.168.1.12 eq www
access-group 120 in interface outside
```

TurboACL is a feature introduced with Cisco PIX Firewall OS version 6.2 that improves the average search time for access control lists(ACLs) containing a large number of entries. TurboACL feature is only applied to access lists with a minimum of 19 access list entries (ACE) to a maximum of 16000 ACE.

The object grouping feature enables you to group objects such as hosts (servers and clients), services, and networks, and apply security policies and rules to the group. The four types of object groups are:

- Network
- Protocol
- Service
- icmp-type

The PIX supports several popular multimedia applications. Its application inspection function dynamically opens and closes UDP ports for secure multimedia connections. Popular multimedia applications such as RealPlayer, Microsoft NetMeeting, and others are supported by the Cisco PIX Firewall.

Q&A

The questions in this section do not attempt to cover more breadth or depth than the exam; however, they are designed to make sure that you know the answer. Hopefully, these questions will help limit the number of exam questions on which you narrow your choices to two options and then guess. Be sure to use the CD and take the simulated exams.

The answers to these questions can be found in Appendix A.

1 What is the maximum number of access list entries in one access list that TurboACL supports?

A 19

B 2000

C 16,000

D 10

2 What is the minimum number of access list entries needed in an access list for TurboACL to compile?

A 4

B 19

C 16,000

D No minimum is required

3 Which of the following is *not* one of four options for object types when you create an object group?

A Network

B Protocol

C Application

D Services

4 True or false: By default, traffic initiated from the outside (external to the PIX) is allowed in through the PIX.

5 What command lets you create a network object group?

   A   **object-group network** *group-id*

   B   **enable object-group network** *group-id*

   C   **create network object-group**

   D   **network object-group enable**

6 What command enables TurboACL globally on the PIX Firewall?

   A   **turboacl global**

   B   **access-list compiled**

   C   **access-list turboacl**

   D   You cannot enable TurboACL globally

7 What is the minimum memory requirement for TurboACL to work?

   A   8 MB

   B   100 Kb

   C   2.1 MB

   D   4 MB

This chapter covers the following exam topics for the Cisco Secure PIX Firewall Advanced Exam:

11. Syslog configuration

CHAPTER 8

Syslog

System logging, otherwise known as syslog, on the Cisco PIX Firewall makes it possible for you as an administrator to gather information about the PIX unit's traffic and performance. You can use syslog messages generated by the PIX to troubleshoot and analyze suspicious activity on the network.

This chapter describes how to configure syslog on the Cisco PIX Firewall and interpret the messages it generates.

"Do I Know This Already?" Quiz

The purpose of this quiz is to help you determine your current understanding of the topics covered in this chapter. Write down your answers and compare them to the answers in Appendix A. If you have to look at any references to correctly answer the questions, it is a good idea to read the chapter. Device activity and performance logging are very important network functions that too often are given a lower priority by many network administrators. This chapter helps you understand how syslog works on the Cisco PIX Firewall unit and how to configure it. The concepts in this chapter are the foundation of much of what you need to understand to pass the CSPFA Certification Exam. Unless you do exceptionally well on the "Do I Know This Already?" pretest and are 100% confident in your knowledge of this area, you should read through the entire chapter.

1 What port does syslogd listen on by default?

2 What is the total number of logging facilities available for syslog configuration?

3 True or false: If the PIX is set to Warning level, critical, alert, and emergency messages are sent in addition to warning messages.

4 What is the command for sending syslog messages to Telnet sessions?

5 What is the **logging trap** command used for?

6 What is the command used to enable logging on the failover PIX unit?

7 Why would you use the *timestamp* command parameter?

8 What is PFSS?

Foundation Topics

How Syslog Works

The syslog message facility in the Cisco PIX Firewall is a useful means to view trouble-shooting messages and to watch for network events such as attacks and denials of service. The Cisco PIX Firewall reports on events and activities via syslog messages, which report on the following:

- **System status**—When the Cisco PIX Firewall reboots or a connection via Telnet or the console is made or disconnected.

- **Accounting**—The number of bytes transferred per connection.

- **Security**—Dropped UDP packets and denied TCP connections.

- **Resources**—Notification of connection and translation slot depletion.

It is important to become familiar with the logging process and logging command parameters on the PIX before you dive in and start configuring the PIX for logging. Syslog messages can be sent to a couple of different output destinations on or off the PIX unit:

- **PDM logging**—Logging messages can be sent to the PIX Device Manager (PDM).

- **Console**—Syslog messages can be configured to be sent to the console interface, where the PIX administrator (you) can view the messages in real time as they happen when you're connected to the console interface.

- **Internal memory buffer**—Syslog messages can be sent to the buffer.

- **Telnet console**—Syslog messages can also be configured to be sent to Telnet sessions. This configuration helps you remotely administer and troubleshoot PIX units without your being physically present at the same location as the firewall.

- **Syslog servers**—This type of configuration is particularly useful for storing syslog messages for analysis on performance, trends, and packet activities on the PIX unit. Syslog messages are sent to UNIX servers/workstations running a syslogd daemon or to Windows NT servers running PIX Firewall Syslog Server (PFSS).

- **SNMP Management station**—Syslog traps can be configured to be sent to an SNMP management station.

After you decide where to send the syslog messages, you have to decide what type of messages you want to see at your output destination.

All syslog messages have a severity level; however, not all syslog messages are required to have a facility.

Logging Facilities

When syslog messages are sent to a server, it is important to indicate what *pipe* the PIX will send the messages through. The single syslog service, syslogd, can be thought of as having multiple pipes. It uses the pipes to decide where to send incoming information based on the pipe on which the information arrives. Syslogd is a daemon/service that runs on UNIX machines. In this analogy, the *logging facilities* are the pipes by which syslogd decides *where* to send information it receives—that is, which file to write to.

Eight *logging facilities* (16 through 23) are commonly used for syslog on the PIX. On the syslog server, the facility numbers have a corresponding identification—local0 to local7. The following are the facility numbers and their corresponding syslog identification:

- local0(16)
- local1(17)
- local2(18)
- local3(19)
- local4(20)
- local5(21)
- local6(22)
- local7(23)

The default facility is local4(20). To change the default logging facility on the PIX, you use the **logging facility** *facility* command. The following command shows the logging facility changed to 21:

```
Pix(config)# logging facility 21
```

Logging Levels

Different *severity levels* are attached to incoming messages. You can think of these levels as indicating the type of message. The PIX can be configured to send messages at different levels. Table 8-1 lists these levels from highest to lowest importance.

Table 8-1   *Logging Severity Levels*

Level	Numeric Code	System Condition
Emergency	0	System unusable message
Alert	1	Take immediate action
Critical	2	Critical condition
Error	3	Error message
Warning	4	Warning message
Notification	5	Normal but significant condition
Informational	6	Information message
Debug	7	Debug message, log FTP commands, and WWW URLs

Many of the **logging** commands require that you specify a severity level threshold to indicate which syslog messages can be sent to the output locations. The lower the level number, the more severe the syslog message. The default severity level is 3 (Error). During configuration, you can specify the severity level as either a number or a keyword, as described in Table 8-1. The level you specify causes the Cisco PIX Firewall to send the messages of that level and below to the output location. For example, if you specify severity level 3 (error), the PIX sends 0 (emergency);severity level 1 (alert); 2 (critical); and 3 (error) messages to the output location.

Configuring Syslog on the Cisco PIX Firewall

The **logging** command is used to configure logging on the PIX. Logging is disabled by default. Table 8-2 describes the **logging** command's parameters.

Table 8-2   **logging** *Command Parameters*

Command	Description
logging on	Enables the transmission of syslog messages to all output locations. You can disable sending syslog messages with the **no logging on** command.
no logging message *n*	Allows you to disable specific syslog messages. Use the **logging message** *message_number* command to resume logging of specific disabled messages.
logging buffered *n*	Stores syslog messages in the PIX Firewall so that you can view them with the **show logging** command. Cisco recommends that you use this command to view syslog messages when the PIX Firewall is in use in a network.
clear logging	Clears the message buffer created with the **logging buffered** command.
clear logging message	Re-enables all disabled syslog messages.
logging console *n*	Displays syslog messages on the PIX Firewall console as they occur. Use this command when you are debugging problems or when there is minimal load on the network. Do not use this command when the network is busy, because it can reduce PIX Firewall performance.
logging monitor *n*	Displays syslog messages when you access the PIX Firewall console with Telnet.
logging host [*interface*] *ip_address* [*protocol/ port*]	Specifies the host that receives the syslog messages. The PIX Firewall can send messages across UDP or TCP (which you specify by setting the *protocol* variable). The default UDP port is 514. The default TCP port is 1468.
logging history *severity_level*	Sets the logging level for SNMP traps.

Table 8-2   logging *Command Parameters (Continued) (Continued)*

Command	Description
logging queue *msg_count*	Specifies how many syslog messages can appear in the message queue while awaiting processing. The default is 512 messages. Use the **show logging queue** command to view queue statistics.
logging trap *n*	Sets the logging level for syslog messages.
show logging disabled	Displays a complete list of disabled syslog messages.
show logging	Lists the current syslog messages and which **logging** command options are enabled.
logging standby	Lets the failover standby unit send syslog messages.

Configuring the PIX Device Manager to View Logging

The PDM Logging panel, shown in Figure 8-1, allows you to view syslog messages that are captured in the PDM Log buffer in PIX Firewall memory. You may select the level of syslog messages you want to view. When you view the PDM Log, all the buffered syslog messages at and below the logging level you choose are displayed.

Figure 8-1   *PDM Logging Interface*

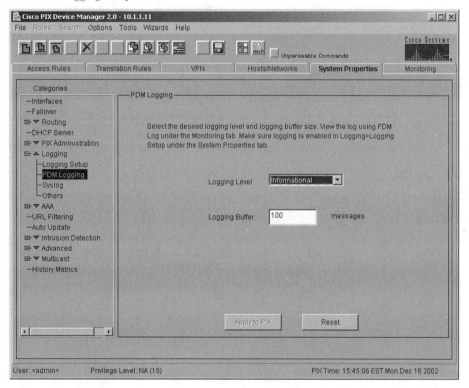

The PDM Logging panel has the following fields:

- **Logging Level**—Allows you to choose the level of syslog messages to view.

PDM is discussed in further detail in Chapter 11, "PIX Device Manager."

Configuring Syslog Messages at the Console

Use the **logging console** command to send the syslog messages to the console interface on the Cisco PIX Firewall:

Step 1 After logging into configuration mode, enter the following:

```
logging on
logging console 5
```

The **5** indicates the logging level. In this case, it is logging notification.

Step 2 View the messages with the following command:

```
show logging
```

Viewing Messages in a Telnet Console Session

Use the **logging monitor** command to configure the PIX to send syslog messages to Telnet sessions. For example, after logging into configuration mode, enter the following:

```
logging monitor 6
terminal monitor
```

In this example, syslog messages 0 to 6, or emergency to informational, are sent to a Telnet session. To disable logging to Telnet, you use the **no logging monitor** command.

The *terminal monitor* displays messages directly to the Telnet session. You can disable the direct display of messages by entering the **terminal no monitor** command. A Telnet session sometimes is lost in busy networks when the **logging monitor** command is used.

Configuring the Cisco PIX Firewall to Send Syslog Messages to a Log Server

PIX syslog messages are usually sent to a syslog server or servers. The syslog servers run the syslogd daemon, which is already built into UNIX systems and that comes as the add-on PFSS in Windows NT 4.0. PIX uses UDP 514 by default to send syslog messages to a syslog server. The following steps show you how to configure the PIX to send syslog messages:

Step 1 Designate a host to receive the messages with the **logging host** command:

```
logging host inside  10.1.1.10
```

You can specify additional servers so that if one goes offline, another is available to receive messages.

Step 2   Set the logging level with the **logging trap** command:

```
logging trap informational
```

If needed, set the **logging facility** command to a value other than its default of 20. Most UNIX systems expect the messages to arrive at facility 20.

NOTE   In the event that all syslog servers are offline, the Cisco PIX Firewall stores up to 100 messages in its memory. Subsequent messages that arrive overwrite the buffer starting from the first line.

Step 3   Start sending messages with the **logging on** command. To disable sending messages, use the **no logging** command.

Configuring a Syslogd Server

Because syslogd was originally a UNIX concept, the features available in the syslogd products on non-UNIX systems depend on the vendor implementation. Features might include dividing incoming messages by facility or debug level or both, resolving the names of the sending devices, and reporting facilities. For information on configuring the non-UNIX syslog server, refer to the vendor's documentation.

NOTE   Configuring the syslog server is not covered on the PIX exam.

To configure syslog on UNIX, follow these steps:

Step 1   On SunOS, AIX, HPUX, or Solaris, as root, make a backup of the /etc/ syslog.conf file before modifying it.

Step 2   Modify /etc/syslog.conf to tell the UNIX system how to sort out the syslog messages coming in from the sending devices—that is, which *logging_facility.level* goes in which file. Make sure there is a tab between the *logging_facility.level* and *file_name*.

Step 3   Make sure the destination file exists and is writable.

Step 4   The **#Comment** section at the beginning of syslog.conf usually explains the syntax for the UNIX system.

Step 5   Do not put file information in the **ifdef** section.

Step 6   As root, restart syslogd to pick up changes.

For example, if /etc/syslog.conf is set for

```
local7.warn       /var/log/local7.warn
```

warning, error, critical, alert, and emergency messages coming in on the local7 logging facility are logged in the local7.warn file. Notification, informational, and debug messages coming in on the local7 facility are not logged anywhere.

If /etc/syslog.conf is set for

```
*.debug           /var/log/all.debug
```

all message levels from all logging facilities go to this file.

PIX Firewall Syslog Server (PFSS)

PFSS lets you view PIX Firewall event information from a Windows NT system. It includes special features not found on other syslog servers:

- The ability to receive syslog messages via TCP or UDP
- Full reliability, because messages can be sent via TCP

PFSS can receive syslog messages from up to ten PIX units. You can install this product for use with any model of Cisco PIX Firewall. If you have specified that the PIX send syslog messages via TCP, the Windows NT disk might become full, and the PIX unit stops its traffic. If the Windows NT file system is full, the Windows system beeps, and the PFSS disables all TCP connections from the PIX unit(s) by closing its TCP listen socket. The PIX tries to reconnect to the PFSS five times, and during the retry, it stops all new connections through the PIX.

Configuring SNMP Traps and SNMP Requests

SNMP requests can be used to query the PIX on its system status information. If you want to send only the cold start, link up, and link down generic traps, no further configuration is required. SNMP traps send information about a particular event *only* when the configured threshold is reached.

To configure the PIX to receive SNMP requests from a management station, you need to

- Configure the IP address of the SNMP management station with the **snmp-server host** command.
- Set the **snmp-server** options for **location**, **contact**, and the **community** password as required.

To configure SNMP traps on the PIX, you need to

- Configure the IP address of the SNMP management station with the **snmp-server host** command.
- Set the **snmp-server** options for **location**, **contact**, and the **community** password as required.
- Set the trap with the **snmp-server enable traps** command.
- Set the logging level with the **logging history** command.

How Log Messages Are Organized

Syslog messages are listed numerically by message code. Each message is followed by a brief explanation and a recommended action. If several messages share the same explanation and recommended action, the messages are presented together, followed by the common explanation and recommended action.

The explanation of each message indicates what kind of event generated the message. Possible events include the following:

- AAA (accounting, authentication, and authorization) events
- Connection events (for example, connections denied by the PIX configuration or address translation errors)
- Failover events reported by one or both units of a failover pair
- FTP/URL events (for example, successful file transfers or blocked Java applets)
- Mail Guard/SNMP events
- PIX management events (for example, configuration events or Telnet connections to the PIX console port)
- Routing errors

How to Read System Log Messages

System log messages received at a syslog server begin with a percent sign (%) and are structured as follows:

`%PIX-level-message_number: message_text`

- **PIX** identifies the message facility code for messages generated by the PIX Firewall.

- *level* reflects the severity of the condition described by the message. The lower the number, the more serious the condition.

- *message_number* is the numeric code that uniquely identifies the message.

- *message_text* is a text string describing the condition. This portion of the message sometimes includes IP addresses, port numbers, or usernames.

You can find more information on syslog messages at www.cisco.com/univercd/cc/td/doc/product/iaabu/pix/pix_v52/syslog/pixemsgs.htm#11493.

Disabling Syslog Messages

It is possible to single out syslog messages that you do not want to receive by simply instructing the PIX not to log that particular message. Table 8-3 shows the commands used to manage the type of individual syslog messages sent by the Cisco PIX Firewall.

Table 8-3 *Syslog Message Management Commands*

Command	Description
no logging message *message_number*	Disables syslog messages.
show logging disabled	Displays a list of disabled syslog messages.
logging message *message_number*	Re-enables disabled syslog messages.
clear logging message	Re-enables all disabled syslog messages.

Foundation Summary

The syslog message facility in the Cisco PIX Firewall is a useful means to view trouble-shooting messages and to watch for network events such as attacks and service denials. Syslog messages can be configured to be sent to

- PDM logging
- Console
- Telnet console
- Internal memory/buffer
- Syslog server
- SNMP management station

Common to all ways of viewing syslog messages is the message's level, or severity. The level specifies the types of messages sent to the syslog host, as shown in Table 8-4.

Table 8-4 *Logging Severity Levels*

Level	Numeric Code	System Condition
Emergency	0	System unusable message
Alert	1	Take immediate action
Critical	2	Critical condition
Error	3	Error message
Warning	4	Warning message
Notification	5	Normal but significant condition
Informational	6	Information message
Debug	7	Debug message, log FTP commands, and WWW URLs

System log messages received at a syslog server begin with a percent sign (%) and are structured as follows:

```
%PIX-level-message_number: message_text
```

You can set the *level* with the **logging** command so that you can view syslog messages on the PIX Firewall console, from a syslog server, or with SNMP.

Q&A

The questions in this section are designed to ensure your understanding of the concepts discussed in this chapter and adequately prepare you to complete the exam. You should use the simulated exams on the CD to practice for the exam.

The answers to these questions can be found in Appendix .

1 What is the command for sending syslog messages to the Telnet session?

A **logging console**

B **logging monitor**

C **telnet logging**

D send log telnet

2 What is the **logging trap** command used for?

3 True or false: PFSS stands for PIX Firewall System Solution.

4 PIX Firewall can be configured to send syslog messages to all of the following except which one?

A Console

B Telnet

C Serial

D Syslog server

5 Which of the following is *not* an example of a severity level for syslog configuration?

A Emergency

B Alert

C Prepare

D Warning

6 What is syslogd?

A A message type that forms the syslog services

B A service that runs on UNIX machines

C A hardware subcomponent that is required for syslog configuration on the PIX

D It gathers information on IT businesses in Japan.

7 What port does syslogd use by default?

    A UDP 512

    B TCP 514

    C TCP 512

    D UDP 514

8 True or false: The default facility number on the PIX Firewall is 18.

9 How are syslog messages organized?

    A They are listed numerically by message code.

    B They are listed by importance level.

    C They are listed by date.

    D They are not organized.

10 True or false: It is possible to disable specific syslog messages.

11 Windows NT 4.0 server can work as a syslog server with what?

    A IIS configured for logging

    B PIX Firewall Syslog Server application installed

    C PIX Device Manager

    D UNIX

This chapter covers the following exam topics for the Cisco Secure PIX Firewall Advanced Exam:

33. Understanding failover
34. Failover configuration
35. LAN-based failover configuration

CHAPTER 9

Cisco PIX Firewall Failover

Today, most businesses rely heavily on critical application servers that support the business process. The interruption of these services due to network device failures or other causes has a great financial cost, not to mention the irritation it causes in the user community. It is with this in mind that most of Cisco's devices, including the firewall products (models 515 and up), can be configured in a redundant or highly available configuration.

The failover feature makes the Cisco PIX Firewall a highly available firewall solution. The purpose of this feature is to ensure continuity of service in case of a failure on the primary unit.

The failover process requires two PIX firewalls—one primary (active mode) and one secondary (standby mode). The idea is to have the primary PIX Firewall handle all the traffic from the network and to have the secondary PIX wait in standby mode in case the primary fails, at which point it takes over the process of handling all the network traffic. In the event of a primary (active) unit failure, the secondary PIX changes its state from standby mode to active and assumes the IP address and MAC address of the previously active unit and begins accepting traffic for it. The new standby unit assumes the IP address and MAC address of the unit that was previously the standby unit, thus completing the failover process.

"Do I Know This Already?" Quiz

The purpose of this quiz is to help you determine your current understanding of the topics covered in this chapter. Write down your answers and compare them to the answers in Appendix A. The concepts in this chapter are the foundation of much of what you need to understand to pass the CSPFA Certification Exam. Unless you do exceptionally well on the "Do I Know This Already?" pretest and are 100% confident in your knowledge of this area, you should read through the entire chapter.

1 What are some things that trigger a failover event?

2 What command assigns an IP address to the standby PIX Firewall?

3 How many PIX Firewall devices can be configured in a failover configuration?

4 What is the benefit of using LAN-based failover?

5 What is some of the information that is updated to the standby unit in a stateful failover configuration?

6 What command forces replication to the standby unit?

7 What command configures a LAN-based failover?

8 What is the default failover poll in seconds?

Foundation Topics

What Causes a Failover Event

In a PIX failover configuration, one of the PIX firewalls is considered the *active* unit, and the other is the *standby* unit. As the name implies, the active unit performs normal network functions, and the standby unit monitors and is ready to take control should the active unit fail to perform its functionality. A failover event occurs after a series of tests determines that the primary (active) unit can no longer continue providing its services and the standby Cisco PIX Firewall assumes the role of the primary. The main causes of failover are as follows:

- **Loss of power**—When the primary (active) unit loses power or is turned off, the standby unit assumes the active role.

- **Cable errors**—The cable is wired so that each unit can distinguish between a power failure in the other unit and an unplugged cable. If the standby unit detects that the active unit is turned off (or resets), it takes active control.

- **Standby active**—An administrator can force the standby unit to change state using the **standby active** command, which causes failover to occur. This is the only time when failover takes place without the primary (active) unit's having problems.

- **Memory exhaustion**—If block memory exhaustion occurs for 15 straight seconds on the active unit.

- **Failover communication loss**—If the standby unit does not hear from the active unit for more than twice the configured poll time (or a maximum of 30 seconds), and the cable status is OK, a series of tests are conducted before the standby unit takes over as active.

What Is Required for a Failover Configuration

The hardware and software for the primary and standby PIX firewalls must match for failover configuration to work properly. Both must be the same for:

- Firewall model
- Software version
- Flash memory size
- RAM size
- Activation key

The only additional hardware needed to support failover is the failover cable. Both units in a failover pair communicate through the failover cable. The failover cable is a modified

RS-232 serial link cable that transfers data at 115 kbps. It is through this cable that the two units maintain the heartbeat network. Some of the messages that are communicated over the failover cable are

- Hello (keepalive packets)
- Configuration replication
- Network link status
- State of the unit (active/standby)
- MAC address exchange

It is also important to examine the labels on each end of the failover cable. One end of the cable is labeled "primary," and the other end is labeled "secondary." To have a successful failover configuration, the end labeled "primary" should be connected to the primary unit, and the end labeled "secondary" should be connected to the secondary unit. Changes made to the standby unit are never replicated to the active unit.

Failover Monitoring

The failover feature in the Cisco PIX Firewall monitors failover communication, the power status of the other unit, and hello packets received at each interface. If two consecutive hello packets are not received within an amount of time determined by the failover feature, failover starts testing the interfaces to determine which unit has failed and transfers active control to the standby unit.

NOTE   The **failover poll** *seconds* command allows you to determine how long failover waits before sending special failover "hello" packets between the primary and standby units over all network interfaces and the failover cable. The default is 15 seconds. The minimum value is 3 seconds, and the maximum is 15 seconds.

Failover uses the following tests to check the status of the units for failure:

- **Link up/down test**—If an interface card has a bad network cable or a bad port, if it is administratively shut down, or if it is connected to failed switch, it is considered failed.

- **Network activity test**—The unit counts all received packets for up to 5 seconds. If any packets are received at any time during this interval, the interface is considered operational, and testing stops. If no traffic is received, the ARP test begins.

- **Address Resolution Protocol (ARP) test**—The ARP test involves evaluating the unit's ARP cache for the ten most recently acquired entries. One at a time, the PIX sends ARP requests to these machines, attempting to stimulate network traffic. After each request, the unit counts all received traffic for up to 5 seconds. If traffic is received, the interface is considered operational. If no traffic is received, an ARP request is sent to the next machine. If at the end of the list no traffic has been received, the ping test begins.

- **Ping test**—This test consists of sending out a broadcast ping request. The unit then counts all received packets for up to 5 seconds. If any packets are received at any time during this interval, the interface is considered operational, and testing stops. If no traffic is received, the testing starts over again with the ARP test.

TIP   Portfast should be enabled on all the ports where the PIX interface directly connects, and trunking and channeling should be turned off. This way, if the PIX's interface goes down during failover, the switch does not have to wait 30 seconds while the port is transitioned from a listening state to a learning state to a forwarding state.

Configuration Replication

Configuration changes including initial failover configurations to the Cisco PIX Firewall are done on the primary unit. The standby unit keeps the current configuration through the process of configuration replication. For configuration replication to occur, the two PIX units should be running the same software release. Configuration replication usually occurs when:

- The standby unit completes its initial bootup, and the active unit replicates its entire configuration to the standby unit.

- Configurations are made (commands) on the active unit, and the commands/changes are sent across the failover cable to the standby unit.

- Issuing the **write standby** command on the active unit forces the entire configuration in memory to be sent to the standby unit.

When the replication starts, the PIX console displays the message "Sync Started." When the replication is complete, the PIX console displays the message "Sync Completed." During the replication, information cannot be entered on the PIX console.

The **write memory** command is important, especially when failover is being configured for the first time. During the configuration replication process, the configuration is replicated from the active unit's running configuration to the running configuration of the standby unit. Because the running configuration is saved in RAM (which is unstable), the **write memory** command should be issued to save the configuration to Flash on the standby unit.

Stateful Failover

In stateful failover mode, more information is shared about the connections that have been established with the standby unit by the active unit. The active unit shares per-connection state information with the standby unit. If and when an active unit fails over to the standby unit, an application does not reinitiate its connection. This is because stateful information from the active unit updates the standby unit.

NOTE   Some applications are latency-sensitive. In some cases, the application times out before the failover sequence is completed. In these cases, the application must reestablish the session.

Replicated state information includes the following:

- TCP connection table, including timeout information for each connection
- Translation (xlate) table and status
- Negotiated H.323 UDP ports
- Port allocation table bitmap for PAT

Because failover cannot be prescheduled, the state update for the connection is packet-based. This means that every packet passes through the PIX and changes a connection's state, which might trigger a state update.

However, some state information does not get updated to the standby unit in a stateful failover:

- The user authentication (uauth) table
- ISAKMP and the IPSec SA table
- ARP table
- Routing information

Most UDP state tables are not transferred, with the exception of dynamically opened ports corresponding to multichannel protocols such as H.323.

In addition to the failover cable, stateful failover setup requires a 100-Mbps or Gigabit Ethernet interface to be used exclusively for passing state information between the active and standby units. IP protocol 105 is used to pass data over this interface.

The stateful failover interface can be connected to any of the following:

- Category 5 crossover cable directly connecting the primary unit to the secondary unit
- 1000BASE-TX half-duplex switch using straight Category 5 cables
- 100BASE-TX full duplex on a dedicated switch or a switch's dedicated VLAN
- 1000BASE-TX full duplex on a switch's dedicated VLAN

NOTE	A Cisco PIX Firewall with two FDDI cards cannot use stateful failover, because an additional Ethernet interface with FDDI is not supported in stateful failover.

LAN-Based Failover

The distance restriction of 6 feet of serial cable between two PIX devices in a failover configuration is no longer a limitation starting with PIX version 6.2. LAN-based failover is a new feature (available only on PIX 6.2) that extends PIX failover functionality to operate through a dedicated LAN interface without the serial failover cable. This feature provides for a choice of configuration when it comes to failover configuration on the PIX.

The obvious benefit of LAN-based failover is removing the 6-foot distance limitation from the PIX devices in a failover configuration. However, another benefit is not so obvious. It provides an alternative path for stateful information if the failover interface goes down. For example, if the failover interface goes down, the PIX informs the peer through the other interfaces of the active PIX's status. To configure LAN-based failover, you need a dedicated switch or hub (or VLAN) to connect the PIX failover pair so that the secondary unit can detect the failure of the primary unit's dedicated LAN failover interface and become active.

The weakness of LAN-based failover is the delayed detection of its peer power loss, consequently causing a relatively longer period for failover to occur.

NOTE	Crossover Ethernet cables cannot be used to connect the LAN-based failover interface. Additionally, it is recommended that you dedicate a LAN interface for LAN-based failover, but the interface can be shared with stateful failover under lightly loaded configurations.

Cisco PIX Firewall software version 6.2 enhances failover functionality so that the standby unit in a PIX failover pair can be configured to use a virtual MAC address. This eliminates potential "stale" ARP entry issues for devices connected to the PIX failover pair in the unlikely event that both firewalls in a failover pair fail at the same time and only the standby unit remains operational.

Configuring Failover

Now for the fun stuff! To configure failover, you need to become familiar with a few key commands. Table 9-1 shows the commands used to configure and verify failover.

Table 9-1   *Configuring and Verifying Failover*

Command	Description
failover	The **failover** command without an argument enables the failover function on the PIX. Use this command after you connect the failover cable between the primary and secondary unit. Use the **no failover** command to disable the failover feature.
failover active	Makes the PIX unit it is issued on the active unit. This command is usually used to make the primary unit active again after repairs have been made to it.
failover ip address *if_name ip_address*	Issued on the primary unit to configure the standby unit's IP address. This is the IP address that the standby interface uses to communicate with the active unit. Therefore, it has the same subnet as the system address[*]. The *if_name* argument is for the interface name, such as **outside**. The *ip_address* is the interface name's IP address.
failover link *stateful_if_name*	Enables stateful failover on the specified interface.
show failover	This popular command displays the status of the failover configuration.
failover poll *seconds*	Specifies how long failover waits before sending special hello packets between the primary and secondary units. The default is 15 seconds. The minimum is 3 seconds, and the maximum is 15 seconds.
failover reset	Can be entered from either unit (active or standby), preferably the active unit. This forces the units back to their state and is used after repairs have been made.
write standby	Enter the **write standby** command from the active unit to synchronize the current configuration to the Flash memory on the standby unit.
failover lan interface *interface_name*	Configures LAN-based failover.
**failover lan unit primary	secondary**	Specifies the primary or secondary PIX to use for LAN-based failover.
failover replicate http	Allows the stateful replication of HTTP sessions in a stateful failover environment.

*The system address is the same address as the active unit IP address. When the active unit fails, the standby assumes the system address so that there is no need for the network devices to be reconfigured for a different firewall address.

Figure 9-1 shows two PIX units in a failover configuration. Example 9-1 shows the steps required to configure failover and stateful failover on the PIX Firewall.

Figure 9-1   *Network Diagram of Failover Configuration*

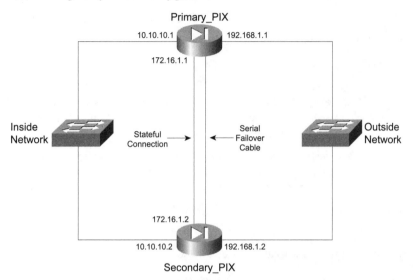

Example 9-1   *Sample Configuration for primary-PIX*

```
hostname primary-PIX
nameif ethernet0 outside security0
nameif ethernet1 inside security100
nameif ethernet2 failover security10
interface ethernet0 10baset
interface ethernet1 10baset
interface ethernet2 100full
ip address outside 192.168.1.1 255.255.255.224
ip address inside 10.10.10.1 255.255.255.0
global (outside) 1 192.168.1.15-192.168.1.40 netmask 255.255.255.224
nat (inside) 1 0.0.0.0 0.0.0.0 0 0
```

Before beginning the failover configuration, be sure that you connect the failover cable to the units correctly. Also be sure that the standby unit is not powered on.

Step 1   Enable failover:

    Primary-pix (config)# **failover**

Step 2   Assign interface ethernet2 a name for stateful failover:

    Primary-pix (config)# **nameif ethernet2 failover**

Step 3 Set the interface speed:

```
Primary-pix (config)# interface ethernet2 100full
```

Step 4 Assign an IP address to the interface:

```
Primary-pix (config)# ip address failover 172.16.1.1 255.255.255.240
```

Step 5 Verify your failover configuration:

```
Primary-pix (config)# show failover
```

Step 6 Configure the secondary unit IP address from the primary unit by the **failover ip address** command. Add the **failover ip address** command for *all* interfaces, including the one for the dedicated failover interface and any unused interfaces:

```
Primary-pix (config)# failover ip address outside 192.168.1.2
Primary-pix (config)# failover ip address inside 10.10.10.2
Primary-pix (config)# failover ip address failover 172.16.1.2
```

Step 7 Save your configuration:

```
Primary-pix (config)# write memory
```

Step 8 Use the **show ip address** command to view the addresses you specified:

```
Primary-pix (config)# show ip address
System IP Addresses:
     ip address outside 192.168.1.1 255.255.255.0
     ip address inside 10.10.10.1 255.255.255.0
     ip address failover 172.16.1.1 255.255.255.240
Current IP Addresses:
     ip address outside 192.168.1.1 255.255.255.0
     ip address inside 10.10.10.1 255.255.255.0
     ip addressfailover 172.16.1.2 255.255.255.240
```

The Current IP Addresses are the same as the System IP Addresses on the failover active unit. When the primary unit fails, the Current IP Addresses become those of the standby unit.

Step 9 Enable stateful failover:

```
Primary-pix (config)# failover link failover
```

Step 10 Power up the secondary unit. At this point, the primary unit starts replicating the configuration to the secondary.

Step 11 Verify your failover configuration:

```
Primary-pix (config)# show failover
Failover On
Cable status: Normal
Reconnect timeout 0:00:00
```

```
Poll frequency 15 seconds
      This host: primary - Active
            Active time: 240 (sec)
            Interface st_failover (172.16.1.1): Normal
            Interface outside (192.168.1.1): Normal
            Interface inside (10.10.10.1): Normal
      Other host: secondary - Standby
            Active time: 0 (sec)
            Interface st_failover (172.16.1.1): Normal
            Interface outside (192.168.1.1): Normal
            Interface inside (10.10.10.1): Normal

Stateful Failover Logical Update Statistics
      Link : failover
      Stateful Obj   xmit      xerr       rcv        rerr
      General        2701         0         0           0
      sys cmd        2653         0         0           0
      up time           0         0         0           0
      xlate             0         0         0           0
      tcp conn          0         0         0           0
      udp conn          0         0         0           0
      ARP tbl           0         0         0           0
      RIP Tbl           0         0         0           0

      Logical Update Queue Information
                     Cur       Max      Total
      Recv Q:          0         0          0
      Xmit Q:          0         0       2701
```

The first part of the **show failover** command output describes the cable status. Each interface on the PIX unit has one of the following values:

— **Normal**—The active unit is working, and the standby unit is ready.

— **Waiting**—Monitoring of the other unit's network interfaces has not yet started.

— **Failed**—The PIX Firewall has failed.

— **Shutdown**—The interface is turned off.

The second part of the **show failover** command describes the status of the stateful failover configuration. Each row is for a particular static object count:

— **General**—The sum of all stateful objects.

— **Sys cmd**—Refers to logical update system commands, such as **login** and **stay alive**.

- **Up time**—The value for PIX up time that the active PIX unit passes on to the standby unit.

- **Xlate**—The PIX translation information.

- **Tcp conn**—The PIX dynamic TCP connection information.

- **Udp conn**—The PIX dynamic UDP connection information.

- **ARP tbl**—The PIX dynamic ARP table information.

- **RIF tbl**—The dynamic router table information.

The **Stateful Obj** has these values:

- **Xmit**—Indicates the number of packets transmitted.

- **Xerr**—Indicates the number of transmit errors.

- **Rcv**—Indicates the number of packets received.

- **rerr**—Indicates the number of receive errors.

Step 12 Enter the **write standby** command from the active unit to synchronize the current configuration to the Flash memory on the standby unit.

Foundation Summary

Failover allows you to connect a second PIX Firewall unit to your network to protect your network should the first unit go offline. If you use Stateful Failover, you can maintain operating state for the TCP connection during the failover from the primary unit to the standby unit.

Failover is triggered by some of the following events:

- Losss Of Power
- Standy unit forced by an Administrator to be active
- Cable errors
- Memory exhaustion
- Failover communication loss

Failover requires you to purchase a second PIX Firewall unit sold as a failover unit that only works as a failover unit. You need to ensure that both units have the same software version, activation key type, Flash memory, and the same RAM. Once you configure the primary unit and attach the necessary cabling, the primary unit automatically copies the configuration over to the Standby unit.

If a failure is due to a condition other than a loss of power on the other unit, failover will begin a series of tests to determine which unit failed. This series of tests will begin when "hello" messages are not heard for two consecutive 15-second intervals (the interval depends on how you set the **failover poll** command). Hello messages are sent over both network interfaces and the failover cable. Failover uses the following tests to determine the other units availability:

- Link up/Down
- Network activity
- Address resolution Protocol
- Ping

The Stateful Failover feature passes per-connection stateful information to the Standby unit. After a failover occurs, the same connection information is available at the new Active unit. End user applications are not required to do a reconnect to keep the same communication session.

Q&A

The questions in this section are designed to ensure your understanding of the concepts discussed in this chapter and adequately prepare you to complete the exam. Use the simulated exams on the CD to practice for the exam.

The answers to these questions can be found in Appendix A.

1 Which two of the following cause a failover event?

   A   A reboot or power interruption on the active PIX Firewall

   B   Low HTTP traffic on the outside interface

   C   The **failover active** command is issued on the standby PIX Firewall

   D   Block memory exhaustion for 15 consecutive seconds or more on the active PIX

2 What is the command to view failover configuration?

   A   **show failover**

   B   **failover**

   C   **view failover**

   D   **show me failover**

3 Which of the following is/are replicated during a stateful failover?

   A   Configuration

   B   TCP connection table, including timeout information for each connection

   C   Translation (xlate) table

   D   Negotiated H.323 UDP protocols

   E   All of the above

4 Which of the following is *not* replicated in a stateful failover?

   A   User authentication (uauth) table

   B   ISAKMP and IPSec SA table

   C   ARP table

   D   Routing information

   E   All of the above

5 What is the command to force configuration replication to the standby unit?

   A   **write standby**

   B   **copy to secondary**

   C   **force secondary**

   D   **force conf**

6 Which of the following is a stateful failover hardware restriction?

   A   The stateful failover configuration is supported only by PIX 535 models.

   B   Only fiber connections can be used in a stateful failover hardware configuration.

   C   A PIX with two FDDI cards cannot use stateful failover, because an additional Ethernet interface with FDDI is not supported.

   D   There is no hardware restriction for stateful failover configuration.

7 What command assigns an IP address to the standby Cisco PIX Firewall?

   A   **secondary ip address** *ip address*

   B   **failover ip address** *if_name ip_address*

   C   **ip address** *ip address* **secondary**

   D   **ip address** *ip address* **failover**

8 What is the command to configure a LAN-based failover?

   A   **conf lan failover**

   B   **failover ip LAN**

   C   **failover lan interface** *if_name*

   D   **lan interface failover**

9 What is an advantage of a LAN-based failover?

   A   It quickly fails over to a peer when a power failure on the active unit takes place.

   B   It does not have the 6-foot cable distance limitation for failover communication.

   C   It is preconfigured on the PIX.

   D   All of the above

10 What is the default failover poll in seconds?

   A   10 seconds

   B   15 seconds

   C   30 seconds

   D   25 seconds

This chapter covers the following exam topics for the Cisco Secure PIX Firewall Advanced Exam:

36. PIX Firewall enables a secure VPN
37. IPSec configuration tasks
38. Prepare to configure VPN support
39. Configure IKE parameters
40. Configure IPSec parameters
41. Test and verify VPN configuration
42. Cisco VPN Client
43. Scale PIX Firewall VPNs
44. PPPoE and the PIX Firewall

CHAPTER 10

Virtual Private Networks

Virtual private networks (VPNs) have become a crucial portion of nearly all enterprise networks. The ability of VPN technologies to create a secure link interconnecting offices over the Internet saves companies the expense of dedicated connections. Additionally, VPN connections allow remote users to connect to their headquarters securely.

How to Best Use This Chapter

This chapter provides an overview of the different VPN technologies available and discusses where the Cisco PIX Firewall can be used as an endpoint for VPNs. You need to become very familiar with the methodology used to implement VPNs and how that method-ology is applied to the PIX. As you read through this chapter, consider how encryption technology is applied in general, and then focus on the configuration steps required to configure the PIX. If you are at all familiar with configuring VPNs on any Cisco product, you will probably find this chapter very easy.

"Do I Know This Already?" Quiz

The purpose of this quiz is to help you determine your current understanding of the topics covered in this chapter. Write down your answers and compare them to the answers in Appendix A. If you have to look at any references to correctly answer the questions about PIX functionality, you should read that portion and double-check your thinking by reviewing the Foundation Summary. The concepts in this chapter are the foundation of much of what you need to understand to pass the CSPFA Certification Exam. Unless you do exceptionally well on the "Do I Know This Already?" pretest and are 100% confident in your knowledge of this area, you should read through the entire chapter.

  1 Which encryption is stronger, Group 2 Diffie-Hellman or 3DES?

  2 What is the command to apply an access list to a crypto map?

  3 What is the difference between ESP and AH?

  4 What service uses UDP 500?

5 What is the size of an MD5 hash?

6 Why is **manual-ipsec** not recommended by Cisco?

7 What is the most scalable VPN solution?

8 What is the difference between an access VPN and an intranet VPN?

9 Which hash algorithm is configured by default for phase 1?

10 What are the two methods of identifying SA peers?

11 What happens if you have different ISAKMP policies configured on your potential SA peers, and none of them match?

12 What command should you use to watch your IKE negotiation?

13 Where do you define your authentication method?

14 What are the three types of VPNs?

Foundation Topics

Overview of VPN Technologies

Before the creation of VPN technologies, the only way for companies to secure network communications between different locations was to purchase costly dedicated connections. VPNs allow companies to create secure encrypted tunnels between locations over a shared network infrastructure such as the Internet. A VPN is a service that offers secure, reliable connectivity over a shared public network infrastructure. VPNs are broken into three types based on their usage:

- **Access VPNs**—An access VPN, shown in Figure 10-1, provides secure communications with remote users. Access VPNs are used by users who connect via dialup or other mobile connections. A user working from home would most likely use an access VPN to connect to work. Access VPNs usually require some type of client software running on the user's computer. This type of VPN is commonly called a *remote-access VPN*.

Figure 10-1   *Access VPN*

- **Intranet VPNs**—An intranet VPN is used to securely interconnect a company's different locations. This allows all locations to have access to the resources available on the enterprise network. Intranet VPNs link headquarters, offices, and branch offices over a shared infrastructure using connections that are always encrypted. This type of VPN is normally configured as a *site-to-site VPN*.

- **Extranet VPNs**—Extranet VPNs provide a secure tunnel between customers, suppliers, and partners over a shared infrastructure using connections that are always encrypted. This type of VPN is also normally configured as a site-to-site VPN. The difference between an intranet VPN and an extranet VPN is the network access that is granted at either end of the VPN. Figure 10-2 shows a site-to-site VPN, the configuration commonly used for both intranet and extranet VPNs.

Figure 10-2   *Site-to-Site VPN*

Internet Protocol Security (IPSec)

IPSec is not a protocol. It is a framework of open-standard protocol suites designed to provide data authentication, data integrity, and data confidentiality. IPSec runs at the IP layer and uses IKE to negotiate the security association (SA) between the peers. The following items must be negotiated as part of IKE SA negotiation:

- Encryption algorithm

- Hash algorithm

- Authentication method

- Diffie-Hellman group

As soon as the IKE SA negotiation is complete, the established SA is bidirectional.

IPSec's function is to establish security associations between two IPSec peers. The security associations determine the keying, protocols, and algorithms to be used between the peers. IPSec SAs can be established only as unidirectional. Two primary security protocols are included as part of the IPSec standard supported by the PIX:

- **Encapsulating Security Payload (ESP)**—ESP provides data authentication, encryption, and antireplay services. ESP is protocol number 50 assigned by the Internet Assigned Numbers Authority (IANA). ESP is primarily responsible for getting the data from the source to the destination in a secure manner, verifying that the data has not been altered and ensuring that the session cannot be hijacked. ESP can also be used to authenticate the sender, either by itself or in conjunction with AH. ESP can be configured to encrypt the entire data packet or only the packet's payload. Figure 10-3 shows how ESP encapsulates the IPv4 packet, which portions are encrypted, and which are authenticated.

Figure 10-3 *ESP Encapsulation*

IPV4 Packet without ESP Encapsulation

IPV4 Packet with ESP Encapsulation

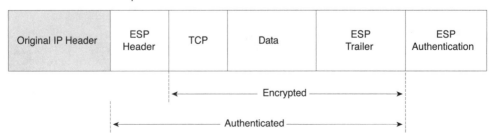

- **Authentication Header (AH)**—AH provides data authentication and antireplay services. AH is protocol number 51 assigned by the IANA. The primary function of AH is origin authentication. AH does not provide any data encryption. It provides only origin authentication or verifies that the data is from the sender. This functionality also prevents session hijacking. Figure 10-4 shows how AH is inserted into the IPv4 packet.

Figure 10-4   *AH Insertion into the IPv4 Packet*

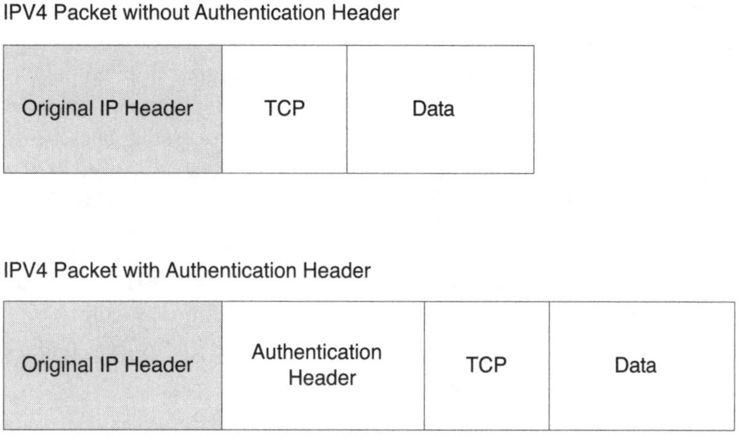

IPV4 Packet without Authentication Header

Original IP Header	TCP	Data

IPV4 Packet with Authentication Header

Original IP Header	Authentication Header	TCP	Data

It is important to note that ESP authenticates only the payload, and AH authenticates the IP header. You might want to use both ESP and AH if you use NAT for any of your IPSec traffic.

Both ESP and AH must be configured to use a specific encryption algorithm and hash algorithms. An encryption algorithm is the mathematical algorithm used to encrypt and decrypt the data. The hash algorithm is used to ensure data integrity.

NOTE   The Cisco PIX Firewall requires an activation key (license) to implement the IPSec features.

The encryption algorithms supported on the PIX are as follows:

- **Data Encryption Standard (DES)**—DES is a 56-bit symmetric encryption algorithm. Although it is still widely used, DES is somewhat outdated and should not be used if your data is highly sensitive. It is commonly used for VPN connections to locations outside the U.S. that cannot purchase higher levels of encryption due to U.S. technology export policies.

- **Triple Data Encryption Standard (3DES)**—3DES is a 168-bit symmetric encryption algorithm.

A hash algorithm takes a message as input and creates a fixed-length output called the *message digest*. The message digest is put into the digital signature algorithm, which generates or verifies the signature for the message. Signing the message digest rather than the actual message usually improves the message's processing, because the message digest is smaller than the message. The same hash algorithm must be used by the message's originator and verifier. The Cisco PIX Firewall supports the Keyed-Hash Message Authentication Code (HMAC) variant of the following hash algorithms:

- **Secure Hash Algorithm 1 (SHA-1)**—The output of SHA-1 is 160-bit. Because the output is larger than MD5, SHA-1 is considered more secure.

- **Message Digest 5 (MD5)**—The output of MD5 is 128-bit. MD5 is slightly faster to process because of its smaller message digest.

Internet Key Exchange (IKE)

IKE is the protocol that is responsible for negotiation. IKE is the short name for ISAKMP/Oakley, which stands for Internet Security Association and Key Management Protocol (with Oakley distribution). The terms *IKE* and *ISAKMP* are used interchangeably throughout this chapter. IKE operates over UDP port 500 and negotiates the key exchange between peers to establish the SA. This process requires that the IPSec systems first authenticate themselves to each other and establish ISAKMP (IKE) shared keys. This negotiation is called *phase 1* negotiation, and it is during this phase that the Diffie-Hellman key agreement is performed. During phase 1, IKE creates the IKE security association, which is a secure channel between the two IKE peers. IKE authenticates the peer and the IKE messages between the peers during IKE phase 1. Phase 1 consists of *main mode* or *aggressive mode*.

A main-mode negotiation consists of six message exchanges:

- The first two messages simply negotiate the exchange policy.

- The second two messages exchange Diffie-Hellman public-key values and an 8- to 256-bit *nonce*.

- The last two messages authenticate the key exchange.

In an aggressive-mode exchange:

- The first two messages negotiate policy, exchange public-key values, and authenticate the responder.
- The third message authenticates the initiator and is normally postponed until the negotiation is complete and is not sent as clear text.

Figure 10-5 shows main-mode and aggressive-mode key exchanges.

NOTE	Diffie-Hellman is a public-key cryptography protocol that is used between two IPSec peers to derive a shared secret over an unsecured channel without transmitting it to each other. Please change this sentence to read: There are two Diffie-Hellman groups supported by the PIX Firewall: Group 1 is 768-bit, and group 2 is 1024-bit. Diffie-Hellman is discussed in greater detail later in this chapter.

Peers that want to participate in the IPSec session *must* authenticate themselves to each other before IKE can proceed. Peer authentication occurs during the main-mode/aggressive-mode exchange during IKE phase 1. The IKE protocol is very flexible and supports multiple authentication methods as part of the phase 1 exchange. The two entities must agree on a common authentication protocol through a negotiation process. IKE phase 1 has three methods to authenticate IPSec peers in Cisco products:

- **Preshared keys**—A case-sensitive key value entered into each peer manually and used to authenticate the peer.
- **RSA signatures**—RSA is a public-key cryptographic system that uses a digital certificate authenticated by an RSA signature.
- **RSA encrypted nonces**—Uses RSA encryption to encrypt a *nonce value* (a random number generated by the peer) and other values.

Figure 10-5 *Key Exchanges*

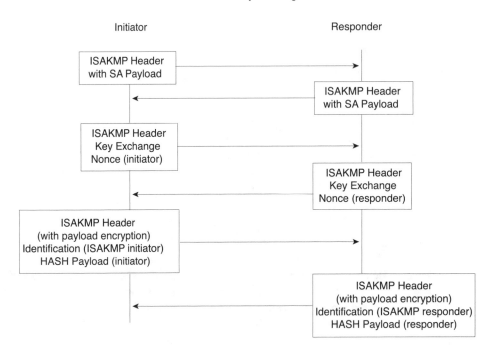

Main Mode Key Exchange

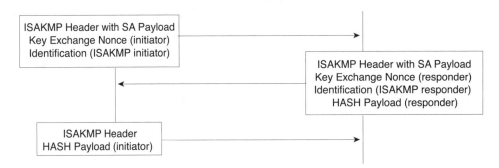

Aggressive Mode Key Exchange

Having completed the phase 1 negotiation, IKE provides a secure channel for the completion of phase 2. The phase 2 exchange occurs only after the IKE SA negotiation is complete. It is used to derive keying material and negotiate policies for non-ISAKMP SA (such as the IPSec SA). IKE performs the following functions and provides the following benefits:

- It automatically negotiates the security parameters for SAs between peers, removing the requirement of manually configuring each peer.
- It provides the capability to configure an SA's lifetime.
- It allows the encryption key to dynamically change while the IPSec session is open.
- It provides antireplay (hijacking) protection to IPSec services.
- It provides dynamic authentication of SA peers.
- It provides support for certification authorities.
- It allows for the scalable implementation of IPSec.

Certification Authorities (CAs)

IKE interoperates with X.509v3 certificates for authentication that requires public keys. Certification authorities (CAs) manage certificate requests, issue digital certificates, and publish certificate revocation lists (CRLs) to list certificates that are no longer valid. A digital certificate contains information about the user or device and includes a copy of its public key. This technology allows IPSec-protected networks to scale, because the peers simply exchange digital certificates that have been authenticated by a certificate authority, removing the requirement to manually configure each IPSec peer. The PIX interoperates with CA server products from the following vendors:

- Baltimore Technologies
- Entrust Corporation
- Microsoft Corporation
- VeriSign

After ensuring that you have correctly configured the firewall host name, domain name, and the system date/time, you can initiate enrollment with a CA server. It is important that your date and time are correctly configured so that you can verify the validity of the certificate when received. The process that a PIX uses to enroll with a CA server is as follows:

Step 1   The firewall generates an RSA key pair.

Step 2   The firewall contacts the CA server and obtains the CA server's certificate, which contains the public key.

Step 3   The firewall requests a signed certificate from the CA server using the generated key and the public key from the CA.

Step 4   The CA administrator verifies the request and returns the signed certificate.

Configuring the PIX Firewall as a VPN Gateway

Configuring the Cisco PIX Firewall as a VPN gateway or VPN termination point is a process that requires four specific tasks:

- Selecting your configuration
- Configuring IKE
- Configuring IPSec
- Testing and troubleshooting your connection

Selecting Your Configuration

Selecting a standardized configuration is perhaps the most important step in creating a VPN. You need to follow these steps when selecting your configuration:

Step 1 Determine which hosts will participate in this connection and what devices to use as VPN gateways. The Cisco PIX Firewall can create a VPN connection to another PIX, VPN appliances, routers, other third-party firewalls, and so on.

Step 2 Gather information about the peers and all hosts and networks that will participate in this VPN.

Step 3 Select which IKE policies (phase 1 and phase 2) to use based on the number and location of the peers.

Step 4 Verify the current configuration of your Cisco PIX Firewall to ensure that you do not select any policies (such as ACLs, ISAKMP policies, or crypto maps) that conflict with the current configuration:

— Ensure that you have connectivity with your peers. If you are unable to connect with a peer in the clear, you will be unable to create an encrypted connection.

— Ensure that perimeter devices such as routers are allowing the traffic required to create and maintain the VPN connection. Most notable are UDP port 500 (used for IKE negotiation), protocol 50 (ESP), and protocol 51 (AH).

It is extremely important to ensure that VPN peers have configurations with matching elements. If both peers are not configured to have compatible VPN components, they will be unable to create the encrypted connection.

Configuring IKE

Remember that IKE is the method used by the peers to negotiate and establish the SA. Determining which IKE configuration to use is not difficult. Most companies have a standard configuration that they employ when creating any VPN connection. If you do not have a pre-established policy, you should select a policy that allows your minimum amount of security to be not less that required for the most sensitive data to travel across the connection. The following steps are required to configure IKE on a Cisco PIX Firewall:

Step 1 **Enable IKE**—This is a simple command on the PIX. You turn on IKE by enabling it on a specific interface. The syntax for the command is **isakmp enable** *if_name*. For example:

```
tgpix (config)# isakmp enable outside
```

Step 2 **Create your IKE policies (phase I)**—To create the IKE policies, you select certain options and configure them as policies. Again, it is extremely important that both peers are configured in the same manner. Any undefined policies use the current default values. You must make the following choices when creating the policy:

— Authentication method: preshared secret or RSA signature

NOTE   You need to configure your SA peer's preshared secret for each IP address.

— Message encryption algorithm: DES or 3DES

— Message integrity algorithm: SHA-1 or MD5

— Key exchange parameters: Diffie-Hellman group 1 or group 2

— IKE established SA lifetime: the default is 86,400 seconds

The **isakmp policy** command is a simple command with several options that all must be selected. Table 10-1 describes the **isakmp policy** command parameters.

Table 10-1 isakmp policy *Command Parameters*

Parameter	Description
priority	Allows you to prioritize your ISAKMP policies. Policy priorities range from 1 to 65,534, with 1 being the highest priority.
authentication pre-share	Specifies that the peer authentication method is the preshared key. This requires that the preshared key be manually configured on both peers.
authentication rsa-sig	Specifies that the peer authentication method is RSA signatures. This method allows peer authentication to be completed automatically and is a more scalable solution. This is the default setting.
encryption des	Specifies that the encryption algorithm is DES. This is the default setting.
encryption 3des	Specifies that the encryption algorithm is 3DES.
group 1	Specifies that Diffie-Hellman group 1 (768-bit) is used. This is the default setting.
group 2	Specifies that Diffie-Hellman group 2 (1024-bit) is used.
hash md5	Specifies that the MD5 hash algorithm is used.
hash sha	Specifies that the SHA-1 hash algorithm is used. This is the default setting.
lifetime	Specifies the SA's lifetime. The range is from 60 to 86,400 seconds. The default setting is 86,400.

For example, to configure ISAKMP policies configured for VPN peers, you would have a configuration similar to this:

```
LOCAL PIX FIREWALL>>>>>>>>>>
tgpix (config)# isakmp policy 10 authentication pre-share
tgpix (config)# isakmp policy 10 encryption 3des
tgpix (config)# isakmp policy 10 group 2
tgpix (config)# isakmp policy 10 hash md5
tgpix (config)# isakmp policy 10 lifetime 86400
tgpix (config)# isakmp enable outside

REMOTE PIX FIREWALL>>>>>>>>>>
gonderpix (config)# isakmp policy 10 authentication pre-share
gonderpix (config)# isakmp policy 10 encryption 3des
gonderpix (config)# isakmp policy 10 group 2
gonderpix (config)# isakmp policy 10 hash md5
gonderpix (config)# isakmp policy 10 lifetime 86400
gonderpix (config)# isakmp enable outside
```

Note that the policies are the same on both peers.

Step 3   **Configuring the preshared key**—It is possible to configure the same preshared key for all your SAs. This method is not recommended, because it is more secure to specify a different key for each SA. To configure the preshared key, you need to determine how the peers identify themselves. SA peers can identify themselves by IP address or host name. It is recommended that you use the same method of identification for all SAs. If you choose to identify the peers by host name, the negotiations could fail if a DNS issue prevents the host name from resolving correctly. Here is the command for configuring identification:

```
isakmp identity (address | hostname)
```

Here is the command for configuring the preshared key:

```
isakmp key string address | hostname peer-address netmask peer netmask |
    hostname
```

NOTE   You can configure your preshared key with a wildcard IP address and netmask, but this is not recommended and could be considered a security risk.

To configure ISAKMP policies for both Cisco PIX Firewalls with the ISAKMP identities and **isakmp key** commands added, you would have a configuration similar to this:

```
LOCAL PIX FIREWALL>>>>>>>>>>>
tgpix (config)# isakmp policy 10 authentication pre-share
tgpix (config)# isakmp policy 10 encryption 3des
tgpix (config)# isakmp policy 10 group 2
tgpix (config)# isakmp policy 10 hash md5
tgpix (config)# isakmp policy 10 lifetime 86400
tgpix (config)# isakmp enable outside
tgpix (config)# isakmp identity address
tgpix (config)# isakmp key abc123 192.168.1.2 netmask 255.255.255.255
```

```
REMOTE PIX FIREWALL>>>>>>>>>>
gonderpix (config)# isakmp policy 10 authentication pre-share
gonderpix (config)# isakmp policy 10 encryption 3des
gonderpix (config)# isakmp policy 10 group 2
gonderpix (config)# isakmp policy 10 hash md5
gonderpix (config)# isakmp policy 10 lifetime 86400
gonderpix (config)# isakmp enable outside
gonderpix (config)# isakmp identity address
gonderpix (config)# isakmp key abc123 192.168.1.1 netmask
    255.255.255.255
```

Step 4 **Verify your configuration**—Because of the configurations' complexity,
it is a good idea to verify your configuration. Remember that both peers
must have an exactly matched phase 1 policy for the key exchange to
occur, which is the first step in establishing the VPN connection. As
always, the **show** command is a very effective tool for checking your
configuration. It is possible to get extended output with **show isakmp
policy**, or you can see the commands that were input with **show isakmp**.
You get slightly more detailed output with **write terminal** than with
show isakmp. Here is some sample output from **show isakmp**:

```
tgpix# show isakmp
isakmp policy 10 authentication pre-share
isakmp policy 10 encryption 3des
isakmp policy 10 group 2
isakmp policy 10 hash md5
isakmp policy 10 lifetime 86400
isakmp enable outside
```

You can see that policy 10 uses preshared secrets for authentication,
3DES encryption, the group 2 (1024-bit) Diffie-Hellman key exchange,
MD5 HASH, and a connection lifetime of 86,400 seconds (24 hours),
and it is enabled on the outside interface.

Here is some sample output from **write terminal**:

```
tgpix# write terminal
isakmp policy 10 authentication pre-share
isakmp policy 10 encryption 3des
isakmp policy 10 group 2
isakmp policy 10 hash md5
isakmp policy 10 lifetime 86400
isakmp enable outside
isakmp key abc123 192.168.1.2 netmask 255.255.255.255
```

Here you see much the same information as with **show isakmp**, but you
also see the shared secret (**isakmp key**) for peer 192.168.1.2.

Here is some sample output from **show isakmp policy**:

```
tgpix# show isakmp policy
Protection suite or priority  10
    encryption algorithm:    Three key triple DES
    hash algorithm:          Message Digest 5
    authentication method:     Pre-Shared Key
    Diffie-Hellman group:    #2 (1024 bit)
    lifetime:        86400 seconds, no volume limit
Default protection suite
    encryption algorithm:   DES - Data Encryption Standard (56-bit keys)
```

```
hash algorithm:          Secure Hash Standard
authentication method:    Rivest-Shamir-Adleman Signature
Diffie-Hellman group:    #1 (768 bit)
lifetime:         86400 seconds, no volume limit
```

In this output, you can see the two ISAKMP policies that are configured on the firewall (policy 10 and default). If you do not configure a specific ISAKMP policy, the default values are used.

Configuring IPSec

Now that you have successfully configured IKE on your firewall, you are ready to configure IPSec. Follow these steps:

Step 1   Create a crypto access list to define the traffic to protect.

Step 2   Configure a transform set that defines how the traffic is protected.

Step 3   Create a crypto map entry.

Step 4   Apply the crypto map set to an interface.

Step 5   Specify that IPSec traffic is permitted.

Creating a Crypto Access List

Crypto access lists are used to identify which IP traffic is to be protected by encryption and which traffic is not. After the access list is defined, the crypto maps reference it to identify the type of traffic that IPSec protects. The **permit** keyword in the access list causes IPSec to protect all IP traffic that matches the access list criteria. If the **deny** keyword is used in the access list, the traffic is not encrypted. It is good practice to have the same set of crypto access lists specified in the local peer defined at the remote peer. This ensures that traffic that has IPSec protection applied locally can be processed correctly at the remote peer. The crypto map entries themselves should also support common transforms and should refer to the other system as a peer.

It is not recommended that you use the **permit any any** command, because it causes all outbound traffic to be encrypted (and all encrypted traffic to be sent to the peer specified in the corresponding crypto map entry), and it requires encryption of all inbound traffic. With this type of access list, the firewall drops all inbound packets that are not encrypted.

The syntax for the **access-list** command is as follows:

```
access-list acl_name [permit | deny] protocol src_addr src_mask
  [operator port[port]] dest_addr dest_mask [operator port[port]]
```

Table 10-2 lists and describes the command arguments and options for the **access-list** command.

Table 10-2   **access-list** *Command Parameters*

Parameter	Description
acl_name	Specifies the access list's name or number.
permit	Encrypts the packet.
deny	Does not encrypt the packet.
protocol	Specifies the protocol by name or IP protocol number. Protocols include **icmp**, **tcp**, **udp**, and **ip**. (**ip** is the keyword for any.)
src_addr, *dest_addr*	Specifies the IP address of the network or host for the source and destination. The term **any** is the wildcard for 0.0.0.0 0.0.0.0. It is also possible to use the word **host** to indicate a 32-bit mask.
src_mask, *dest_mask*	Specifies the subnet masks of the source or destination network.
operator	An optional field. It includes the following options: **lt** = less than **gt** = greater than **eq** = equal to **neq** = not equal to **range** = inclusive range
port	Specifies the TCP or UDP port used for the IP service.

NOTE   The configuration examples in this chapter build on each other (they include the previous portion). The specific items that are being addressed as part of the current configuration are highlighted.

Example 10-1 shows the current ISAKMP policy configuration with the access list added.

Example 10-1   *Crypto Access List*

```
tgpix (config)# isakmp policy 10 authentication pre-share
tgpix (config)# isakmp policy 10 encryption 3des
tgpix (config)# isakmp policy 10 group 2
tgpix (config)# isakmp policy 10 hash md5
tgpix (config)# isakmp policy 10 lifetime 86400
tgpix (config)# isakmp enable outside
tgpix (config)# isakmp identity address
tgpix (config)# isakmp key abc123 192.168.1.2 netmask 255.255.255.255
tgpix (config)# access-list 90 permit ip 10.10.10.0 255.255.2550.0 10.10.20.0
  255.255.255.0
```

Configuring a Transform Set

A transform set defines the combination of encryption algorithms and message integrity algorithms to be used for the IPSec tunnel. Both peers agree on the transform set during the IPSec negotiation. It is possible to define multiple transform sets, because both peers search for a common transform set during the IKE negotiation. If a common transform set is found, it is selected and applied to the protected traffic. Table 10-3 shows the transform sets supported on the Cisco PIX Firewall.

Table 10-3   *PIX-Supported IPSec Transform Sets*

Transform	Description
ah-md5-hmac	AH-md5-hmac transform used for authentication.
ah-sha-hmac	AH-sha-hmac transform used for authentication.
esp-des	ESP transform using DES encryption (56-bit).
esp-3des	ESP transform using 3DES encryption (168-bit).
esp-md5-hmac	ESP transform with HMAC-MD5 authentication, used with either esp-des or esp-3des to provide additional integrity of ESP packets.
esp-sha-hmac	ESP transform with HMAC-SHA authentication, used with either esp-des or esp-3des to provide additional integrity of ESP packets.

The syntax for the **transform-set** command is as follows:

```
crypto ipsec transform-set transform-set name transform1 [transform2 transform3]
```

Example 10-2 shows the current ISAKMP policy configuration with the access list and transform set defined.

Example 10-2   *Crypto Transform Set*

```
tgpix (config)# isakmp policy 10 authentication pre-share
tgpix (config)# isakmp policy 10 encryption 3des
tgpix (config)# isakmp policy 10 group 2
tgpix (config)# isakmp policy 10 hash md5
tgpix (config)# isakmp policy 10 lifetime 86400
tgpix (config)# isakmp enable outside
tgpix (config)# isakmp identity address
tgpix (config)# isakmp key abc123 address 192.168.1.2 netmask 255.255.255.255
tgpix (config)# access-list 90 permit ip 10.10.10.0 255.255.255.0.0 10.10.20.0
  255.255.255.0
tgpix (config)# crypto ipsec transform-set strong esp-3des esp-md5-hmac
```

Configuring IPSec SA Lifetimes

To preclude any opportunity to gather sufficient network traffic using a single encryption key, it is important to limit the key lifetime. This forces a key exchange, changing the encryption scheme and greatly reducing the possibility of cracking the key. Technology continues to advance, producing computers that can break code at faster rates. However, these systems require a certain amount of traffic encrypted under a single key. The idea is to change encryption keys before any system can feasibly crack your encryption. The PIX allows you to configure your SA lifetimes, forcing a key exchange. It is possible to limit the SA lifetime either by the amount of traffic passing through the connection or by how long the encrypted connection remains open. The command for configuring SA lifetimes is as follows:

```
crypto ipsec security-association lifetime [kilobytes | seconds]
```

Example 10-3 shows the current configuration, including an SA lifetime of 15 minutes (900 seconds).

Example 10-3 *Crypto IPSec SA Lifetime*

```
tgpix (config)# isakmp policy 10 authentication pre-share
tgpix (config)# isakmp policy 10 encryption 3des
tgpix (config)# isakmp policy 10 group 2
tgpix (config)# isakmp policy 10 hash md5
tgpix (config)# isakmp policy 10 lifetime 86400
tgpix (config)# isakmp enable outside
tgpix (config)# isakmp identity address
tgpix (config)# isakmp key abc123 address 192.168.1.2 netmask 255.255.255.255
tgpix (config)# access-list 90 permit ip 10.10.10.0 255.255.2550.0 10.10.20.0
  255.255.255.0
tgpix (config)# crypto ipsec transform-set strong esp-3des esp-md5-hmac
tgpix (config)# crypto ipsec security-association lifetime seconds 900
```

Configuring Crypto Maps

Just as the **isakmp-policy** configures the parameters for the IKE negotiations, **crypto-map**s tell the PIX how to negotiate the IPSec SA. The **crypto-map** is the final piece of the puzzle that is used on both peers to establish the SA. Again, it is extremely important that the settings are compatible on both ends. If both peers do not have a compatible configuration, they cannot establish the VPN connection. This does not mean that the configuration must be an exact match (like the **isakmp** configurations), but the peers must have matching elements within the **crypto-map**. Many different components are covered by the **crypto-map** command. The following parameters are set using this command:

- **What traffic is to be encrypted and what traffic is not?**—Earlier in this chapter, the **access-list** command was said to designate what traffic the PIX should encrypt. This is correct; however, the access list is applied by the **crypto-map**.

- **What type of IPSec to apply to the connection?**—The **crypto-map** tells the firewall which transform set to use.

- **How the SA is to be initially established?**—This tells the firewall if the SA is manually established or established using IKE.

- **Who is the peer for this SA?**—This can be one or more peers. You can configure a primary peer and backup peers. In the event that the firewall cannot establish the connection with the primary peer, it attempts to connect to the secondary, and so on. These additional peers are called *backup gateways*.

- **What is the SA's local address?**—The crypto map is applied to a specific interface on the PIX.

- **Any additional options that should be configured for this SA?**—This can include setting a specific timeout in kilobytes or adding a AAA server.

Three steps are required for configuring crypto maps:

Step 1   Creating a crypto map entry

Step 2   Applying the crypto map set to an interface

Step 3   Specifying that IPSec traffic be permitted

It is important that you ensure that all three steps are completed. Although each line of the crypto map is considered "creating the crypto map," specific lines apply the crypto map and specify the IPSec traffic. These lines are discussed next.

Normally you have at least five **crypto-map** entries with the same name. These entries combine to list your IPSec SA configuration. Each line of the configuration has its own purpose. The following text shows and explains the syntax of each line.

```
crypto-map map-name seq-num ipsec-isakmp
```

This line establishes the crypto map by name and sequence number and specifies that IKE negotiates the SA.

```
crypto-map map-name seq-num match address acl_name
```

This line binds the access list to the crypto map. It establishes what traffic is encrypted and what is not. This line specifies which IPSec traffic is permitted. It defines the traffic as "interesting."

```
crypto-map map-name seq-num set transform-set transform-set name
```

This line identifies which transform set is to be used. The *transform-set name* is assigned to the transform set in the **crypto ipsec transform-set** command.

```
crypto-map map-name seq-num set peer ip-address
```

This line identifies the SA peer by IP address.

```
crypto-map map-name seq-num interface if_name
```

This line applies the crypto map to a specific interface. In much the same way that the **access-group** command is used to bind the access lists to an interface for standard ACLs, this command binds the entire crypto map process (including the crypto access list) to the interface. This line applies the crypto map set to a specific interface on the firewall.

Additional **crypto-map** entries can include **pfs**, **set security-association lifetime**, and **aaa-authentication settings**.

Example 10-4 shows the current configuration, including the crypto map entries. Note that the access list is numbered 90 and the **match address** command references **90**. The **ipsec transform-set** is named **strong**, and the **set transform-set** references the name **strong**.

Example 10-4   *Crypto Map Entries*

```
tgpix (config)# isakmp policy 10 authentication pre-share
tgpix (config)# isakmp policy 10 encryption 3des
tgpix (config)# isakmp policy 10 group 2
tgpix (config)# isakmp policy 10 hash md5
tgpix (config)# isakmp policy 10 lifetime 86400
tgpix (config)# isakmp enable outside
tgpix (config)# isakmp identity address
tgpix (config)# isakmp key abc123 address 192.168.1.2 netmask 255.255.255.255
tgpix (config)# access-list 90 permit ip 10.10.10.0 255.255.2550.0 10.10.20.0
   255.255.255.0
tgpix (config)# crypto ipsec transform-set strong esp-3des esp-md5-hmac
tgpix (config)# crypto map gonder 10 ipsec-isakmp
tgpix (config)# crypto map gonder 10 match address 90
tgpix (config)# crypto map gonder 10 set transform-set strong
tgpix (config)# crypto map gonder 10 set peer 192.168.1.2
tgpix (config)# crypto map gonder interface outside
```

Table 10-4 describes the different **crypto-map** command arguments and options that are available when you're configuring crypto maps.

Table 10-4   **crypto-map** *Arguments and Options*

Argument/Option	Description
map-name	You can apply multiple **crypto-map**s on a single PIX Firewall. It is a good idea to assign a name that allows you to keep track of which **crypto-map** goes with which **access-list**. The easiest way to do this is to use the same name or number for both components.
seq-num	Because you can add multiple **crypto-map**s to the PIX, you must give each a sequence number so that the system can process each in the correct order. The lower the number, the higher the priority.
ipsec-isakmp	Indicates that the PIX uses IKE to negotiate the SA. This is the recommended configuration.
ipsec-manual	Indicates that the SA is configured manually and that IKE is not used to negotiate it. This is not the recommended configuration, because it is difficult to ensure that both peers are configured correctly and because a manual session does not expire (no renegotiation of the keys).
set session-key	Manually specifies the session keys within the crypto map entry.
inbound	Manual IPSec requires that session keys be configured directionally. You must specify both inbound and outbound session keys.
outbound	Manual IPSec requires that session keys be configured directionally. You must specify both inbound and outbound session keys.

Table 10-4   **crypto-map** *Arguments and Options (Continued)*

Argument/Option	Description
match address	Identifies the access list for the IPSec SA.
acl_name	The name of the access list that indicates that the traffic should be encrypted.
set peer	Specifies the SA peer using either of the following two arguments.
hostname	Identifies the SA peer's host name and any backup gateways.
ip-address	Identifies the SA peer's IP address(es) and any backup gateways.
interface	Identifies the interface that is to be used for the local SA peer address.
if_name	The interface name.
set pfs	Initiates Perfect Forward Secrecy (PFS). PFS provides an additional layer of security to the SA negotiation and renegotiation. It requires that a new Diffie-Hellman exchange occur every time a key negotiation takes place. This causes the key exchange to use a new key for every negotiation rather than renegotiating based on a key that is currently being used. This process increases the processor load on both peers.
group 1	Indicates that the Diffie-Hellman group 1 (768-bit) modulus should be used when the key exchange for the **esp-des** and **esp-3des** transforms is performed.
group 2	Indicates that the Diffie-Hellman group 2 (1024-bit) modulus should be used when the key exchange for the **esp-des** and **esp-3des** transforms is performed.
set transform-set	Specifies the transform to be used for the **crypto-map** entry. You can list multiple **transform-set**s by priority. The PIX automatically selects the most secure transform that is listed on both peers.
transform-set name	Specifies the **transform-set** by name.
set security-association lifetime	A second location for configuring the SA lifetime.
seconds *seconds*	The SA lifetime in seconds.
kilobytes *kilobytes*	The SA lifetime in kilobytes.
dynamic	Specifies that the **crypto-map** entry must reference a preexisting dynamic crypto map.
dynamic-map-name	Specifies the dynamic crypto-map.
aaa-server-name	Specifies the AAA server that authenticates the user during IKE authentication. The PIX Firewall supports TACACS+ and RADIUS for this function.

sysopt connection permit-ipsec

The **sysopt** command reconfigures the system options. The command **sysopt connection permit-ipsec** implicitly permits all packets that arrive via the IPSec tunnel to bypass any checking of access lists, conduits, or **access-group** command statements for IPSec connections. If the **sysopt connection permit-ipsec** command is not specified, an explicit rule (conduit or ACL) must be coded to allow the traffic arriving from the IPSec tunnel through the firewall.

Example 10-5 shows the current configuration with this command included.

Example 10-5   sysopt connection permit-ipsec

```
tgpix (config)# isakmp policy 10 authentication pre-share
tgpix (config)# isakmp policy 10 encryption 3des
tgpix (config)# isakmp policy 10 group 2
tgpix (config)# isakmp policy 10 hash md5
tgpix (config)# isakmp policy 10 lifetime 86400
tgpix (config)# isakmp enable outside
tgpix (config)# isakmp identity address
tgpix (config)# isakmp key abc123 address 192.168.1.2 netmask 255.255.255.255
tgpix (config)# access-list 90 permit ip 10.10.10.0 255.255.2550.0 10.10.20.0
  255.255.255.0
tgpix (config)# crypto ipsec transform-set strong esp-3des esp-md5-hmac
tgpix (config)# crypto map gonder 10 ipsec-isakmp
tgpix (config)# crypto map gonder 10 match address 90
tgpix (config)# crypto map gonder 10 set transform-set strong
tgpix (config)# crypto map gonder 10 set peer 192.168.1.2
tgpix (config)# crypto map gonder interface outside
tgpix (config)# sysopt connection permit-ipsec
```

Troubleshooting Your VPN Connection

Configuring an SA peer can be extremely complicated and must be exact. If both peers are not configured correctly, they cannot successfully establish the VPN connection. The most common VPN issue is an incorrect configuration of either of the SA peers. The first step of troubleshooting a VPN should always be to compare the configurations of both peers and verify that they match. Three commands and a variety of command options are available to help you troubleshoot VPN issues:

* **show**
* **clear**
* **debug**

show Command

The **show** command lets you view different portions of the configuration and see the condition of ISAKMP and IPSec SAs. Table 10-5 explains the different **show** commands.

Table 10-5   show *Commands*

Command	Description
show isakmp	Displays all ISAKMP configurations.
show isakmp policy	Displays only configured ISAKMP policies.
show access-list	Displays configured access lists.
show crypto-map	Displays all configured crypto map entries.
show crypto ipsec transform-set	Displays all configured IPSec transform sets.
show crypto ipsec security-association lifetime	Displays configured SA lifetimes, including the default value.
show crypto isakmp sa	Displays the status of current IKE SAs.
show crypto ipsec sa	Displays the status of current IPSec SAs.

Example 10-6 displays the output from the **show crypto isakmp sa** command on the PIX Firewall in Los Angeles that is configured for a VPN connection to Boston.

Example 10-6   **show crypto isakmp sa** *Command Output*

```
tgpix# show crypto isakmp sa
dst          src          state     conn-id    slot
192.168.2.1  192.168.1.1  QM_IDLE   1          0
```

Example 10-7 displays the output from **show crypto ipsec sa** for the same firewall.

Example 10-7   **show crypto ipsec sa** *Command Output*

```
tgpix# show crypto ipsec sa
interface: outside
    Crypto map tag: 10, local addr. 192.168.1.1
   local  ident (addr/mask/prot/port): (10.10.10.0/255.255.255.0/0/0)
   remote ident (addr/mask/prot/port): (192.168.2.1/255.255.255.255/0/0)
   current_peer: 10.10.2.5
   dynamic allocated peer ip: 192.168.2.1
     PERMIT, flags={}
    #pkts encaps: 345, #pkts encrypt: 345, #pkts digest 0
    #pkts decaps: 366, #pkts decrypt: 366, #pkts verify 0
    #pkts compressed: 0, #pkts decompressed: 0
    #pkts not compressed: 0, #pkts compr. failed: 0, #pkts decompress failed: 0
    #send errors 0, #recv errors 0
     local crypto endpt.: 192.168.1.1, remote crypto endpt.: 192.168.2.1
     path mtu 1500, ipsec overhead 56, media mtu 1500
     current outbound spi: 9a46ecae
     inbound esp sas:
```

continues

Example 10-7   **show crypto ipsec sa** *Command Output (Continued)*

```
        spi: 0x50b98b5(84646069)
          transform: esp-3des esp-md5-hmac ,
          in use settings ={Tunnel, }
          slot: 0, conn id: 1, crypto map: Chapter10
          sa timing: remaining key lifetime (k/sec): (460800/21)
          IV size: 8 bytes
          replay detection support: Y
      inbound ah sas:
      inbound pcp sas:
      outbound esp sas:
       spi: 0x9a46ecae(2588339374)
          transform: esp-3des esp-md5-hmac ,
          in use settings ={Tunnel, }
          slot: 0, conn id: 2, crypto map: Chapter10
          sa timing: remaining key lifetime (k/sec): (460800/21)
          IV size: 8 bytes
          replay detection support: Y
     outbound ah sas:
```

clear Command

The **clear** command allows you to remove current settings. You must be very careful when using the **clear** command to ensure that you do not remove portions of your configuration that are needed. The most common use of the **clear** command for troubleshooting VPN connectivity is to clear current sessions and force them to regenerate. Table 10-6 explains the two **clear** commands used to troubleshoot VPN connectivity.

Table 10-6   **clear** *Commands*

Command	Description
clear crypto isakmp sa	Clears all active ISAKMP SAs.
clear crypto ipsec sa	Clears all active IPSec SAs.

debug Command

The **debug** command lets you watch the VPN negotiation take place. This command is available only from configuration mode on the PIX. Table 10-7 explains the two **debug** commands most commonly used to troubleshoot VPN connectivity.

Table 10-7   **debug** *Commands*

Command	Description
debug crypto isakmp	Displays IKE communication between the PIX and its IPSec peers.
debug crypto ipsec	Displays IPSec communication between the PIX and its IPSec peers.

Example 10-8 displays the output from the **debug crypto isakmp** command on the PIX Firewall in Los Angeles that is configured for a VPN connection to Boston. Note the highlighted comments "atts are not acceptable" and "atts are acceptable" that are generated during the negotiation as address transforms attempt to find a match.

Example 10-8   **debug crypto isakmp** *Command Output*

```
crypto_isakmp_process_block: src 192.168.1.1, dest 192.168.2.1
OAK_AG exchange
ISAKMP (0): processing SA payload. message ID = 0
ISAKMP (0): Checking ISAKMP transform 1 against priority 1 policy
ISAKMP:        encryption DES-CBC
ISAKMP:        hash MD5
ISAKMP:        default group 1
ISAKMP:        auth pre-share
ISAKMP (0): atts are not acceptable. Next payload is 3
ISAKMP (0): Checking ISAKMP transform 3 against priority 1 policy
ISAKMP:        encryption ESP_3DES
ISAKMP:        hash HMAC-MD5
ISAKMP:        default group 2
ISAKMP:        auth pre-share
ISAKMP (0): atts are acceptable. Next payload is 3
ISAKMP (0): processing KE payload. message ID = 0
ISAKMP: Created a peer node for 192.168.2.1
OAK_QM exchange
ISAKMP (0:0): Need config/address
ISAKMP (0:0): initiating peer config to 192.168.2.1. ID = 2607270170 (0x9b67c91a)
return status is IKMP_NO_ERROR
crypto_isakmp_process_block: src 192.168.2.1, dest 192.168.1.1
ISAKMP_TRANSACTION exchange
ISAKMP (0:0): processing transaction payload from 192.168.2.1. message ID =
   2156506360
ISAKMP: Config payload CFG_ACK
ISAKMP (0:0): peer accepted the address!
ISAKMP (0:0): processing saved QM.
oakley_process_quick_mode:
OAK_QM_IDLE
ISAKMP (0): processing SA payload. message ID = 448324052
ISAKMP : Checking IPSec proposal 1
ISAKMP: transform 1, ESP_DES
ISAKMP:   attributes in transform:
ISAKMP:        authenticator is HMAC-MD5
ISAKMP:        encaps is 1
IPSec(validate_proposal): transform proposal (prot 3, trans 2, hmac_alg 1) not
   supported
ISAKMP (0): atts not acceptable. Next payload is 0
ISAKMP : Checking IPSec proposal 2
ISAKMP: transform 1, ESP_3DES
ISAKMP:   attributes in transform:
ISAKMP:        authenticator is HMAC-MD5
ISAKMP:        encaps is 1
ISAKMP (0): atts are acceptable.
ISAKMP (0): processing NONCE payload. message ID = 448324052
ISAKMP (0): processing ID payload. message ID = 44
ISAKMP (0): processing ID payload. message ID = 44
INITIAL_CONTACTIPSec(key_engine): got a queue event...
```

Example 10-9 displays the output from **debug crypto ipsec** for the same firewall. Notice that this **debug** command actually depicts the real address of the node behind the firewall that is initiating the VPN connection.

Example 10-9   **debug crypto ipsec** *Command Output*

```
IPSec(key_engine): got a queue event...
IPSec(spi_response): getting spi 0xd532efbd(3576885181) for SA
        from  192.168.2.1  to  192.168.1.1  for prot 3
return status is IKMP_NO_ERROR
crypto_isakmp_process_block: src 192.168.2.1, dest 192.168.1.1
OAK_QM exchange
oakley_process_quick_mode:
OAK_QM_AUTH_AWAIT
ISAKMP (0): Creating IPSec SAs
        inbound SA from  192.168.2.1  to  192.168.1.1  (proxy 10.10.10.3 to
   192.168.1.1.)
        has spi 3576885181 and conn_id 2 and flags 4
        outbound SA from  192.168.1.1  to  192.168.2.1  (proxy 192.168.1.1 to
   10.10.10.3)
        has spi 2749108168 and conn_id 1 and flags 4IPSec(key_engine): got a queue
   event...
IPSec(initialize_sas): ,
  (key eng. msg.) dest= 192.168.1.1, src= 192.168.2.1,
    dest_proxy= 192.168.1.1/0.0.0.0/0/0 (type=1),
    src_proxy= 10.10.10.3/0.0.0.0/0/0 (type=1),
    protocol= ESP, transform= esp-3des esp-md5-hmac ,
    lifedur= 0s and 0kb,
    spi= 0xd532efbd(3576885181), conn_id= 2,        keysize= 0, flags= 0x4
IPSec(initialize_sas): ,
  (key eng. msg.) src= 192.168.1.1, dest= 192.168.2.1,
    src_proxy= 192.168.1.1/0.0.0.0/0/0 (type=1),
    dest_proxy= 10.10.10.3/0.0.0.0/0/0 (type=1),
    protocol= ESP, transform= esp-3des esp-md5-hmac ,
    lifedur= 0s and 0kb,
    spi= 0xa3dc0fc8(2749108168), conn_id= 1, keysize= 0, flags= 0x4
return status is IKMP_NO_ERROR
```

Cisco VPN Client

The VPN client is used to connect to access VPNs because one of the peers is mobile and the VPN does not remain up at all times. Cisco VPN Client for Windows is a package that is installed on a remote system to create VPN connections from remote locations. Sales personnel and executives who spend time traveling but still need access to the corporate network commonly use this package. It is possible to use the VPN client after connecting to the Internet using the following connections:

- Dialup
- Cable modem
- Digital Subscriber Line (DSL)
- Integrated Services Digital Network (ISDN)
- Local-area network (LAN)

After connecting to the Internet, you open the VPN client and initiate the connection to your peer (corporate network). The VPN client negotiates the connection using IKE and secures the connection with IPSec. After it is established, the VPN connection functions the same way as the intranet or extranet VPN. The main difference is that one peer is remote and the VPN client handles the connection negotiation and the encryption. Usually the only thing left for the user to do is to input his or her password.

VPN Groups

Cisco VPN 3000 clients can be combined into a single group or multiple groups that have like policies applied using the **vpn group** command. Table 10-8 lists the commands and options available when configuring VPN groups.

Table 10-8   *VPN Group Commands and Options*

Command	Description
vpngroup *group_name*	Assigns a name of up to 128 ASCII characters to a specific VPN group.
address-pool *ip pool name*	Specifies a pool of local addresses to be assigned to VPN clients as they connect to the network.
default-domain *domain_name*	Assigns a default domain name to all VPN clients.
dns-server *dns_ip_prim/sec*	Assigns primary and secondary DNS server information that is given to the VPN clients as they negotiate the connection.
wins-server *wins_ip_prim/sec*	Assigns primary and secondary WINS server information that is passed to the VPN clients as they negotiate the connection.
idle-time *idle_seconds*	Sets the inactivity timeout.
max-time *max seconds*	Sets the maximum time for a VPN connection to remain up.
password *preshared_key*	Specifies a group preshared key.
split-tunnel *acl_name*	Specifies an ACL that allows the user to maintain an encrypted tunnel into the network and a clear tunnel out to the Internet.

Point-to-Point Tunneling Protocol (PPTP) and Layer 2 Tunneling Protocol (L2TP)

The PIX Firewall can be configured for VPN connections to Microsoft products using either PPTP or L2TP. The command necessary to implement this feature is **vpdn**. After **vpdn** is enabled on a specific interface with **vpdn enable** *if_name,* all other **vpdn** commands are grouped into **vpdn group**, which is specified using the command **group** *group_name* (where *group_name* can be an ASCII string of up to 128 characters). Table 10-9 lists the configuration options that can be set for VPDN groups.

Table 10-9 *VPDN Configuration Commands and Options*

Command	Description
accept {dialin pptp l l2tp}	Configures the PIX Firewall to accept dial-in PPTP or L2TP requests.
ppp authentication {PAP l CHAP l MSCHAP}	Configures the firewall to authenticate connections using either Point-to-Point Protocol (PPP), Challenge Handshake Authentication Protocol (CHAP), or Microsoft CHAP (MS-CHAP). The default setting is PPP.
ppp encryption mppe {40 l 128 l auto l required}	Specifies the bit value for Microsoft Point-to-Point Encryption, whether autonegotiation is allowed, and whether a negotiation is required.
client configuration address local *address_pool_name*	Identifies the pool of addresses to be assigned to dial-in users.
client configuration dns *dns_server_ip1* [*dns_server_ip2*]	Specifies primary and secondary Domain Name Servers for dial-in users.
client configuration wins *wins_server_ip1* [*wins_server_ip2*]	Specifies primary and secondary Windows Internet Naming Service servers for dial-in users.
client authentication aaa *aaa_server_group*	Specifies a AAA server group for user authentication.
client authentication local	Authenticates users from a local user database (on the PIX).
client accounting aaa *aaa_server_group*	Specifies a AAA server group for accounting. (This can be different from the authentication group.)
password	Specifies a local user password.
pptp echo *echo_timeout*	Specifies a PPTP timeout value in seconds. The PIX terminates the connection if this value is exceeded.
l2tp tunnel hello *hello_timeout*	Specifies an L2TP timeout value in seconds. The PIX terminates the connection if this value is exceeded.

Table 10-10 lists and describes the **show** commands associated with VPDNs.

Table 10-10   *VPDN* **show** *Commands and Options*

Command	Description
show vpdn tunnel	Displays tunnel information.
show vpdn session	Displays session information to include the interface ID used for the **show pppinterface id** command.
l2tp | pptp	Selects the protocol used (L2TP or **PPTP**).
id	Identifies a tunnel or session.
id *tunnel_id*	Indicates the unique tunnel ID.
id *session_id*	Indicates the unique session ID.
pppinterface id *intf_id*	Shows the virtual interface created for the tunnel.
username	Enters or displays the local username.
packets	Displays the packet and byte count.
state	Displays the session state.
summary	Displays tunnel summary information.
transport	Displays tunnel transport information.
window	Displays window information.

The **clear** command is also available to allow you to reset certain portions of the configuration. Table 10-11 lists the available **clear** command options.

Table 10-11   *VPDN* **clear** *Commands and Options*

Command	Description
username	Removes VPDN username commands from the configuration.
tunnel	Removes one or more tunnels from the configuration.
id *tunnel_id*	Removes a specific tunnel (based on *tunnel_id*) from the configuration.
all	Removes all tunnels from the configuration.

Configuring PIX Firewalls for Scalable VPNs

Earlier in this chapter, you learned about the different methods of negotiating an IPSec connection:

- Manual IPSec, which requires you to manually configure each peer. This method is not recommended by Cisco, because it does not allow for key exchanges and therefore would be rather easy to decrypt, given enough time and traffic. Obviously, manual IPSec is not a scalable solution.

- IKE, which dynamically negotiates your SA using preshared keys or digital certificates. Preshared keys still require you to manually enter a preshared key into each IPSec peer.

- IKE with digital certificates is the most dynamic solution that lets IKE negotiate your IPSec SA and a CA server authenticating each peer. This system is completely dynamic, very secure, and very scalable.

PPPoE Support

Cisco PIX Firewall software version 6.2 supports Point-to-Point Protocol over Ethernet (PPPoE). PPPoE provides a standard method of using PPP authentication over an Ethernet network and is used by many Internet service providers (ISPs) to grant client machine access to their networks, commonly through DSL. PPPoE is supported only on the outside interfaces of the PIX 501 and PIX 506/506E.

Foundation Summary

There are three different VPN types: access, intranet, and extranet. Access VPNs are used for remote users and normally require client software. Intranet and extranet VPNs are configured as site-to-site VPNs.

VPN peers need to authenticate each other and negotiate the IPSec SA. The negotiation is completed automatically using IKE. The authentication is completed using preshared keys, RSA signatures (certificates), or RSA nonces. To configure IKE on the PIX, you use the following commands:

- **isakmp policy**:
    - Configures the authentication type.
    - Configures the message encryption algorithm.
    - Configures the message integrity algorithm.
    - Configures the key exchange parameters.
    - Defines the SA lifetime (reinitiates the Diffie-Hellman key exchange).
- **isakmp enable**—Applies the ISAKMP policy to an interface, allowing that interface to receive UDP500 traffic.
- **isakmp identity**—Identifies the local peer by IP address or host name.
- **isakmp key**—If you're using a preshared key, define the key and the peer (by IP address or host name).

After you configure IKE, you are ready to configure IPSec. Follow these steps:

Step 1   Configure **access-list** so that the PIX knows what traffic should be encrypted.

Step 2   Create **transform-set**s to define the encryption and integrity to be used for the session.

Step 3   Define **ipsec security-association lifetime** (optional) to reduce the opportunity of others to crack your encryption.

Step 4   Configure **crypto-map**:

- Define SA negotiation (manual or IKE).
- Apply **access-list** to **crypto-map**.
- Apply **transform-set** to **crypto-map**.
- Identify the SA peer by IP address or host name.
- Apply **crypto-map** to an interface.

Three commands (and many options for each) are available to troubleshoot VPN connectivity:

- **show**—Displays the current configuration or current SA status.
- **clear**—Removes the current configuration or setting (usually used to regenerate the connection).
- **debug**—Allows you to see ongoing sessions and key negotiations.

Cisco VPN Client is used to connect remote users to internal resources via an encrypted tunnel. The package handles all the negotiation and encryption and can operate using any connection to the Internet.

To develop a scalable VPN solution, you must implement a dynamic means of authentication. The most effective and scalable method today is the use of IKE and certification authorities.

Q&A

The questions in this section are designed to ensure your understanding of the concepts discussed in this chapter and adequately prepare you to complete the exam. You should use the simulated exams on the CD to practice for the exam.

The answers to these questions can be found in Appendix A.

1 What is the default lifetime if not defined in **isakmp policy**?

2 Do your transform sets have to match exactly on each peer?

3 True or false: The X509v3 standard applies to the ESP header's format.

4 What is the difference between the **isakmp** lifetime and the **crypto-map** lifetime?

5 What command do you use to delete any active SAs?

6 What is the command for defining a preshared key?

7 What is the first thing you should check if you are unable to establish a VPN?

8 What is the function of the access list with regard to VPNs?

9 What PIX firewalls support PPPoE?

Scenario

VPN Configurations

Clearly the most detail-oriented and time-consuming portion of configuring VPNs is ensuring that both peers have matching configurations. This task usually becomes more complicated, because you might have access to only one peer and are relying on someone else to configure the other end. A single discrepancy between the configurations can prevent the key exchange from completing or prevent the encryption from occurring. It is best to compare the configurations on both peers before attempting the connection rather than trying to troubleshoot the VPN after an unsuccessful connection.

In this scenario, you are working as a consultant and have been assigned the task of configuring a full-mesh VPN between corporate headquarters and two branch offices. Figure 10-6 shows the layout of each network and how the VPNs are to connect.

Figure 10-6 *VPN Network Layout*

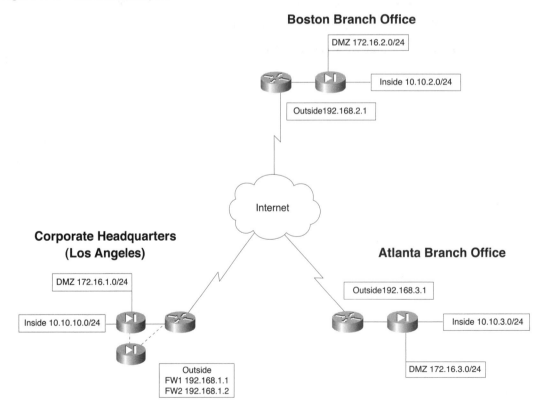

The three locations have all provided their current PIX configurations, but each has a significant amount of information missing. It is your responsibility to complete each of the configurations and ensure that they are correct. Example 10-10 shows the configuration for the corporate headquarters in Los Angeles.

Example 10-10 *PIX Configuration for Los Angeles*

```
1.    : Saved
2.    :
3.    PIX Version 6.2(2)
4.    nameif ethernet0 outside security0
5.    nameif ethernet1 inside security100
6.    nameif ethernet2 DMZ security70
7.    enable password HtmvK15kjhtlyfvcl encrypted
8.    passwd Kkjhlkf1568Hke encrypted
9.    hostname LosAngeles
10.   domain-name www.Chapter10.com
11.   fixup protocol ftp 21
12.   fixup protocol http 80
13.   fixup protocol h323 1720
14.   fixup protocol rsh 514
15.   fixup protocol smtp 25
16.   fixup protocol sqlnet 1521
17.   fixup protocol sip 5060
18.   fixup protocol skinny 2000
19.   names
20.   access-list inbound permit icmp any host 192.168.1.10
21.   access-list inbound permit tcp any host 192.168.1.10  eq www
22.   access-list inbound permit tcp any host 192.168.1.10 eq 443
23.   access-list inbound permit tcp any host 192.168.1.11  eq www
24.   access-list inbound permit tcp any host 192.168.1.11 eq 443
25.   access-list inbound permit tcp any host 192.168.1.12  eq www
26.   access-list inbound permit tcp any host 192.168.1.12 eq 443
27.   access-list inbound permit tcp any host 192.168.1.13  eq ftp
28.   access-list inbound permit tcp any host 192.168.1.10 eq 443
29.   access-list DMZ permit udp 172.16.1.0 255.255.255.0 host 10.10.10.240 eq ntp
30.   access-list VPN permit ip 10.10.10.0 255.255.255.0 10.10.2.0 255.255.255.0
31.   _____
32.   _____
33.   _____
34.   pager lines 24
35.   logging on
36.   logging timestamp
37.   interface ethernet0 auto
38.   interface ethernet1 auto
39.   interface ethernet2 auto
40.   mtu outside 1500
41.   mtu inside 1500
42.   ip address outside 192.168.1.1 255.255.255.0
43.   ip address inside 10.10.10.1 255.255.255.0
44.   ip address DMZ 172.16.1.1 255.255.255.0
45.   failover
46.   failover timeout 0:00:00
```

continues

Example 10-10   *PIX Configuration for Los Angeles (Continued)*

```
47.  failover poll 15
48.  failover ip address outside 192.168.1.2
49.  failover ip address inside 10.10.10.2
50.  failover ip address DMZ 172.16.1.2
51.  arp timeout 14400
52.  global (outside) 1 192.168.1.20-250
53.  nat (inside) 1 0.0.0.0 0.0.0.0
54.  nat (inside) 0 access-list VPN
55.  static (DMZ,outside) 192.168.1.10 172.16.1.10 netmask 255.255.255.255 0 0
56.  static (DMZ,outside) 192.168.1.11 172.16.1.11 netmask 255.255.255.255 0 0
57.  static (DMZ,outside) 192.168.1.12 172.16.1.12 netmask 255.255.255.255 0 0
58.  static (DMZ,outside) 192.168.1.13 172.16.1.13 netmask 255.255.255.255 0 0
59.  access-group inbound in interface outside
60.  access-group DMZ in interface DMZ
61.  route outside 0.0.0.0 0.0.0.0 192.168.1.254 1
62.  timeout xlate 3:00:00
63.  timeout conn 1:00:00 half-closed 0:10:00 udp 0:02:00 rpc 0:10:00 h323 0:05:00
     sip 0:30:00 sip_media 0:02:00
64.  timeout uauth 0:05:00 absolute
65.  aaa-server TACACS+ protocol tacacs+
66.  aaa-server RADIUS protocol radius
67.  no snmp-server location
68.  no snmp-server contact
69.  snmp-server community public
70.  no snmp-server enable traps
71.  floodguard enable
72.  sysopt connection permit-ipsec
73.  no sysopt route dnat
74.  crypto ipsec transform-set
75.  crypto ipsec transform-set NothingNew esp-3des esp-sha-hmac
76.  _____
77.  _____
78.  _____
79.  crypto map Chapter10 10 set transform-set Chapter10
80.  crypto map Chapter10 20 ipsec-isakmp
81.  _____
82.  _____
83.  _____
84.  crypto map Chapter10 interface outside
85.  _____
86.  _____
87.  _____
88.  _____
89.  _____
90.  _____
91.  _____
92.  _____
93.  _____
94.  terminal width 80
95.  Cryptochecksum:e0clmj3546549637cbsFds54132d5
```

Example 10-11 shows the configuration for the Boston branch office.

Example 10-11 *PIX Configuration for Boston*

```
1.    : Saved
2.    :
3.    PIX Version 6.2(2)
4.    nameif ethernet0 outside security0
5.    nameif ethernet1 inside security100
6.    nameif ethernet2 DMZ security70
7.    enable password ksjfglkasglc encrypted
8.    passwd kjngczftglkacytiur encrypted
9.    hostname Boston
10.   domain-name www.Chapter10.com
11.   fixup protocol ftp 21
12.   fixup protocol http 80
13.   fixup protocol smtp 25
14.   fixup protocol skinny 2000
15.   names
16.   access-list inbound permit icmp any host 192.168.2.10
17.   access-list inbound permit tcp any host 192.168.2.10  eq www
18.   access-list inbound permit tcp any host 192.168.2.10 eq 443
19.   access-list DMZ permit udp 172.16.2.0 255.255.255.0 host 10.10.2.240 eq ntp
20.   access-list
21.   access-list
22.   access-list
23.   access-list
24.   pager lines 24
25.   logging on
26.   logging timestamp
27.   interface ethernet0 auto
28.   interface ethernet1 auto
29.   interface ethernet2 auto
30.   mtu outside 1500
31.   mtu inside 1500
32    ip address outside 192.168.2.1 255.255.255.0
33.   ip address inside 10.10.2.1 255.255.255.0
34.   ip address DMZ 172.16.2.1 255.255.255.0
35.   arp timeout 14400
36.   global (outside) 1 192.168.2.20-200
37.   nat (inside) 1 0.0.0.0 0.0.0.0 0 0
38.   nat (inside) 0 access-list VPN
39.   static (DMZ,outside) 192.168.2.10 172.16.2.10 netmask 255.255.255.255 0 0
40.   access-group inbound in interface outside
41.   access-group DMZ in interface DMZ
42.   route outside 0.0.0.0 0.0.0.0 192.168.2.254 1
43.   timeout xlate 3:00:00
44.   timeout conn 1:00:00 half-closed 0:10:00 udp 0:02:00
45.   timeout uauth 0:05:00 absolute
46.   aaa-server TACACS+ protocol tacacs+
47.   aaa-server RADIUS protocol radius
48.   no snmp-server location
49.   no snmp-server contact
50.   snmp-server community public
```

continues

Example 10-11 *PIX Configuration for Boston (Continued)*

```
51.   no snmp-server enable traps
52.   floodguard enable
53.   _____
54.   _____
55.   _____
56.   crypto map Chapter10 10 ipsec-isakmp
57.   crypto map Chapter10 10 match address LosAngeles
58.   _____
59.   crypto map Chapter10 10 set transform-set Chapter10
60.   crypto map Chapter10 20 ipsec-isakmp
61.   crypto map Chapter10 20 match address Atlanta
62.   crypto map Chapter10 20 set peer 192.168.3.1
63.   _____
64.   _____
65.   isakmp enable outside
66.   isakmp key ******** address 192.168.1.1 netmask 255.255.255.255
67.   isakmp key ******** address 192.168.3.1 netmask 255.255.255.255
68.   isakmp identity address
69.   isakmp policy 20 authentication pre-share
70.   _____
71.   _____
72.   _____
73.   _____
74.   terminal width 80
75.   Cryptochecksum:e0c04954fcabd239ae291d58fc618dd5
```

Example 10-12 shows the configuration for the Atlanta branch office.

Example 10-12 *PIX Configuration for Atlanta*

```
1.    : Saved
2.    :
3.    PIX Version 6.2(2)
4.    nameif ethernet0 outside security0
5.    nameif ethernet1 inside security100
6.    nameif ethernet2 DMZ security70
7.    enable password ksjfglkasglc encrypted
8.    passwd kjngczftglkacytiur encrypted
9.    hostname Atlanta
10.   domain-name www.Chapter10.com
11.   fixup protocol ftp 21
12.   fixup protocol http 80
13.   fixup protocol smtp 25
14.   fixup protocol skinny 2000
15.   names
16.   access-list inbound permit icmp any host 192.168.3.10
17.   access-list inbound permit tcp any host 192.168.3.10   eq www
18.   access-list inbound permit tcp any host 192.168.3.10 eq 443
19.   access-list DMZ permit udp 172.16.3.0 255.255.255.0 host 10.10.3.240 eq ntp
20.   access-list
21.   access-list
22.   access-list
```

Example 10-12 *PIX Configuration for Atlanta (Continued)*

```
23.  access-list
24.  pager lines 24
25.  logging on
26.  logging timestamp
27.  interface ethernet0 auto
28.  interface ethernet1 auto
29.  interface ethernet2 auto
30.  mtu outside 1500
31.  mtu inside 1500
32.  ip address outside 192.168.3.1 255.255.255.0
33.  ip address inside 10.10.3.1 255.255.255.0
34.  ip address DMZ 172.16.3.1 255.255.255.0
35.  arp timeout 14400
36.  global (outside) 1 192.168.3.20-200
37.  nat (inside) 1 0.0.0.0 0.0.0.0 0 0
38.  nat (inside) 0 access-list VPN
39.  static (DMZ,outside) 192.168.3.10 172.16.3.10 netmask 255.255.255.255 0 0
40.  access-group inbound in interface outside
41.  access-group DMZ in interface DMZ
42.  route outside 0.0.0.0 0.0.0.0 192.168.3.254 1
43.  timeout xlate 3:00:00
44.  timeout conn 1:00:00 half-closed 0:10:00 udp 0:02:00
45.  timeout uauth 0:05:00 absolute
46.  aaa-server TACACS+ protocol tacacs+
47.  aaa-server RADIUS protocol radius
48.  no snmp-server location
49.  no snmp-server contact
50.  snmp-server community public
51.  no snmp-server enable traps
52.  floodguard enable
53.  sysopt connection permit-ipsec
54.  crypto ipsec transform-set
55.  crypto ipsec transform-set NothingNew esp-3des esp-sha-hmac
56.  crypto map Chapter10 10 ipsec-isakmp
57.  crypto map
58.  crypto map
59.  crypto map Chapter10 10 set transform-set Chapter10
60.  crypto map
61.  crypto map
62.  crypto map
63.  crypto map Chapter10 20 set transform-set Chapter10
64.  crypto map
65.  isakmp
66.  isakmp key ********
67.  isakmp key
68.  isakmp identity address
69.  isakmp policy 20
70.  isakmp policy 20 encryption 3des
71.  isakmp policy 20 hash md5
72.  isakmp policy 20 group 2
73.  isakmp policy 20 lifetime 86400
74.  terminal width 80
75.  Cryptochecksum:e0c04954fcabd239ae291d58fc618dd5
```

Each line of the configuration is numbered, and certain lines have not been completed. Your job is to complete the lines and verify each configuration against the configuration of the VPN peer. The following sections give the blank lines for each configuration. The completed configurations are listed at the end of the chapter, along with a complete description of each element from the configuration in Los Angeles. You will not find all the information needed to complete the configuration on a single firewall. Remember that the configurations must match on each end of the VPN.

Los Angeles Configuration

Fill in the missing lines in Example 10-10:

Line 31: _____

Line 32: _____

Line 33: _____

Line 74: _____

Line 76: _____

Line 77: _____

Line 78: _____

Line 81: _____

Line 82: _____

Line 83: _____

Line 85: _____

Line 86: _____

Line 87: _____

Line 88: _____

Line 89: _____

Line 90: _____

Line 91: _____

Line 92: _____

Line 93: _____

Boston Configuration

Fill in the missing lines in Example 10-11:

Line 20: _____

Line 21: _____

Line 22: _____

Line 23: _____

Line 53: _____

Line 54: _____

Line 55: _____

Line 58: _____

Line 63: _____

Line 64: _____

Line 70: _____

Line 71: _____

Line 72: _____

Line 73: _____

Atlanta Configuration

Fill in the missing lines in Example 10-12:

Line 20: _____

Line 21: _____

Line 22: _____

Line 23: _____

Line 54: _____

Line 57: _____

Line 58: _____

Line 60: _____

Line 61: _____

Line 62: _____

Line 64: _____

Line 65: _____

Line 66: _____

Line 67: _____

Line 69: _____

Completed PIX Configurations

It is a good idea to use a common naming convention when creating access lists, transforms, and crypto maps to reduce confusion. Example 10-13 shows the completed configuration for the Los Angeles headquarters.

Example 10-13 *Completed Configuration for Los Angeles*

```
 1.   : Saved
 2.   :
 3.   PIX Version 6.2(2)
 4.   nameif ethernet0 outside security0
 5.   nameif ethernet1 inside security100
 6.   nameif ethernet2 DMZ security70
 7.   enable password HtmvK15kjhtlyfvcl encrypted
 8.   passwd Kkjhlkf1568Hke encrypted
 9.   hostname LosAngeles
10.   domain-name www.Chapter10.com
11.   fixup protocol ftp 21
12.   fixup protocol http 80
13.   fixup protocol h323 1720
14.   fixup protocol rsh 514
15.   fixup protocol smtp 25
16.   fixup protocol sqlnet 1521
17.   fixup protocol sip 5060
18.   fixup protocol skinny 2000
19.   names
20.   access-list inbound permit icmp any host 192.168.1.10
21.   access-list inbound permit tcp any host 192.168.1.10  eq www
22.   access-list inbound permit tcp any host 192.168.1.10 eq 443
23.   access-list inbound permit tcp any host 192.168.1.11  eq www
24.   access-list inbound permit tcp any host 192.168.1.11 eq 443
25.   access-list inbound permit tcp any host 192.168.1.12  eq www
26.   access-list inbound permit tcp any host 192.168.1.12 eq 443
27.   access-list inbound permit tcp any host 192.168.1.13  eq ftp
28.   access-list inbound permit tcp any host 192.168.1.10 eq 443
29.   access-list DMZ permit udp 172.16.1.0 255.255.255.0 host 10.10.10.240 eq ntp
30.   access-list VPN permit ip 10.10.10.0 255.255.255.0 10.10.2.0 255.255.255.0
31.   access-list VPN permit ip 10.10.10.0 255.255.255.0 10.10.3.0 255.255.255.0
32.   access-list Boston permit ip 10.10.10.0 255.255.255.0 10.10.2.0 255.255.255.0
33.   access-list Atlanta permit ip 10.10.10.0 255.255.255.0 10.10.3.0 255.255.255.0
34.   pager lines 24
35.   logging on
36.   logging timestamp
37.   interface ethernet0 auto
38.   interface ethernet1 auto
39.   interface ethernet2 auto
40.   mtu outside 1500
41.   mtu inside 1500
42.   ip address outside 192.168.1.1 255.255.255.0
43.   ip address inside 10.10.10.1 255.255.255.0
44.   ip address DMZ 172.16.1.1 255.255.255.0
```

continues

Example 10-13   *Completed Configuration for Los Angeles (Continued)*

```
45.  failover
46.  failover timeout 0:00:00
47.  failover poll 15
48.  failover ip address outside 192.168.1.2
49.  failover ip address inside 10.10.10.2
50.  failover ip address DMZ 172.16.1.2
51.  arp timeout 14400
52.  global (outside) 1 192.168.1.20-250
53.  nat (inside) 1 0.0.0.0 0.0.0.0 0 0
54.  nat (inside) 0 access-list VPN
55.  static (DMZ,outside) 192.168.1.10 172.16.1.10 netmask 255.255.255.255 0 0
56.  static (DMZ,outside) 192.168.1.11 172.16.1.11 netmask 255.255.255.255 0 0
57.  static (DMZ,outside) 192.168.1.12 172.16.1.12 netmask 255.255.255.255 0 0
58.  static (DMZ,outside) 192.168.1.13 172.16.1.13 netmask 255.255.255.255 0 0
59.  access-group inbound in interface outside
60.  access-group DMZ out interface DMZ
61.  route outside 0.0.0.0 0.0.0.0 192.168.1.254 1
62.  timeout xlate 3:00:00
63.  timeout conn 1:00:00 half-closed 0:10:00 udp 0:02:00 rpc 0:10:00 h323 0:05:00
     sip 0:30:00 sip_media 0:02:00
64.  timeout uauth 0:05:00 absolute
65.  aaa-server TACACS+ protocol tacacs+
66.  aaa-server RADIUS protocol radius
67.  no snmp-server location
68.  no snmp-server contact
69.  snmp-server community public
70.  no snmp-server enable traps
71.  floodguard enable
72.  sysopt connection permit-ipsec
73.  no sysopt route dnat
74.  crypto ipsec transform-set Chapter10 esp-3des esp-md5-hmac
75.  crypto ipsec transform-set NothingNew esp-3des esp-sha-hmac
76.  crypto map Chapter10 10 ipsec-isakmp
77.  crypto map Chapter10 10 match address Boston
78.  crypto map Chapter10 10 set peer 192.168.2.1
79.  crypto map Chapter10 10 set transform-set Chapter10
80.  crypto map Chapter10 20 ipsec-isakmp
81.  crypto map Chapter10 20 match address Atlanta
82.  crypto map Chapter10 20 set peer 192.168.3.1
83.  crypto map Chapter10 20 set transform-set Chapter10
84.  crypto map Chapter10 interface outside
85.  isakmp enable outside
86.  isakmp key ******** address 192.168.2.1 netmask 255.255.255.255
87.  isakmp key ******** address 192.168.3.1 netmask 255.255.255.255
88.  isakmp identity address
89.  isakmp policy 20 authentication pre-share
90.  isakmp policy 20 encryption 3des
91.  isakmp policy 20 hash md5
92.  isakmp policy 20 group 2
93.  isakmp policy 20 lifetime 86400
94.  terminal width 80
95.  Cryptochecksum:e0clmj3546549637cbsFds54132d5
```

Example 10-14 shows the completed configuration for the Boston branch office.

Example 10-14 *Completed Configuration for Boston*

```
1.    : Saved
2.    :
3.    PIX Version 6.2(2)
4.    nameif ethernet0 outside security0
5.    nameif ethernet1 inside security100
6.    nameif ethernet2 DMZ security70
7.    enable password ksjfglkasglc encrypted
8.    passwd kjngczftglkacytiur encrypted
9.    hostname Boston
10.   domain-name www.Chapter10.com
11.   fixup protocol ftp 21
12.   fixup protocol http 80
13.   fixup protocol smtp 25
14.   fixup protocol skinny 2000
15.   names
16.   access-list inbound permit icmp any host 192.168.2.10
17.   access-list inbound permit tcp any host 192.168.2.10  eq www
18.   access-list inbound permit tcp any host 192.168.2.10 eq 443
19.   access-list DMZ permit udp 172.16.2.0 255.255.255.0 host 10.10.2.240 eq ntp
20.   access-list VPN permit ip 10.10.2.0 255.255.255.0 10.10.10.0 255.255.255.0
21.   access-list VPN permit ip 10.10.2.0 255.255.255.0 10.10.3.0 255.255.255.0
22.   access-list LosAngeles permit ip 10.10.2.0 255.255.255.0 10.10.10.0
      255.255.255.0
23.   access-list Atlanta permit ip 10.10.2.0 255.255.255.0 10.10.3.0 255.255.255.0
24.   pager lines 24
25.   logging on
26.   logging timestamp
27.   interface ethernet0 auto
28.   interface ethernet1 auto
29.   interface ethernet2 auto
30.   mtu outside 1500
31.   mtu inside 1500
32  ip address outside 192.168.2.1 255.255.255.0
33.   ip address inside 10.10.2.1 255.255.255.0
34.   ip address DMZ 172.16.2.1 255.255.255.0
35.   arp timeout 14400
36.   global (outside) 1 192.168.2.20-200
37.   nat (inside) 1 0.0.0.0 0.0.0.0 0 0
38.   nat (inside) 0 access-list VPN
39.   static (DMZ,outside) 192.168.2.10 172.16.2.10 netmask 255.255.255.255 0 0
40.   access-group inbound in interface outside
41.   access-group DMZ in interface DMZ
42.   route outside 0.0.0.0 0.0.0.0 192.168.2.254 1
43.   timeout xlate 3:00:00
44.   timeout conn 1:00:00 half-closed 0:10:00 udp 0:02:00
45.   timeout uauth 0:05:00 absolute
46.   aaa-server TACACS+ protocol tacacs+
47.   aaa-server RADIUS protocol radius
48.   no snmp-server location
49.   no snmp-server contact
50.   snmp-server community public
```

continues

Example 10-14 *Completed Configuration for Boston (Continued)*

```
51.  no snmp-server enable traps
52.  floodguard enable
53.  sysopt connection permit-ipsec
54.  crypto ipsec transform-set Chapter10 esp-3des esp-md5-hmac
55.  crypto ipsec transform-set NothingNew esp-3des esp-sha-hmac
56.  crypto map Chapter10 10 ipsec-isakmp
57.  crypto map Chapter10 10 match address LosAngeles
58.  crypto map Chapter10 10 set peer 192.168.1.1
59.  crypto map Chapter10 10 set transform-set Chapter10
60.  crypto map Chapter10 20 ipsec-isakmp
61.  crypto map Chapter10 20 match address Atlanta
62.  crypto map Chapter10 20 set peer 192.168.3.1
63.  crypto map Chapter10 20 set transform-set Chapter10
64.  crypto map Chapter10 interface outside
65.  isakmp enable outside
66.  isakmp key ******** address 192.168.1.1 netmask 255.255.255.255
67.  isakmp key ******** address 192.168.3.1 netmask 255.255.255.255
68.  isakmp identity address
69.  isakmp policy 20 authentication pre-share
70.  isakmp policy 20 encryption 3des
71.  isakmp policy 20 hash md5
72.  isakmp policy 20 group 2
73.  isakmp policy 20 lifetime 86400
74.  terminal width 80
75.  Cryptochecksum:e0c04954fcabd239ae291d58fc618dd5
```

Example 10-15 shows the completed configuration for the Atlanta branch office.

Example 10-15 *Completed Configuration for Atlanta*

```
1.   : Saved
2.   :
3.   PIX Version 6.2(2)
4.   nameif ethernet0 outside security0
5.   nameif ethernet1 inside security100
6.   nameif ethernet2 DMZ security70
7.   enable password ksjfglkasglc encrypted
8.   passwd kjngczftglkacytiur encrypted
9.   hostname Atlanta
10.  domain-name www.Chapter10.com
11.  fixup protocol ftp 21
12.  fixup protocol http 80
13.  fixup protocol smtp 25
14.  fixup protocol skinny 2000
15.  names
16.  access-list inbound permit icmp any host 192.168.3.10
17.  access-list inbound permit tcp any host 192.168.3.10  eq www
18.  access-list inbound permit tcp any host 192.168.3.10 eq 443
19.  access-list DMZ permit udp 172.16.3.0 255.255.255.0 host 10.10.3.240 eq ntp
20.  access-list VPN permit ip 10.10.3.0 255.255.255.0 10.10.2.0 255.255.255.0
21.  access-list VPN permit ip 10.10.3.0 255.255.255.0 10.10.10.0 255.255.255.0
22.  access-list LosAngeles permit ip 10.10.3.0 255.255.255.0 10.10.10.0
     255.255.255.0
```

Example 10-15 *Completed Configuration for Atlanta (Continued)*

```
23.  access-list Boston permit ip 10.10.3.0 255.255.255.0 10.10.2.0 255.255.255.0
24.  pager lines 24
25.  logging on
26.  logging timestamp
27.  interface ethernet0 auto
28.  interface ethernet1 auto
29.  interface ethernet2 auto
30.  mtu outside 1500
31.  mtu inside 1500
32.  ip address outside 192.168.3.1 255.255.255.0
33.  ip address inside 10.10.3.1 255.255.255.0
34.  ip address DMZ 172.16.3.1 255.255.255.0
35.  arp timeout 14400
36.  global (outside) 1 192.168.3.20-200
37.  nat (inside) 1 0.0.0.0 0.0.0.0 0 0
38.  nat (inside) 0 access-list VPN
39.  static (DMZ,outside) 192.168.3.10 172.16.3.10 netmask 255.255.255.255 0 0
40.  access-group inbound in interface outside
41.  access-group DMZ in interface DMZ
42.  route outside 0.0.0.0 0.0.0.0 192.168.3.254 1
43.  timeout xlate 3:00:00
44.  timeout conn 1:00:00 half-closed 0:10:00 udp 0:02:00
45.  timeout uauth 0:05:00 absolute
46.  aaa-server TACACS+ protocol tacacs+
47.  aaa-server RADIUS protocol radius
48.  no snmp-server location
49.  no snmp-server contact
50.  snmp-server community public
51.  no snmp-server enable traps
52.  floodguard enable
53.  sysopt connection permit-ipsec
54.  crypto ipsec transform-set Chapter10 esp-3des esp-md5-hmac
55.  crypto ipsec transform-set NothingNew esp-3des esp-sha-hmac
56.  crypto map Chapter10 10 ipsec-isakmp
57.  crypto map Chapter10 10 match address LosAngeles
58.  crypto map Chapter10 10 set peer 192.168.1.1
59.  crypto map Chapter10 10 set transform-set Chapter10
60.  crypto map Chapter10 20 ipsec-isakmp
61.  crypto map Chapter10 20 match address Boston
62.  crypto map Chapter10 20 set peer 192.168.2.1
63.  crypto map Chapter10 20 set transform-set Chapter10
64.  crypto map Chapter10 interface outside
65.  isakmp enable outside
66.  isakmp key ******** address 192.168.1.1 netmask 255.255.255.255
67.  isakmp key ******** address 192.168.2.1 netmask 255.255.255.255
68.  isakmp identity address
69.  isakmp policy 20 authentication pre-share
70.  isakmp policy 20 encryption 3des
71.  isakmp policy 20 hash md5
72.  isakmp policy 20 group 2
73.  isakmp policy 20 lifetime 86400
74.  terminal width 80
75.  Cryptochecksum:e0c04954fcabd239ae291d58fc618dd5
```

How the Configuration Lines Interact

Figure 10-7 shows the completed configuration for Los Angeles, with a brief explanation for each entry. Note that each entry is connected to one or more other entries on the right. This diagram depicts how the lines of the configuration are dependent on each other. Keep this in mind when trying to troubleshoot a VPN configuration. It might help you to find which line is missing or incorrectly configured.

Figure 10-7 *LA Configuration with Comments*

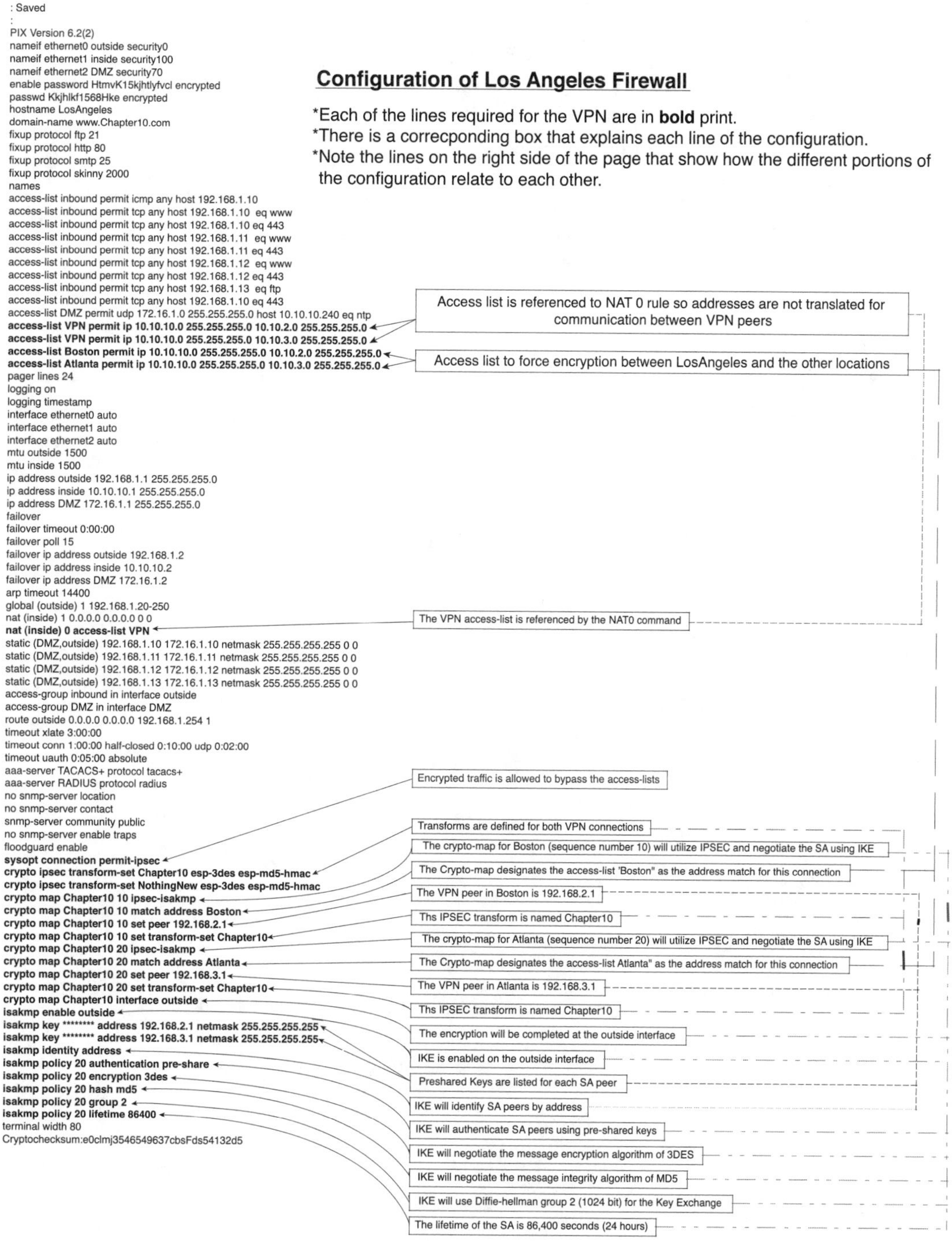

```
: Saved
:
PIX Version 6.2(2)
nameif ethernet0 outside security0
nameif ethernet1 inside security100
nameif ethernet2 DMZ security70
enable password HtmvK15kjhtlyfvcl encrypted
passwd Kkjhlkf1568Hke encrypted
hostname LosAngeles
domain-name www.Chapter10.com
fixup protocol ftp 21
fixup protocol http 80
fixup protocol smtp 25
fixup protocol skinny 2000
names
access-list inbound permit icmp any host 192.168.1.10
access-list inbound permit tcp any host 192.168.1.10  eq www
access-list inbound permit tcp any host 192.168.1.10 eq 443
access-list inbound permit tcp any host 192.168.1.11  eq www
access-list inbound permit tcp any host 192.168.1.11 eq 443
access-list inbound permit tcp any host 192.168.1.12  eq www
access-list inbound permit tcp any host 192.168.1.12 eq 443
access-list inbound permit tcp any host 192.168.1.13  eq ftp
access-list inbound permit tcp any host 192.168.1.13 eq 443
access-list DMZ permit udp 172.16.1.0 255.255.255.0 host 10.10.10.240 eq ntp
access-list VPN permit ip 10.10.10.0 255.255.255.0 10.10.2.0 255.255.255.0
access-list VPN permit ip 10.10.10.0 255.255.255.0 10.10.3.0 255.255.255.0
access-list Boston permit ip 10.10.10.0 255.255.255.0 10.10.2.0 255.255.255.0
access-list Atlanta permit ip 10.10.10.0 255.255.255.0 10.10.3.0 255.255.255.0
pager lines 24
logging on
logging timestamp
interface ethernet0 auto
interface ethernet1 auto
interface ethernet2 auto
mtu outside 1500
mtu inside 1500
ip address outside 192.168.1.1 255.255.255.0
ip address inside 10.10.10.1 255.255.255.0
ip address DMZ 172.16.1.1 255.255.255.0
failover
failover timeout 0:00:00
failover poll 15
failover ip address outside 192.168.1.2
failover ip address inside 10.10.10.2
failover ip address DMZ 172.16.1.2
arp timeout 14400
global (outside) 1 192.168.1.20-250
nat 1 0.0.0.0 0.0.0.0 0 0
nat (inside) 0 access-list VPN
static (DMZ,outside) 192.168.1.10 172.16.1.10 netmask 255.255.255.255 0 0
static (DMZ,outside) 192.168.1.11 172.16.1.11 netmask 255.255.255.255 0 0
static (DMZ,outside) 192.168.1.12 172.16.1.12 netmask 255.255.255.255 0 0
static (DMZ,outside) 192.168.1.13 172.16.1.13 netmask 255.255.255.255 0 0
access-group inbound in interface outside
access-group DMZ in interface DMZ
route outside 0.0.0.0 0.0.0.0 192.168.1.254 1
timeout xlate 3:00:00
timeout conn 1:00:00 half-closed 0:10:00 udp 0:02:00
timeout uauth 0:05:00 absolute
aaa-server TACACS+ protocol tacacs+
aaa-server RADIUS protocol radius
no snmp-server location
no snmp-server contact
snmp-server community public
no snmp-server enable traps
floodguard enable
sysopt connection permit-ipsec
crypto ipsec transform-set Chapter10 esp-3des esp-md5-hmac
crypto ipsec transform-set NothingNew esp-3des esp-md5-hmac
crypto map Chapter10 10 ipsec-isakmp
crypto map Chapter10 10 match address Boston
crypto map Chapter10 10 set peer 192.168.2.1
crypto map Chapter10 10 set transform-set Chapter10
crypto map Chapter10 20 ipsec-isakmp
crypto map Chapter10 20 match address Atlanta
crypto map Chapter10 20 set peer 192.168.3.1
crypto map Chapter10 20 set transform-set Chapter10
crypto map Chapter10 interface outside
isakmp enable outside
isakmp key ******** address 192.168.2.1 netmask 255.255.255.255
isakmp key ******** address 192.168.3.1 netmask 255.255.255.255
isakmp identity address
isakmp policy 20 authentication pre-share
isakmp policy 20 encryption 3des
isakmp policy 20 hash md5
isakmp policy 20 group 2
isakmp policy 20 lifetime 86400
terminal width 80
Cryptochecksum:e0clmj3546549637cbsFds54132d5
```

Configuration of Los Angeles Firewall

*Each of the lines required for the VPN are in **bold** print.
*There is a correcponding box that explains each line of the configuration.
*Note the lines on the right side of the page that show how the different portions of the configuration relate to each other.

> Access list is referenced to NAT 0 rule so addresses are not translated for communication between VPN peers

> Access list to force encryption between LosAngeles and the other locations

> The VPN access-list is referenced by the NAT0 command

> Encrypted traffic is allowed to bypass the access-lists

> Transforms are defined for both VPN connections

> The crypto-map for Boston (sequence number 10) will utilize IPSEC and negotiate the SA using IKE

> The Crypto-map designates the access-list 'Boston" as the address match for this connection

> The VPN peer in Boston is 192.168.2.1

> Ths IPSEC transform is named Chapter10

> The crypto-map for Atlanta (sequence number 20) will utilize IPSEC and negotiate the SA using IKE

> The Crypto-map designates the access-list Atlanta" as the address match for this connection

> The VPN peer in Atlanta is 192.168.3.1

> Ths IPSEC transform is named Chapter10

> The encryption will be completed at the outside interface

> IKE is enabled on the outside interface

> Preshared Keys are listed for each SA peer

> IKE will identify SA peers by address

> IKE will authenticate SA peers using pre-shared keys

> IKE will negotiate the message encryption algorithm of 3DES

> IKE will negotiate the message integrity algorithm of MD5

> IKE will use Diffie-hellman group 2 (1024 bit) for the Key Exchange

> The lifetime of the SA is 86,400 seconds (24 hours)

This chapter covers the following exam topics for the Cisco Secure PIX Firewall Advanced Exam:

CHAPTER 11

PIX Device Manager

The *Cisco PIX Device Manager*, hereafter referred to as *PDM*, is a browser-based configuration tool designed to help you set up, configure, and monitor your Cisco PIX Firewall graphically, without requiring extensive knowledge of the Cisco PIX Firewall command-line interface (CLI).

"Do I Know This Already?" Quiz

The purpose of this quiz is to help you determine your current understanding of the topics covered in this chapter. Write down your answers and compare them to the answers in Appendix A. If you have to look at any references to correctly answer the questions about PDM functionality, you should read the chapter.

1 What happens to traffic that is not explicitly permitted by an access rule in an access control list?

2 True or false: PDM supports a mixed configuration with **outbound** or **conduit** commands and **access-list** commands.

3 What is a translation exemption rule?

4 What are the six tabs on the PDM?

5 How do you connect to the PDM?

6 What version of PIX Software is required of PDM version 1.1?

7 Which models of Cisco PIX Firewall are supported by PDM?

8 What versions of Windows does PDM support?

9 What steps should you take before installing PDM?

10 True or false: PDM comes preinstalled on all PIX 5.3 and later software versions.

11 Where does PDM reside?

Foundation Topics

PDM Overview

PDM is a browser-based configuration tool designed to help you set up, configure, and monitor your Cisco PIX Firewall graphically. It is installed as a separate software image on the Cisco PIX Firewall and resides in the Flash memory of all PIX units running PIX version 6.0 and higher. PDM uses tables, drop-down menus, and task-oriented selection menus to assist you in administering your Cisco PIX Firewall. Additionally, PDM maintains compatibility with the PIX command-line interface (CLI) and includes a tool for using the standard CLI commands within the PDM application. PDM also lets you print or export graphs of traffic through the Cisco PIX Firewall and system activity.

NOTE   PDM is a signed Java applet that downloads from the PIX Firewall to your web browser.

Figure 11-1 shows the PDM graphical user interface (GUI).

Figure 11-1 *PIX Device Manager GUI*

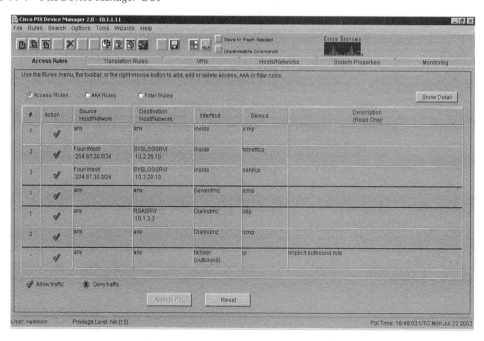

If your Cisco PIX Firewall unit is new and came with PIX version 6.0, the software is already loaded in Flash memory. If you are upgrading from a previous version of Cisco PIX Firewall, you need to use TFTP from the PIX unit's inside interface to copy the PDM image to your Cisco PIX Firewall. PDM works with PIX Firewall version 6.0 and can operate on the PIX 506, 515, 520, 525, and 535 units as soon as they are upgraded to version 6.0.

PDM is designed to assist you in managing your network security by

- Letting you visually monitor your Cisco PIX Firewall system, connections, IDS, and traffic on the interfaces.

- Creating new PIX Firewall configurations or modifying existing configurations that were originally implemented using the PIX Firewall CLI or Cisco Secure Policy Manager (Cisco Secure PM).

- Using visual tools such as task-oriented selections and drop-down menus to configure your Cisco PIX Firewall.

- Using Secure Socket Layer (SSL) to secure communication between the PDM and the PIX.

- Monitoring and configuring PIX units individually.

Multiple Cisco PIX Firewalls can be monitored and configured from a single workstation via the web browser. It is also possible to have up to five administrators accessing a given PIX via PDM at the same time.

NOTE   PDM cannot be used to configure PIX units that are being managed by Cisco Secure PM, because all changes made using PDM are overwritten the next time Cisco Secure PM synchronizes with the PIX. If there is a need to use both Cisco Secure PM and PDM, it is recommended that you use PDM for monitoring only, not configuration.

PIX Firewall Requirements to Run PDM

A PIX Firewall unit must meet the following requirements to run PDM:

- You must have an activation (license) key that enables Data Encryption Standard (DES) or the more secure 3DES, which PDM requires for support of the SSL protocol.

- PIX OS version 6.0 or higher.

- Minimum of 8 MB of Flash memory on the PIX unit.

The optimal configuration file size to use with PDM is less than 100 KB (which is approximately 1500 lines). Cisco PIX Firewall configuration files larger than 100 KB might interfere with PDM's performance on your workstation. You can determine the size of your configuration file by entering the command **show flashfs** at a PIX CLI prompt. Then, look for a line in the output that begins with **file 1**. The **length** number on the same line is the configuration file size in bytes. Example 11-1 provides sample output from **show flashfs**.

Example 11-1   **show flashfs** *Command Output*

```
pix# show flashfs
flash file system:  version:2  magic:0x12345679
  file 0: origin:        0 length:1540152
  file 1: origin: 1572864 length:6458
  file 2: origin:        0 length:0
  file 3: origin: 2752512 length:4539600
  file 4: origin:16646144 length:280
Pix#
```

PDM Operating Requirements

PDM's requirements depend on the platform from which you run it. PDM is not supported on Macintosh, Windows 3.1, or Windows 95 operating systems.

Browser Requirements

The following are required to access PDM from a browser:

- PDM requires JavaScript and Java to be enabled. If you are using Microsoft Internet Explorer, your JDK version should be 1.1.4 or higher. To check which version you have, launch PDM. When the PDM information window comes up, the field JDK Version indicates your JDK version. If you have an older JDK version, you can get the latest JVM from Microsoft by downloading the product called Virtual Machine.

- Browser support for SSL must be enabled. The supported versions of Internet Explorer and Netscape Navigator support SSL without requiring additional configuration.

Windows Requirements

The following are required to access PDM from a Windows NT/2000 operating system:

- Windows 2000 (Service Pack 1), Windows NT 4.0 (Service Pack 4 and higher), Windows 98, or Windows Me.

- Supported browsers: Internet Explorer 5.0 (Service Pack 1) or higher (5.5 recommended), Netscape Communicator 4.51 or higher (4.76 recommended). Internet Explorer is recommended due to its faster load times.

- Any Pentium or Pentium-compatible processor running at 350 MHz or higher.

- At least 128 MB of RAM. 192 MB or more is recommended.

- An 800×600-pixel display with at least 256 colors. A 1024×768-pixel display and at least High Color (16-bit) colors are recommended.

SUN Solaris Requirements

The following requirements apply to the use of PDM with Sun SPARC:

- Sun Solaris 2.6 or later running CDE or OpenWindows window manager.
- SPARC microprocessor.
- Supported browser: Netscape Communicator 4.51 or higher (4.76 recommended).
- At least 128 MB of RAM.
- 800×600 pixel display with at least 256 colors. A 1024×768 pixel display and at least High Color (16-bit) colors are recommended.

NOTE   PDM does not support Solaris on IBM PCs.

Linux Requirements

The following requirements apply to the use of PDM with Linux:

- Red Hat Linux 7.0 running the GNOME or KDE 2.0 desktop environment.
- Supported browser: Netscape Communicator 4.75 or a later version.
- At least 64 MB of RAM.
- An 800×600-pixel display with at least 256 colors. A 1024×768-pixel display and at least High Color (16-bit) colors are recommended.

PDM Installation and Configuration

Two versions of PDM are currently available:

- **PDM version 1.1**—Requires PIX software 6.0 or 6.1
- **PDM version 2.1**—Requires PIX software 6.2

Both PDM versions are available on all PIX 501, 506/506E, 515/515E, 520, 525, and 535 platforms that are running Cisco PIX Firewall software version 6.0 or later. PDM version 2.0 requires Cisco PIX Firewall software version 6.2. If you are using Cisco PIX Firewall software version 6.0 or 6.1, use PDM version 1.1.

Before installing PDM, follow these steps:

Step 1   Save or print your PIX configuration, and write down your activation key.

Step 2   If you are upgrading from a previous version of PIX, you need to obtain the PDM software from Cisco in the same way you download the Cisco PIX Firewall software. Then use TFTP to download the image to your PIX unit.

Step 3   If you upgrade your Cisco PIX Firewall software to version 6.0 or higher and you plan to use PDM, both the PIX image and the PDM image must be installed on your failover units.

The upgrade procedure is very similar to that of the Cisco PIX Firewall image upgrade. Example 11-2 shows the installation procedures for PDM installation.

Example 11-2   *PDM Installation Procedures*

```
PIXFIREWALL(config)# copy tftp flash:pdm
Address or name of remote host [127.0.0.1] 10.1.1.10
Source file name [cdisk]pdm-202.bin
copying tftp://10.1.1.10/cdisk to flash:pdm
[yes |no |again]y
```

After you succesfully install your PDM, you are ready to access it using your web browser. On a browser running on a workstation connected to the PIX unit, enter the following:

    https://PIX_Inside_Interface_IP_Address

This launches the PDM applet. Use your enable password and leave the username blank to access the PDM interface when prompted to provide a username and password.

NOTE   Remember that you have to use HTTPS and not HTTP when accessing the PDM. Otherwise, the browser cannot get connected.

Using the PDM to Configure the Cisco PIX Firewall

The Cisco PIX Firewall Device Manager Startup Wizard, shown in Figure 11-2, walks you through the initial configuration of your Cisco PIX Firewall. You are prompted to enter information about your PIX Firewall. The Startup Wizard applies these settings, so you should be able to start using your PIX Firewall right away.

Figure 11-2 *Cisco PIX Firewall Device Manager Startup Wizard Screen*

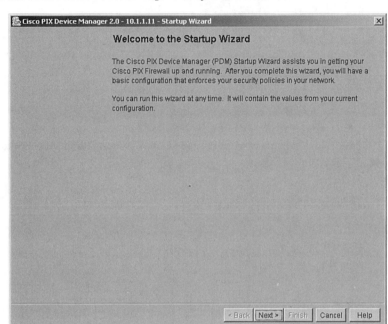

The Startup Wizard configures the following attributes on your Cisco PIX Firewall:

- A host name for your PIX.
- A domain name for your PIX.
- A default gateway for your PIX.
- An enable password that is required to access PDM or the PIX's CLI.
- The speed and IP address information of the outside interface on the PIX.

- Your PIX's other interfaces, such as the inside or DMZ interfaces, can be configured from the Startup Wizard.

- Network Address Translation (NAT) or Port Address Translation (PAT) rules for your PIX.

- Dynamic Host Configuration Protocol (DHCP) settings for the inside interface, as a DHCP server.

- If you are using a PIX 501 or 506, the Startup Wizard lets you configure Cisco Easy VPN Remote device settings, which let the PIX act as a VPN client and establish a VPN tunnel to the VPN server.

The Startup Wizard helps you set up a *shell configuration*—a basic configuration for your Cisco PIX Firewall. To customize and modify your PIX configuration, PDM provides you with six main tabs:

- System Properties

- Hosts/Networks

- Translation Rules

- Access Rules

- VPN

- Monitoring

The sections that follow examine the System Properties, Hosts/Networks, Translation Rules, Access Rules, and Monitoring tabs of the PIX Device Manager in more detail. The section, "Using PDM to Create a Site-to-Site VPN," describes all actions associated with the VPN tab.

System Properties

The System Properties tab, shown in Figure 11-3, lets you view and configure all the parameters that can be configured using the Startup Wizard. Basic configurations such as interface definition and configurations, password, clock, and Telnet configuration are all done at this tab. In addition to the basic configuration, the System Properties tab lets you perform advanced configuration typically done at the CLI. You can configure logging; authentication, authorization, and accounting (AAA); multicast; TurboACL; intrusion detection; and more through the user-friendly interface of the System Properties panel.

Figure 11-3   *System Properties Tab on the PDM*

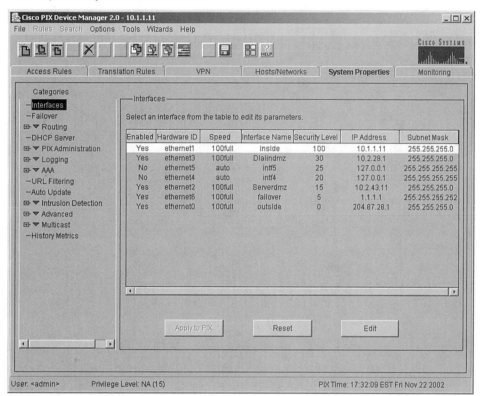

Complicated configurations such as AAA have been made significantly more intuitive and easier with the system properties under AAA. The AAA Server Groups panel, shown in Figure 11-4, allows you to specify up to 14 AAA server groups for your network.

Figure 11-4 *AAA Server Groups Panel Under the System Properties Tab*

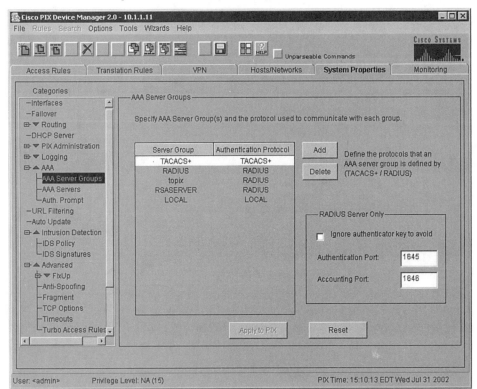

Each AAA server group directs different types of traffic to the authentication servers in its group. If the first authentication server listed in the group fails, the PIX seeks authentication from the next server in the group. You can have up to 16 groups, and each group can have up to 16 AAA servers for a total of up to 256 AAA servers.

The Authentication Prompt panel lets you change the AAA challenge text for HTTP, FTP, and Telnet access. Figure 11-5 shows prompt messages that can be configured when users authenticate by a AAA server.

Figure 11-5 *Configurable Prompt Messages*

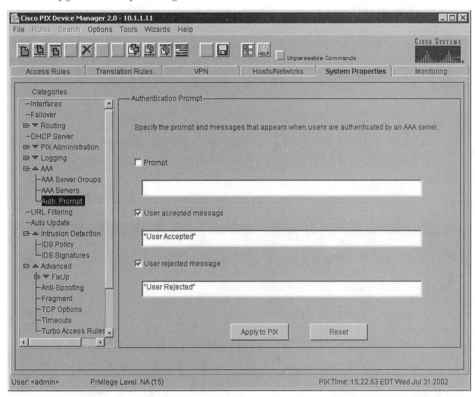

If configured, the prompt text appears above the username and password prompts that users view when logging in. If you do not use this feature, FTP users view FTP authentication, HTTP users view HTTP authentication, and challenge text does not appear for Telnet access. If the user authentication occurs from Telnet, you can use the **user accepted** and **user rejected** options to display different authentication prompts if the authentication server accepts or rejects the authentication attempt. Chapters 13 and 14 discuss AAA in further detail.

Another example of a command-line task that has been streamlined by the System Properties page is URL filtering. The URL Filtering panel lets you prevent internal users from accessing external URLs that you designate using the Websense URL filtering server. After you have defined your URL filtering server(s) and related parameters on this panel, use the Filter Rules panel to define the rules that will be used to enforce URL filtering.

NOTE   A total of 16 URL servers can be configured.

The PIX Firewall can be configured to use either N2H2 or Websense, but not both. For example, if the PIX unit is configured to use two Websense servers, when N2H2 is selected, a warning appears after you add the first N2H2 server and click Apply To PIX. All the previously configured Websense servers are dropped, and the new N2H2 server is added. This also takes place when you switch from N2H2 to Websense. Content filtering is discussed further in Chapter 12, "Content Filtering on the PIX Firewall."

Hosts/Networks

The Hosts/Networks tab, shown in Figure 11-6, lets you view, edit, add to, and delete from the list of hosts and networks defined for the selected interface defined previously on the System Properties tab.

Figure 11-6 *Hosts/Networks Tab on the PDM*

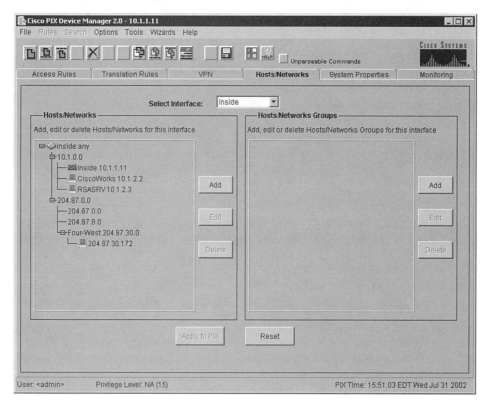

The PDM requires that you define any host or network that you intend to use in access rules and translations. These hosts or networks are organized below the interface from which they can be reached.

Access rules reference these hosts or networks in a rule's source and destination conditions, whereas translation rules reference them in a rule's original address condition. When defining either type of rule, you can reference a host or network by clicking Browse in the appropriate Add or Edit Rule dialog box. Additionally, you can reference the host or network by name if a name is defined for it.

In addition to defining the basic information for these hosts or networks, you can define route settings and NAT rules for any host or network. You can also configure route settings on the System Properties tab and translation rules on the Translation Rules tab. These different configuration options accomplish the same results. The Hosts/Networks tab provides another way to modify these settings on a per-host or per-network basis.

Translation Rules

The Translation Rules tab, shown in Figure 11-7, lets you view all the address translation rules or NAT exemption rules applied to your network.

Figure 11-7 *Translation Rules Tab on the PDM*

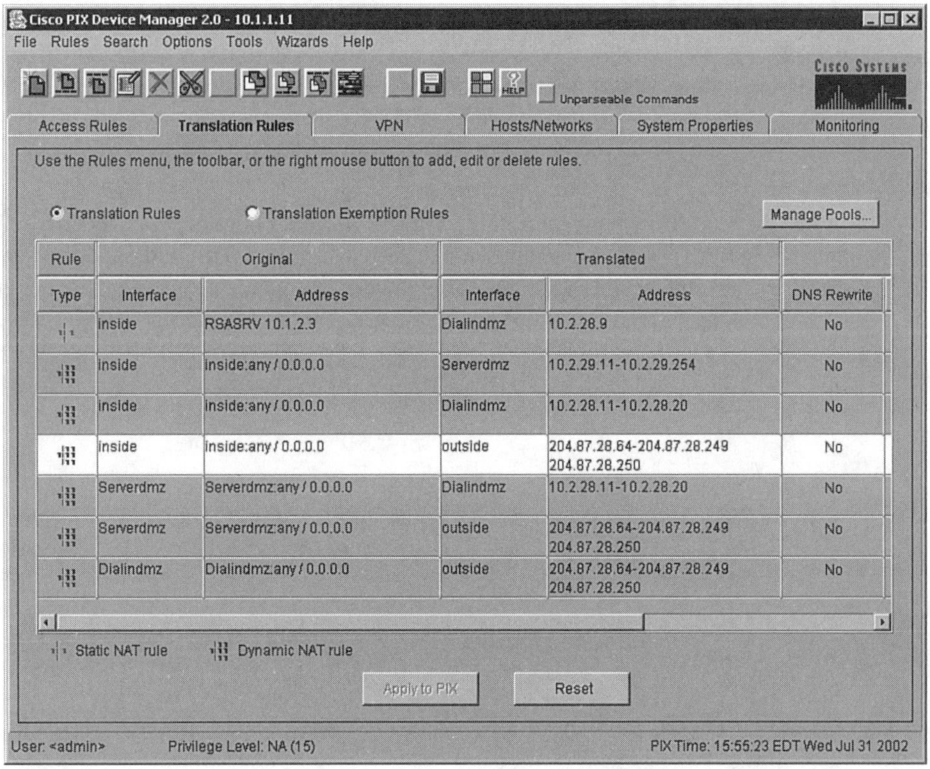

The Cisco PIX Firewall supports both NAT, which provides a globally unique address for each outbound host session, and PAT, which provides a single, unique global address for up to 64,000 simultaneous outbound or inbound host sessions. The global addresses used for NAT come from a pool of addresses to be used specifically for address translation. The unique global address that is used for PAT can be either one global address or the IP address of a given interface.

From the Translation Rules tab you can also create a translation exemption rule, which lets you specify traffic that is exempt from being translated or encrypted. The exemption rules are grouped by interface in the table, and then by direction. If you have a group of IP addresses that will be translated, you can exempt certain addresses from being translated using the exemption rules. If you have a previously configured access list, you can use that to define your exemption rule. PDM writes a **nat 0** command to the CLI. You can re-sort your exemption's view by clicking the column heading.

It is important to note that the order in which you apply translation rules can affect how the rules operate. PDM lists the static translations first and then the dynamic translations. When processing NAT, the Cisco PIX Firewall first translates the static translations in the order they are configured. You can select Rules > Insert Before or Rules > Insert After to determine the order in which static translations are processed. Because dynamically translated rules are processed on a best-match basis, the option to insert a rule before or after a dynamic translation is disabled.

Access Rules

The Access Rules tab, shown in Figure 11-8, shows your entire network security policy expressed in rules. This tab combines the concepts of access lists, outbound lists, and conduits to describe how a specific host or network interacts with another host or network to permit or deny a specific service and/or protocol. This tab also lets you define AAA rules and filter rules for ActiveX and Java.

Figure 11-8 *Access Rules Tab on the PDM*

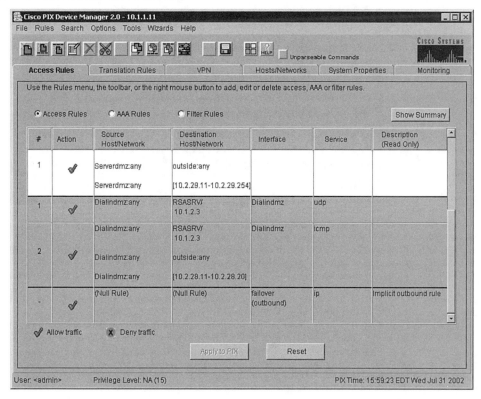

Access rules are categorized into two modes:

- Access control list mode (the default)
- Conduit and outbound list mode

If your PIX currently has a working configuration using either **conduit** commands, **outbound** commands, or access lists, PDM continues using your current model. If the Cisco PIX Firewall is currently using **conduit** commands to control traffic, PDM adds more **conduit** commands to your configuration as you add rules. Similarly, if your PIX is currently configured using **access-list** commands, the PDM adds more **access-list** commands to your configuration as you add rules. If you have a Cisco PIX Firewall with no previous configuration, PDM adds **access-list** commands to the CLI by default. PDM does not support a mixed configuration with **outbound** commands or **conduit** commands and **access-list** commands.

Keep in mind the following points when creating access rules with the PDM:

- It is important to remember that you cannot define any access rules until static or dynamic NAT has been configured for the hosts or networks on which you want to permit or deny traffic.

- You cannot use unavailable commands until your rule meets certain conditions, such as defining hosts or networks. Unavailable commands appear dimmed on the Rules menu. For example, Insert Before and Insert After are available only after a rule is highlighted. Paste is available only when a rule has been copied or cut.

- Access rules are listed in sequential order and are applied in the order in which they appear on the Access Rules tab. This is the order in which the PIX evaluates them. An implicit, unwritten rule denies all traffic that is not permitted. If traffic is not explicitly permitted by an access rule, it is denied.

Null Rules

A null rule indicates that an access rule was configured for a host that is not visible on another interface. This rule is null because no traffic can flow between these two hosts even though the access rule would permit it. Table 11-1 shows an example of a null rule.

Table 11-1   *Null Rule Example*

#	Action	Source Host/ Network	Destination Host/ Network	Interface	Service	Description
1	√	(null rule)	(null rule)	[inbound]	tcp	

This can happen when PDM reads in an existing configuration where any of the following exists:

- Inbound rules without a static translation
- Outbound rules without NAT
- No hosts or networks are defined for either source or destination

Monitoring

The Monitoring tab, shown in Figure 11-9, is one of the most useful tools to help you make sense of the different statistics that the Cisco PIX Firewall can generate. The different panels on the monitoring tab help you analyze your PIX's performance using colorful graphs.

Figure 11-9 *Monitoring Tab on the PDM*

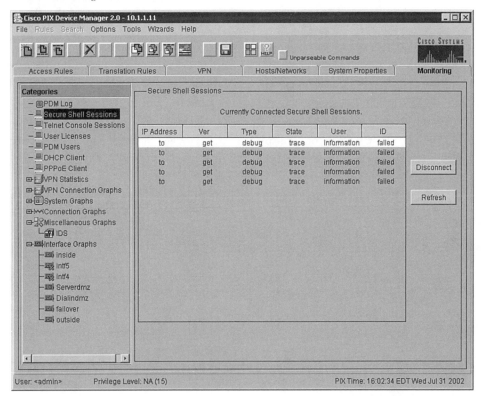

The Monitoring tab features two types of graphing and monitoring functions:

- The first type has a unique screen for each menu selection that shows the table of statistics, numeric values, or settings for that menu selection.

- The second type uses the same screen, which allows the building of graph windows that combine up to four graphs in a single window.

The graphs displayed in the New Graph window can be printed or bookmarked in your browser for later recall, or the data may be exported for use by other applications.

The following options can provide monitoring statistics on the Cisco PIX:

- The PDM Log panel displays the syslog messages currently in the PDM Log buffer on the PIX. A snapshot of the PDM Log buffer contents on the PIX can be displayed.

- The Secure Shell Sessions panel allows you to monitor connections made to the PIX Firewall using Secure Shell (SSH). When the Secure Shell panel is displayed, a snapshot of the current SSH sessions to the PIX Firewall is available.

- The Telnet Console Sessions panel allows you to monitor connections made to the PIX Firewall using Telnet. A snapshot of current Telnet sessions to the PIX Firewall is displayed.

- The User Licenses panel displays the number of current users, which is subtracted from the maximum number of users for your PIX Firewall licensing agreement.

- The PDM Users panel allows you to monitor connections made to the PIX Firewall using PDM. A snapshot of the current PDM user sessions to the PIX Firewall is displayed.

- The DHCP Client panel displays DHCP-assigned interface parameters when DHCP addressing is configured on the outside interface of the PIX Firewall. A snapshot of the current DHCP lease information is displayed.

- The PPPoE Client panel allows the PIX Firewall to automatically connect users on the inside interface to Internet service providers (ISPs) via the outside interface.

- The VPN Statistics panel lets you graphically monitor the following functions:

  — Number of active Phase 2 IPSec tunnels

  — Number of active Phase 2 IKE tunnels

  — L2TP active tunnels

  — L2TP active sessions

  — PPTP active tunnels

  — PPTP active sessions

  — Detailed IPSec information (similar to the CLI command **show ipsec sa detail**)

- The System Graphs panel allows you to build the New Graph window, which monitors the PIX Firewall's system resources, including block utilization, CPU utilization, failover statistics, and memory utilization

- The Connection Graphs panel allows you to monitor a wide variety of performance statistics for PIX Firewall features, including statistics for xlates, connections, AAA, fixups, URL filtering, and TCP intercept

- The IDS panel under the Miscellaneous panel allows you to monitor intrusion detection statistics, including packet counts for each Intrusion Detection System (IDS) signature supported by the PIX Firewall.

- The Interface Graphs panel allows you to monitor per-interface statistics, such as packet counts and bit rates, for each enabled interface on the PIX Firewall.

NOTE   If an interface is not enabled using the System Properties tab panel, no graphs are available for that interface.

Using PDM for VPN Configuration

Chapter 10, "Virtual Private Networks," explained how to configure VPN on the Cisco PIX Firewall via the command-line interface. One of the difficult configuration and trouble-shooting issues occurs with VPNs. Quite often, typos occur when you create a VPN config-uration via the CLI. For novice administrators of the Cisco PIX Firewall, the commands and remembering their sequence can be overwhelming. The PDM presents a user-friendly VPN Wizard that creates both site-to-site and remote VPNs for the Cisco PIX Firewall. Admin-istrators are prompted for unique parameters such as IP addresses, and they use drop-down menus to configure their VPN. The following sections present step-by-step instructions on using the PDM to create both a site-to-site VPN and a remote-access VPN.

Using PDM to Create a Site-to-Site VPN

The following steps and figures show a sample site-to-site VPN configuration using the VPN Wizard on the PDM:

Step 1   Select the Site to Site VPN button, as shown in Figure 11-10, to create a site-to-site VPN configuration. This configuration is used between two IPSec security gateways, which can include Cisco PIX Firewalls, VPN concentrators, or other devices that support site-to-site IPSec connectivity. Use this panel to also select the type of VPN tunnel you are defining and to identify the interface on which the tunnel will be enabled. In Figure 11-10, the outside interface is selected as the VPN termination point.

Figure 11-10 *VPN Wizard with Site-to-Site VPN Selected*

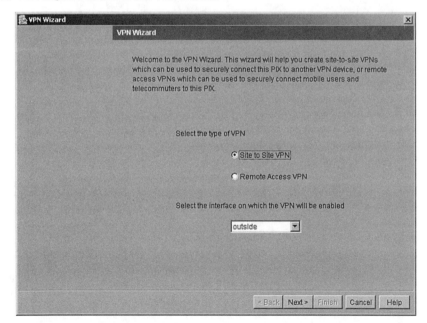

Step 2 On the Remote Site Peer panel, shown in Figure 11-11, you specify the IP address of the remote IPSec peer that will terminate the VPN tunnel you are configuring. Also, you use this panel to identify which of the following methods of authentication you want to use:

— Preshared keys

— Certificates

Figure 11-11 shows the Remote Site Peer panel configured with the remote IPSec peer and the preshared authentication keys.

Figure 11-11 *Remote Site Peer Panel*

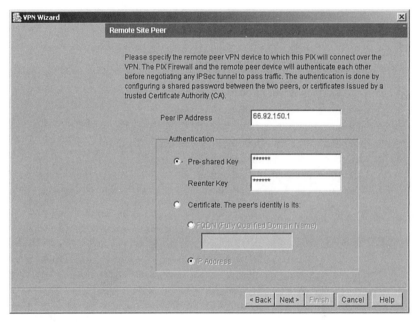

Step 3 Configure the encryption and authentication algorithms for IKE Phase I. Figure 11-12 shows the IKE Policy panel.

Step 4 Configure the transform set to specify the encryption and authentication algorithms used by IPSec, as shown in Figure 11-13. IPSec provides secure communication over an insecure network, such as the public Internet, by encrypting traffic between two IPSec peers, such as your local PIX and a remote PIX or VPN concentrator.

Figure 11-12 *IKE Policy Panel*

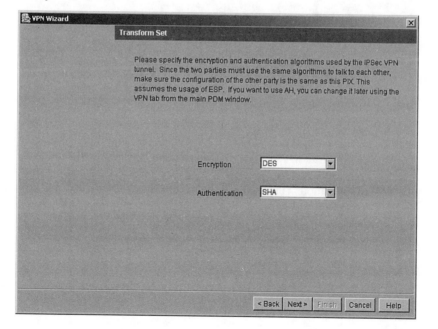

Figure 11-13 *Transform Set Panel*

Step 5 Identify the traffic you want to protect using the current IPSec tunnel, as shown in Figure 11-14. The current IPSec tunnel protects packets that are sent to or received from the hosts or networks you select on this panel. Use this panel to identify the hosts and networks protected by your local Cisco PIX Firewall. In Figure 11-14, packets that are sent to and received from the 10.1.0.0/16 network are protected.

Figure 11-14 *IPSec Traffic Selector Panel: On Local Site*

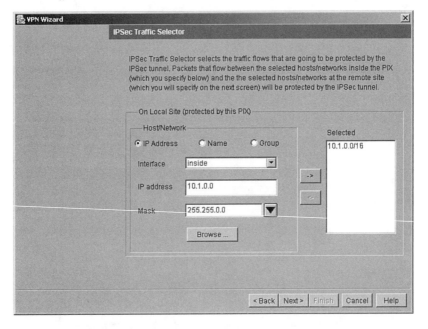

Step 6 Identify the hosts and networks protected by the remote IPSec peer, as shown in Figure 11-15.

Step 7 At this point, the site-to-site VPN configuration has been completed but not yet written to the PIX. When you click Finish, a dialog box with CLI commands appears, as shown in Figure 11-16. You can review your configuration in that dialog box and click Send to write the configuration to the PIX.

Figure 11-15 *IPSec Traffic Selector Panel: On Remote Site*

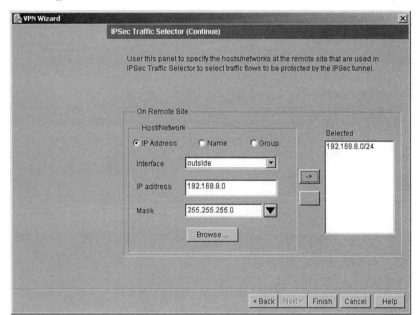

Figure 11-16 *CLI Command Preview in PDM*

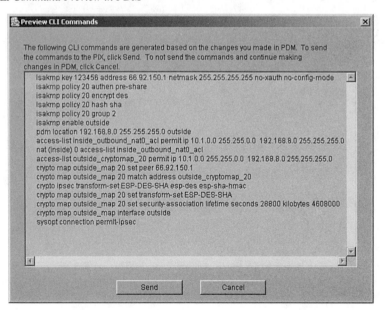

Using PDM to Create a Remote-Access VPN

With a remote-access VPN, your local Cisco PIX Firewall provides secure connectivity between individual remote users and the LAN resources protected by your local PIX.

Step 1   From the opening screen of the PDM VPN Wizard, shown in Figure 11-17, select the Remote Access VPN button to create a remote-access VPN configuration. This configuration allows secure remote access for VPN clients, such as mobile users. A remote-access VPN allows remote users to securely access centralized network resources. When you select this option, the system displays a series of panels that let you enter the configuration required for this type of VPN. In Figure 11-17, the outside interface is selected as the interface on which the current VPN tunnel will be enabled.

Figure 11-17 *VPN Wizard with Remote Access VPN Selected*

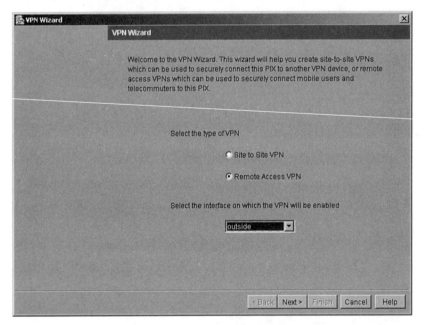

Step 2   On the Remote Access Client panel, shown in Figure 11-18, identify the type of remote access client that will use the current VPN tunnel to connect to your local Cisco PIX Firewall. The options are as follows:

—   **Cisco VPN Client**—Select this button to support remote-access clients using Cisco VPN Client v3.*x* or higher (Cisco Unified VPN Client Framework).

— **Cisco VPN 3000 Client**—Select this button to support remote-access clients using Cisco VPN 3000 Client, Release 2.5/2.6.

— **Microsoft Windows client using PPTP**—Select this button to support remote-access clients using Microsoft Windows client using Point-to-Point Tunneling Protocol (PPTP).

— **Microsoft Windows client using L2TP**—Select this button to support remote-access clients using Microsoft Windows client using Layer 2 Tunneling Protocol (L2TP).

Figure 11-18 *Remote Access Client Panel*

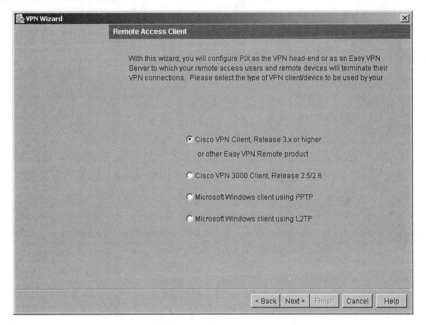

Step 3   Create a VPN client group to group remote-access users who are using the Cisco VPN client. The attributes associated with a group are applied and downloaded to the client(s) that are part of a given group. The Group Password is a preshared key to be used for IKE authentication. Figure 11-19 shows the VPN Client Group panel with Sales as a group name and Pre-shared key selected for IKE authentication.

Figure 11-19 *VPN Client Group Panel*

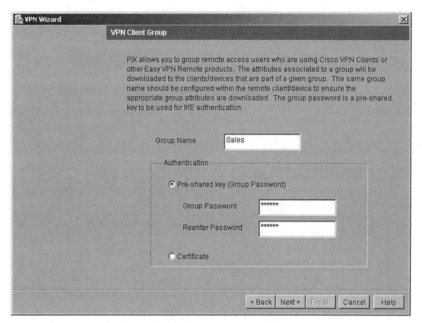

A preshared key is a quick and easy way to set up communication with a limited number of remote peers. To use this method of authentication, exchange the preshared key with the remote-access user through a secure and convenient method, such as an encrypted e-mail message.

NOTE   Preshared keys must be exchanged between each pair of IPSec peers that need to establish secure tunnels. This authentication method is appropriate for a stable network with a limited number of IPSec peers. It might cause scalability problems in a network with a large or increasing number of IPSec peers.

Step 4   Use the Extended Client Authentication panel, shown in Figure 11-20, to require VPN client users to authenticate from a AAA server for access to the private network on your PIX Firewall. Extended client authentication is optional and is not required for VPN client access to the private network.

Figure 11-20 *Extended Client Authentication Panel*

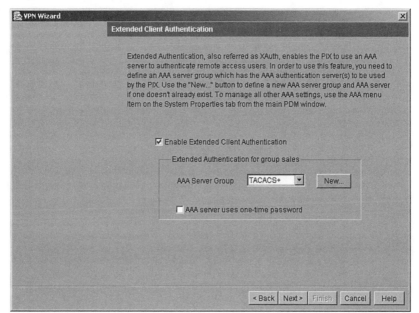

Extended authentication (Xauth) is a feature within the IKE protocol. Xauth lets you deploy IPSec VPNs using TACACS+ or RADIUS as your user authentication method. This feature, which is designed for VPN clients, provides user authentication by prompting the user for a username and password and verifies them with the information stored in your TACACS+ or RADIUS database. Xauth is negotiated between IKE Phase 1 (the IKE device authentication phase) and IKE Phase 2 (the IPSec SA negotiation phase). If Xauth fails, the IPSec security association is not established, and the IKE security association is deleted.

The AAA server must be defined before Xauth will work on the Cisco PIX Firewall. You can define the AAA server using the New button. This opens the AAA Server Group panel, where you can define the location of the AAA server, the group name, and the protocol used for AAA.

Step 5 Define the location of the AAA server, the group name, and the protocol used for AAA, as shown in Figure 11-21.

Step 6 Create a pool of local addresses that can be used to assign dynamic addresses to remote VPN clients. Enter a descriptive identifier for the address pool. Figure 11-22 shows a sample configuration for the remote sales group in the Address Pool panel.

Figure 11-21 *AAA Server Group Window*

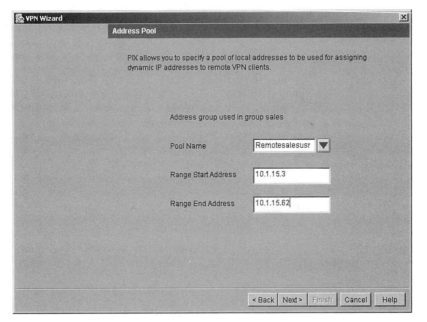

Figure 11-22 *Address Pool Panel*

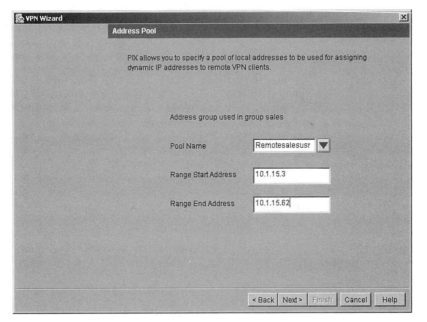

Step 7   (Optional) Configure the DNS and WINS addresses that can be pushed down to the remote client, as shown in Figure 11-23.

Figure 11-23 *Attributes Pushed to Client Panel*

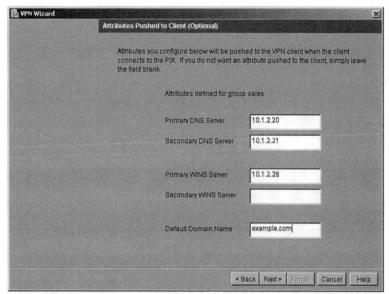

Step 8   Specify the encryption and authentication algorithms used by IKE (Phase 1), as shown in Figure 11-24.

Figure 11-24 *IKE Policy Panel*

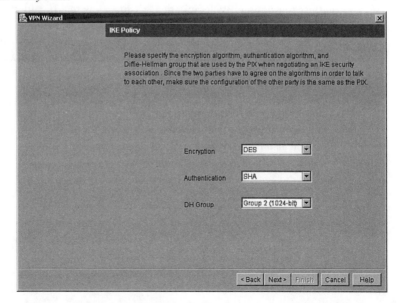

Step 9   Specify the encryption and authentication algorithms used by the IPSec
VPN tunnel, as shown in Figure 11-25.

Figure 11-25 *Transform Set Panel*

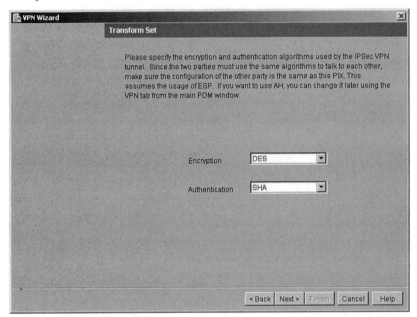

Step 10   (Optional) The Address Translation Exemption panel, shown in Figure
11-26, identifies local hosts/networks that are to be exempted from
address translation. By default, the PIX hides the real IP address of
internal networks from outside hosts through dynamic or static NAT. The
security provided by NAT is essential to minimize the risk of being
attacked by untrusted outside hosts, but it might be inappropriate for
those who have been authenticated and protected by VPN.

Step 11   After you click Finish, the PDM VPN Wizard displays your
configuration in CLI format, as shown in Figure 11-27. When you click
Send, the commands that were configured via the PDM are sent to the
PIX. You also have the option of canceling the configuration.

Figure 11-26 *Address Translation Exemption Panel*

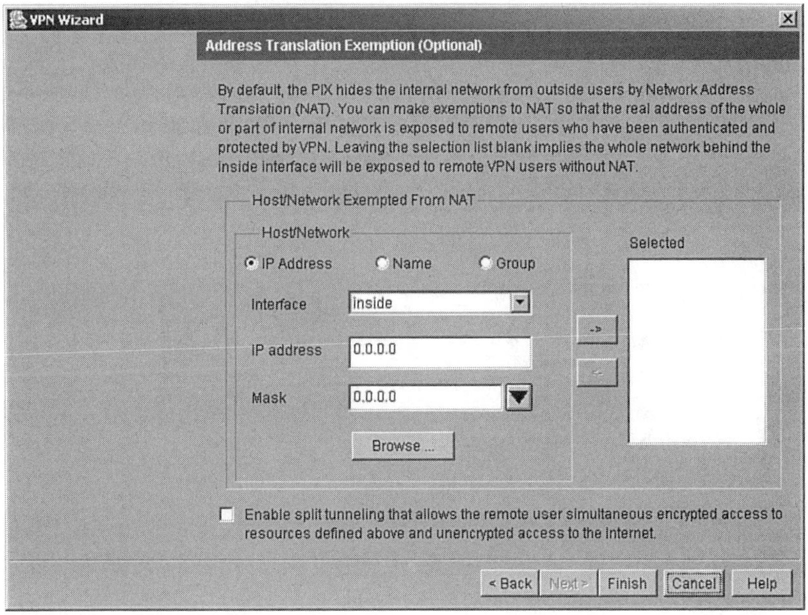

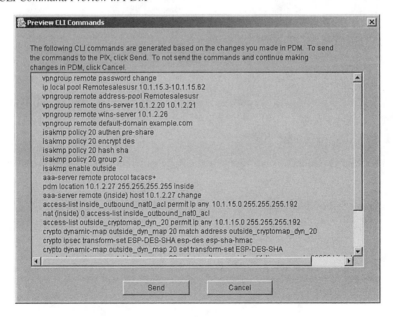

Figure 11-27 *CLI Command Preview in PDM*

Foundation Summary

PDM is a browser-based configuration tool designed to help you set up, configure, and monitor your Cisco PIX Firewall graphically. It is installed as a separate software image on the Cisco PIX Firewall and resides in the Flash memory of all PIX units running PIX version 6.0 and higher. Multiple PIX units can be monitored and configured using the PDM from a single workstation via the web browser.

PDM works with the following operating systems:

Windows Requirements

- Windows 2000 (Service Pack 1), Windows NT 4.0 (Service Pack 4 and higher), Windows 98, or Windows Me.

- Supported browsers: Internet Explorer 5.0 (Service Pack 1) or higher (5.5 recommended), Netscape Communicator 4.51 or higher (4.76 recommended). Internet Explorer is recommended due to its faster load times.

- Any Pentium or Pentium-compatible processor running at 350 MHz or higher.

- At least 128 MB of RAM. 192 MB or more is recommended.

- An 800×600-pixel display with at least 256 colors. A 1024×768-pixel display and at least High Color (16-bit) colors are recommended.

SUN Solaris Requirements

- Sun Solaris 2.6 or later running CDE or OpenWindows window manager.

- SPARC microprocessor.

- Supported browser: Netscape Communicator 4.51 or higher (4.76 recommended).

- At least 128 MB of RAM.

- An 800×600 pixel display with at least 256 colors. A 1024×768 pixel display and at least High Color (16-bit) colors are recommended.

Linux Requirements

- Red Hat Linux 7.0 running the GNOME or KDE 2.0 desktop environment.

- Supported browser: Netscape Communicator 4.75 or a later version.

- At least 64 MB of RAM.

- An 800×600-pixel display with at least 256 colors. A 1024×768-pixel display and at least High Color (16-bit) colors are recommended.

PDM uses tables, drop-down menus, and task-oriented selection menus to assist you in administering your Cisco PIX Firewall. Connection to the PDM is only allowed for SSL connection. There are six main tabs available on the PDM used to configure the Cisco PIX Firewall:

- System Properties
- Hosts/Networks
- Translation Rules
- Access Rules
- VPN
- Monitoring

The optimal configuration file size to use with PDM is less than 100 KB (which is approximately 1500 lines). Cisco PIX Firewall configuration files larger than 100 KB might interfere with PDM's performance on your workstation.

Q&A

The questions in this book are more difficult than what you should experience on the exam. The questions do not attempt to cover more breadth or depth than the exam; however, they are designed to make sure that you know the answer. Hopefully, these questions will help limit the number of exam questions on which you narrow your choices to two options and then guess. Be sure to use the CD and take the simulated exams.

The answers to these questions can be found in Appendix A.

1 How many tabs does the PDM have for configuring and monitoring the Cisco PIX Firewall?

   A Three

   B Five

   C Eight

   D Six

2 How do you connect to the PDM?

   A By accessing the PIX through Telnet and entering **PDM**

   B By entering **http://inside_interface_ip** in your browser

   C By entering **https://inside_interface_ip** in your browser

   D By entering **https://PIX_PDM**

3 What version of the PIX is required for PDM to run?

   A 5.1

   B 5.2

   C 5.3

   D 6.0

4 Which model of the Cisco PIX Firewall does PDM support?

   A 506

   B 515

   C 520

   D 525

   E 535

   F All of the above

5 Where does PDM reside?

    A   On a Windows NT/2000 server

    B   On a Red Hat Linux 7.0 server

    C   On a Solaris server

    D   All of the above

    E   In the PIX Flash memory

6 What default security mechanism does PDM employ for browsers to connect to it?

    A   RSA

    B   SSL

    C   Biometrics

    D   None of the above

7 True or false: The PDM lets conduits and access lists exist together on the PIX Firewall configuration.

8 Which of the following is a prerequisite for access rules to be created?

    A   Hosts or networks must be defined before access rule creation.

    B   Dynamic or static translation must be defined before access rule creation.

    C   There are no prerequisites.

    D   A and B

9 What is a translation exemption rule?

    A   A rule that exempts addresses from being encrypted or translated

    B   A rule that denies access to addresses

    C   A rule that increases security on selected addresses

    D   None of the above

10 PDM does *not* run on which of the following?

    A   Windows 3.1

    B   Windows 2000

    C   Linux 7.0

    D   Windows NT 4.0

This chapter covers the following exam topics for the Cisco Secure PIX Firewall Advanced Exam:

20. URL filtering

CHAPTER 12

Content Filtering with the Cisco PIX Firewall

Up to now, you have focused on how to configure the PIX and how to protect against unwanted traffic from outside in. This chapter focuses specifically on outbound traffic and content filtering—traffic moving from inside out.

More and more companies today have some form of network policy in place. Websites that are not related to their business or that are otherwise considered inappropriate are prohibited for use by their employees. This chapter discusses how the Cisco PIX Firewall mitigates some of the threats posed by Java applets and ActiveX objects and how Cisco PIX Firewall enforces URL filtering.

"Do I Know This Already?" Quiz

The purpose of this quiz is to help you determine your current understanding of the topics covered in this chapter. Write down your answers and compare them to the answers in Appendix A. The concepts in this chapter are the foundation for much of what you need to understand to pass the CSPFA Certification Exam. Unless you do exceptionally well on the "Do I Know This Already?" pretest and are 100% confident in your knowledge of this area, you should read through the entire chapter.

1 What two URL filtering servers does the PIX work with?

2 What command filters out Java applets from HTML pages?

3 Why are Java applets and ActiveX objects considered a threat?

4 How does PIX filter Java applets and ActiveX objects?

5 True or false: PIX blocks HTML tags split across network packets or tags longer than the number of bytes in the MTU.

6 What is the command to designate or identify the filtering server?

7 True or false: Cisco PIX Firewall version 5.3 supports N2H2.

8 What PIX Firewall version supports the Websense filtering server?

9 What is the longest URL filter, in bytes, that is possible with Cisco PIX Firewall version 6.1 and older?

10 What is the longest URL filtering that is supported by Cisco PIX Firewall 6.2?

11 What is the command to filter URLs?

12 If the filtering server does not respond before the web content server does, the reply from the web content server is dropped. What can you do to avoid this problem?

ActiveX controls and Java applets are designed to make the browsing experience more interactive. Based on the Component Object Model (COM), ActiveX controls are written for a specific platform of Microsoft Windows. When the user displays a page containing ActiveX or Java, the browser downloads the control dynamically. ActiveX controls are native programs, so they can do all the things that one local program can do. For example, they can read and write to the hard drive, execute programs, perform network administration tasks, and determine which system configuration they are running on. While ActiveX and Java applets can perform powerful tasks, they can also be used maliciously to damage systems.

One way to prevent the threats posed by ActiveX Java applets is at the browser or user level. Users can configure their web browsers not to run ActiveX or Java applets. Although you can disable ActiveX and Java applets within the browser, this requires a lot of effort for a large enterprise network. In these cases, it is easier to prevent the ActiveX objects and Java applets before they reach the browser.

When configured for filtering, the Cisco PIX Firewall filters or renders ActiveX objects and Java applets ineffective from HTML web pages before they reach the browser. Java and ActiveX filtering of HTML files is performed by selectively replacing the <APPLET> and </APPLET> and <OBJECT CLASSID> and </OBJECT> tags with comments.

Filtering Java Applets

The **filter java** command filters out Java applets that return to the Cisco PIX Firewall from an outbound connection. The user still receives the HTML page, but the web page source for the applet is commented out so that the applet cannot execute:

```
filter java port[-port] local_ip mask foreign_ip mask
```

The following example specifies that Java applet blocking applies to web traffic on port 80 from local subnet 10.10.10.0 and for connections to any foreign host:

```
filter java http 10.10.10.0 255.255.255.0 0 0
```

Table 12-1 describes the different parameters for the **filter** command.

Table 12-1   **filter** *Command Parameters*

Parameter	Description
activex	Blocks outbound ActiveX, Java applets, and other HTML <OBJECT> tags from outbound packets.
allow	Filters URL only. When the server is unavailable, lets outbound connections pass through Cisco PIX Firewall without filtering. If you omit this option, and if the N2H2 or Websense server goes offline, Cisco PIX Firewall stops outbound port 80 (Web) traffic until the N2H2 or Websense server is back online.
cgi_truncate	Sends a CGI script as an URL.
except	Filters URL only. Creates an exception to a previous filter condition.
foreign_ip	The IP address of the lowest security level interface to which access is sought. You can use 0.0.0.0 (or, in shortened form, 0) to specify all hosts.
foreign_mask	Network mask of *foreign_ip*. Always specify a mask value. You can use 0.0.0.0 (or, in shortened form, 0) to specify all hosts.
http	Specifies port 80. You can enter **http** or **www** instead of **80** to specify port 80.
java	Filters out Java applets returning from an outbound connection.
local_ip	The IP address of the highest security level interface from which access is sought. You can set this address to 0.0.0.0 (or, in shortened form, 0) to specify all hosts.
local_mask	Network mask of *local_ip*. You can use 0.0.0.0 (or, in shortened form, 0) to specify all hosts.
longurl-deny	Denies the URL request if the URL is over the URL buffer size limit or if the URL buffer is unavailable.
longurl-truncate	Sends only the originating host name or IP address to the Websense server if the URL is over the URL buffer limit.
mask	Subnet mask.
Parameter	**Description**
port	The port that receives Internet traffic on the Cisco PIX Firewall. Typically, this is port 80, but other values are accepted. The **http** or **url** literal can be used for port 80.
proxy-block	Prevents users from connecting to an HTTP proxy server.
url	Filters URLs from data moving through the Cisco PIX Firewall.

Filtering ActiveX Objects

The **filter activex** command filters out ActiveX and other HTML <OBJECT> usages from outbound packets. These controls include custom forms, calendars, and extensive third-party forms for gathering or displaying information. The syntax for filtering ActiveX objects is as follows:

```
filter activex port local_ip mask foreign_ip mask
```

Note that if the <OBJECT> or </OBJECT> HTML tags split across network packets or if the code in the tags is longer than the number of bytes in the MTU, Cisco PIX Firewall cannot block the tag.

Filtering URLs

Most organizations today have human resources policies whereby indecent materials cannot be brought into the workplace. Similarly, network security policies prohibit users from visiting websites that are categorized as indecent or irrelevant to business mission of organization.

Using other content-filtering vendor products, Cisco PIX Firewall enforces network security policy as it relates to URL filtering. When a user issues an HTTP request to a website, the Cisco PIX Firewall sends the request to the web server and to the filtering server at the same time. If the policy on the filtering server permits the connection, the Cisco PIX Firewall allows the reply from the website to reach the user who issued the original request. If the policy on the filtering server denies the connection, the Cisco PIX Firewall redirects the user to a block page, indicating that access was denied.

PIX works in conjunction with two types of URL filtering application servers:

- **Websense Enterprise content-filtering application**—Supported by Cisco PIX Firewall version 5.3 or later

- **N2H2 web content-filtering application**—Supported by Cisco PIX Firewall version 6.2

Identifying the Filtering Server

The **url-server** command designates the server running the N2H2 or Websense URL filtering application. The limit is 16 URL servers, and you can use only one application server at a time, either N2H2 or Websense. Additionally, changing your configuration on the Cisco PIX Firewall does not update the configuration on the application server; this must be done separately, according to the individual vendor's instructions.

The syntax for identifying the two URL filtering servers, Websense and N2H2, is slightly different. The syntax for identifying an N2H2 filtering server is as follows:

```
PIX(config)# url-server [if_name] vendor n2h2 host local_ip[:port number]
  [timeout seconds] [protocol tcp | udp]
```

The following example identifies an N2H2 filtering server with an IP address of 10.10.10.13:

```
url-server (inside) vendor n2h2 host 10.0.1.13
```

The default port used by the N2H2 server to communicate with the Cisco PIX Firewall via TCP or UDP is 4005.

The syntax for identifying a Websense filtering server is as follows:

```
PIX(config)# url-server [if_name] host local_ip [timeout seconds] [protocol tcp |
   udp version 1 | 4]
```

The following example identifies a Websense filtering server with an IP address of 10.10.10.14:

```
PIX(config)# url-server (inside) host 10.10.10.14
```

To the view the filtering server, use the **show url-server** command, as shown in Example 12-1.

Example 12-3 *Displaying the Filtering Server Information*

```
PIX(config)# show url-server
URL Server Statistics:
--------------------
URL Server Vendor              n2h2
URLs total/allowed/denied      100/95/5

URL Server Status:
-----------------
192.168.1.22          UP
171.69.1.234             DOWN
```

Configuring Filtering Policy

The **filter url** command lets you prevent outbound users from accessing URLs that you designate as inadmissible. The syntax for filtering URLs is as follows:

```
filter url port[-port] local_ip local_mask foreign_ip foreign_mask [allow]
   [proxy-block]
```

With filtering enabled, the Cisco PIX Firewall stops outbound HTTP traffic until a filtering server permits the connection. If the primary filtering server does not respond, the Cisco PIX Firewall directs the filtering request to the secondary filtering server. The **allow** option causes the Cisco PIX Firewall to forward HTTP traffic without filtering when the primary filtering server is unavailable.

The following example filters all HTTP traffic:

```
filter url http 0.0.0.0 0.0.0.0 0.0.0.0 0.0.0.0
```

You can make an exception to URL filtering policies by using the **except** parameter in the **filter url** command. For example:

```
filter url http 0 0 0 0
filter url except 10.10.10.20 255.255.255.255 0 0
```

This policy filters all HTTP traffic with the exception of HTTP traffic originating from host 10.10.10.20.

Websense protocol version 4 contains the following enhancements:

- URL filtering allows the Cisco PIX Firewall to check outgoing URL requests against the policy defined on the Websense server.

- Username logging tracks the username, group, and domain name on the Websense server.

- Username lookup lets the Cisco PIX Firewall use the user authentication table to map the host's IP address to the username.

There are instances in which the web server replies to a user HTTP request faster than the URL filtering servers. In these instances, the **url-cache** command provides a configuration option to buffer the response from a web server if its response is faster than that from the N2H2 or Websense filtering service server. This prevents the web server's response from being loaded twice, improving throughput. The syntax of the **url-cache** command is as follows:

```
url-cache {dst | src_dst} size kbytes
```

Table 12-2 describes the parameters for the **url-cache** command.

Table 12-2   url-cache *Command Parameters*

Parameter	Description
dst	Caches entries based on the URL destination address. Select this mode if all users share the same URL filtering policy on the N2H2 or Websense server.
src_dst	Caches entries based on the source address initiating the URL request and the URL destination address. Select this mode if users do not share the same URL filtering policy on the N2H2 or Websense server.
size kbytes	Specifies a value for the cache size within the range 1 to 128 KB.

Use the **url-cache** command to enable URL caching, set the size of the cache, and display cache statistics.

Caching also stores URL access privileges in memory on the Cisco PIX Firewall. When a host requests a connection, the Cisco PIX Firewall first looks in the URL cache for matching access privileges instead of forwarding the request to the N2H2 or Websense server.

The **clear url-cache** command removes **url-cache** command statements from the configuration, and the **no url-cache** command disables caching.

Filtering Long URLs

Cisco PIX Firewall version 6.1 and earlier versions do not support filtering URLs longer than 1159 bytes. Cisco PIX Firewall version 6.2 supports filtering URLs up to 6000 bytes for the Websense filtering server. The default is 2000 bytes. In addition, Cisco PIX Firewall version 6.2 introduces the **longurl-truncate** and **cgi-truncate** parameters to allow handling of URL requests longer than the maximum permitted size. The format for these options is as follows:

```
filter url [http | port[-port] local_ip local_mask foreign_ip foreign_mask] [allow]
   [proxy-block] [longurl-truncate | longurl-deny | cgi-truncate]
```

- **longurl-truncate** causes the Cisco PIX Firewall to send only the host name or IP address portion of the URL for evaluation to the filtering server when the URL is longer than the maximum length permitted.

- **longurl-deny** denies outbound traffic if the URL is longer than the maximum permitted.

- **cgi-truncate** sends a CGI script as the URL.

Cisco PIX Firewall version 6.2 supports a maximum URL length of 1159 bytes for the N2H2 filtering server. To increase the maximum length of a single URL (for Websense only), enter the following command:

```
url-block url-size size
```

The value of the *size* variable is 2 to 6 KB.

Viewing Filtering Statistics and Configuration

The **show url-cache** command with the **stat** option displays the URL caching statistics. Example 12-2 demonstrates sample output from this command.

Example 12-4   **show url-cache** *Command Output*

```
PIX(config)# show url-cache stat
URL Filter Cache Stats
----------------------
    Size:      128KB
 Entries:      1415
  In Use:         1
 Lookups:         0
    Hits:         0
```

The significant fields in this output are as follows:

- **Size**—The size of the cache in kilobytes, set with the **url-cache** *size* option.

- **Entries**—The maximum number of cache entries based on the cache size.

- **In Use**—The current number of entries in the cache.

- **Lookups**—The number of times the Cisco PIX Firewall has looked for a cache entry.

- **Hits**—The number of times the Cisco PIX Firewall has found an entry in the cache.

You can view more statistics about URL filtering and performance with the **show url-server stats** and **show perfmon** commands, respectively. Example 12-3 shows output from **show url-server stats**.

Example 12-5 **show url-server stats** *Command Output*

```
PIX(config)# show url-server stats
URL Server Statistics:
----------------------
Vendor                          Websense
URLs total/allowed/denied       2370/1958/412
URL Server Status:
------------------
10.10.10.13     UP
10.10.10.14     DOWN
```

Example 12-4 shows output from the **show perfmon** command.

Example 12-6 **show perfmon** *Command Output*

```
PIX(config)# show perfmon
PERFMON STATS:    Current      Average
Xlates            0/s          0/s
Connections       0/s          2/s
TCP Conns         0/s          2/s
UDP Conns         0/s          0/s
URL Access        0/s          2/s
URL Server Req    0/s          3/s
TCP Fixup         0/s          0/s
TCPIntercept      0/s          0/s
HTTP Fixup        0/s          3/s
FTP Fixup         0/s          0/s
AAA Authen        0/s          0/s
AAA Author        0/s          0/s
AAA Account       0/s          0/s
```

Foundation Summary

The **filter url** command lets you prevent outbound users from accessing World Wide Web URLs that you designate using one of the following URL filtering applications:

- Websense Enterprise web filtering application—Supported by PIX Firewall version 5.3 or later

- Filtering by N2H2 for IFP-Enabled Devices—Supported by PIX Firewall version 6.2

When a user issues an HTTP request to a website, the PIX Firewall sends the request to the web server and to the filtering server at the same time. If the filtering server permits the connection, the PIX Firewall allows the reply from the website to reach the user who issued the original request. If the filtering server denies the connection, the PIX Firewall redirects the user to a block page, indicating that access was denied.

Q&A

The questions in this section are designed to ensure your understanding of the concepts discussed in this chapter and adequately prepare you to complete the exam. You should use the simulated exams on the CD to practice for the exam.

The answers to these questions can be found in Appendix A.

1 How does PIX filter Java applets and ActiveX objects?

   A By commenting out the <OBJECT> </OBJECT> or <APPLET> </APPLET> tags in the HTML page.

   B By deleting the <OBJECT> </OBJECT> or <APPLET> </APPLET> tags in the HTML page.

   C It notifies the content filtering server, which in turn disables the ActiveX objects and Java applets.

   D PIX does not filter ActiveX objects or Java applets.

2 What is the command to designate or identify the filtering server?

   A **filter url-server**

   B **url-server**

   C **filtering server**

   D **server url**

3 True or false: Cisco PIX Firewall version 4.4 supports N2H2.

4 What is the longest URL filtering that is supported by Cisco PIX Firewall 6.2 with Websense Enterprise filtering software?

   A 12 KB

   B 15 KB

   C 4 KB

   D 6 KB

5 What is the command to filter URLs?

   A **filter url**

   B **url-filter**

   C **url-server**

   D .**filter web page**

6 What happens when the only filtering server is unavailable?

    A If the **allow** option is set, the PIX forwards HTTP traffic without filtering.

    B HTTP traffic is dropped, because the filtering server is unavailable.

    C HTTP requests are queued until the filtering server is available.

    D PIX reverts to the onboard filtering engine to filter HTTP traffic.

7 What is the default port used by the N2H2 server to communicate with the Cisco PIX Firewall?

    A TCP/UDP 1272

    B TCP 5004 only

    C TCP/UDP 4005

    D UDP 5004 only

8 What command identifies Websense servers on a Cisco PIX Firewall?

    A **websense url filter** *server_ip*

    B **filter url** *server_ip* **vendor n2h2**

    C **url-server** [*if_name*] **vendor n2h2 host** *local_ip*

    D All of the above

9 How many URL servers can be configured on a single Cisco PIX Firewall?

    A 5

    B 12

    C 3

    D 16

10 What command disables URL caching on the Cisco PIX Firewall?

    A **no url-cache**

    B **caching-url**

    C **disable url-cache**

    D None of the above

This chapter covers the following exam topics for the Cisco Secure PIX Firewall Advanced Exam:

29. Introduction to AAA
30. Installation of CSACS for Windows NT/2000

CHAPTER 13

Overview of AAA and the Cisco PIX Firewall

This chapter presents authentication, authorization, and accounting, more commonly known as AAA. It discusses how the Cisco PIX Firewall is incorporated with AAA servers and the relationship between the Cisco PIX Firewall and the AAA server(s). This chapter also introduces the Cisco Secure Access Control Server (CSACS), a AAA server product offered by Cisco.

Chapter 6, "Getting Started with the Cisco PIX Firewall," addresses the commands necessary to configure the Cisco PIX Firewall. You might remember that the importance of remembering the PIX commands was mentioned in the Introduction. In the real world, it is possible to navigate your way around a PIX and figure out a command's correct syntax. This is not possible in the testing environment. You are asked to select a command that performs a certain function from a list of very similar commands. It is very important that you under-stand the correct syntax for each PIX command.

How to Best Use This Chapter

If you are very familiar with AAA, but you aren't very familiar with the CSACS, you should skim the first half of this chapter to reinforce your knowledge of AAA and focus on the installation of CSACS. The AAA process is relatively simple to understand, although there are quite a few different configuration options. This chapter explains the AAA process, discusses how the Cisco PIX Firewall fits into this process, and covers the installation of CSACS.

"Do I Know This Already?" Quiz

The purpose of this quiz is to help you determine your current understanding of the topics covered in this chapter. Write down your answers and compare them to the answers in Appendix A. If you have to look at any references to correctly answer the questions about PIX functionality, you should read that portion and double-check your thinking by reviewing the Foundation Summary. The concepts in this chapter are the foundation for much of what you need to understand to pass the CSPFA Certification Exam. Unless you do exceptionally well on the "Do I Know This Already?" pretest and are 100% confident in your knowledge of this area, you should read through the entire chapter.

1 What is the relationship between the Cisco PIX Firewall and the AAA server?

2 What three methods are used to authenticate to the Cisco PIX Firewall?

3 How does the Cisco PIX Firewall process cut-through proxy?

4 What are the main differences between RADIUS and TACACS+?

5 What patch level must you have Windows 2000 Professional configured to before you install CSACS?

6 Why is it important to authenticate a user before completing authorization?

7 What are the three layers of authentication?

8 What is the purpose of the explain box during the CSACS installation?

9 What do you need to verify before installing CSACS?

10 Why is it important to have Internet Explorer up to date on your CSACS?

Foundation Topics

Overview of AAA and the Cisco PIX Firewall

Authentication, authorization, and accounting (AAA) has become an extremely important component in any network infrastructure. AAA is used in our everyday lives not only for network security, but also for physical security, or any other function that requires access control. This chapter discusses the AAA process, its components, the responsibilities of each component, and how the Cisco PIX Firewall fits into the equation.

Definition of AAA

The best way to understand AAA is to break up the pieces and look at them individually. The three components of AAA are distinctly different, and each has its own responsibility. AAA is now integrated into nearly every situation that requires access control. Access control can be applied to users, hosts on a network (such as servers and workstations), networking components (such as routers, switches, VPN appliances, and firewalls), and other automated devices that require access and that perform a function. This chapter discusses AAA as it pertains to a user, but you will see how the principles can apply to many automated functions. The three components of AAA are as follows:

- **Authentication**—The process of validating an identity. The identity that is being validated could be a user, a computer, a networking component, and so on. Authentication is by far the most important step. No access is granted until the requestor has been authenticated. There are three layers of user authentication:

  - **What the user knows**—This normally is a user password or passphrase.

  - **What a user has**—This normally is a user token or badge issued to the user by whomever has authority over what the user is attempting to access.

  - **What a user is**—This area includes biometrics—checking the user's fingerprint or retinal scan against a stored image in the database.

  Many organizations do not incorporate all three layers of authentication; however, it is very common to use a minimum of two layers at one time.

- **Authorization**—After the user has been authenticated, he or she is granted access rights to perform specific functions.

- **Accounting**—After the user is granted access, the accounting function tracks what tasks the user performed and saves that information is a log that can be reviewed later. Accountability of users and their actions is an issue that is becoming increasingly important in the security of enterprise networks.

The three functions of AAA can be performed by a single server or can be divided among several servers. Most large enterprise networks create a hierarchy of AAA servers, with the lower-level servers tending to user functions and the upper-level servers working as a central point for updating and distributing user information.

AAA and the Cisco PIX Firewall

So how does the PIX factor into the AAA equation? Any user requesting access or a service that is configured for authentication and who goes through the PIX is prompted by the firewall for a username and password. If the PIX has a local database configured for user authentication, it matches this user information against that database and permits or denies access. If the PIX is configured to use a separate AAA server, it forwards the user information to that server for authentication and authorization. In this case, the PIX and the AAA server act in a client/server mode, with the PIX being the client. The PIX acts as a *Network Access Server (NAS)* but operates as a client to the AAA server. It is a common practice to configure redundant AAA servers. It is also possible to configure a local database on the PIX for use when no other AAA servers can be contacted.

NOTE   The local user database on a Cisco PIX Firewall can be processor-intensive and should be used only for small organizations with a limited number of users.

Remember that the AAA server not only authenticates the user but also tells the firewall what the user is authorized to do. If a user is authorized to access websites via HTTP and attempts to connect to the same servers over FTP, that connection is dropped at the firewall even though that user has been authenticated. Additionally, the AAA server should log the fact that the user attempted to make a connection that was outside his or her authority.

Cut-Through Proxy

Cut-through proxy is a feature on the Cisco PIX Firewall that allows transparent AAA services and a seamless connection through the firewall to the destination. It provides significantly better performance than application proxy firewalls because it completes user authentication at the application layer, verifies authorization against the security policy, and then opens the connection as authorized by the security policy. In other words, the connection request needs to go up to the application layer only once to be authorized. After that, all authorized traffic is passed at the lower layers, dramatically increasing the rate at which it can pass through the firewall.

There are three ways to connect to the Cisco PIX Firewall and activate the cut-through proxy:

* HTTP
* FTP
* Telnet

The firewall responds to each of these connections with a username and password prompt. Figure 13-1 shows the Telnet user authentication prompt. The user information is either authenticated against a local database on the PIX or forwarded to a AAA server for authentication. After the user is authenticated, the firewall completes the connection that is requested (if authorized).

Figure 13-1   *Telnet Logon Prompt*

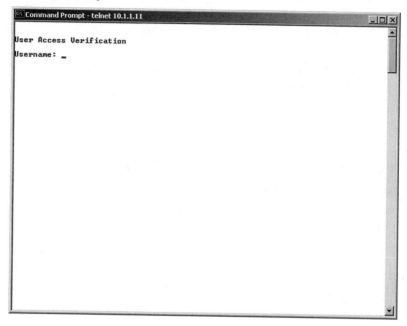

Figure 13-2 shows the steps for cut-through proxy on a Cisco PIX Firewall.

Figure 13-2   *Cut-Through Proxy Steps*

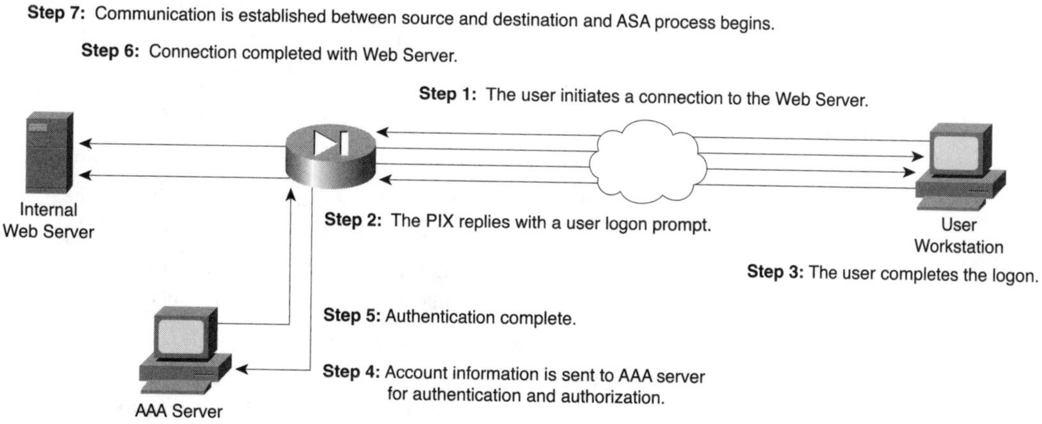

Step 7: Communication is established between source and destination and ASA process begins.

Step 6: Connection completed with Web Server.

Step 1: The user initiates a connection to the Web Server.

Internal
Web Server

Step 2: The PIX replies with a user logon prompt.

User
Workstation

Step 3: The user completes the logon.

Step 5: Authentication complete.

Step 4: Account information is sent to AAA server
for authentication and authorization.

AAA Server

Supported AAA Server Technologies

The Cisco PIX Firewall supports two AAA server authentication protocols:

- **Remote Authentication Dial-In User Service (RADIUS)**—RADIUS was developed by Livingston Enterprises as a AAA server. It uses a UDP connection between the client (NAS) and the server (AAA). RADIUS combines the authentication and authorization into a single response to a query from the NAS.

- **Terminal Access Controller Access Control System (TACACS+)**—TACACS+ was developed by Cisco Systems as an alternative to RADIUS. TACACS+ uses a TCP connection between the client and server and divides the authentication and authorization into separate transmissions.

Cisco Secure Access Control Server (CSACS)

CSACS is a AAA server product developed by Cisco that can run on Windows NT/2000 Server. It supports a number of NASs, including the Cisco PIX Firewall. CSACS supports both RADIUS and TACACS+.

Minimum Hardware and Operating System Requirements for CSACS

Table 13-1 documents the minimum requirements needed by a system to run CSACS.

Table 13-1 *CSACS System Requirements*

System Requirement Type	Requirements
Hardware	Pentium III Processor, 550 MHz or greater
	256 MB of RAM
	250 MB of available drive space. Additional space is required if you intend to run the CSACS database on this system.
	Screen resolution of 800×600 256-color display
Operating system	Microsoft Windows NT Server with Service Pack 6a
	Microsoft Windows 2000 Server with Service Pack 1 or 2
	Microsoft Windows 2000 Advanced Server with Service Pack 1 or 2, without Microsoft Clustering Services installed
	Microsoft Windows 2000 Datacenter Server with Service Pack 1 or 2, without Microsoft Clustering Services installed
Browser	Microsoft Internet Explorer 5.0 or 5.5 with Java and JavaScript enabled
	Netscape Communicator 4.76 with Java and JavaScript enabled

Installing CSACS on Windows 2000/NT Server

You can download a 90-day trial version of CSACS from the Cisco Software Center at
www.cisco.com. You must register as a user to receive your *CCO login*. You must have the
CCO login to download software from the software center. The installation of CSACS is an
easy step-by-step process. It is a good idea to verify that your Windows NT or Windows
2000 Server is up to the current patch level. When you are ready to begin the installation,
just run setup.exe. Figure 13-3 shows the initial CSACS installation screen.

Figure 13-3   *CSACS Splash Screen*

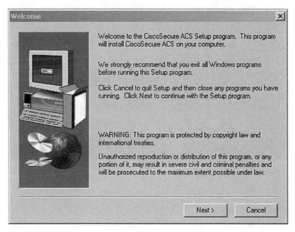

The second screen, shown in Figure 13-4, prompts you to verify that your system is ready
for this installation. Before this installation, you should verify that your NT/2000 server is
up to date, including Internet Explorer, and that you have connectivity with the NAS. In this
case, the PIX functions as the NAS.

Figure 13-4   *Before Installation Screen*

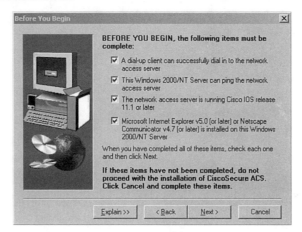

You are prompted to specify the installation directory, as shown in Figure 13-5. You can use the default directory, C:\Program Files\Cisco Secure ACS V3.0, or you can select another directory for the installation.

Figure 13-5 *Installation Directory (Default)*

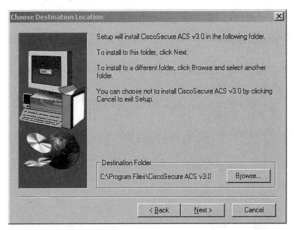

You also select either the CSACS user database or the CSACS database and the Windows NT/2000 user database combined. The latter selection lets you use Windows username/password management and integrate Windows performance monitoring, which provides you with real-time login statistics.

For the purpose of this installation, the CSACS database only is used. Figure 13-6 shows this installation screen.

Figure 13-6 *User Database Screen*

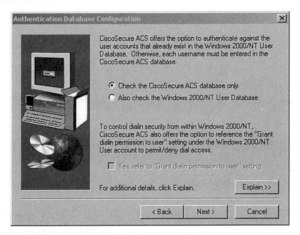

You are prompted to select any of ten possible choices for the connection type to the NAS, as shown in Figure 13-7. Remember that the Cisco PIX Firewall is acting as the NAS. For this configuration, **TACACS+ (Cisco IOS)** is selected. Having selected the **Authenticate Users Using** selection, you need to finish the NAS information to complete the connection between the AAA server and the NAS. Figure 13-8 shows the NAS information box. Note the **Explain** button in the lower-right corner. Click this button to get an explanation of each of the settings, as shown in Figure 13-9.

Figure 13-7 *NAS Technology*

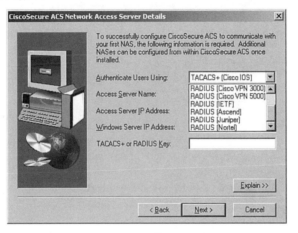

Figure 13-8 *NAS Information*

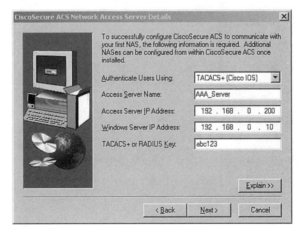

Figure 13-9 *Explanation of Settings*

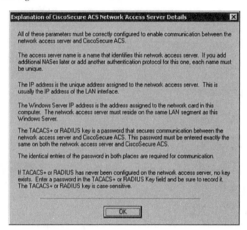

You are prompted to select the advanced features you want to appear on the user interface. This allows you to determine how much (or how little) detail you want to see when working in the user interface. Figure 13-10 shows the available selections, and Figure 13-11 shows the explanation screen that describes each of the available options.

Figure 13-10 *Available Options in the User Interface*

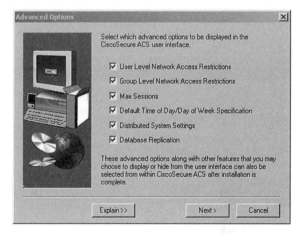

Figure 13-11 *Explanation of Options*

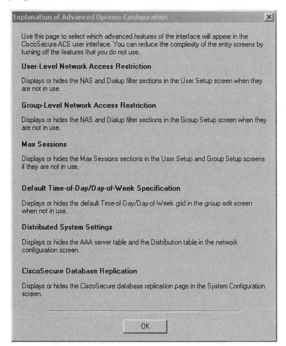

Next you select from three actions for the AAA server to initiate in the event of a communications failure between the CSACS and the NAS. These settings also include SMTP settings and the user account for the CSACS to send an alert to if a failure occurs. Figures 13-12 and 13-13 show the settings screen and the settings explanation screen.

Figure 13-12 *Alert Action and Notification Settings*

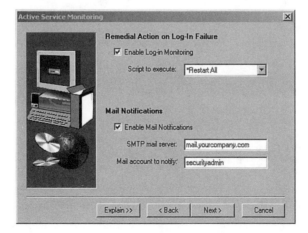

Figure 13-13 *Explanations for Alert Action and Notification Settings*

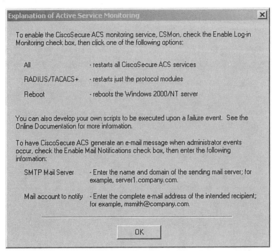

Congratulations! You have completed the installation of CSACS on a Windows 2000 Server. After completing the review questions, feel free to proceed to Chapter 14, "Configuration of AAA on the PIX Firewall," to configure CSACS.

Foundation Summary

Authentication, authorization, and accounting are three separate functions performed by AAA servers to allow access to resources. Each of these functions has a specific goal. No one is granted access of any kind until he or she is authenticated.

- **Authentication**—Identifies the entity (user).
- **Authorization**—Gives the user access based on his or her profile.
- **Accounting**—Maintains a record of user access.

The Cisco PIX Firewall can maintain an internal user database or connect to an external AAA server. The PIX supports both RADIUS and TACACS+ technologies. Figure 13-14 shows the steps that the AAA server takes during the entire AAA process.

Figure 13-14 *AAA Server Steps*

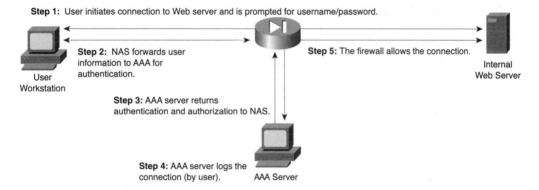

CSACS is available for both Windows NT/2000 Server and UNIX and can be configured for TACACS+ and RADIUS. The CSACS installation on Windows 2000 is an easy step-by-step (Install Wizard) installation.

Q&A

As mentioned in the Introduction, the questions in this book are more difficult than what you should experience on the exam. The questions do not attempt to cover more breadth or depth than the exam; however, they are designed to make sure that you know the answer. Hopefully, these questions will help limit the number of exam questions on which you narrow your choices to two options and then guess. Be sure to use the CD and take the simulated exams.

The answers to these questions can be found in Appendix A.

1 What platforms does CSACS support?

   A Windows XP Professional

   B UNIX

   C Windows NT Workstation

   D Windows 2000 Professional

2 Why is it important to do accounting on your network?

3 What options are available to authenticate users on a PIX Firewall?

   A Local user database

   B Remote RADIUS server

   C Remote TACACS+ server

   D All of the above

4 What two technologies does the CSACS support?

5 True or false: Cut-through proxy authenticates users and then allows them to connect to anything.

6 True or false: The CSACS installation on Windows NT/2000 Server is a relatively simple Installation Wizard.

7 Which of the following are *not* connection types for authenticating to a PIX Firewall? (Select all that apply.)

   A Telnet

   B SSH

   C FTP

   D HTTPS

This chapter covers the following exam topics for the Cisco Secure PIX Firewall Advanced Exam:

29. Overview of AAA
20. Installation of CSACS for Windows NT/2000
31. Authentication configuration
32. Downloadable ACLs

Configuration of AAA on the Cisco PIX Firewall

This chapter addresses the commands necessary to configure authentication, authorization, and accounting (AAA) on the Cisco PIX Firewall. You might remember that the importance of remembering the PIX commands was mentioned in the Introduction. In the real world, it is possible to navigate your way around a PIX and figure out the correct syntax for a command. This is not possible in the testing environment. You will be asked to select a command that performs a certain function from a list of very similar commands. It is *very* important that you understand the correct syntax for each PIX command.

How to Best Use This Chapter

This chapter covers the communication between the Cisco PIX Firewall and the Cisco Secure Access Control Server (CSACS). You will learn to configure the PIX to work with a AAA server, and you will learn to configure the CSACS to work with the PIX. The configurations for authentication, authorization, and accounting are very similar and should be relatively simple to remember. Quite a few commands and options are available for configuring each AAA component, but each is used for nearly every component. The CSACS is a simple GUI-controlled package that includes online help. You need to become familiar with the tabs on the navigation bar and how the different configurations interact.

"Do I Know This Already?" Quiz

The purpose of this quiz is to help you determine your current understanding of the topics covered in this chapter. Write down your answers and compare them to the answers in Appendix A. If you have to look at any references to correctly answer the questions about PIX functionality, you should read that portion and double-check your thinking by reviewing the Foundation Summary. The concepts in this chapter are the foundation of much of what you need to understand to pass the CSPFA Certification Exam. Unless you do exceptionally well on the "Do I Know This Already?" pretest and are 100% confident in your knowledge of this area, you should read through the entire chapter.

1 True or false: The **show aaa** command shows you everything that has to do with your AAA server in its configuration.

2 Both your Cisco PIX Firewall and your CSACS are configured for TACACS+, but you cannot configure the downloadable PIX ACLs. What is the problem?

3 What is the command to get authorization to work with access lists?

4 What is the one type of database you do *not* want to implement for a large enterprise network with many users?

5 What tab on the CSACS is used to configure the PIX, and what is the firewall considered?

6 What three services are used to authenticate by default in the PIX?

7 How do you put text messages into the logon prompt for a Telnet session?

8 What three messages can you change with the **auth-prompt** command?

9 If your **timeout uauth** is set to 0:58:00, when is the user prompted to reauthenticate after the session times out?

10 What does the option **inactivity** in the **timeout uauth** command mean?

11 What two formats can logs be written to using the CSACS?

12 If you create a user on the CSACS and do not assign that user to a group, what group is he or she automatically assigned to?

13 You have added a new RSA SecurID Token Server to the network. In which two places do you configure the CSACS to use it?

14 What command is most commonly used to check your AAA configuration on the PIX?

Foundation Topics

Chapter 13, "Overview of AAA and the Cisco PIX Firewall," provided a good overview of the AAA process and the CSACS for Windows 2000. This chapter addresses the configuration of the Cisco PIX Firewall and the CSACS required to build an operational AAA solution. The PIX must be configured to communicate with the CSACS, and the CSACS must be configured to control the PIX. Although the PIX configuration is completed using the command-line interface, the commands required are rather simple and fairly intuitive. The CSACS is completely web-based, with instructions on every page, and it is very simple to configure. After completing this chapter, you should be intimately familiar with the configurations of both the Cisco PIX Firewall and the CSACS combined as a functional AAA solution.

Specifying Your AAA Servers

Only two components are required to build a AAA solution:

- AAA server
- Network Access Server (NAS)

It is possible to divide the AAA functions between multiple devices to reduce the processing required by any single server. It is also possible for a single AAA server to support multiple NASs. The point is that there is no single solution. The number of AAA servers and NASs should be tailored to support the size and scope of the network being accessed. Configuring the PIX to connect to a AAA server requires only a few commands. Of course, quite a few options are available with each command. In this exercise, the Cisco PIX Firewall is configured to connect to a CSACS located on the DMZ segment. Figure 14-1 depicts the network configuration used for the examples in this chapter. Note that the CSACS is located on a DMZ segment rather than on the inside or outside segments. This allows you to restrict access to the CSACS from either segment, making the system more secure.

Figure 14-1 *Cisco PIX Firewall and CSACS Topology for This Chapter*

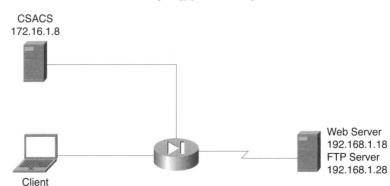

Configuring AAA on the Cisco PIX Firewall

Four steps are required to configure AAA on the PIX Firewall. Each of these steps must be completed for the PIX to communicate with the AAA servers:

Step 1 Identify the AAA server

Step 2 Configure authentication

Step 3 Configure authorization

Step 4 Configure accounting

Step 1: Identifying the AAA Server and NAS

You must be sure to have the correct information about your AAA server before attempting to configure your PIX. The **aaa-server** command is used (from configuration mode on the PIX) to specify the AAA server. Remember that you are dealing with at least two devices: the PIX and the CSACS.

You must configure the PIX to recognize the CSACS as its AAA server for authentication. You must also configure the CSACS to communicate with the PIX with the necessary account information so that the CSACS can validate authentication requests from the PIX. To accomplish both tasks, you need to use the following commands:

```
aaa-server group_tag protocol auth_protocol
aaa-server group_tag (if_name) host server_ip key timeout seconds
```

You must define the following command options and parameters for the configuration to be successful:

- **aaa-server**—Designates the AAA server or server group. A group can have up to 14 servers, and the PIX can handle up to 14 groups of AAA servers, for a total of 196 AAA servers. This allows you to tailor which AAA servers handle certain services and lets you configure your AAA servers for redundancy. When a user logs in, the NAS contacts the first server in the group (see the *group_tag* description). If it does not receive a response within the designated timeout period, it moves to the next server in the group.

- *group_tag*—The name used for the AAA server group. The *group_tag* is also used in the **aaa authentication**, **aaa authorization**, and **aaa accounting** commands.

- **protocol** *auth_protocol*—The type of AAA server used—TACACS+ or RADIUS.

- *if_name*—The interface name for the interface on which the AAA server resides. This designates how the firewall connects to the AAA server.

- **host** *server_ip*—The AAA server's IP address.

- *key*—A shared secret between the CSACS (server) and the PIX (client). It is an alphanumeric password that can be up to 127 characters.

- **timeout** *seconds*—How long the PIX waits between transmission attempts to the AAA server. The PIX makes four attempts to connect with the AAA server before trying to connect to the next AAA server in the group. The default timeout is 5 seconds; the maximun timeout is 30. Using the default timeout of 5 seconds, the PIX attempts four transmissions, waiting 5 seconds between each attempt, for a total of 20 seconds.

For the network example in this chapter, you would enter the syntax shown in Example 14-1.

Example 14-7 *Identifying AAA Servers on the PIX*

```
tgpix (config)# aaa-server TACACS+ protocol tacacs+
tgpix (config)# aaa-server TACACS+ (DMZ) host 172.16.1.8 abc123 timeout 20
```

For smaller networks with a limited number of users, you can authenticate to a database configured locally on the Cisco PIX Firewall. This is not a recommended configuration for medium to large networks, because the processing required to maintain and authenticate against a local database reduces the firewall's performance. The command to configure authentication to a local database is

```
aaa-server local
```

You finish configuring the CSACS to connect to the PIX by selecting the PIX during the CSACS installation, as shown in Figure 14-2.

Figure 14-2 *Selecting the Network Access Server*

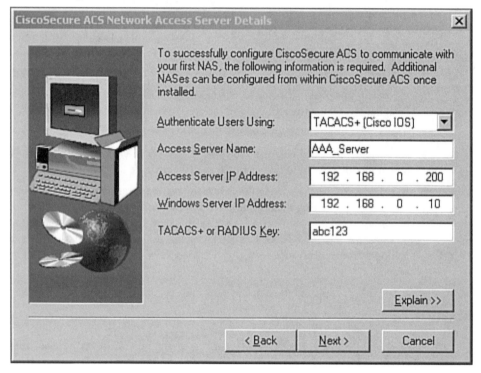

You also can create additional NASs or edit the current NAS settings in CSACS by selecting the Network Configuration tab on the CSACS main screen. Remember that the CSACS calls the NAS the "AAA client." Figure 14-3 shows the settings for the PIX Firewall in the CSACS.

Figure 14-3 *Configuring NAS in CSACS*

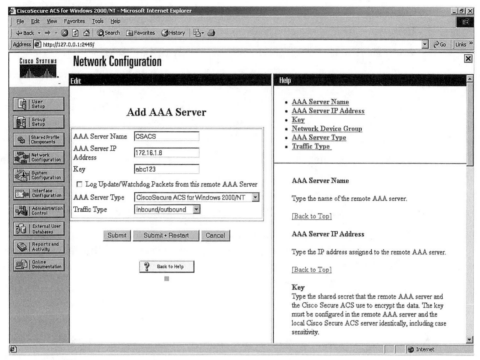

NOTE	The TACACS+ or RADIUS key specified on CSACS must exactly match the key specified in the **aaa-server** command for communication between the CSACS server and the NAS to be established.

Step 2: Configuring Authentication

Now that you have the AAA server and the NAS configured to communicate with each other, you need to configure both for user authentication. First you need to configure the authentication parameters on the Cisco PIX Firewall, and then you need to create the user accounts on the CSACS. Three types of authentication are supported on the PIX Cisco Firewall:

- TACACS+
- RADIUS
- LOCAL

The **aaa authentication** command has three different types. The following list describes the options and variables you find collectively within all three:

- **include**—Creates a rule with a specified service.

- **exclude**—Creates an exception to a previously defined rule.

- *authen_service*—The service that is included or excluded. It is the application with which the user accesses the network. The PIX Firewall can authenticate only via FTP, HTTP, and Telnet. You can configure the *authen_service* as "any" to allow the PIX to authenticate any of the three, but this does not allow your users to authenticate using any protocol other than FTP, HTTP, or Telnet.

- **inbound**—Specifies that the PIX is to authenticate inbound traffic (originates on the inside interface and is directed to the outside interface).

- **outbound**—Specifies that the PIX is to authenticate outbound traffic (originates on the outside interface and is directed to the inside interface).

- *if_name*—The interface name from which the users should be authenticated. This is optional. By default, the user must authenticate before being allowed through the PIX Firewall. Therefore, outbound traffic authenticates at the inside interface, and inbound traffic authenticates at the outside interface.

- *local_ip*—The host address or network segment with the highest security level. As with the other address definitions on the PIX Firewall, 0 is used to define "any."

- *local_mask*—The subnet mask that applies to the *local_ip*. 0 is used to define "any."

- *foreign_ip*—Defines the address space with the lowest security level. The use of 0 defines "any."

- *foreign_mask*—The subnet mask that applies to the *foreign_ip*. 0 is used to define "any."

- *group_tag*—The name used for the AAA server group. The *group_tag* is also used in the **aaa-server**, **aaa authorization**, and **aaa accounting** commands.

The following sections describe the three different formats and functions of the **aaa authentication** command in greater detail.

Manually Designating AAA Authentication Parameters

The first command allows you to manually designate the authentication parameters using the items in the preceding list. The syntax for this command is as follows:

```
aaa authentication include/exclude authen_service inbound/outbound if_name local_ip
  local_mask foreign_ip foreign_mask group_tag
```

Example 14-2 shows the syntax for requiring all inbound traffic to authenticate except for traffic connecting to host 192.168.1.28 based on the network shown in Figure 14-1.

Example 14-8   *Configuring AAA Authentication on the PIX*

```
tgpix (config)# aaa authentication include any inbound 0 0 0 0 TACACS+
tgpix (config)# aaa authentication exclude http inbound 192.168.1.28
  255.255.255.255 0 0 TACACS+
```

Note that the *local_ip* listed is a public address. This is because inbound traffic cannot route to a private address. To configure this authentication, you must ensure that you have a static address translation or NAT configured for your *local_ip* and that you list the translated address as the *local_ip*.

Designating AAA Authentication Parameters Via Access Lists

It is also possible to configure your AAA authentication to reference access lists using the **match** command. This configuration removes the requirement of manually defining the local and foreign addresses. The syntax for AAA authentication using access lists is as follows:

> aaa authentication match *acl_name* inbound | outbound *if_name group_tag*

Example 14-3 is an example of the **aaa authentication** command including the referenced access list.

Example 14-9   *Configuring* **aaa authentication match**

```
tgpix (config)# static (inside.outside) 192.168.200.1 10.10.10.10 netmask
  255.255.255.255
tgpix (config)# access-list PIXTEST permit tcp any host  192.168.200.2 eq 80
tgpix (config)# access-group PIXTEST in interface outside

tgpix (config)# aaa authentication match PIXTEST inbound TACACS+
```

The static translation and access group are also included in this example because each is required in order to have the correct public address and to apply the access list.

NOTE   Chapter 7, "Configuring Access," discusses access lists in greater detail.

One additional command you should use when configuring authentication is **sysopt uauth allow-http-cache**. This command allows the HTTP cache for user authentication, which prevents the user from having to reauthenticate when navigating the Internet when HTTP authentication is required.

Console Access Authentication

The final type of AAA authentication is for direct connections to the Cisco PIX Firewall. It is very important to restrict access to the firewalls as much as possible. One way to increase your firewall's security is to require all access to the firewall to be authenticated by a AAA server. The **aaa authentication console** command prompts the user to authenticate differently, depending on the method used to access the Cisco PIX Firewall:

- **serial**—Causes the user to be prompted before the first command of the command-line prompt when connecting directly to the firewall via a serial cable. The user is continually prompted until he or she successfully logs in.

- **telnet**—Causes the user to be prompted before the first command-line prompt when attempting a Telnet session to the CLI. The user is continually prompted until he or she successfully logs in.

- **ssh**—Causes the user to be prompted before the first command-line prompt when attempting a Secure Shell (SSH) session to the CLI. If the user is unable to successfully authenticate within three attempts, he or she is disconnected and receives the message "Rejected by Server."

- **http**—This option is selected when you use the PIX Device Manager (PDM) to manage your Cisco PIX Firewall. PDM users see a pop-up window in their browser (PIX Device Manager). The user is continually prompted until he or she successfully logs in.

- **enable**—With this option, the PIX requires AAA server authentication to enter privileged mode. The **enable** option prompts the user for a username and password before entering privileged mode for serial, Telnet, and SSH connections. If the user is unable to successfully authenticate after three attempts, he sees the "Access Denied" message.

NOTE   By default, the PDM can access the Cisco PIX Firewall with no username and the enable password unless the **aaa authentication http console** *group_tag* command is set.

The PIX supports usernames up to 127 characters and passwords up to 63 characters. Usernames and passwords cannot contain the @ character. The PDM is limited to a maximum of 30 characters for the username and 15 characters for the password.

NOTE   To remove the **aaa authentication** from the configuration, enter **no aaa authentication**.

Authentication of Services

The Cisco PIX Firewall is designed to authenticate users via FTP, HTTP, and Telnet. Many other services passing through the PIX require authentication. To fulfill this requirement, the PIX supports *virtual services*. The Cisco PIX Firewall can perform functions for servers that do not exist and allow the PIX to authenticate users who want to connect to services other than FTP, HTTP, and Telnet. After the user has been authenticated, he can access whatever authorized services he is requesting.

Your company uses Microsoft NetMeeting to communicate between its many different branch offices. NetMeeting runs on the H.323 protocol, which uses a number of different ports. To allow this access, users must authenticate via FTP, HTTP, or Telnet. If you do not have a server available to accept the FTP, HTTP, or Telnet connections, you can configure the Cisco PIX Firewall to accept the connections via a virtual service.

Virtual Telnet

Vitrual Telnet allows the user to authenticate using Telnet and use a service that does not support authentication. The PIX accepts the user's connection and challenges him for a username and password. The username and password are verified by the TACACS+ or RADIUS server. If the user successfully authenticates, the connection to his requested service is completed. An additional server is not required to accept the connection, because the Cisco PIX Firewall creates a virtual server to handle the authentication requests. Virtual Telnet sessions can be inbound or outbound on the PIX.

To configure virtual Telnet on the Cisco PIX Firewall, you must first create the virtual server on a segment that can be reached via the PIX. Normally this is an address on the firewall's outside interface. In Figure 14-4, the virtual IP address is 192.168.1.4. This public IP address can be accessed from both inside networks and public networks (such as the Internet). The syntax of the **virtual telnet** command is as follows:

```
virtual telnet ip_address
```

Figure 14-4 *Assigning the IP for Virtual Services*

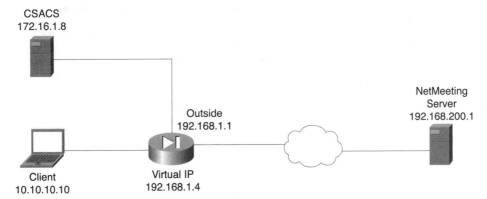

Example 14-4 shows the virtual Telnet configuration that authenticates host 10.10.10.10 when you make an outbound connection to a NetMeeting server located on the Internet.

Example 14-10 *Configuring Virtual Telnet Outbound Connections*

```
tgpix (config)# ip address outside 192.168.1.1 255.255.255.0
tgpix (config)# ip address inside 10.10.10.1 255.255.255.0
tgpix (config)# global (outside) 1 192.168.1.20-192.168.1.40 netmask 255.255.255.0
tgpix (config)# nat (inside) 1 0 0 0
tgpix (config)# aaa-server TACACS+ protocol tacacs+
tgpix (config)# aaa-server TACACS+ (DMZ) host 172.16.1.8 abc123 timeout 20
tgpix (config)# aaa authentication include telnet outbound 0 0 0 0 TACACS+
tgpix (config)# virtual telnet 192.168.1.4
tgpix (config)# static (inside, outside) 192.168.1.5 10.10.10.10 netmask
  255.255.255.255 0 0
tgpix (config)# access-list NetMeeting permit tcp 192.168.200.1 255.255.255.255
  10.10.10.10 255.255.255.255 any eq H323
tgpix (config)# access-group NetMeeting in outside
```

Now let's change the positions of the client and server. This time the NetMeeting server is behind the Cisco PIX Firewall, and the client is on the Internet. The PIX configuration must change to allow the inbound traffic to connect to the NetMeeting server. First, the NetMeeting server needs to have a public IP address, which means that you need to perform static translation. Second, you need to configure the access lists to allow the inbound traffic. Example 14-5 shows the configuration required to allow inbound connections to a destination on the protected network.

Example 14-11 *Configuring Virtual Telnet Inbound Connections*

```
tgpix (config)# ip address outside 192.168.1.1 255.255.255.0
tgpix (config)# ip address inside 10.10.10.1 255.255.255.0

tgpix (config)# global (outside) 1 192.168.1.20-192.168.1.40 netmask 255.255.255.0
tgpix (config)# nat (inside) 1 0 0 0
tgpix (config)# aaa-server TACACS+ protocol tacacs+
tgpix (config)# aaa-server TACACS+ (DMZ) host 172.16.1.8 abc123 timeout 20
tgpix (config)# aaa authentication include telnet outbound 0 0 0 0 TACACS+
tgpix (config)# virtual telnet 192.168.1.4
tgpix (config)# static (inside, outside) 192.168.1.5 10.10.10.10 netmask
  255.255.255.255 0 0
tgpix (config)# access-list NetMeeting permit tcp 192.168.200.1 255.255.255.255
  10.10.10.10 255.255.255.255 any eq H323
tgpix (config)# access-group NetMeeting in outside
```

NOTE   To remove the **virtual telnet** from the configuration, enter **no virtual telnet**.

Virtual HTTP

Virtual HTTP functions similarly to virtual Telnet in that the PIX acts as the HTTP server via an additional IP assigned to the firewall. The user might believe that he is accessing the web server, but he is actually accessing the virtual server for the authentication prompt, being authenticated by a AAA server, and ridirected to his destination after successful authentication. The syntax for **virtual http** is

```
virtual http ip_address
```

Normally the *ip_address* should be an address in the inside network segment. This way, the internal users access it directly, and the external users connect to it via static address translation at the firewall. Of course, the inbound users require authentication and also must be permitted by an access list or conduit. Example 14-6 depicts the configuration for virtual HTTP on the PIX Firewall.

Example 14-12 *Configuring Virtual HTTP Inbound Connections*

```
tgpix (config)# ip address outside 192.168.1.1 255.255.255.0

tgpix (config)# ip address inside 10.10.10.1255.255.255.0

tgpix (config)# global (outside) 1 192.168.1.20-192.168.1.40 netmask 255.255.255.0
tgpix (config)# nat (inside) 1 0 0 0
tgpix (config)# aaa-server TACACS+ protocol tacacs+
tgpix (config)# aaa-server TACACS+ (DMZ) host 172.16.1.8 abc123 timeout 20
tgpix (config)# static (inside, outside) 192.168.1.5 10.10.10.5 netmask
  255.255.255.255 0 0
tgpix (config)# aaa authentication include any inbound 192.168.1.5 255.255.255.255
  0 0 TACACS+
tgpix (config)# access-list WebTest permit tcp any host 192.168.1.5 255.255.255.255
  eq www
tgpix (config)# access-group WebTest in outside
tgpix (config)# virtual http 192.168.1.5
```

NOTE	To remove the **virtual http** from the configuration, enter **no virtual http**.

Authentication Prompts

The **auth-prompt** command is used to configure the exact text used when the user is challenged to authenticate, successfully authenticates, or does not authenticate. This command sets the text for FTP, HTTP, and Telnet session authentication. The syntax of this command is

```
auth-prompt [prompt | accept | reject] string
```

The *string* is the text that is displayed. It can be up to 235 characters in length for FTP and Telnet connections. It is limited to 120 characters for HTTP connections using Netscape Navigator and 37 characters for HTTP connections using Microsoft Internet Explorer. The *string* should not include any special characters. It ends with either a question mark (?) or by pressing the enter key.

The **auth-prompt** command has three options:

- **prompt**—The text that is displayed when the user is prompted to authenticate: "Access to this location is restricted, please provide username and password".

- **accept**—Configures the text displayed if the user successfully authenticates using a Telnet session: "User Authentication complete, please continue". No text is displayed for authentication using FTP or HTTP.

- **reject**—Configures the text displayed if the user is unable to successfully authenticate using a Telnet session: "Authentication unsuccessful, if you feel that you have received this message in error please contact your systems administrator". The text for FTP and HTTP authentication sessions cannot be configured on the PIX.

Authentication Timeout

After a user is successfully authenticated, his or her user information is saved in cache for a predetermined amount of time. You set this time by configuring the **timeout uauth** command. It is specified in hours, minutes, and seconds. If the user session idle time exceeds the timeout, the session is terminated, and the user is prompted to authenticate during the next connection. To disable caching of users, use the **timeout uauth 0** command. Be sure not to use **timeout uauth 0** when using **virtual http**. This setting prevents any connections to the real web server after successful authentication at the Cisco PIX Firewall.

NOTE   If the firewall is performing NAT, the **timeout uauth** value must be less than the **timeout xlate** value to ensure that the user authentication times out before the address translation.

Two command options or settings are associated with the **timeout uauth** command:

- **absolute**—The default setting for the **uauth** timer. This setting sets the timer to prompt the user to reauthenticate after the timer elapses only when the user starts a new connection. If the user leaves the session open and the timer elapses, and he closes the browser without clicking another link, he is not prompted to reauthenticate. Setting the **uauth** timer to **0** disables caching of user authentication and therefore disables the **absolute** option.

- **inactivity**—The period of inactivity that must occur before the timer starts. This is how long the system waits before it considers a connection idle.

Example 14-7 depicts the **timeout** command with the **absolute** and **inactivity** settings. The first command sets the timer to 4 hours and tells the system not to prompt the user after the session times out unless he initiates another session. The second command defines a 30-minute period of inactivity as an idle session and tells the system to start the timer at that point.

Example 14-13 *Configuring Timeout on the PIX*

```
tgpix (config)# timeout uauth 4:00:00 absolute
tgpix (config)# timeout uauth 0:30:00 inactivity
```

The final command associated with timeouts is **clear uauth.** This command forces the system to delete the authorization cache for all users. This makes the system reauthenticate every user when they initiate their next connection.

Step 3: Configuring Authorization

When discussing authorization, you should first understand the difference between authentication and authorization:

- Authentication identifies who the user is.

- Authorization determines what the user can do.

- Authentication is valid without authorization.

- Authorization is invalid unless the user has successfully authenticated.

Authorization is not a requirement, but rather a method of allowing you to become more granular in what access you give specific users. After users have successfully authenticated, they can be given the access they have requested. This access is configured using the **aaa authorization** command. The syntax for the **aaa authorization** command is very similar to the **aaa authentication** command, except for the service. The Cisco PIX Firewall does not permit or deny any traffic based solely on the **aaa authorization** commands. This configuration merely tells the firewall which services it needs to reference the AAA server for authorization before allowing or denying the connection. A TACACS+ server performs AAA authorization. The server is configured using the following syntax:

```
aaa authorization tacacs_server_tag
```

tacacs_server_tag specifies the TACACS+ server to be used for authorization.

author_service is the service defined for **aaa authorization**. The *author_service* parameter defines any service that requires authorization by listing them as **include** or **exclude** and defining the direction the request is travleing as **outbound** or **inbound**. Services not listed are implicitly authorized. *author_service* can be **any, ftp, http, telnet,** or *protocol/port*. Authorization of services is configured using the following syntax:

```
aaa authorization include | exclude author_service inbound | outbound if_name local_ip
   local_mask foreign_ip foreigh_mask
```

Example 14-8 shows the commands used to authorize outbound DNS requests and all inbound services except HTTP requests from 192.168.1.28 to any destination.

Example 14-14 *Configuring Authorization on the PIX*

```
tgpix (config)# aaa authorization include any inbound outside 0 0 0 0 TACACS+
tgpix (config)# aaa authorization exclude http inbound outside 192.168.1.28
  255.255.255.255 0 0 TACACS+
tgpix (config)# aaa authorization include udp/53 outbound inside 0 0 0 0 TACACS+
```

NOTE   To remove the **aaa authorization** from the configuration, enter **no aaa authorization**.

CSACS and Authorization

After the Cisco PIX Firewall is configured correctly, you must configure authorization on your CSACS. If your CSACS is already configured with the PIX as the NAS, a few steps remain to configure authorization:

Step 1   Configure user accounts within the CSACS.

Step 2   Assign users to a group.

Step 3   Apply authorization rules to the group.

Steps 1 and 2: Configuring User Accounts Within the CSACS and Assigning Users to a Group

To configure new users in CSACS, select the User Setup tab on the left navigation bar. When the User Setup windows appears, enter the username in the User: box, and then click Add/Edit, as shown in Figure 14-5. You see the screen shown in Figure 14-6.

In the User Setup window, the administrator can configure many options pertaining to the user account:

- **Account Disabled**—Lets you create accounts for users who are not yet ready to begin using the system. For example, suppose you are told that the company has hired a new employee who is scheduled to begin working in three weeks. You can configure the user account and then turn it on when the new employee starts work.

- **Supplementary User Info**—An optional field for entering user information. It is a very good idea to complete these fields, because they help you keep track of your user accounts as your user base grows:

  - **Real Name**—The user's name, not the user account name.

  - **Description**—A desription of the user. Normally this field describes the user's position within the company.

Figure 14-5 *Creating User Accounts on the CSACS*

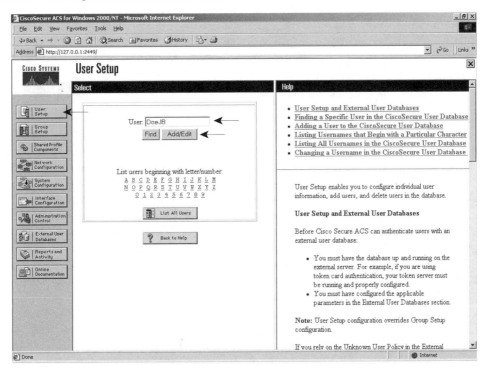

- **User Setup**—Select the type of authentication database, and enter the user password:

  — **Password Authentication**—Two types of password authentication are available on the CSACS by default. You can add a number of additional authentication types using the External User Databases tab on the left navigation bar. Select the authentication type from the drop-down menu:

  CiscoSecure Database—Authenticates the user from a database installed locally on the CSACS.

  Windows NT/2000—Authenticates the user against a Windows NT/2000 that is located on the same system that is running the CSACS.

  External User Database—You can add multiple configurations for each of the following authentication services: Vasco Token Server, RSA SecurID Token Server, RADIUS Token Server, External ODBC Database, Windows NT/2000, Novell NDS, Leap Proxy RADIUS Server, Generis LDAP, SafeWord Token Server, CryptoCard Token Server, AXENT Token Server, and ActivCard Token Server.

Figure 14-6 *Configuring User Accounts on the CSACS*

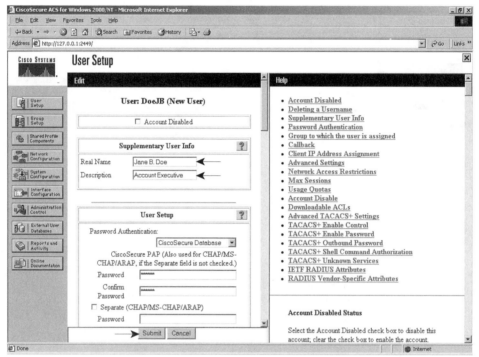

— **Password and Confirm Password**—Enter and confirm the user's password.

— **Separate (CHAP/MS-CHAP/ARAP) Password**—This feature is not used on the PIX Firewall.

— **Group to which the user is assigned**—Select a user group from the drop-down box. All users are assigned to the Default Group unless they are specifically assigned to another group. Grouping the users and applying rules to groups allows you to efficiently administer the authentication services.

— **Callback**—This feature is not used on the PIX Firewall.

— **Client IP Address Assignment**—This feature is not used on the PIX Firewall.

• **Network Access Restrictions**—Defines per-user network access restrictions.

• **Max Sessions**—Contains three radio buttons that define the maximum number of concurrent sessions the user can have:

— **Unlimited**—The user can maintain an unlimited number of concurrent sessions through the firewall.

— **Fill in the box**—Defines the maximum number of concurrent sessions.

— **Use group settings**—The default setting. The maximum number is defined at the group level.

- **Account Disable**—Configures the parameters for disabling a user account based on the date or a number of failed logon attempts. Do not confuse this option with the **Account Disabled** option at the top of the User Setup page.

    — **Never**—The default setting. It allows the user unlimited attempts to log on.

    — **Disable account if**:

    Date exceeds—Select the date from the drop-down boxes. The default setting is 30 days after the account is created.

    Failed attempts exceed—Add the number of allowed failed attempts to the box.

    An indicator shows the number of failed attempts since the last successful logon.

    There is a check box for you to reset the failed attempts count on submit.

Step 3: Applying Authorization Rules to the Group

Now that the user account is created and the user is assigned to a group, it is time to apply authorization rules to the group. Select the Group Setup tab on the navigation bar on the left.

Figure 14-7 shows the available selections in the initial Group Setup window.

Figure 14-7 *Configuring a Group Setup on the CSACS*

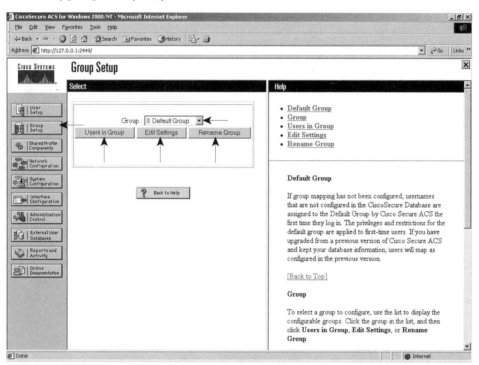

You can select the group from the drop-down box and select any of three options for that group:

- **Users in Group**—Replaces the Help window on the right side of the screen with a list of the users assigned to the selected group, as shown in Figure 14-8. Each username is a link to that user's configuration in the User Setup.

- **Edit Settings**—This option allows you to edit the specific settings for the selected group. This is where the authorization rules are applied to the group.

- **Rename Group**—Groups can be renamed to simplify administration. Users can be added to groups based on like positions or job functions (such as marketing, sales, infrastructure, and security).

Figure 14-8 *Users in Group*

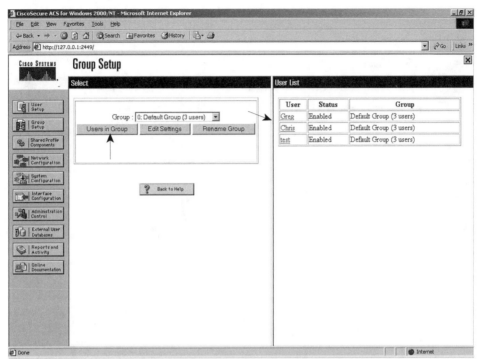

- You configure commands by editing the settings for a specific group. Select Group Setup from the navigation bar, click Edit Settings, and scroll down to the Shell Command Authorization Set. You see radio buttons and a Command box that is a subset, as shown in Figure 14-9.

To configure shell command authorization for AAA clients using TACACS+, set the options in this section as applicable:

- **None**—If you do not want to apply TACACS+ shell command authorization for users belonging to this group, select this option (This is the option selected in Figure 14-9).

- **Assign a Shell Command Authorization Set for any network device**—To apply a shell command authorization set to all TACACS+ AAA clients, select this option and then select the set you want from the corresponding list.

Figure 14-9 *Command Authorization Sets*

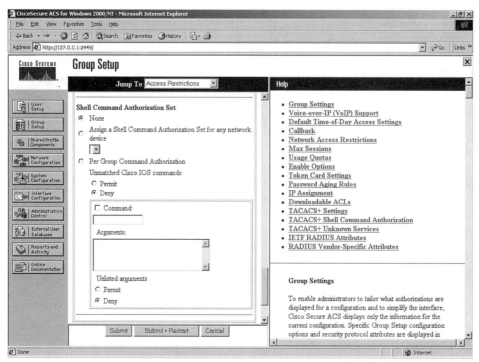

- **Assign a Shell Command Authorization Set on a per Network Device Group Basis**—To apply a shell command authorization set to the TACACS+ AAA clients belonging to a particular Network Device Group (NDG), select this option, and then use the following options:

  - **Device Group**—From the list, select the NDG to which you want to assign a shell command authorization set.

  - **Command Set**—From the list, select the shell command authorization set you want to apply to the NDG.

  - **Add Association**—Click to add the NDG and command set selected to the Device Group/Command Set list.

  - **Remove Associate**—To remove an NDG/command set association, select from the Device Group/Privilege list the NDG/command set association you want to remove, and then click Remove Associate.

NOTE   Shell command authorization sets are created and configured in the Shared Profile Components window.

- **Per Group Command Authorization**—To set TACACS+ shell command authorization on a command-by-command basis, select this option, and then use the following options:
  - **Unmatched Cisco IOS commands**—To determine how CSACS handles commands that you do not specify in this section, select either Permit or Deny as applicable.
  - **Command**—Select this check box, and then enter the Cisco IOS command in the corresponding box.
  - **Arguments**—For each argument of the Cisco IOS command, specify whether the argument is to be permitted or denied. These should be entered in the format **permit** *argument* or **deny** *argument*. This allows you to specify which commands are permitted or denied.
  - **Unlisted Arguments**—To permit only the arguments listed, select Deny. To allow users to issue all arguments not specifically listed, select Permit. This setting allows you to permit or deny all commands and arguments not listed previously.

Step 4: Configuring Accounting

You have successfully configured both your Cisco PIX Firewall and CSACS for authentication and authorization. The final portion is to configure accounting. Accounting is used to track specific traffic passing through the firewall. It also ensures that users are performing functions in keeping with company policies. Log data is commonly stored and can be used to investigate employees who are using their Internet connections for activities not authorized by the employer. The general syntax for the command that accomplishes accounting is as follows:

```
aaa accounting include | exclude acctg_service inbound | outbound | if_name local_ip
  local_mask foreign_ip foreign_mask group_tag
```

The following items are defined within the **aaa accounting** command:

- **include**—Create a rule with a specified service.
- **exclude**—Create an exception to a previously defined rule.
- *acctg_service*—The service that is included or excluded. It is the service that the user is requesting access to the network. You can configure *acctg_service* as **any**, **ftp**, **http**, **telnet**, or *protocol/port*. When you configure *protocol/port,* the *protocol* is listed as a number:

- ICMP—1
- TCP—6
- UDP—17

- **inbound**—Specifies that the PIX is to authenticate inbound traffic (originates on the inside interface and is directed to the outside interface).

- **outbound**—Specifies that the PIX is to authenticate outbound traffic (originates on the outside interface and is directed to the inside interface).

- *if_name*—The interface name from which the users should be authenticated. This is optional. By default, the user must authenticate before being allowed through the PIX Firewall. Therefore, outbound traffic authenticates at the inside interface, and inbound traffic authenticates at the outside interface.

- *local_ip*—The host address or network segment with the highest security level. As with the other address definitions on the PIX Firewall, 0 is used to define "any."

- *local_mask*—The subnet mask that applies to the *local_ip*. 0 is used to define "any."

- *foreign_ip*—Defines the address space with the lowest security level. The use of 0 defines "any."

- *foreign_mask*—The subnet mask that applies to the *foreign_ip*. 0 is used to define "any."

- *group_tag*—The name used for the AAA server group. The *group_tag* is also used in the **aaa-server**, **aaa authorization**, and **aaa accounting** commands.

Example 14-9 shows how to configure AAA accounting on the PIX.

Example 14-15 *Configuring AAA Accounting on the PIX*

```
tgpix (config)# aaa accounting include any inbound 0 0 0 0 TACACS+
tgpix (config)# aaa accounting include any outbound 0 0 0 0 TACACS+
```

As with authentication and authorization, it is possible to configure the PIX to match an access list, as demonstrated in Example 14-10.

Example 14-16 *Configuring AAA Accounting to Match an ACL*

```
tgpix (config)# static (inside.outside) 192.168.200.2 10.10.10.10 netmask
  255.255.255.255
tgpix (config)# access-list PIXTEST permit tcp any host 65.197.254.5 eq 80
tgpix (config)# access-group PIXTEST in interface outside
tgpix (config)# aaa accounting match PIXTEST inbound TACACS+
```

NOTE   To remove the **aaa accounting** from the configuration, enter **no aaa accounting**.

Viewing Accounting Information in Cisco Secure

Now that the Cisco PIX Firewall is configured to perform accounting, you need to ensure that the CSACS is properly configured to log the events. Select System Configuration, as shown in Figure 14-10, select the Logging tab on the navigation bar, and check off the log format and the items you want to log (see Figure 14-11). Logs can be saved in a .CSV (flat file) or ODBC (database) format.

Figure 14-10 *CSACS System Configuration Options Screen*

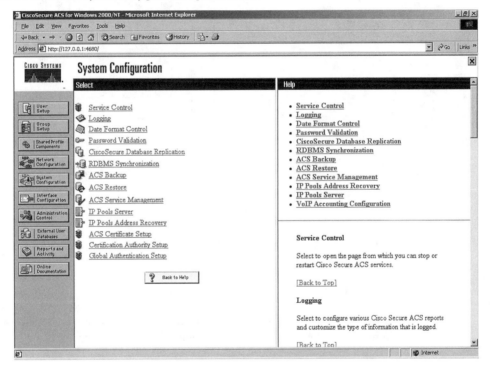

Figure 14-11 *CSACS Logging Targets and Options Screen*

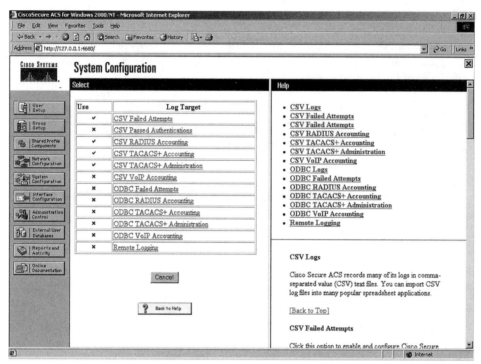

You can view several reports from the CSACS browser interface. Select Reports and Activity from the navigation bar (see Figure 14-12) and choose the report you want by clicking the applicable button in the left window. Reports are available for TACACS+ and/ or RADIUS only if a AAA client has been configured to use that protocol.

Figure 14-12 *CSACS Reports and Activity Options Screen*

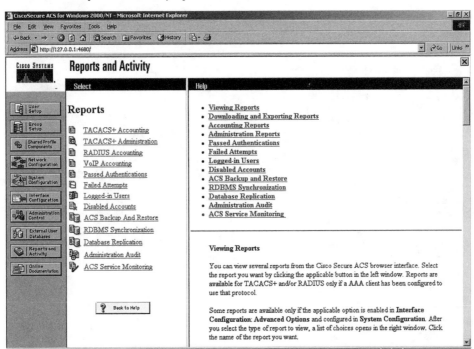

Some reports are available only if the applicable option is enabled in the Interface Config-uration: Advanced Options panel (see Figure 14-13) and configured in System Configu-ration. After you select the type of report to view, a list of choices appears in the right window. Click the name of the report you want.

Figure 14-13 *Interface Configuration Options for CSACS Reports*

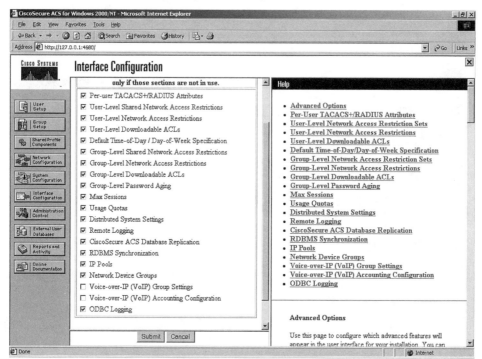

Cisco Secure and Cut-Through Configuration

Cut-through proxy is a feature of the Cisco PIX Firewall that allows it to open connections after authenticating and authorizing a user with the AAA server. This feature was discussed in Chapters 1 and 2. The user initiates a connection to his or her destination and is prompted for a username and password by the PIX. The user-provided information is verified by the AAA server, and the connection is allowed by the firewall.

Configuring Downloadable PIX ACLs

Version 3.0 of CSACS allows you to create a "downloadable ACL" using the shared profile component. The downloadable ACL configuration is supported for RADIUS servers only. To verify that your configuration is for a RADIUS server, select Network Configuration from the navigation bar and click AAA Client. Verify that RADIUS (Cisco IOS/PIX) is selected, as shown in Figure 14-14.

Figure 14-14 *RADIUS (Cisco IOS/PIX) Configuration*

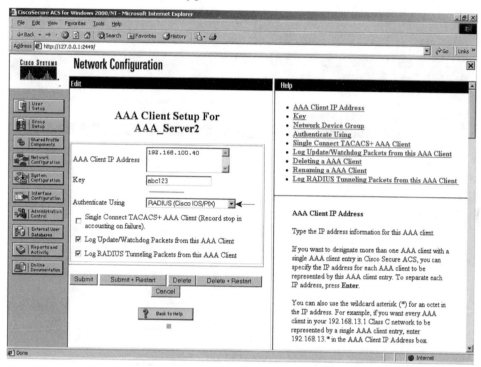

Select Shared Profile Components from the navigation bar, click the link for Downloadable PIX ACL, and select Add.

NOTE   If you are not configured for a RADIUS server, the Downloadable PIX ACL link is unavailable.

Add the following information in the Downloadable PIX ACLs configuration box, and click Submit:

- **Name**—The access list name.
- **Description**—A description of the access list.
- **ACL Definitions**—A test of the command. This should use the same format as the command used on the PIX Firewall, except for the access list name. It is also not necessary to add the access list to an access group. This is done automatically when the ACL is downloaded to the PIX Firewall.

Figure 14-15 shows a downloadable ACL configured to allow outbound access to www.cisco.com.

Figure 14-15 *Creating a Downloadable ACL*

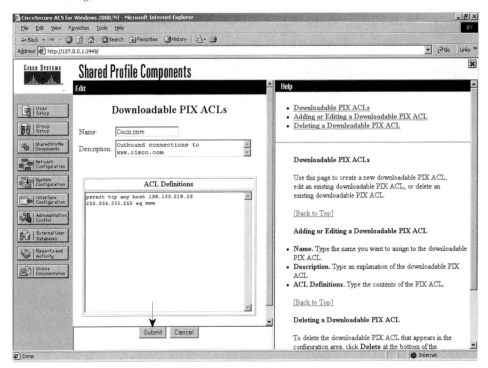

After you configure the downloadable ACL in Shared Profile Components, you can add it to either an individual user setup or a group setup. Figure 14-16 shows the Downloadable ACLs box in Group Setup. To add the downloadable ACL to the group, simply check the box and select the ACL name from the drop-down box.

Figure 14-16 *Selecting a Downloadable ACL*

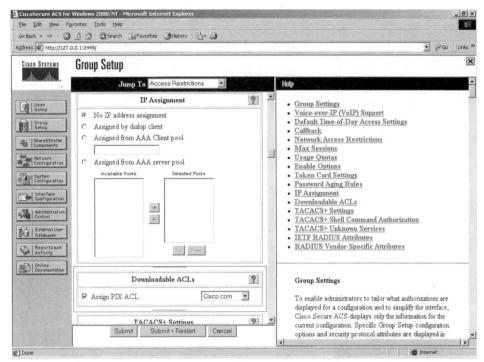

Troubleshooting Your AAA Setup

Troubleshooting your AAA configuration can be a simple function or a difficult process, depending on how complicated the configuration is and how well you documented it. It is always in your best interests to document any configuration and to be as detailed as possible when doing so. It is also recommended that you use best practices such as adding users to groups and applying rules to groups rather than to users, using a *standardized* naming convention, and completing the description fields and comment blocks when creating elements, rules, components, and so on. Neglecting these basic steps can turn a relatively simple issue into an extremely difficult troubleshooting event. It is also a good idea to remember the basic troubleshooting method of "divide and conquer." In other words, don't start checking the PIX or the CSACS configurations until you have verified connectivity between the two devices.

Checking the PIX Firewall

The most effective command for troubleshooting the PIX firewall is **show**. The **show** command is run in configuration mode and can be used to show the configuration for all the AAA components on the PIX. The following is a list of the **show** commands pertaining to the AAA configuration:

- **show aaa-server**—Shows you the different *group_tags*, which protocol is used for each *group_tag,* and the *ip_address, key,* and *timeout* for each AAA server.

- **show aaa**—Provides you with the output of the following commands:

  - **show aaa authentication**—Shows you all AAA authentication rules.

  - **show aaa authorization**—Shows you all AAA authorization rules.

  - **show aaa accounting**—Shows you all AAA accounting rules.

  - **show timeout**—Shows the maximum idle time for a session.

  - **show timeout uauth**—Shows the duration in hours, minutes, and seconds before the authentication and authorization cache times out.

  - **show auth prompt**—Shows the prompt, accept, and reject text messages when a user attempts to authenticate via a Telnet session.

Troubleshooting Authentication

If you encounter issues with your AAA authentication, you can use the **debug aaa authentication** command to display the communication between the Cisco PIX Firewall and the AAA server. This command lets you determine the method of authentication and verify successful communication between the PIX and the AAA server. Example 14-11 shows where a login causes the PIX to initiate a connection to the AAA server at 17.16.1.8, requesting a login using TACACS+ and generating an eight-digit session ID. The session ID is used to distinguish between multiple concurrent authentication requests.

Example 14-17 **debug aaa authentication** *Command Output*

```
tgpix# debug aaa authentication
10:15:01: AAA/AUTHEN: create_user user='' ruser='' port='tty19'
  rem_addr='172.16.1.8' authen_type=1 service=1 priv=1
10:15:01: AAA/AUTHEN/START (0): port='tty19' list='' action=LOGIN service=LOGIN
10:15:01: AAA/AUTHEN/START (0): using "default" list
10:15:01: AAA/AUTHEN/START (12345678): Method=TACACS+
10:15:01: TAC+ (12345678): received authen response status = GETUSER
10:15:02: AAA/AUTHEN (12345678): status = GETUSER
10:15:02: AAA/AUTHEN/CONT (12345678): continue_login
10:15:02: AAA/AUTHEN (12345678): status = GETUSER
10:15:02: AAA/AUTHEN (12345678): Method=TACACS+
10:15:02: TAC+: send AUTHEN/CONT packet
10:15:03: TAC+ (12345678): received authen response status = GETPASS
10:15:03: AAA/AUTHEN (12345678): status = GETPASS
10:15:03: AAA/AUTHEN/CONT (12345678): continue_login
```

Example 14-17 debug aaa authentication *Command Output (Continued)*

```
10:15:03: AAA/AUTHEN (12345678): status = GETPASS
10:15:03: AAA/AUTHEN (12345678): Method=TACACS+
10:15:03: TAC+: send AUTHEN/CONT packet
10:15:03: TAC+ (12345678): received authen response status = PASS
10:15:03: AAA/AUTHEN (12345678): status = PASS
```

Troubleshooting Authorization

If you encounter issues with your AAA authorization, you can use the **debug aaa authorization** command to display the communication between the PIX Firewall and the AAA server, as demonstrated in Example 14-12.

Example 14-18 debug aaa authorization *Command Output*

```
tgpix# debug aaa authorization
10:15:01: AAA/AUTHOR (0): user='jdoe'
10:15:01: AAA/AUTHOR (0): send AV service=shell
10:15:01: AAA/AUTHOR (0): send AV cmd*
10:15:01: AAA/AUTHOR (123456789): Method=TACACS+
10:15:01: AAA/AUTHOR/TAC+ (123456789): user=jdoe
10:15:01: AAA/AUTHOR/TAC+ (123456789): send AV service=shell
10:15:01: AAA/AUTHOR/TAC+ (123456789): send AV cmd*
10:15:01: AAA/AUTHOR (123456789): Post authorization status = FAIL
```

Troubleshooting Accounting

If you encounter issues with your AAA accounting, you can use the **show accounting** command to step through the sessions and, if necessary, print records of actively accounted sessions. The **debug aaa accounting** command is used to display the output of AAA accounting and is independent of the protocol used to transfer records to the log server, as demonstrated in Example 14-13.

Example 14-19 debug aaa accounting *Command Output*

```
tgpix# debug aaa accounting
10:15:01: AAA/ACCT: EXEC acct start, line 10
10:15:01: AAA/ACCT: Connect start, line 10, glare
10:15:01: AAA/ACCT: Connection acct stop:
task_id=70 service=exec port=10 protocol=telnet address=172.16.1.13 cmd=glare
bytes_in=308 bytes_out=76 paks_in=45 paks_out=54 elapsed_time=14
```

If you believe you have encountered a protocol-specific problem, you can view the individual protocols using the following commands:

- **debug tacacs**—Displays the packet information for communication between the PIX Firewall and the AAA server. Example 14-14 demonstrates typical output from this command.

- **debug tacacs events**—Should be used only if requested by Cisco service personnel.

- **debug radius**—Displays the output of the RADIUS communication. This is more difficult to read, except for the obvious "Access-Accept" or "Access-Reject" message. Example 14-15 demonstrates typical output from this command.

Example 14-20 **debug tacacs** *Command Output*

```
tgpix# debug tacacs
10:15:01: TAC+: Opening TCP/IP connection to 172.16.1.8 using source 172.16.1.1
10:15:01: TAC+: Sending TCP packet number 123456789-1 to 172.16.1.8 (AUTHEN/START)
10:15:01: TAC+: Receiving TCP packet number 123456789-2 from 172.16.1.8
10:15:01: TAC+ (123456789): received authen response status = GETUSER
10:15:01: TAC+: send AUTHEN/CONT packet
10:15:02: TAC+: Sending TCP packet number 123456789-3 to 172.16.1.8 (AUTHEN/CONT)
10:15:02: TAC+: Receiving TCP packet number 123456789-4 from 172.16.1.8
10:15:02: TAC+ (123456789): received authen response status = GETPASS
10:15:02: TAC+: send AUTHEN/CONT packet
10:15:03: TAC+: Sending TCP packet number 123456789-5 to 172.16.1.8 (AUTHEN/CONT)
10:15:03: TAC+: Receiving TCP packet number 123456789-6 from 172.16.1.8
10:15:03: TAC+ (123456789): received authen response status = PASS
10:15:03: TAC+: Closing TCP connection to 172.16.1.8
```

Example 14-21 **debug radius** *Command Output*

```
tgpix# debug radius
10:15:01: Radius: IPC Send 0.0.0.0:1645, Access-Request, id 0xE len 12
10:15:01:        Attribute 5 5 CDA14568
10:15:01:        Attribute 7 9 B475B47A
10:15:01:        Attribute 6 2 45C4E78A
10:15:01:        Attribute 4 1 14568521
10:15:01: Radius: Received from 172.16.1.8:1645, Access-Accept, id 0xE len 33
10:15:01:        Attribute 2 2 0000000F
```

NOTE   It is important that you not run the **debug** command continuously, because these commands can generate a significant amount of output.

The command to terminate the debug is **no debug** *insert your command here*.

Checking the CSACS

After verifying your settings on the Cisco PIX Firewall, you should double-check the settings on the CSACS to ensure that they match the PIX. You can also use the extensive logging information available on the CSACS Reports and Activity page. You can find a list of troubleshooting information for the CSACS in the CSACS online documentation. Simply enter "Troubleshooting Information for Cisco Secure ACS" in the Search box at Cisco.com to find this documentation.

Foundation Summary

The Cisco PIX Firewall and the CSACS combine to make an effective AAA solution. The **aaa-server** command configures the PIX Firewall to communicate with the AAA server. This command determines the authentication protocol used between the PIX and the AAA server, the IP address of the AAA server, and the *group_tag* or the name of the group the AAA server is in. The PIX can group up to 14 servers and handle up to 14 server groups. The CSACS is installed on either a Windows NT server or Windows 2000 server. It considers itself a AAA server and the PIX Firewall the AAA client. Command-line entries are put on the PIX Firewall to configure authentication, authorization, and accounting. User accounts, groups, logging, and downloadable PIX ACLs are all configured on the CSACS. Although you can assign authorization to individual users, it is recommended that you assign users to groups and assign authorization rules to the groups.

There are three main steps for troubleshooting AAA issues:

- Verify connectivity between the PIX and the CSACS.
- Verify the configuration of the Cisco PIX Firewall.
- Verify the configuration of the CSACS.

Table 14-1 outlines the commands and syntax necessary to configure the Cisco PIX Firewall as a NAS.

Table 14-1   *Commands to Configure the Cisco PIX Firewall as a NAS*

Command	Description
aaa authentication include | exclude *authen_service* **inbound | outbound** *if_name local_ip local_mask foreign_ip foreign_mask group_tag*	Implements AAA authentication to include or exclude a specific service that is inbound or outbound in a specific interface for a specific source and destination address assigned to a specific AAA server group as assigned by the group tag.
aaa authentication match *acl_name* **inbound | outbound** *if_name group_tag*	Matches the requirement for AAA authentication with a specific access control list.
show aaa	Displays your AAA configuration.
debug aaa authentication	Displays the authentication communication between the NAS and the AAA server.
aaa authorization include | exclude *author_service* **inbound | outbound** *if_name local_ip local_mask foreign_ip foreign_mask group_tag*	Implements AAA authorization to include or exclude a specific service that is inbound or outbound in a specific interface for a specific source and destination address assigned to a specific AAA server group as assigned by the group tag.

continues

Table 14-1 *Commands to Configure the Cisco PIX Firewall as a NAS (Continued)*

Command	Description
aaa authorization match *acl_name* **inbound** I **outbound** *if_name group_tag*	Matches the requirement for AAA authorization with a specific access control list.
debug aaa authorization	Displays the authorization communication between the NAS and the AAA server.
aaa accounting include I **exclude** *author_service* **inbound** I **outbound** *if_name local_ip local_mask foreign_ip foreign_mask group_tag*	Implements AAA accounting to include or exclude a specific service that is inbound or outbound in a specific interface for a specific source and destination address assigned to a specific AAA server group as assigned by the group tag.
aaa accounting match *acl_name* **inbound** I **outbound** *if_name group_tag*	Matches the requirement for AAA accounting with a specific access control list.
show accounting	Steps through individual recorded logs.
debug aaa accounting	Displays the accounting communication between the NAS and the AAA server.

The commands listed in Table 14-2 let you display protocol-specific communication between the NAS (PIX Firewall) and the AAA server.

Table 14-2 *Commands to Display Communication Between the Cisco PIX Firewall and the AAA Server*

Command	Description
debug tacacs	Debugs TACACS communications between the PIX and the AAA server.
debug radius	Debugs RADIUS communications between the PIX and the AAA server.

Q&A

The questions in this section do not attempt to cover more breadth or depth than the exam; however, they are designed to make sure that you know the answer. Hopefully, these questions will help limit the number of exam questions on which you narrow your choices to two options and then guess. Be sure to use the CD and take the simulated exams.

The answers to these questions can be found in Appendix A.

1 What is the best way to authenticate an H.323 connection?

    A Authenticate to the H.323 server.

    B Telnet to the H.323 server.

    C Virtual Telnet to the PIX for authentication.

    D Virtual HTTP to the CSACS for authentication.

2 What is the total number of AAA servers that the PIX can connect to?

3 How do you disable caching of user authentication?

4 What happens to virtual HTTP if you disable **timeout uauth absolute**?

5 How can you tell you have configured your NAS to authenticate using RADIUS in the CSACS by looking at the Shared Profile Components tab?

6 What are the two default password authentication databases configured on the CSACS?

7 What PIX command establishes the authentication protocol to be used with the AAA server?

8 Which options are mandatory in every **aaa authentication** command on the PIX Firewall? (Select all that apply.)

    A **include/exclude**

    B **inbound/outbound**

    C *local_ip/mask*

    D **group_tag**

    E *acl_name*

9 True or false: You can restrict local access to the PIX Firewall using CSACS.

10 How do you configure client IP address assignment on the CSACS when using the PIX Firewall as the AAA client?

11 By default, what is the maximum number of sessions allowed for a user who is configured on the CSACS?

12 Why is it a good idea to rename your groups in CSACS?

13 Where do you see the logs on the CSACS?

14 You are installing CSACS on your new Windows 2000 Professional, but you cannot get it to load correctly. What is most likely the problem?

    A   CSACS requires server software.

    B   Your patch level is not up to date.

    C   You are running a personal firewall or host-based IDS that is blocking the installation.

    D   You do not have administrative privileges on that system.

    E   All of the above

15 True or false: The CSACS comes with its own online documentation.

This chapter covers the following exam topics for the Cisco Secure PIX Firewall Advanced Exam:

26. Multimedia support
27. Attack guards
28. Intrusion detection

CHAPTER 15

Attack Guards and Multimedia Support

The primary function of the Cisco PIX Firewall is to prevent and protect internal hosts from malicious attacks from the outside network. Some hackers try to gain access to the internal network, but others attack network resources to disrupt network services. This chapter describes some of the features of the Cisco PIX Firewall that are used to mitigate known attacks against network resources. This chapter also discusses how the PIX handles multimedia application protocols.

"Do I Know This Already?" Quiz

The purpose of this quiz is to help you determine your current understanding of the topics covered in this chapter. Write down your answers and compare them to the answers in Appendix A. It is strongly recommended that you go through this self-assessment quiz before you read the "Foundation Topics" section. The concepts in this chapter are the foundation of much of what you need to understand to pass the CSPFA Certification Exam. Unless you do exceptionally well on the "Do I Know This Already?" pretest and are 100% confident in your knowledge of this area, you should read through the entire chapter.

1 What PIX feature mitigates a denial of service (DoS) attack using an incomplete IP datagram?

2 What default port does the PIX inspect for H.323 traffic?

3 How do you enable the PIX's Mail Guard feature?

4 True or false: Floodguard is enabled by default.

5 What is an embryonic connection?

6 Which actions are available in the PIX IDS configuration?

7 How does DNS Guard on the Cisco PIX Firewall prevent DoS attacks that exploit DNS?

8 How does **ip verify reverse-path** secure the PIX?

9 How does the Mail Guard feature prevent SMTP-related attacks?

10 True or false: The shunning feature on the Cisco PIX Firewall *does not* require the aid of the Cisco IDS device.

Foundation Topics

Multimedia Support on the Cisco PIX Firewall

Chapter 7, "Configuring Access," began a discussion of some applications that require special handling by the Cisco PIX Firewall. Multimedia applications have special behaviors that require special handling by the PIX inspection feature.

During normal mode of operation, multimedia application protocols open more than one communication channel and several data channels. For example, a client might transmit a request on TCP, get responses on UDP, or use dynamic ports. The **fixup protocol** command is used to help the PIX identify such protocols so that it can perform inspections.

Here are some of the multimedia applications supported by the PIX Firewall:

- Microsoft Netshow
- Microsoft Netmeeting
- Intel Internet Video Phone
- VDOnet VDOLive
- RealNetworks RealAudio and RealVideo
- VocalTech
- White Pine Meeting Point
- White Pine CuSeeMe
- Xing StreamWorks
- VXtreme WebTheatre

The PIX dynamically opens and closes UDP ports for secure multimedia connections. There is no need to open a range of ports, which creates a security risk, or to reconfigure any application clients.

The PIX supports multimedia with or without NAT. Many firewalls that cannot support multimedia with NAT limit multimedia usage to only registered users or require exposure of inside IP addresses to the Internet.

Many popular multimedia applications use Real-Time Streaming Protocol (RTSP) or the H.323 suite protocol standard.

Real-Time Streaming Protocol (RTSP)

RTSP, described in RFC 2326, controls the delivery of real-time data such as audio and video. It is used for large-scale broadcasts and audio- or video-on-demand streaming. It supports applications such as Cisco IP/TV, RealNetworks RealAudio G2 Player, and Apple QuickTime 4 software.

RTSP applications use port 554 with TCP (and rarely UDP) as a control channel. The TCP control channel is used to negotiate the two UDP data channels that are used to transmit audio/video traffic. RTSP does not typically deliver continuous data streams over the control channel, usually relying on a UDP-based data transport protocol such as standard Real-Time Transport Protocol (RTP) to open separate channels for data and for RTP Control Protocol (RTCP) messages. RTCP carries status and control information, and RTP carries the actual data.

The **fixup protocol** command is used for RTSP connections to let the Cisco PIX Firewall do inspection. The **fixup protocol rtsp** command lets the PIX dynamically create conduits for RTSP UDP channels. For example, the standard RTSP port 554 is enabled by the following command:

```
fixup protocol rtsp 554
```

H.323

The H.323 collection of protocols collectively uses up to two TCP connections and four to six UDP connections. Most of the ports, with the exception of one TCP port, are negotiated just for that particular session. Figure 15-1 shows the H.323 protocols in relation to the OSI reference model.

Figure 15-1   *H.323 Protocols Mapped to the OSI Reference Model*

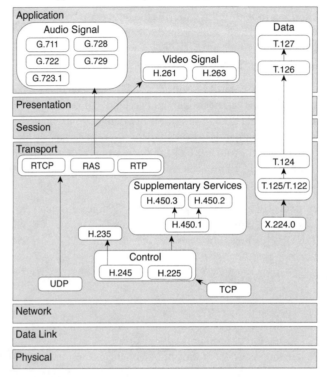

As shown in Figure 15-1:

- RAS manages registration, admission, and status
- Q.931 manages call setup and termination
- H.235 security and authentication
- H.245 negotiates channel usage

The content of the streams in H.323 is far more difficult for firewalls to understand than existing protocols because H.323 encodes packets using Abstract Syntax Notation (ASN.1).

The H.323 control channel handles H.225 and H.245 and H.323 RAS. H.323 inspection uses the following ports:

- 1718—Gatekeeper discovery UDP port
- 1719—RAS UDP port
- 1720—TCP control port

NOTE   PAT support for H.323 is available on the PIX version 6.2 software.

fixup protocol h323 Command

The Cisco PIX Firewall inspects port 1720 (default) connections for H.323 traffic. If you need to change port 1720 because you have applications using H.323 on other ports, use the **fixup** command:

```
fixup protocol h323 7430-7450
```

Use the **no** form of this command to disable the inspection of traffic on the indicated port.

An H.323 client might initially establish a TCP connection to an H.323 server using TCP port 1720 to request Q.931 call setup. The H.323 terminal supplies a port number to the client to use for an H.245 TCP connection.

The two major functions of H.323 inspection are as follows:

- Performs Network Address Translation (NAT) on the embedded IP addresses in the H.225 and H.245 messages. In other words, it translates the H.323 payload to a NAT address. (PIX Firewall uses an ASN.1 decoder to decode the H.323 messages.)
- Dynamically creates conduits for TCP and UDP channels to allocate the negotiated H.245 and RTP/RTCP connections.

Each UDP connection with a packet going through H.323 inspection is marked as an H.323 connection and times out with the H.323 timeout as configured by the administrator using the **timeout** command. To clear all previous **fixup protocol h323** commands and reset port 1720 as the default, use the **clear fixup protocol h323** command.

Attack Guards

Hackers use several methods to cause network service disruption. Denial of service (DoS) is a popular way of causing network disruption. The Cisco PIX Firewall has some attack mitigation features to combat against some of the following attacks:

- Fragmentation
- Domain Name System (DNS) attacks
- SMTP-based attacks
- SYN flooding
- Authentication and authorization attacks

Fragmentation Guard and Virtual Reassembly

Breaking a single IP datagram into two or more smaller IP datagrams is called *IP fragmentation*. DoS attacks overwhelm the host with fragmented IP datagrams. The **sysopt security fragguard** command enables the IP fragmentation guard feature on the PIX. This feature cannot be selectively enabled or disabled at the interface. The **sysopt security fragguard** command is disabled by default. To enable the IP fragmentation guard on the PIX, enter the following:

```
sysopt security fragguard
```

The fragguard feature enforces the checks recommended by RFC 1858, with two additional security checks protecting against many IP fragment-style attacks, such as teardrop:

- The checks ensure that each noninitial IP fragment has an associated valid initial IP fragment.

- IP fragments of more than 12 elements cannot pass through the PIX. IP fragments are rated 100 full fragmented packets per second to each internal host. This means that the PIX can process 1200 packet fragments a second.

Virtual reassembly is enabled by default. This feature uses syslog to log any fragment overlapping and small fragment offset anomalies. Here is an example of such a message:

```
% PIX-2-106020: Deny IP teardrop fragment (size=num, offset=num)from IP_addr to
IP_addr
```

Domain Name System (DNS) Guard

To understand the DNS attack protection provided by the Cisco PIX Firewall, it helps to understand how DNS can be exploited to cause a DoS attack. DNS queries are sent from the attacker to each of the DNS servers. These queries contain the target's spoofed address. The DNS servers respond to the small query with a large response. These responses are routed to the target, causing link congestion and possible denial of Internet connectivity.

The port assignment for DNS cannot be configured on the Cisco PIX Firewall. DNS requires application inspection so that DNS queries will not be subject to generic UDP handling based on activity timeouts. The PIX allows only a single DNS response for outgoing DNS requests. The UDP connections associated with DNS queries and responses are torn down as soon as a reply to a DNS query is received, dropping all other responses and averting a DoS attack. This functionality is called *DNS Guard*. DNS Guard is enabled by default.

DNS inspection performs two tasks:

- It monitors the message exchange to ensure that the DNS reply's ID matches the DNS query's ID.

- It translates the DNS A-record on behalf of the **alias** command.

Only forward lookups are translated via NAT, so pointer (PTR) records are not touched. Alarms can also be set off in the Intrusion Detection System (IDS) module for DNS zone transfers.

NOTE   A pointer record is also called a reverse record. A PTR record associates an IP address with a canonical name.

Cisco PIX Firewall version 6.2 introduces full support for NAT and PAT of DNS messages originating from either inside (more-secure) or outside (less-secure) interfaces. This means that if a client on an inside network requests DNS resolution of an inside address from a DNS server on an outside interface, the DNS A-record is translated correctly. This also means that the use of the **alias** command is now unnecessary.

Mail Guard

An SMTP server responds to client requests with numeric reply codes and optional human-readable strings. SMTP application inspection controls and reduces the commands that the user can use, as well as the messages the server returns. SMTP inspection performs three primary tasks:

- SMTP requests are restricted to seven commands—**HELO**, **MAIL**, **RCPT**, **DATA**, **RSET**, **NOOP**, and **QUIT**.
- It monitors the SMTP command-response sequence.
- It generates an audit trail—audit record 108002—when an invalid character embedded in the mail address is replaced. For more information, see RFC 821.

By default, the Cisco PIX Firewall inspects port 25 connections for SMTP traffic. SMTP inspection monitors the command-response sequence for the following anomalous signatures:

- Truncated commands.
- Incorrect command termination (those not terminated with <CR><LR>).
- The MAIL and RCPT commands specify the mail's sender and recipient. Mail addresses are scanned for strange characters. The pipe character (|) is deleted (changed to a blank space), and < and > are allowed only if they are used to define a mail address (> must be preceded by <).
- An unexpected transition by the SMTP server.
- For unknown commands, the PIX changes all the characters in the packet to X. In this case, the server generates an error code to the client. Because of the change in the packet, the TCP checksum has to be recalculated or adjusted.

The **fixup** command is used to change the default port assignment for SMTP. The command syntax is as follows:

```
fixup protocol smtp [port[-port]]
```

The **fixup protocol smtp** command enables the Mail Guard feature. This restricts mail servers to receiving only the seven commands defined in RFC 821, section 4.5.1 (**HELO**, **MAIL**, **RCPT**, **DATA**, **RSET**, **NOOP**, and **QUIT**). All other commands are rejected.

The strict implementation of RFC 821, section 4.5.1 sometimes causes problems for mail servers that do not adhere to the standard. For example, Microsoft Exchange Server does not strictly comply with RFC 821 section 4.5.1, using extended SMTP commands such as HELO. The Cisco PIX Firewall converts any such commands into NOOP commands, which, as specified by the RFC, forces SMTP servers to fall back to using minimal SMTP commands only. This might cause Microsoft Outlook clients and Exchange servers to function unpredictably when their connection passes through the PIX.

Mail Guard, however, is not the magic bullet for all mail server-related attacks. It protects your mail server only from known attacks.

Flood Defender

The Flood Defender feature of the PIX protects inside systems from a DoS attack that floods an interface with half-open TCP (embryonic) connections, otherwise known as *SYN flooding*. Creating a threshold for the number of embryonic connections or limiting the number of connections to the host mitigates such attacks. When the configured embryonic limit is reached, the PIX intercepts the SYN bound for the host and responds with a SYN/ACK on the host's behalf.

You enable this feature by setting the *emb_limit* (maximum embryonic connections) option or *max_conn* (maximum connection) option on the **nat** and **static** commands. For example:

```
static (inside,outside) 192.168.10.10 10.10.10.10 netmask 255.255.255.255
    max_conn 300 emb_limit 500000
```

This example sets the maximum connection to host 10.10.10.10 to 300 and sets the embryonic connection limit to 500,000.

If you set *max_conn* too low, you deny legitimate user access, creating a denial of service for yourself. There is no magic number for the *max_conn* and *emb_limit* arguments, because every network has a unique environment. The best number is a number that does not negatively affect the network. You can observe the number of connections and embryonic connections to your host, pre- and post- *max_conn* and *emb_limit* implementation, using the **show local-host** *host_ip* command.

The **static** command with the maximum connection or embryonic connection mitigates inbound DoS. The **nat** command with the same arguments can prevent the users in your network from committing TCP SYN attacks on someone else.

AAA Floodguard

The Cisco PIX Firewall has a Floodguard feature that helps it monitor and recover resources tied up in the user authentication (auth) subsystem. As with DNS, the service of authentication is maliciously exploited to create a DoS attack. Authentication attacks are done on the premise that each authentication request has to be processed. Sending an enormous number of authentication requests bogs down the target's finite resources, forcing a shutdown in the worst case.

When the Cisco PIX Firewall is inundated with authentication requests, it displays messages indicating that it is out of resources or out of TCP users. TCP user resources in different states are reclaimed depending on urgency in the following order:

1 Timewait

2 Finwait

3 Embryonic

4 Idle

The Floodguard is enabled by default. It can be disabled using the **floodguard disable** command.

PIX Firewall's Intrusion Detection Feature

The Cisco PIX Firewall includes an IP-only intrusion detection feature. It provides visibility at network perimeters or for locations where additional security between network segments is required.

The PIX's IDS identifies 53 common attacks using signatures to detect patterns of misuse in network traffic. Traffic passing through the PIX can be identified to be audited, logged, and/or dropped.

After it's configured, the IDS feature watches packets and sessions as they flow through the firewall, scanning each for a match with any of the IDS signatures. When suspicious activity is detected, PIX responds immediately and can be configured to

1 Send an alarm to a syslog server

2 Drop the packet

3 Reset the Transmission Control Protocol (TCP) connection

The Cisco PIX Firewall supports both inbound and outbound auditing. Auditing is performed by looking at the IP packets as they arrive at an input interface. If a packet triggers a signature and the configured action does not drop the packet, the same packet can trigger other signatures. The IDS feature allows a signature to be acted upon differently depending on the interface on which it was detected. It also allows signatures to be individually disabled if reoccurring false positives are detected.

TIP   You can find an excellent explanation of the IDS messages that are generated from IDS events in the section "Messages 400000 to 407002" of the document "System Log Messages" at www.cisco.com/univercd/cc/td/doc/product/iaabu/pix/pix_62/syslog/pixemsgs.htm#xtocid5.

Intrusion Detection Configuration

An audit policy (audit rule) defines the attributes of all signatures that can be applied to an interface, along with a set of actions. Using an audit policy can limit the traffic that is audited or specify actions to be taken when the signature matches. Each audit policy is identified by a name and can be defined for informational or attack signatures. Each interface can have two policies—one for informational signatures and one for attack signatures. If a policy is defined without actions, the configured default actions take effect. Each policy requires a different name.

The **ip audit** command enables the IDS feature on the Cisco PIX Firewall. The **ip audit** command can be used to create a global audit policy or a per-interface policy.

The global audit policy specifies the default actions to be taken when an attack or informational signature is matched. The global audit policy is enabled by

```
ip audit attack
ip audit info
```

In all the **ip audit** commands, the **action** can be any combination of **alarm**, **drop**, and **reset**. If nothing is configured, the default action is **alarm**. The **alarm** option indicates that when a signature match is detected in a packet, the PIX reports the event to all configured syslog servers. The **drop** option drops the offending packet. The **reset** option drops the offending packet and closes the connection if it is part of an active connection.

The syntax of the **ip audit attack** command is

```
ip audit attack [[action [alarm] [drop] [reset]]
```

The syntax of the **ip audit info** command is

```
ip audit info [[action [alarm] [drop] [reset]]
```

Table 15-1 describes the complete command parameters for the **ip audit** command.

Table 15-1   **ip audit** *Command Parameters*

Command Parameter	Description
attack	Specifies the default actions to be taken for attack signatures.
action *actions*	**alarm**, **drop**, **reset**
info	Specifies the default actions to be taken for informational signatures.
interface	Applies an audit specification or policy (via the **ip audit name** command) to an interface.
name	Specifies informational signatures, except those disabled or excluded by the **ip audit signature** command, as part of the policy.
signature	Specifies which messages to display, attaches a global policy to a signature, and disables or excludes a signature from auditing.

Table 15-1   **ip audit** *Command Parameters (Continued)*

Command Parameter	Description
name *audit_name*	The name assigned by the PIX Firewall admin for the audit policy.
clear	Resets name, signature, interface, and attack information to its default values.
signature *signature_number*	IDS signature number.

The following example shows the creation and application of policy1 and policy2 on the outside and inside interface:

```
ip audit name policy1_pol info
ip audit name attack_policy2 attack action alarm drop reset
ip audit interface outside policy1_pol
ip audit interface inside policy2_pol
```

Table 15-2 describes the **show** commands used to verify the IP audit configuration.

Table 15-2   **show** *Commands to Verify IP Audit Configuration*

Command	What the Output Displays
show ip audit attack	The default attack actions.
show ip audit info	The default informational actions.
show ip audit interface	The interface configuration.
Command	**What the Output Displays**
show ip audit name [name [info | attack]]	All audit policies or specific policies referenced by name and possibly type.
show ip audit signature [*signature_number*]	Disabled signatures.

The Cisco PIX Firewall IDS feature does not cover the entire intrusion detection signature that is available to a Cisco IDS unit.

Dynamic Shunning

The dynamic shunning feature allows a Cisco PIX Firewall, when combined with a Cisco IDS 3.0 sensor that is configured appropriately, to dynamically respond to an attacking host by preventing new connections and disallowing packets from any existing connection. Just like a router, the IDS unit tells the PIX to stop any new connections and to time out existing connections with the sources of traffic that are determined to be malicious. The **shun** command applies a blocking function to the interface receiving the attack for a user-defined period of time. Packets containing the IP source address of the attacking host are dropped and are logged until the blocking function is removed by the Cisco Secure IDS master unit.

In the following example, the offending host (10.10.10.14) makes a connection with the victim (10.25.25.32) with TCP. The connection in the PIX connection table reads

```
10.10.10.14, 555-> 10.25.25.32, 666 PROT TCP
```

Applying the following **shun** command:

```
shun 10.1.1.27 10.2.2.89 555 666 tcp
```

deletes the connection from the PIX Firewall connection table and also prevents packets from 10.1.1.27 from going through the PIX. The offending host can be inside or outside the PIX.

The application of the blocking function of the **shun** command does not require the specified host to be in active connection. Because the **shun** command is used to block attacks dynamically, it is not displayed in your PIX configuration. Shun statistics are available via **show** commands, syslog messages, and PIX Device Manager (PDM) monitoring.

Although the idea of dynamic shunning seems be an innovative way of dealing with offending hosts, it sometimes produces false positives that might cause a denial of service to legitimate users. This feature is available only on PIX Firewall version 6.0(2) and later.

ip verify reverse-path Command

The **ip verify reverse-path** command is a security feature that does a route lookup based on the source address. Usually, the route lookup is based on the destination address. This is why it is called *reverse path forwarding*. With this command enabled, packets are dropped if no route is found for the packet or the route found does not match the interface on which the packet arrived. This command is disabled by default and provides Unicast Reverse Path Forwarding (Unicast RPF) functionality for the PIX.

The **ip verify reverse-path** command provides both ingress and egress filtering. Ingress filtering checks inbound packets for IP source address integrity and is limited to addresses for networks in the enforcing entity's local routing table. If the incoming packet does not have a source address represented by a route, it is impossible to know whether the packet has arrived on the best possible path back to its origin. This is often the case when routing entities cannot maintain routes for every network.

Egress filtering verifies that packets destined for hosts outside the managed domain have IP source addresses that can be verified by routes in the enforcing entity's local routing table. If an exiting packet does not arrive on the best return path back to the originator, the packet is dropped, and the activity is logged. Egress filtering prevents internal users from launching attacks using IP source addresses outside the local domain, because most attacks use IP spoofing to hide the identity of the attacking host. Egress filtering makes the task of tracing an attack's origin much easier. When employed, egress filtering enforces what IP source addresses are obtained from a valid pool of network addresses. Addresses are kept local to the enforcing entity and therefore are easily traceable.

Unicast RPF is implemented as follows:

- ICMP packets have no session, so each packet is checked.
- UDP and TCP have sessions, so the initial packet requires a reverse route lookup. Subsequent packets arriving during the session are checked using an existing state maintained as part of the session. Noninitial packets are checked to ensure that they arrived on the same interface used by the initial packet.

NOTE   Before using this command, add static **route** command statements for every network that can be accessed on the interfaces you want to protect. Enable this command only if routing is fully specified. Otherwise, the Cisco PIX Firewall stops traffic on the interface you specify if routing is not in place.

The following example protects traffic between the inside and outside interfaces and provides **route** command statements for two networks, 10.1.2.0 and 10.1.3.0, that connect to the inside interface via a hub:

```
ip address inside 10.1.1.1 255.255.0.0
route inside 10.1.2.0 255.255.0.0 10.1.1.1 1
route inside 10.1.3.0 255.255.0.0 10.1.1.1 1
ip verify reverse-path interface outside
ip verify reverse-path interface inside
```

The **ip verify reverse-path interface outside** command protects the outside interface from network ingress attacks from the Internet, whereas the **ip verify reverse-path interface inside** command protects the inside interface from network egress attacks from users on the internal network.

The **clear ip verify** command removes **ip verify** commands from the configuration. Unicast RPF is a unidirectional input function that screens inbound packets arriving on an interface. Outbound packets are not screened.

Because of the danger of IP spoofing in the IP protocol, measures need to be taken to reduce this risk when possible. Unicast RPF, or reverse route lookup, prevents such manipulation under certain circumstances.

Foundation Summary

The Cisco PIX Firewall has built-in features that help it mitigate most known attacks:

- **DNS Guard**—DNS queries and responses are torn down as soon as a reply to a DNS query is received, dropping all other responses and averting a DoS attack.

- **Mail Guard**—The **fixup protocol smtp** command enables the Mail Guard feature. This restricts mail servers to receiving only the seven commands defined in RFC 821, section 4.5.1 (**HELO, MAIL, RCPT, DATA, RSET, NOOP,** and **QUIT**). All other commands are rejected.

- **Flood Defender**—Protects inside systems from a DoS attack that floods an interface with half-open TCP (embryonic) connections, otherwise known as SYN flooding.

- **AAA Floodguard**—Monitors and recovers resources tied up in the user authentication (auth) subsystem, averting a DoS attack.

- **Fragmentation guard**—Prevents a DoS attack caused by fragmented IP datagrams overwhelming the hosts.

The Cisco PIX Firewall also includes an intrusion detection feature with 53 common attack signatures. The PIX supports both inbound and outbound auditing. When an attack signature is detected, the PIX can send an alarm, drop the packet, or reset the TCP connection.

Q&A

As mentioned in the Introduction, the questions in this book are more difficult than what you should experience on the exam. The questions do not attempt to cover more breadth or depth than the exam; however, they are designed to make sure that you know the answer. Hopefully, these questions will help limit the number of exam questions on which you narrow your choices to two options and then guess. Be sure to use the CD and take the simulated exams.

The answers to these questions can be found in Appendix A.

1 What does the Flood Defender feature on the PIX Firewall do?

   A It prevents the PIX from being flooded with water.

   B It protects the inside network from being engulfed by rain.

   C It protects against SYN flood attacks.

   D It protects against AAA attacks.

2 What PIX feature mitigates a DoS attack that uses an incomplete IP datagram?

   A Floodguard

   B Incomplete guard

   C Fragguard

   D Mail Guard

3 Which of the following multimedia application(s) is/are supported by the PIX Firewall?

   A CuSeeMe

   B VDOLive

   C Netmeeting

   D Internet Video Phone

   E All of the above

4 What is the default port that PIX inspects for H.323 traffic?

   A 1628

   B 1722

   C 1720

   D 1408

5 How do you enable the Mail Guard feature on the PIX?

A **mail guard on**

B **enable mail guard**

C **fixup protocol mailguard**

D **fixup protocol smtp**

6 Which of the following describes how the Mail Guard works on the PIX Firewall?

A It lets all mail in except for mail described by an access list.

B It restricts SMTP requests to seven commands.

C It revokes mail messages that contain attacks.

D It performs virus checks on each mail message.

7 Which of the following statements about DNS Guard are true?

A It is disabled by default.

B It allows only a single DNS response for outgoing requests.

C It monitors the DNS servers for suspicious activities.

D It is enabled by default.

8 Which of the following are PIX Firewall attack mitigation features?

A DNS Guard

B Floodgate Guard

C Mail Guard

D Webguard

9 What command enables the PIX Firewall IDS feature?

A **ids enable**

B **ip audit**

C **ip ids audit**

D **audit ip ids**

10 What is the default action of the PIX IDS feature?

   A Nothing

   B Drop

   C Alarm

   D Reset

11 What does the reset action do in the PIX Firewall IDS configuration?

   A Warns the source of the offending packet before it drops the packet.

   B Drops the offending packet and closes the connection if it is part of an active connection with a TCP RST.

   C Waits 2000 offending packets and then permanently bans the connection to the source host.

   D Reports the incident to the syslog server and waits for more offending packets from the same source to arrive.

12 Which of the following is true of the **ip verify reverse-path** command?

   A It provides both ingress and egress filtering.

   B It is disabled by default.

   C It is very complicated to configure.

   D It works only with the PIX 520 model.

Answers to the "Do I Know This Already?" Quizzes and Q&A Questions

Chapter 1

Q&A

1 True or false: Network security means locking your computer in a filing cabinet.

Answer: False

2 What is the goal of a reconnaissance attack?

Answer: To determine what vulnerabilities can be exploited

3 True or false: A horizontal scan affects more hosts on a network than a vertical scan.

Answer: True. A horizontal scan scans all hosts across a specific network segment for a specific service (port). A vertical scan scans a specific host for a number of services.

4 True or false: To secure your network, you only need to install a firewall.

Answer: False. A firewall provides perimeter security, which is a piece of the puzzle. To secure the network, you need to implement security in depth.

5 What is the difference between a security policy and a security process?

Answer: The security policy is a written policy that spells out how security is implemented within a company. The security process is a four-step process that ensures that the security policy is constantly being improved.

Chapter 2

"Do I Know This Already?" Quiz

1 What are the three basic firewall technologies?

Answer: Packet filtering, proxy, stateful inspection

2 Of the three firewall technologies, which one generates a separate connection on behalf of the requestor and usually operates at the upper layers of the OSI model?

Answer: Proxy firewalls generate a new connection on behalf of the requestor and operate at the upper layers of the OSI model.

3 Which firewall technology is commonly implemented on a router?

Answer: The technology commonly applied to routers is packet filtering.

4 What items does a packet filter look at to determine whether to allow the traffic?

Answer: Source address/port, destination address/port, protocol

5 What firewall technology does the Cisco PIX Firewall use?

   A   Proxy filtering

   B   Packet filtering

   C   Stateful inspection

   D   Proxy inspection

   Answer: C

6 What are the advantages of the Cisco PIX Firewall over competing firewall products?

Answer: A single embedded operating environment, the Adaptive Security Algorithm, cut-through proxy, redundancy

7 How many PIX firewalls can you operate in a high-availability cluster?

Answer: The Cisco PIX Firewall can operate as a high-availability pair (two systems).

8 What is the ASA, and how does the Cisco PIX Firewall use it?

Answer: The Adaptive Security Algorithm is what the PIX uses to perform stateful inspection. It not only tracks the session information in the state table, but also randomly generates TCP sequence numbers to ensure that a session cannot be hijacked.

9 Why is cut-through proxy more efficient than traditional proxy?

Answer: Cut-through proxy is a feature that the Cisco PIX Firewall uses to authenticate and authorize a user before opening his or her connection. Cut-through proxy uses the ASA to track session information but does not perform any proxy services. This greatly increases the firewall's performance as compared to traditional proxy firewalls.

Q&A

1 True or false: Packet filtering can be configured on Cisco routers.

   Answer: True

2 What design feature allows the Cisco Secure PIX Firewall to outperform conventional application firewalls?

   A The Packet Selectivity Algorithm

   B Super-packet filtering

   C A single embedded operating environment

   D Hot standby proxy processing

   Answer: C

3 True or false: Cut-through proxy technology allows users to do anything they want after authenticating at the firewall.

   Answer: False

4 What steps are required to add an ARP entry to a Cisco PIX Firewall?

   A Edit the /etc/interfaces/outside/arp.conf file.

   B You don't need to add an ARP entry on a PIX Firewall.

   C Add the ARP entry using the GUI interface.

   D Use the **set arp** command in interface config mode.

   Answer: B

5 True or false: There is no limit on the number of connections an application proxy firewall can handle.

   Answer: False

6 True or false: The Adaptive Security Algorithm requires a tremendous amount of processing by the firewall. Even though it is not very efficient, the PIX can handle it.

   Answer: False

7 True or false: Redundancy allows you to configure two or more PIX firewalls in a cluster to protect critical systems.

   Answer: False

Chapter 3

"Do I Know This Already?" Quiz

1 What is the ASA, and how does the Cisco PIX Firewall use it?

Answer: The Adaptive Security Algorithm is what the PIX uses to perform stateful inspection. It not only tracks the session information in the state table, but also randomly generates TCP sequence numbers to ensure that a session cannot be hijacked.

2 What three authentication methods can the PIX Firewall use when performing cut-through proxy?

Answer: Remote Authentication Dial-In User Service (RADIUS), Terminal Access Controller Access Control System (TACACS+), or a local user database on the PIX itself. Note that the local user database is a feature that became available with OS version 6.2.

3 Why does the ASA generate random TCP sequence numbers?

Answer: Because it makes it extremely difficult for a potential attacker to predict the initial sequence number when attempting to hijack a TCP session.

4 If a user has successfully authenticated but cannot establish a connection to the server, what is most likely the problem?

Answer: The user is not authorized to access that server.

5 What is the best way to remove the ASA from a PIX Firewall?

Answer: The ASA is part of the embedded operating environment. It cannot be removed from the PIX.

6 What components of a TCP session does the ASA write to the state table?

Answer: Source and destination addresses, source and destination port numbers, TCP sequencing information, additional TCP/UDP flags

7 What can cause a session object to be deleted from the state table?

Answer: The connection is not authorized by the security policy, the connection is completed (the session has ended), or the session has timed out

8 What are the three ways to initiate a cut-through proxy session?

Answer: HTTP, FTP, Telnet

9 What happens to a reply that does not have the correct TCP sequence number?

Answer: The firewall drops it.

10 How many interfaces does a PIX 501 have, and how many network segments does it support?

Answer: The PIX 501 has five Ethernet interfaces but supports only two segments (inside and outside).

11 What X509 certificates do all PIX firewalls support?

Answer:

Entrust Technologies, Inc.—Entrust/PKI 4.0

Microsoft Corporation—Windows 2000 Certificate Server 5.0

VeriSign—Onsite 4.5

Baltimore Technologies—UniCERT 3.05

12 What is the maximum throughput of the PIX 535?

Answer: 1 Gbps

13 How many interfaces can you install in a PIX 515?

Answer: Six

14 What is the lowest model number of the PIX Firewall family to support failover?

Answer: PIX 515

15 What are three methods of managing a Cisco PIX Firewall?

Answer: Command-line interface (CLI), PIX Device Manager (PDM), Cisco Secure Policy Manager

Q&A

1 List four advantages of ASA.

Answer:

It is more secure than packet filtering.

It is more efficient than proxy services.

It can guard against session hijacking.

It is part of the embedded PIX operating environment.

2 What are the three firewall technologies?

A Packet filtering, proxy, connection dropping

B Stateful inspection, packet filtering, proxy

    C   Stateful proxy, stateful filtering, packet inspection

    D   Cut-through proxy, ASA, proxy

Answer: B

3 How does cut-through proxy work in a PIX Firewall?

Answer: The user is authenticated against a user database of AAA server, the connection is compared to the security policy, and the connection is opened or dropped.

4 What happens to the session object after a connection ends?

Answer: It is deleted from the state table.

5 True or false: A PIX 501 is designed to support five network segments.

Answer: False. It supports only two segments.

6 How many interfaces can the PIX 525 handle?

Answer: Eight

7 How many PCI slots does the PIX 506 have?

Answer: None

8 True or false: If the ACT LED on the front of a PIX 525 is lit, it means that everything is working correctly.

Answer: False

9 True or false: The interfaces on a PIX 520 are numbered top to bottom and left to right.

Answer: True

10 True or false: You don't need a license for any Cisco PIX Firewall. If you own the appliance, you can do anything you want with it.

Answer: False

Chapter 4

"Do I Know This Already?" Quiz

1 How many ways can you access the PIX Firewall?

Answer: You can access the PIX through Telnet, SSH, PIX Device Manager, and the console port.

2 What is the command to change the Telnet password?

Answer: passwd

3 Which version of SSH does PIX support?

Answer: The PIX Firewall supports SSH version 1.

4 What is the activation key?

Answer: The activation key is the license key or number for the PIX Firewall.

5 Give one reason why you would need to change the activation key on your PIX Firewall.

Answer: The PIX failover feature is not activated.

Q&A

1 What command upgrades a PIX 525 device running a 5.3 OS version to 6.11?

A install

B setup

C copy 6.11

D copy tftp flash

Answer: D

2 What binary file is required to perform a password recovery procedure on a PIX device running OS version 5.2?

A np52.bin

B pix52.bin

C bh52.bin

D pass52.bin

Answer: A

3 What circumstance(s) warrant(s) the use of a boothelper disk in the OS upgrade procedure?

A A corrupt binary image

B A PIX 520 device

C A PIX device running a 5.0 or earlier PIX OS

D No circumstance warrants the use of a boothelper disk.

Answer: B, C

4 What is the console password set to after a successful password recovery procedure?

   A password

   B cisco

   C secret

   D It is erased and set to blank.

   Answer: D

5 What is the Telnet password set to after a successful password recovery procedure?

   A password

   B cisco

   C secret

   D It is erased and set to blank.

   Answer: B

6 Which of the following could be reasons to change (upgrade) your activation key for the PIX?

   A You are upgrading your memory.

   B Your current PIX Firewall does not have failover activated.

   C You are upgrading the processor on your PIX Firewall.

   D Your current PIX Firewall does not have VPN-3DES enabled.

   Answer: B, D

7 What command changes the SSH password for login?

   A change ssh password

   B password

   C passwd

   D ssh pass

   Answer: C

8 What is the default amount of time a Telnet session can be idle?

   A 2 minutes

   B 15 minutes

   C 5 minutes

   D 12 minutes

   Answer: C

9 What is the command to configure Auto Update on the Cisco PIX Firewall?

    A   **auto update**

    B   **auto-update server** *url*

    C   **config auto-update**

    D   **update server** *url*

    Answer: C

10 Which version of SSH does the PIX support?

    A   2.1

    B   2.2

    C   3.1

    D   1

    Answer: D

Chapter 5

"Do I Know This Already?" Quiz

1 What is the difference between TCP and UDP?

Answer: TCP is a connection-oriented transport protocol, and UDP is a connectionless transport protocol.

2 On which transport protocol does PIX change the sequence number?

Answer: PIX changes the TCP sequence number with a randomized number.

3 What is the default security for traffic origination on the inside network segment going to the outside network?

Answer: By default, traffic is permitted from the inside (higher security level) to the outside (lower security level) network as long as the appropriate nat/global command has been configured.

4 True or false: You can have multiple translations in a single connection.

Answer: False. It is actually the opposite. Multiple connections can take place under a single translation.

5 What commands are required to complete NAT on a Cisco PIX Firewall?

Answer: nat and global

6 How many external IP addresses must be used to configure PAT?

Answer: Port Address Translation requires only a single external IP address.

7 True or false: NAT requires that you configure subnets for the external IP addresses.

Answer: False. To configure NAT, you need to define an external address range, not a subnet.

8 How many nodes can you hide behind a single IP address when configuring PAT?

Answer: Approximately 64,000. This is derived from 65,535 ports minus the 1024 already-assigned lower ports.

9 How does PAT support multimedia protocols?

Answer: PAT does not support multimedia protocols.

10 What is an embryonic connection?

Answer: It is a half-open TCP session.

11 What is the best type of translation to use to allow connections to web servers from the Internet?

Answer: Static translation provides a one-to-one translation from external to internal addresses.

12 How does the Cisco PIX Firewall handle outbound DNS requests?

Answer: PIX allows multiple outbound queries but allows only the first response to that query. All other responses to the initial query are dropped.

Q&A

1 When should you run the command **clear xlate**?

   A When updating a conduit on the firewall

   B When editing the NAT for the inside segment

   C When adding addresses to the global pool

   D All of the above

Answer: D

2 What happens if you configure two interfaces with the same security level?

Answer: Traffic cannot pass between those interfaces.

3 True or false: The quickest way to clear the translation table is to reboot the PIX.

Answer: False. The command to do this is clear xlate.

4 True or false: If you configure a static translation for your web server, everyone can connect to it.

Answer: False. You also need to configure a rule in the security policy allowing the connection.

5 Which of the following is not a method of address translation supported by the PIX?

A   Network Address Translation

B   Socket Address Translation

C   Port Address Translation

D   Static

Answer: B

6 True or false: It is easy to hack into a PIX over UDP 53, because it accepts DNS resolves from anyone.

Answer: False. The PIX allows queries to go out to multiple DNS servers but allows only the first response to return to the requesting host. All other responses are dropped.

7 What the does the PIX normally change when allowing a TCP handshake between nodes on different interfaces and performing NAT?

Answer: It translates the local address and randomizes the TCP sequence number.

8 What the does the PIX normally change when allowing a TCP handshake between nodes on different interfaces and performing PAT?

Answer: It translates the local address and source port number and randomizes the TCP sequence number.

9 You have configured two additional DMZ interfaces on your PIX Firewall. How do you prevent nodes on DMZ1 from accessing nodes on DMZ2 without adding rules to the security policy?

A   Route all traffic for DMZ2 out the outside interface.

B   Dynamically NAT all DMZ2 nodes to a multicast address.

C   Assign a higher security level to DMZ2.

D   All of the above

Answer: C

10 True or false: It is possible to hide an entire Class C network behind a single IP using PAT.

Answer: True. PAT supports approximately 64,000 nodes.

11 True or false: TCP is a much better protocol than UDP, because it does handshakes and randomly generates TCP sequence numbers.

Answer: False. Each transport protocol has its strengths and weaknesses. Because UDP is connectionless, it has much less overhead and is faster than TCP.

12 Which of the following **nat** commands is/are correct?

A LabPIX(config)# **nat (inside) 1 0.0.0.0 0.0.0.0**

B LabPIX(config)# **nat (inside) 1 0.0**

C LabPIX(config)# **nat (inside) 1 0 0**

D A and B

E A and C

F All of the above

Answer: E

13 When would you want to configure NAT and PAT for the same inside segment?

Answer: When you have more users than addresses in your global pool.

14 What is RFC 1918?

Answer: It sets aside IP addresses for private networks.

15 True or false: By default, an embryonic connection terminates after 2 minutes.

Answer: False. The default timeout for an embryonic connection is unlimited.

16 What command shows all active TCP connections on the PIX?

Answer: show conn

17 Why is there an *id* field in the **nat** command?

Answer: So that the PIX can tell what nat statement applies to what global statement.

Chapter 6

"Do I Know This Already?" Quiz

1 How do you access privileged mode?

Answer: Enter enable and the enable password.

2 What is the function of the **nameif** command?

Answer: You use it to name a Cisco PIX Firewall interface and assign a security level.

3 What six commands produce a basic working configuration for a Cisco PIX Firewall?

Answer: nameif, interface, ip address, nat, global, route

4 Why is the **route** command important?

Answer: It tells the PIX where to send packets. It is important especially because it is used to create the default route.

5 What is the command to flush out the ARP cache on a Cisco PIX Firewall?

Answer: clear arp

6 True or false: It is possible to configure the outside interface on a Cisco PIX Firewall to accept DHCP requests.

Answer: False. Only the inside interface can be configured to accept DHCP requests and assign IP addresses.

7 What type of environment uses the PIX DHCP client feature?

Answer: Small office/home office (SOHO)

8 What command releases and renews an IP address on the PIX?

Answer: ip address outside dhcp

9 Give at least one reason why it is beneficial to use NTP on the Cisco PIX Firewall.

Answer: 1. For certificate revocation list (CRL) because it is time-stamp-sensitive. 2. Troubleshooting events is easier.

10 Why would you want to secure the NTP messages between the Cisco PIX Firewall and the NTP server?

Answer: To prevent the Cisco PIX Firewall from synchronizing the unauthorized NTP servers.

Q&A

1 What command tests connectivity?

  A ping

  B nameif

  C ip address

  D write terminal

  Answer: A

2 What command saves the configuration you made on the Cisco PIX Firewall?

   A write terminal

   B show start-running config

   C write memory

   D save config

   Answer: C

3 What command assigns security levels to interfaces on the PIX?

   A ip address

   B route

   C nameif

   D secureif

   Answer: C

4 What command flushes the ARP cache on a PIX?

   A flush arp cache

   B no arp cache

   C clear arp

   D You cannot flush the ARP cache.

   Answer: C

5 True or false: The DHCP client feature is primarily designed for large corporate enterprise networks and ISPs.

   Answer: False. The DHCP server is usually used in SOHO environments with lower-end models of the Cisco PIX Firewall, such as the 501 and 506 units.

6 Why would you want authentication enabled between the PIX and the NTP server? (Select all that apply.)

   A To ensure that the PIX does not synchronize with an unauthorized NTP server

   B To maintain the integrity of the communication

   C To increase the speed of communication

   D To reduce latency

   Answer: A, B

7 True or false: The DHCP client feature can be configured on the PIX's inside interface.

Answer: False. The DHCP client can be enabled only on the PIX's outside interface.

8 How do you access privileged mode?

A Enter the **enable** command and the enable password.

B Enter the **privilege** command and the privilege password.

C Enter the super-secret password.

D Enter the **privilege** command only.

Answer: A

9 How do you view the current configuration on your PIX? (Select all that apply.)

A **write terminal**

B **show current**

C **write memory**

D **save config**

Answer: A

10 In a DHCP client configuration, what is the command to release and renew the IP address on the outside interface?

A **ipconfig release**

B **ip address dhcp outside**

C **outside ip renew**

D **ip address renew outside**

Answer: B

Chapter 7

"Do I Know This Already?" Quiz

1 What do static NAT settings do?

Answer: They create a one-to-one mapping between a host/network on the inside to a global IP address that can be accessed by external hosts.

2 True or false: Static NAT is the only configuration that lets inbound access in.

Answer: False. ACL/conduits are required to decide what type of access should be made available to the host/network identified by the static nat command.

3 Can the **conduit** command be used in place of the **access-list** command?

Answer: Yes. However, the preferred command is access-list beginning with PIX version 5.3. ACLs provide improved flexibility compared to conduits.

4 About how many access list entries (ACEs) in one access list does TurboACL support?

Answer: 16,000

5 What is the minimum memory required to run TurboACL?

Answer: 2.1 MB

6 What is the command to enable TurboACL globally on the PIX Firewall?

Answer: access-list compiled

7 What is the minimum number of access list entries needed for TurboACL to compile?

Answer: 19

8 What is the function of object groups?

Answer: Object groups are used to group hosts/networks, services, and more. A single security policy (ACL) can be applied to the group.

9 What is the command to enable a network object group?

Answer: object-group network *group id*

10 What are the four object type options when you're creating object groups?

Answer: network, protocol, service, icmp-type

Q&A

1 What is the maximum number of access list entries in one access list that TurboACL supports?

A 19

B 2000

C 16,000

D 10

Answer: C

2 What is the minimum number of access list entries needed in an access list for TurboACL to compile?

A   4

B   19

C   16,000

D   No minimum is required

Answer: B

3 Which of the following is *not* one of four options for object types when you create an object group?

A   Network

B   Protocol

C   Application

D   Services

Answer: C

4 True or false: By default, traffic initiated from the outside (external to the PIX) is allowed in through the PIX.

Answer: False

5 What command lets you create a network object group?

A   **object-group network** *group-id*

B   **enable object-group network** *group-id*

C   **create network object-group**

D   **network object-group enable**

Answer: A

6 What command enables TurboACL globally on the PIX Firewall?

A   **turboacl global**

B   **access-list compiled**

C   **access-list turboacl**

D   You cannot enable TurboACL globally

Answer: B

7 What is the minimum memory requirement for TurboACL to work?

   A   8 MB

   B   100 Kb

   C   2.1 MB

   D   4 MB

   Answer: C

Chapter 8

"Do I Know This Already?" Quiz

1 What port does syslogd listen on by default?

   Answer: Syslogd listens on UDP port 514 by default. This can be changed, however.

2 What is the total number of logging facilities available for syslog configuration?

   Answer: Eight logging facilities are commonly used for syslog—facilities 16 to 23.

3 True or false: If the PIX is set to Warning level, critical, alert, and emergency messages are sent in addition to warning messages.

   Answer: True

4 What is the command for sending syslog messages to Telnet sessions?

   Answer: logging monitor

5 What is the **logging trap** command used for?

   Answer: It determines what level of syslog messages are sent to the syslog server.

6 What is the command used to enable logging on the failover PIX unit?

   Answer: logging standby

7 Why would you use the *timestamp* command parameter?

   Answer: The *timestamp* command parameter specifies timestamp values on the syslog messages sent to the syslog server for later analyses of the logs.

8 What is PFSS?

   Answer: The PIX Firewall Syslog Server (PFSS) lets you view PIX Firewall event information from the Windows NT system.

Q&A

1 What is the command for sending syslog messages to the Telnet session?

   A **logging console**

   B **logging monitor**

   C **telnet logging**

   D **send log telnet**

   Answer: B

2 What is the **logging trap** command used for?

   Answer: It determines what level of syslog messages are sent to the syslog server.

3 True or false: PFSS stands for PIX Firewall System Solution.

   Answer: False. PFSS stands for PIX Firewall Syslog Server.

4 PIX Firewall can be configured to send syslog messages to all of the following except which one?

   A Console

   B Telnet

   C Serial

   D Syslog server

   Answer: C

5 Which of the following is *not* an example of a severity level for syslog configuration?

   A Emergency

   B Alert

   C Prepare

   D Warning

   Answer: C

6 What is syslogd?

   A A message type that forms the syslog services

   B A service that runs on UNIX machines

   C A hardware subcomponent that is required for syslog configuration on the PIX

   D It gathers information on IT businesses in Japan.

   Answer: B

7 What port does syslogd use by default?

    A UDP 512

    B TCP 514

    C TCP 512

    D UDP 514

    Answer: D

8 True or false: The default facility number on the PIX Firewall is 18.

    Answer: False. The default facility number is 20.

9 How are syslog messages organized?

    A They are listed numerically by message code.

    B They are listed by importance level.

    C They are listed by date.

    D They are not organized.

    Answer: A

10 True or false: It is possible to disable specific syslog messages.

    Answer: True

11 Windows NT 4.0 server can work as a syslog server with what?

    A IIS configured for logging

    B PIX Firewall Syslog Server application installed

    C PIX Device Manager

    D UNIX

    Answer: B

Chapter 9

"Do I Know This Already?" Quiz

1 What are some things that trigger a failover event?

    Answer: Loss of power, cable errors, memory exhaustion, administratively forcing the standby

2 What command assigns an IP address to the standby PIX Firewall?

Answer: failover ip address *if_name ip_address*

3 How many PIX Firewall devices can be configured in a failover configuration?

Answer: Two

4 What is the benefit of using LAN-based failover?

Answer: The serial cable distance restriction of 6 feet is no longer a factor. Also, an alternative path for stateful information can be communicated in the event of a failure by the failover interface.

5 What is some of the information that is updated to the standby unit in a stateful failover configuration?

Answer: TCP connection table, translation table (xlate), negotiated H.323 UDP ports, port allocation table bitmap for PAT

6 What command forces replication to the standby unit?

Answer: failover active

7 What command configures a LAN-based failover?

Answer: failover lan interface *interface_name*

8 What is the default failover poll in seconds?

Answer: 15 seconds

Q&A

1 Which two of the following cause a failover event?

A A reboot or power interruption on the active PIX Firewall

B Low HTTP traffic on the outside interface

C The **failover active** command is issued on the standby PIX Firewall

D Block memory exhaustion for 15 consecutive seconds or more on the active PIX

Answer: A, D

2 What is the command to view failover configuration?

A **show failover**

B **failover**

C **view failover**

D **show me failover**

Answer: A

3 Which of the following is/are replicated during a stateful failover?

   A Configuration

   B TCP connection table, including timeout information for each connection

   C Translation (xlate) table

   D Negotiated H.323 UDP protocols

   E All of the above

Answer: E

4 Which of the following is *not* replicated in a stateful failover?

   A User authentication (uauth) table

   B ISAKMP and IPSec SA table

   C ARP table

   D Routing information

   E All of the above

Answer: E

5 What is the command to force configuration replication to the standby unit?

   A **write standby**

   B **copy to secondary**

   C **force secondary**

   D **force conf**

Answer: A

6 Which of the following is a stateful failover hardware restriction?

   A The stateful failover configuration is supported only by PIX 535 models.

   B Only fiber connections can be used in a stateful failover hardware configuration.

   C A PIX with two FDDI cards cannot use stateful failover, because an additional Ethernet interface with FDDI is not supported.

   D There is no hardware restriction for stateful failover configuration.

Answer: C

7 What command assigns an IP address to the standby Cisco PIX Firewall?

    A **secondary ip address** *ip address*

    B **failover ip address** *if_name ip_address*

    C **ip address** *ip address* **secondary**

    D **ip address** *ip address* **failover**

    Answer: B

8 What is the command to configure a LAN-based failover?

    A **conf lan failover**

    B **failover ip LAN**

    C **failover lan interface** *if_name*

    D **lan interface failover**

    Answer: C

9 What is an advantage of a LAN-based failover?

    A It quickly fails over to a peer when a power failure on the active unit takes place.

    B It does not have the 6-foot cable distance limitation for failover communication.

    C It is preconfigured on the PIX.

    D All of the above

    Answer: B

10 What is the default failover poll in seconds?

    A 10 seconds

    B 15 seconds

    C 30 seconds

    D 25 seconds

    Answer: B

Chapter 10

"Do I Know This Already?" Quiz

1   Which encryption is stronger, Group 2 Diffie-Hellman or 3DES?

Answer: 3DES. Diffie-Hellman is not an encryption protocol.

2   What is the command to apply an access list to a crypto map?

Answer: crypto-map *map-name seq-num* **match address** *acl_name*

3   What is the difference between ESP and AH?

Answer: AH does only header authentication. ESP can both authenticate and encrypt the header and the data.

4   What service uses UDP 500?

Answer: IKE

5   What is the size of an MD5 hash?

Answer: 128 bits

6   Why is **manual-ipsec** not recommended by Cisco?

Answer: The session keys are manually coded and never change.

7   What is the most scalable VPN solution?

Answer: IKE using certification authorities (CAs)

8   What is the difference between an access VPN and an intranet VPN?

Answer: Access VPNs require VPN client software on the remote machine.

9   Which hash algorithm is configured by default for phase 1?

Answer: SHA

10   What are the two methods of identifying SA peers?

Answer: IP address and host name

11   What happens if you have different ISAKMP policies configured on your potential SA peers, and none of them match?

Answer: They cannot negotiate the connection.

12   What command should you use to watch your IKE negotiation?

Answer: debug crypto isakmp

13 Where do you define your authentication method?

Answer: isakmp policy

14 What are the three types of VPNs?

Answer: Access, intranet, extranet

Q&A

1 What is the default lifetime if not defined in **isakmp policy**?

Answer: 86,400 seconds

2 Do your transform sets have to match exactly on each peer?

Answer: No. The peers continue to go through the transforms until they find a match. If there is no match, they are unable to negotiate the connection.

3 True or false: The X509v3 standard applies to the ESP header's format.

Answer: False. X509v3 applies to digital certificates.

4 What is the difference between the **isakmp** lifetime and the **crypto-map** lifetime?

Answer: The isakmp lifetime initiates a renegotiation of IKE based on time only. The crypto-map lifetime initiates a renegotiation of the IPSec SA based on time of traffic (kilobytes).

5 What command do you use to delete any active SAs?

Answer: clear crypto isakmp sa

6 What is the command for defining a preshared key?

Answer: isakmp key *string* **address | hostname** *peer-address* **netmask** *peer netmask | hostname*

7 What is the first thing you should check if you are unable to establish a VPN?

Answer: Verify that the peers' configurations match.

8 What is the function of the access list with regard to VPNs?

Answer: It tells the PIX what traffic should be encrypted.

9 What PIX firewalls support PPPoE?

Answer: 501, 506, 506E

Chapter 11

"Do I Know This Already?" Quiz

1 What happens to traffic that is not explicitly permitted by an access rule in an access control list?

   Answer: It is denied.

2 True or false: PDM supports a mixed configuration with **outbound** or **conduit** commands and **access-list** commands.

   Answer: False

3 What is a translation exemption rule?

   Answer: The translation exemption rule specifies traffic that is exempt from being translated or encrypted. It is possible to create an exemption rule for traffic that is not to be encrypted and sent to the Internet or a less-secure interface. This makes it possible to allow certain traffic between hosts or networks to remain unencrypted. This can be useful if you want to encrypt some traffic to another remote VPN network but you want traffic destined for anywhere else to be unencrypted.

4 What are the six tabs on the PDM?

   Answer: System Monitoring, Hosts/Networks, Access Rules, Translation Rules, VPN, Monitoring

5 How do you connect to the PDM?

   Answer: Through your browser by entering the PIX's inside interface IP address: https://*inside_interface_ip*

6 What version of PIX Software is required of PDM version 1.1?

   Answer: PDM Version 1.1 requires PIX version 6.0(1) at a minimum

7 Which models of Cisco PIX Firewall are supported by PDM?

   Answer: 501, 506, 515, 520, 525, 535

8 What versions of Windows does PDM support?

   Answer: Windows NT and Windows 2000

9 What steps should you take before installing PDM?

Answer: Ensure that you have 8 MB or more of Flash memory and that PIX OS version 6.0 or later is on the PIX.

10 True or false: PDM comes preinstalled on all PIX 5.3 and later software versions.

Answer: False. PDM is available only for Cisco PIX 6.0 and later.

11 Where does PDM reside?

Answer: In the PIX's Flash memory

Q&A

1 How many tabs does the PDM have for configuring and monitoring the Cisco PIX Firewall?

A Three

B Five

C Eight

D Six

Answer: D

2 How do you connect to the PDM?

A By accessing the PIX through Telnet and entering **PDM**

B By entering **http://inside_interface_ip** in your browser

C By entering **https://inside_interface_ip** in your browser

D By entering **https://PIX_PDM**

Answer: C

3 What version of the PIX is required for PDM to run?

A 5.1

B 5.2

C 5.3

D 6.0

Answer: D

4 Which model of the Cisco PIX Firewall does PDM support?

  A 506

  B 515

  C 520

  D 525

  E 535

  F All of the above

  Answer: F

5 Where does PDM reside?

  A On a Windows NT/2000 server

  B On a Red Hat Linux 7.0 server

  C On a Solaris server

  D All of the above

  E In the PIX Flash memory

  Answer: E

6 What default security mechanism does PDM employ for browsers to connect to it?

  A RSA

  B SSL

  C Biometrics

  D None of the above

  Answer: B

7 True or false: The PDM lets conduits and access lists exist together on the PIX Firewall configuration.

  Answer: False. If your PIX currently has a working configuration using either conduit commands, outbound commands, or access lists, PDM continues using your current model. If the PIX Firewall is currently using conduit commands to control traffic, PDM adds more conduit commands to your configuration as you add rules. Similarly, if the PIX Firewall is currently configured using access-list commands, PDM adds more access-list commands to your configuration as you add rules. If you have a PIX Firewall with no previous configuration, PDM adds access-list commands to the CLI by default. PDM does not support a mixed configuration with outbound commands or conduit commands and access-list commands.

8 Which of the following is a prerequisites for access rules to be created?

  A   Hosts or networks must be defined before access rule creation.

  B   Dynamic or static translation must be defined before access rule creation.

  C   There are no prerequisites.

  D   A and B

  Answer: D

9 What is a translation exemption rule?

  A   A rule that exempts addresses from being encrypted or translated

  B   A rule that denies access to addresses

  C   A rule that increases security on selected addresses

  D   None of the above

  Answer: A

10 PDM does *not* run on which of the following?

  A   Windows 3.1

  B   Windows 2000

  C   Linux 7.0

  D   Windows NT 4.0

  Answer: A

Chapter 12

"Do I Know This Already?" Quiz

1 What two URL filtering servers does the PIX work with?

  Answer: Websense and N2H2

2 What command filters out Java applets from HTML pages?

  Answer: filter java port *local_ip mask foreign_ip mask*

3 Why are Java applets and ActiveX objects considered a threat?

  Answer: They can be used to execute malicious tasks on the network and the local machine.

4 How does PIX filter Java applets and ActiveX objects?

Answer: Java and ActiveX filtering of HTML files is performed by selectively replacing the <APPLET> and </APPLET> and <OBJECT CLASSID> and </OBJECT> tags with comments.

5 True or false: PIX blocks HTML tags split across network packets or tags longer than the number of bytes in the MTU.

Answer: False

6 What is the command to designate or identify the filtering server?

Answer: url-server

7 True or false: Cisco PIX Firewall version 5.3 supports N2H2.

Answer: False

8 What PIX Firewall version supports the Websense filtering server?

Answer: Cisco PIX Firewall version 5.3 or later supports Websense.

9 What is the longest URL filter, in bytes, that is possible with Cisco PIX Firewall version 6.1 and older?

Answer: 1159 bytes

10 What is the longest URL filtering that is supported by Cisco PIX Firewall 6.2?

Answer: 6 KB

11 What is the command to filter URLs?

Answer: filter url

12 If the filtering server does not respond before the web content server does, the reply from the web content server is dropped. What can you do to avoid this problem?

Answer: Use the url-block block block-buffer-limit command so that replies from web content servers are buffered and are forwarded to the requesting user if the filtering server allows the connection.

Q&A

1 How does PIX filter Java applets and ActiveX objects?

  A By commenting out the <OBJECT> </OBJECT> or <APPLET> </APPLET> tags in the HTML page.

  B By deleting the <OBJECT> </OBJECT> or <APPLET> </APPLET> tags in the HTML page.

C   It notifies the content filtering server, which in turn disables the ActiveX objects and Java applets.

D   PIX does not filter ActiveX objects or Java applets.

Answer: A

2   What is the command to designate or identify the filtering server?

A   filter url-server

B   url-server

C   filtering server

D   server url

Answer: B

3   True or false: Cisco PIX Firewall version 4.4 supports N2H2.

Answer: False. Cisco PIX Firewall version 5.3 or later supports Websense.

4   What is the longest URL filtering that is supported by Cisco PIX Firewall 6.2 with Websense Enterprise filtering software?

A   12 KB

B   15 KB

C   4 KB

D   6 KB

Answer: D

5   What is the command to filter URLs?

A   filter url

B   url-filter

C   url-server

D   filter web page

Answer: A

6   What happens when the only filtering server is unavailable?

A   If the **allow** option is set, the PIX forwards HTTP traffic without filtering.

B   HTTP traffic is dropped, because the filtering server is unavailable.

C   HTTP requests are queued until the filtering server is available.

D   PIX reverts to the onboard filtering engine to filter HTTP traffic.

Answer: A

7 What is the default port used by the N2H2 server to communicate with the Cisco PIX Firewall?

   A   TCP/UDP 1272

   B   TCP 5004 only

   C   TCP/UDP 4005

   D   UDP 5004 only

Answer: C

8 What command identifies Websense servers on a Cisco PIX Firewall?

   A   **websense url filter** *server_ip*

   B   **filter url** *server_ip* **vendor n2h2**

   C   **url-server** [*if_name*] **vendor n2h2 host** *local_ip*

   D   All of the above

Answer: C

9 How many URL servers can be configured on a single Cisco PIX Firewall?

   A   5

   B   12

   C   3

   D   16

Answer: D

10 What command disables URL caching on the Cisco PIX Firewall?

   A   **no url-cacheno**

   B   **caching-url**

   C   **disable url-cache**

   D   None of the above

Answer: D

Chapter 13

"Do I Know This Already?" Quiz

1 What is the relationship between the Cisco PIX Firewall and the AAA server?

Answer: The Cisco PIX Firewall acts as a client to the AAA server.

2 What three methods are used to authenticate to the Cisco PIX Firewall?

Answer: HTTP, FTP, Telnet

3 How does the Cisco PIX Firewall process cut-through proxy?

Answer: The user connects to the PIX using HTTP, FTP, or Telnet, and then the PIX either authenticates the user locally or forwards the authentication information to a AAA server. After authenticating the user, the PIX opens the requested connection (if allowed in the security policy).

4 What are the main differences between RADIUS and TACACS+?

Answer: RADIUS travels over UDP and combines authentication and authorization; TACACS+ travels over TCP and sends authentication and authorization separately.

5 What patch level must you have Windows 2000 Professional configured to before you install CSACS?

Answer: Trick question. CSACS can be installed only on Windows NT/2000 Server.

6 Why is it important to authenticate a user before completing authorization?

Answer: You cannot assign any permissions unless you know who the user is.

7 What are the three layers of authentication?

Answer: Something you know, something you have, something you are

8 What is the purpose of the explain box during the CSACS installation?

Answer: The explain box brings up a window that provides explanations for each of the options in the configuration.

9 What do you need to verify before installing CSACS?

Answer: Your system should be up to date, including Internet Explorer, and you need connectivity with the NAS (PIX).

10 Why is it important to have Internet Explorer up to date on your CSACS?

Answer: Because CSACS is controlled through the browser.

Q&A

1 What platforms does CSACS support?

   A Windows XP Professional

   B UNIX

   C Windows NT Workstation

   D Windows 2000 Professional

   Answer: B

2 Why is it important to do accounting on your network?

   Answer: To keep track of who is accessing the network and what they are doing

3 What options are available to authenticate users on a PIX Firewall?

   A Local user database

   B Remote RADIUS server

   C Remote TACACS+ server

   D All of the above

   Answer: D

4 What two technologies does the CSACS support?

   Answer: RADIUS and TACACS+

5 True or false: Cut-through proxy authenticates users and then allows them to connect to anything.

   Answer: False. Cut-through proxy authenticates users and connects them to resources they are authorized to use.

6 True or false: The CSACS installation on Windows NT/2000 Server is a relatively simple Installation Wizard.

   Answer: True

7 Which of the following are *not* connection types for authenticating to a PIX Firewall? (Select all that apply.)

   A Telnet

   B SSH

   C FTP

   D HTTPS

   Answer: B, D

Chapter 14

"Do I Know This Already?" Quiz

1 True or false: The **show aaa** command shows you everything that has to do with your AAA server in its configuration.

   Answer: False. It does not show you the output of aaa-server.

2 Both your Cisco PIX Firewall and your CSACS are configured for TACACS+, but you cannot configure the downloadable PIX ACLs. What is the problem?

   Answer: Downloadable PIX ACLs are supported only by RADIUS server.

3 What is the command to get authorization to work with access lists?

   Answer: aaa authorization match *acl_name* **inbound/outbound** *if_name group_tag*

4 What is the one type of database you do *not* want to implement for a large enterprise network with many users?

   Answer: A PIX local database, because it significantly increases the PIX Firewall's processor workload and can become very difficult to administer as the database's size increases.

5 What tab on the CSACS is used to configure the PIX, and what is the firewall considered?

   Answer: The PIX is configured as a AAA client on the Network Configuration tab.

6 What three services are used to authenticate by default in the PIX?

   Answer: FTP, HTTP, Telnet

7 How do you put text messages into the logon prompt for a Telnet session?

   Answer: auth-prompt command

8 What three messages can you change with the **auth-prompt** command?

   Answer: Prompt, accept, reject

9 If your **timeout uauth** is set to 0:58:00, when is the user prompted to reauthenticate after the session times out?

   Answer: By default, timeout uauth absolute does not prompt the user to reauthenticate until he or she starts a new connection after the uauth timer has expired.

10 What does the option **inactivity** in the **timeout uauth** command mean?

   Answer: This is the period of inactivity that elapses before the timeout timer is started.

11 What two formats can logs be written to using the CSACS?

Answer: .CSV and ODBC (flat file and database)

12 If you create a user on the CSACS and do not assign that user to a group, what group is he or she automatically assigned to?

Answer: The default group

13 You have added a new RSA SecurID Token Server to the network. In which two places do you configure the CSACS to use it?

Answer: It must be configured as an external user database, and you must select it for password authentication in the User Setup field.

14 What command is most commonly used to check your AAA configuration on the PIX?

Answer: show aaa or show aaa-server

Q&A

1 What is the best way to authenticate an H.323 connection?

A Authenticate to the H.323 server.

B Telnet to the H.323 server.

C Virtual Telnet to the PIX for authentication.

D Virtual HTTP to the CSACS for authentication.

Answer: C

2 What is the total number of AAA servers that the PIX can connect to?

Answer: 196 (14 servers per group, 14 groups)

3 How do you disable caching of user authentication?

Answer: timeout uauth 0

4 What happens to virtual HTTP if you disable **timeout uauth absolute**?

Answer: After authentication, the user is prevented from connecting to the destination web server.

5 How can you tell you have configured your NAS to authenticate using RADIUS in the CSACS by looking at the Shared Profile Components tab?

Answer: Downloadable PIX ACLs are unavailable unless the AAA client is configured to authenticate using RADIUS.

6 What are the two default password authentication databases configured on the CSACS?

Answer: CiscoSecure Database and Windows NT/2000

7 What PIX command establishes the authentication protocol to be used with the AAA server?

Answer: aaa-server

8 Which options are mandatory in every **aaa authentication** command on the PIX Firewall? (Select all that apply.)

A   **include/exclude**

B   **inbound/outbound**

C   *local_ip/mask*

D   **group_tag**

E   *acl_name*

Answer: B and D

9 True or false: You can restrict local access to the PIX Firewall using CSACS.

Answer: True. This is done using aaa authentication console.

10 How do you configure client IP address assignment on the CSACS when using the PIX Firewall as the AAA client?

Answer: This function is not used on the PIX Firewall.

11 By default, what is the maximum number of sessions allowed for a user who is configured on the CSACS?

Answer: The user account defaults to the group setting.

12 Why is it a good idea to rename your groups in CSACS?

Answer: So you can identify which group includes which users.

13 Where do you see the logs on the CSACS?

Answer: Reports and Activity

14 You are installing CSACS on your new Windows 2000 Professional, but you cannot get it to load correctly. What is most likely the problem?

A   CSACS requires server software.

B   Your patch level is not up to date.

C   You are running a personal firewall or host-based IDS that is blocking the installation.

D   You do not have administrative privileges on that system.

E   All of the above

Answer: A

15 True or false: The CSACS comes with its own online documentation.

Answer: True

Chapter 15

"Do I Know This Already?" Quiz

1 What PIX feature mitigates a denial of service (DoS) attack using an incomplete IP datagram?

Answer: Fragguard mitigates IP fragmentation attacks that cause denial of service.

2 What default port does the PIX inspect for H.323 traffic?

Answer: 1720

3 How do you enable the PIX's Mail Guard feature?

Answer: fixup protocol smtp

4 True or false: Floodguard is enabled by default.

Answer: True

5 What is an embryonic connection?

Answer: An embryonic connection is a half-open TCP connection.

6 Which actions are available in the PIX IDS configuration?

Answer: Alarm, drop, reset

7 How does DNS Guard on the Cisco PIX Firewall prevent DoS attacks that exploit DNS?

Answer: The PIX allows only a single DNS response for outgoing DNS requests. Any other responses are dropped.

8 How does **ip verify reverse-path** secure the PIX?

Answer: It provides a mechanism for checking source IP addresses before receiving or sending packets.

9 How does the Mail Guard feature prevent SMTP-related attacks?

Answer: Mail Guard allows only a restricted set of SMTP commands—namely, HELO, MAIL, RCPT, DATA, RSET, NOOP, and QUIT.

10 True or false: The shunning feature on the Cisco PIX Firewall *does not* require the aid of the Cisco IDS device.

Answer: False. The Cisco shunning feature works in conjunction with the Cisco IDS device.

Q&A

1 What does the Flood Defender feature on the PIX Firewall do?

  A It prevents the PIX from being flooded with water.

  B It protects the inside network from being engulfed by rain.

  C It protects against SYN flood attacks.

  D It protects against AAA attacks.

  Answer: C

2 What PIX feature mitigates a DoS attack that uses an incomplete IP datagram?

  A Floodguard

  B Incomplete guard

  C Fragguard

  D Mail Guard

  Answer: C

3 Which of the following multimedia application(s) is/are supported by the PIX Firewall?

  A CuSeeMe

  B VDOLive

  C Netmeeting

  D Internet Video Phone

  E All of the above

  Answer: E

4 What is the default port that PIX inspects for H.323 traffic?

  A 1628

  B 1722

  C 1720

  D D.1408

  Answer: C

5 How do you enable the Mail Guard feature on the PIX?

A **mail guard on**

B **enable mail guard**

C **fixup protocol mailguard**

D **fixup protocol smtp**

Answer: D

6 Which of the following describes how the Mail Guard works on the PIX Firewall?

A It lets all mail in except for mail described by an access list.

B It restricts SMTP requests to seven commands.

C It revokes mail messages that contain attacks.

D It performs virus checks on each mail message.

Answer: B

7 Which of the following statements about DNS Guard are true?

A It is disabled by default.

B It allows only a single DNS response for outgoing requests.

C It monitors the DNS servers for suspicious activities.

D It is enabled by default.

Answer: B, D

8 Which of the following are PIX Firewall attack mitigation features?

A DNS Guard

B Floodgate Guard

C Mail Guard

D Webguard

Answer: A, C

9 What command enables the PIX Firewall IDS feature?

A **ids enable**

B **ip audit**

C **ip ids audit**

D **audit ip ids**

Answer: B

10 What is the default action of the PIX IDS feature?

A Nothing

B Drop

C Alarm

D Reset

Answer: C

11 What does the reset action do in the PIX Firewall IDS configuration?

A Warns the source of the offending packet before it drops the packet.

B Drops the offending packet and closes the connection if it is part of an active connection with a TCP RST.

C Waits 2000 offending packets and then permanently bans the connection to the source host.

D Reports the incident to the syslog server and waits for more offending packets from the same source to arrive.

Answer: B

12 Which of the following is true of the **ip verify reverse-path** command?

A It provides both ingress and egress filtering.

B It is disabled by default.

C It is very complicated to configure.

D It works only with the PIX 520 model.

Answer: A

Appendix B

1 The VPN session is established, but no traffic, or just one-way traffic, is passing between the firewalls. Ellen starts enabled logging and starts a **debug icmp trace.** She pings the other end of the VPN node and gets the following results:

```
LOCAL_PIX(config)# 609001: Built local-host inside:192.168.4.1
106014: Deny inbound icmp src outside:192.168.2.6 dst inside:192.168.4.1
  (type 8, code 0)
106014: Deny inbound icmp src outside:192.168.2.6 dst inside:192.168.4.1
  (type 8, code 0)
106014: Deny inbound icmp src outside:192.168.2.6 dst inside:192.168.4.1
  (type 8, code 0)
```

```
106014: Deny inbound icmp src outside:192.168.2.6 dst inside:192.168.4.1
   (type 8, code 0)
106014: Deny inbound icmp src outside:192.168.2.6 dst inside:192.168.4.1
   (type 8, code 0)
609002: Teardown local-host inside:192.168.4.1 duration 0:00:15
```

What do these results indicate and what could be causing this problem? How would you help Ellen resolve this issue?

Answer: The sysopt connection permit-ipsec statement is missing from the configuration on the local PIX. Add it.

On the PIX Firewall, by default, any inbound session must be explicitly permitted by a conduit or access-list command statement. With IPSec-protected traffic, the secondary access list check could be redundant. To make sure the IPSec authenticated/cipher inbound sessions are always permitted, use the following command:

```
sysopt connection permit-ipsec
```

2 Eric cannot get the VPN tunnel to work from HQ to the Philadelphia branch office. He starts a debug and gets the following results:

```
crypto_isakmp_process_block: src 172.16.172.40, dest 172.16.172.34
VPN Peer: ISAKMP: Added new peer: ip:172.16.172.40 Total VPN Peers:1
VPN Peer: ISAKMP: Peer ip:172.16.172.40 Ref cnt incremented to:1
   Total VPN Peers:1
OAK_MM exchange
ISAKMP (0): processing SA payload. message ID = 0

ISAKMP (0): Checking ISAKMP transform 1 against priority 10 policy
ISAKMP:       encryption DES-CBC
ISAKMP:       hash MD5
ISAKMP:       default group 1
ISAKMP:       auth pre-share
ISAKMP:       life type in seconds
ISAKMP:       life duration (basic) of 2400
ISAKMP (0): atts are acceptable. Next payload is 0
ISAKMP (0): SA is doing pre-shared key authentication using id type
ID_IPV4
  _ADDR
return status is IKMP_NO_ERROR
crypto_isakmp_process_block: src 172.16.172.40, dest 172.16.172.34
OAK_MM exchange

ISAKMP (0): processing KE payload. message ID = 0
ISAKMP (0): processing NONCE payload. message ID = 0
ISAKMP (0): processing vendor id payload
ISAKMP (0): processing vendor id payload
```

```
ISAKMP (0): remote peer supports dead peer detection
ISAKMP (0): processing vendor id payload
ISAKMP (0): speaking to another IOS box!

return status is IKMP_NO_ERROR
crypto_isakmp_process_block: src 172.16.172.40, dest 172.16.172.34
OAK_MM exchange
ISAKMP (0): processing ID payload. message ID = 0
ISAKMP (0): processing HASH payload. message ID = 0
ISAKMP (0): SA has been authenticated

ISAKMP (0): ID payload
        next-payload : 8
        type         : 1
        protocol     : 17
        port         : 500
        length       : 8
ISAKMP (0): Total payload length: 12
return status is IKMP_NO_ERROR
crypto_isakmp_process_block: src 172.16.172.40, dest 172.16.172.34
ISAKMP (0): processing NOTIFY payload 24578 protocol 1
        spi 0, message ID = 2457631438
ISAKMP (0): processing notify INITIAL_CONTACTIPSEC(key_engine): got a
queue
  event...
IPSEC(key_engine_delete_sas): rec'd delete notify from ISAKMP
IPSEC(key_engine_delete_sas): delete all SAs shared with   172.16.172.40

return status is IKMP_NO_ERR_NO_TRANS
crypto_isakmp_process_block: src 172.16.172.40, dest 172.16.172.34
OAK_QM exchange
oakley_process_quick_mode:
OAK_QM_IDLE
ISAKMP (0): processing SA payload. message ID = 133935992

ISAKMP : Checking IPSec proposal 1
ISAKMP: transform 1, ESP_DES
ISAKMP:    attributes in transform:
ISAKMP:        encaps is 1
ISAKMP:        SA life type in seconds
ISAKMP:        SA life duration (basic) of 28800
ISAKMP:        SA life type in kilobytes
ISAKMP:        SA life duration (VPI) of  0x0 0x46 0x50 0x0
ISAKMP:        authenticator is HMAC-MD5
IPSEC(validate_proposal): invalid local address 172.16.172.34
ISAKMP (0): atts not acceptable. Next payload is 0
```

```
ISAKMP (0): SA not acceptable!
ISAKMP (0): sending NOTIFY message 14 protocol 0
return status is IKMP_ERR_NO_RETRANS
crypto_isakmp_process_block: src 172.16.172.40, dest 172.16.172.34
ISAKMP (0:0): phase 2 packet is a duplicate of a previous packet.
```

What could be the cause of this problem?

Answer: This is a common mistake. The crypto map has not been applied to the correct interface. To fix the problem, apply the crypto map to the correct interface using the following command:

crypto map mymap interface outside

3   Bruce is having problems establishing a VPN session to the Seattle office. He gets the following debug results:

```
IPSEC(crypto_map_check): crypto map mymap 10 incomplete. No peer or
    access-list specified. Packet discarded
```

What is causing this problem, and how would you help Bruce successfully establish a VPN tunnel to the Seattle office?

Answer: To fix this problem, examine the crypto map statements on both peers. A match address statement is missing from the HQ PIX crypto map.

The configuration should contain the following statement:

crypto map *map-name map-number* match address *access-list-number*

4   The web administrator in Los Angeles needs to maintain the web servers in the DMZ from the internal network using terminal services (TCP Port 3389). Is the firewall in Los Angeles configured to allow this access? Explain your answer.

Answer: Yes. The web administrator is coming from the inside interface, which has a security level of 100, and is going to the DMZ interface, which has a security level of 70. Traffic traveling from a higher security level to a lower security level does not require a specific access list to be allowed.

5   The web administrator in Los Angeles also needs to administer the web servers in Boston and Atlanta. Are the three firewalls configured to allow this access? Explain your answer.

Answer: No. Although the VPNs are configured between Los Angeles and the other two locations, and the sysopt connection permit ipsec line is in the configuration, the VPNs are only between each location's internal network segments. To connect to the web servers, you need to configure a VPN connection from the internal network in Los Angeles and the DMZ segments of Boston and Atlanta.

6 The web server 172.16.1.13 needs to access an Oracle database server that sits on a segment connected to the internal network at 10.10.11.221. The web server initiates the connection on TCP port 1521 and retrieves inventory data. Can this connection be completed? Explain your answer.

Answer: No. Although an access list allows access between the web server and the database server on port 1521, there is no route to the 10.10.11.X network segment. Therefore, the traffic is routed to 192.168.1.254 instead of going to the database server on the internal network.

7 The web server 172.16.1.13 needs to access an Oracle database server on the DMZ in Boston using the address 172.16.2.11. The web server initiates the connection on TCP port 1521 to retrieve financial data. Can this connection be completed? Explain your answer.

Answer: Yes. An access list is not required to allow the web server in Los Angeles outbound to Boston. An access list on the Boston firewall allows the inbound connection, and static translations are in place on both ends.

8 Is the configuration solution to Question 7 a good idea? Explain your answer.

Answer: No. With this configuration, the financial data would be transmitted across the Internet in the clear, not through an encrypted connection.

9 The company has installed an FTP server on the DMZ segment in Los Angeles that customers can access to download updates. The FTP server's address is 172.16.1.9. Can all external users access this FTP server? Explain your answer.

Answer: No. An access list is configured to allow this access, but it only allows traffic to 192.168.1.9, which is an external address. No static translation is configured for this FTP server.

10 The exchange server is installed on the DMZ segment in Los Angeles using the address 172.16.1.14. The firewall is configured to allow SMTP access for inbound mail and SSL access for users who want to connect using Outlook Web Access via an HTTPS connection. Will any users be able to receive their mail with this configuration? Explain your answer.

Answer: No. The access list allowing access to the mail server is using the name "Exchange." The access group "Exchange" is applied to the outside interface. Unfortunately, only one access group can be applied to an interface at a time, and the "Inbound" access group is already applied to that interface.

11 What needs to be done in Los Angeles to allow access to the mail server?

Answer: Change the access list name from "Exchange" to "Inbound."

Case Study and Sample Configuration

The DUKEM consulting firm is a medium-sized company with 700 employees. It has three offices across the continental U.S. Twenty percent of DUKEM's employees are mobile or telecommute. Figure B-1 shows the current DUKEM network infrastructure.

Figure B-1 *DUKEM Network Infrastructure*

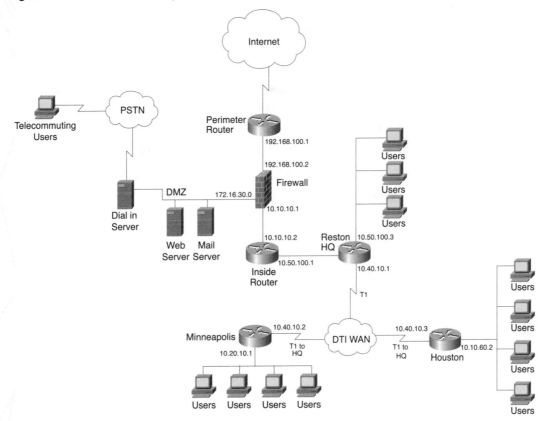

Remote Offices

The branch offices are connected to headquarters (Reston) via T1 connections. All Internet-bound traffic goes out through Reston. Telecommuting and mobile users call an 800 number that connects to a pool of modems at Reston.

Firewall

A Microsoft Windows server-based application firewall is used at headquarters (HQ). The firewall cannot be configured for IPSec or GRE. The firewall has a history of irregular behavior, which has created network disruptions.

Growth Expectation

DUKEM has grown by 13% during each of the past two years and expects to have an average growth rate of 15% over the next few years. It also has seen an increase in the number of employees who telecommute.

DUKEM's CIO has put forth the following requirements:

- A highly available firewall solution
- Secure communication channels between branch offices and HQ, telecommuters and HQ, and possible business partners

An IT consulting firm hired by DUKEM has recommended Cisco PIX Firewall to replace the existing firewall system. You have been selected to do the Cisco PIX Firewall configuration for DUKEM.

Figure B-2 shows the Cisco PIX Firewall solution in the new network design.

Use the information in Figure B-2 to configure your firewalls by completing the following tasks:

> Task 1—Basic configuration for the Cisco PIX Firewall
> Task 2—Configuring access rules on HQ
> Task 3—Configuring authentication
> Task 4—Configuring logging
> Task 5—Configuring VPN
> Task 6—Configuring failover

Good luck!

Figure B-2 *Proposed Network Design with PIX Firewall*

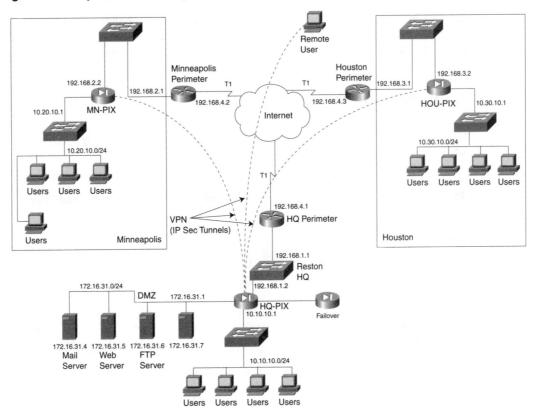

Task 1: Basic Configuration for the Cisco PIX Firewall

Tables B-1 through B-5 list the information required for you to configure the Cisco PIX Firewall at the Reston headquarters. Use the information from the tables to configure your Cisco PIX Firewall according to the network diagram shown in Figure B-2.

Basic Configuration Information for PIX HQ

Table B-1 lists the physical interfaces of the Cisco PIX Firewall that is installed in the Reston headquarters. This table includes the interface name, physical interface ID, assigned address, and speed/duplex.

Table B-1   *PIX Interface Information for HQ*

Interface Name	Hardware ID	Interface IP Address	Interface Speed
Outside	Ethernet0	192.168.1.2	100full
Inside	Ethernet1	10.10.10.1	100full
DMZ	Ethernet2	172.16.31.1	100full
Failover	Ethernet3	1.1.1.1	100full

Table B-2 shows what routing information needs to be configured on the PIX. Note that the only route required is the default route. No specific routes are defined on the firewall.

Table B-2   *PIX Routing Information for HQ*

Interface Name	Destination Network IP Address	Network Mask	Gateway (Router) IP Address
Outside	0.0.0.0	0.0.0.0	192.168.1.1

Table B-3 shows what outside addresses or address ranges are available for the global address pool. Remember that the global addresses are used in conjunction with the **nat** command to assign what addresses the PIX is translating to (this is not the original source, but the translated source).

Table B-3   *Recording Global IP Information for HQ*

Interface Name	NAT ID Number	Beginning IP Address Range	End of IP Address Range
Outside	1	192.168.1.12	192.168.1.250
Outside	1	192.168.1.252	—
DMZ	1	172.16.31.12	172.16.31.100

Table B-4 shows what IP addresses or network segments are to be translated (into the global addresses) as they pass through the firewall.

Table B-4   *NAT IP Information for HQ*

Interface Name	NAT ID Number	Network Address	Network Mask for This Address
Inside	1	10.10.10.0	255.255.255.0
DMZ	1	172.16.31.0	255.255.255.0

Table B-5 shows static IP address mapping for resources that are accessed from the outside (public) network. The static IP address is the address that is configured on the individual server, and the host IP address is the IP address that the PIX uses when answering for the server.

Table B-5   *Static IP Address Mapping Information for HQ*

Interface on Which the Host Resides	Interface Name Where the Global Address Resides	Host IP Address	Static IP Address	Description
DMZ	Outside	192.168.1.4	172.16.31.4	Mail server
DMZ	Outside	192.168.1.5	172.16.31.5	Web server
DMZ	Outside	192.168.1.6	172.16.31.6	FTP server
Inside	Outside	192.168.1.7	10.10.10.7	TACACS+ server
DMZ	Outside	192.168.1.8	172.16.31.7	Logging server

Example B-1 shows the individual configuration commands for all the items documented in Tables B-1 through B-5.

Example B-1   *Firewall Configuration for the Reston Headquarters*

```
nameif ethernet0 outside security0
nameif ethernet1 inside security100
nameif ethernet2 DMZ security80

interface ethernet0 100full
interface ethernet1 100full
interface ethernet2 100full

ip address inside 10.10.10.2 255.255.255.0
ip address outside 192.168.1.2 255.255.255.0
ip address outside 172.16.31.1 255.255.255.0

hostname HQ-PIX
nat (inside) 1 10.10.10.0 255.255.255.0
global (outside) 1 192.168.1.12-192.168.1.250 netmask 255.255.255.0
global (outside) 1 192.168.1.252 netmask 255.255.255.0
```

continues

Example B-1 *Firewall Configuration for the Reston Headquarters (Continued)*

```
global (DMZ) 1 172.16.31.12-172.16.31.100 netmask 255.255.255.0

static (DMZ,outside) 192.168.1.4  172.16.31.4 netmask 255.255.255.255 0 0
static (DMZ,outside) 192.168.1.5  172.16.31.5 netmask 255.255.255.255 0 0
static (DMZ,outside) 192.168.1.6  172.16.31.6 netmask 255.255.255.255 0 0
static (DMZ,outside) 192.168.1.8  172.16.31.7 netmask 255.255.255.255 0 0
static (inside,outside) 192.168.1.7  10.10.10.7 netmask 255.255.255.255 0 0

route outside 0.0.0.0 0.0.0.0 192.168.1.1
```

Basic Configuration Information for PIX Minneapolis

Tables B-6 through B-9 provide the information needed to configure the PIX Firewall at the Minneapolis office.

Table B-6 shows information about the physical interfaces on the PIX Firewall.

Table B-6 *PIX Interface Information for Minneapolis*

Interface Name	Hardware ID	Interface IP Address	Interface Speed
Outside	Ethernet0	192.168.2.2	100full
Inside	Ethernet1	10.20.10.1	100full

Table B-7 depicts what routes need to be configured on the PIX Firewall in the Minneapolis office.

Table B-7 *Routing Information for the Minneapolis PIX*

Interface Name	Destination Network IP Address	Network Mask	Gateway (Router) IP Address
Outside	0.0.0.0	0.0.0.0	192.168.2.1

Table B-8 lists the global IP addresses or address ranges that are used in conjunction with NAT for translation purposes.

Table B-8 *Global IP Address Information for the Minneapolis PIX*

Interface Name	NAT ID Number	Beginning of IP Address Range	End of IP Address Range
Outside	1	192.168.2.12	192.168.2.250
Outside	1	192.168.2.252	—

Table B-9 lists what addresses are dynamically translated on the PIX Firewall.

Table B-9   *NAT IP Address Information for the Minneapolis PIX*

Interface Name	NAT ID Number	Network Address	Network Mask for This Address
Inside	1	10.20.10.0	255.255.255.0

Example B-2 depicts the individual configuration commands for each of the items listed in Tables B-6 through B-9.

Example B-2   *Firewall Configuration for the Minneapolis Office*

```
nameif ethernet0 outside security0
nameif ethernet1 inside security100

interface ethernet0 100full
interface ethernet1 100full

ip address inside 10.20.10.1 255.255.255.0
ip address outside 192.168.2.2 255.255.255.0

hostname MN-PIX

nat (inside) 1 10.20.10.0 255.255.255.0
global (outside) 1 192.168.2.12-192.168.2.250 netmask 255.255.255.0
global (outside) 1 192.168.2.252 netmask 255.255.255.0


route outside 0.0.0.0 0.0.0.0 192.168.2.1
```

Basic Configuration Information for PIX Houston

Tables B-10 through B-13 provide the information needed to configure the PIX Firewall in the Houston office.

Table B-10 shows information about the physical interfaces of the Cisco PIX Firewall.

Table B-10   *Interface Information for the Houston PIX*

Interface Name	Hardware ID	Interface IP Address	Interface Speed
Outside	Ethernet0	192.168.3.2	100full
Inside	Ethernet1	10.30.10.1	100full

Table B-11 depicts what routes need to be configured on the PIX Firewall in the Houston office.

Table B-11 *Routing Information for the Houston PIX*

Interface Name	Destination Network IP Address	Network Mask	Gateway (Router) IP Address
Outside	0.0.0.0	0.0.0.0	192.168.3.1

Table B-12 lists the global IP addresses or address ranges that are used in conjunction with NAT for translation purposes.

Table B-12 *Global IP Address Information for the Houston PIX*

Interface Name	NAT ID Number	Beginning IP Address Range	End of IP Address Range
Outside	1	192.168.3.12	192.168.3.250
Outside	1	192.168.3.252	—

Table B-13 lists what addresses are dynamically translated on the PIX Firewall.

Table B-13 *NAT IP Address Information for the Houston PIX*

Interface Name	NAT ID Number	Network Address	Network Mask for This Address
Inside	1	10.30.10.0	255.255.255.0

Example B-3 depicts the individual configuration commands for each of the items listed in Tables B-10 through B-13.

Example B-3 *Firewall Configuration for the Houston Office*

```
nameif ethernet0 outside security0
nameif ethernet1 inside security100

interface ethernet0 100full
interface ethernet1 100full


ip address inside 10.30.10.1 255.255.255.0
ip address outside 192.168.3.2 255.255.255.0


hostname HOU_PIX

nat (inside) 1 10.30.10.0 255.255.255.0
global (outside) 1 192.168.3.12-192.168.3.250 netmask 255.255.255.0
global (outside) 1 192.168.3.252 netmask 255.255.255.0


route outside 0.0.0.0 0.0.0.0 192.168.3.1
```

Step 5 Define a crypto map for both Houston and Minneapolis:

```
crypto map Dukem-Map 20 ipsec-isakmp
crypto map Dukem-Map 20 match address 120
crypto map Dukem-Map 20 set peer 192.168.3.2
crypto map Dukem-Map 20 set transform-set myset

crypto map Dukem-Map 30 ipsec-isakmp
crypto map Dukem-Map 30 match address 130
crypto map Dukem-Map 30 set peer 192.168.2.2
crypto map Dukem-Map 30 set transform-set myset
```

Step 6 Apply the crypto map to the outside interface:

```
crypto map Dukem-Map interface outside
```

Step 7 Specify that IPSec traffic is implicitly trusted (permitted):

```
sysopt connection permit-ipsec
```

Step 8 Configure a NAT 0 policy so that traffic between the offices is excluded from NAT:

```
access-list VPN permit ip 10.10.10.0 255.255.255.0 10.30.10.0
  255.255.255.0
access-list VPN permit ip 10.10.10.0 255.255.255.0 10.20.10.0
  255.255.255.0
nat 0 access-list VPN
```

Example B-6 shows the complete configuration for the HQ PIX.

Example B-6 *HQ PIX Firewall Configuration*

```
nameif ethernet0 outside security0
nameif ethernet1 inside security100
nameif ethernet2 DMZ security50

enable password 8Ry2YjIyt7RRXU24 encrypted
passwd 2KFQnbNIdI.2KYOU encrypted
hostname HQ_PIX
fixup protocol ftp 21
fixup protocol http 80
fixup protocol h323 1720
fixup protocol rsh 514
fixup protocol smtp 25
fixup protocol sqlnet 1521
fixup protocol sip 5060
names
access-list dmz permit tcp any host 192.168.1.4 eq smtp
access-list dmz permit tcp any host 192.168.1.5 eq www
access-list dmz permit tcp any host 192.168.1.6 eq ftp
access-list dmz permit tcp any host 192.168.1.8 eq 514
!--- Traffic to HOU-PIX:
access-list 120 permit ip 10.10.10.0 255.255.255.0 10.30.10.0 255.255.255.0
!--- Traffic to MN-PIX:
```

continues

Example B-6 *HQ PIX Firewall Configuration (Continued)*

```
access-list 130 permit ip 10.10.10.0 255.255.255.0 10.20.10.0 255.255.255.0
!--- Do not Network Address Translate (NAT) traffic to other PIXes:
access-list VPN permit ip 10.10.10.0 255.255.255.0 10.30.10.0 255.255.255.0
access-list VPN permit ip 10.10.10.0 255.255.255.0 10.20.10.0 255.255.255.0
pager lines 24
logging on
no logging timestamp
no logging standby
no logging console
no logging monitor
no logging buffered
logging trap
no logging history
logging facility 20
logging queue 512
interface ethernet0 100full
interface ethernet1 100full
interface ethernet2 100full

mtu outside 1500
mtu inside 1500
ip address outside 192.168.1.2 255.255.255.0
ip address inside 10.10.10.1 255.255.255.0
ip address DMZ 172.16.31.1 255.255.255.0

ip audit info action alarm
ip audit attack action alarm
no failover
failover timeout 0:00:00
failover poll 15
failover ip address outside 0.0.0.0
failover ip address inside 0.0.0.0
arp timeout 14400

global (outside) 1 192.168.1.12-192.168.1.250 netmask 255.255.255.0
global (outside) 1 192.168.1.252 netmask 255.255.255.0
nat (inside) 1 10.10.10.0 255.255.255.0
!--- Do not NAT traffic to other PIXes:
nat (inside) 0 access-list VPN

static (DMZ,outside) 192.168.1.4  172.16.31.4 netmask 255.255.255.255 0 0
static (DMZ,outside) 192.168.1.5  172.16.31.5 netmask 255.255.255.255 0 0
static (DMZ,outside) 192.168.1.6  172.16.31.6 netmask 255.255.255.255 0 0
static (DMZ,outside) 192.168.1.8  172.16.31.7 netmask 255.255.255.255 0 0
static (inside,outside) 192.168.1.7  10.10.10.7 netmask 255.255.255.255 0 0

access-group DMZ in interface DMZ
access-group acl_out in interface outside
route outside 0.0.0.0 0.0.0.0 192.168.1.1
timeout xlate 3:00:00
timeout conn 1:00:00 half-closed 0:10:00 udp 0:02:00 rpc 0:10:00
h323 0:05:00 sip 0:30:00 sip_media 0:02:00
```

Example B-6   *HQ PIX Firewall Configuration (Continued)*

```
timeout uauth 0:05:00 absolute

aaa-server TACACS+ protocol tacacs+
aaa-server RADIUS protocol radius
aaa-server TACACS+ (inside) host 10.10.10.7
aaa authentication include ftp inside 0.0.0.0 0.0.0.0 TACACS+
aaa authentication include telnet 0.0.0.0 0 0.0.0.0 TACACS+no snmp-server location
no snmp-server contact
snmp-server community public
snmp-server enable traps
floodguard enable
sysopt connection permit-ipsec
no sysopt route dnat
crypto ipsec transform-set myset esp-des esp-md5-hmac

!--- Traffic to HOU-PIX:
crypto map Dukem-Map  20 ipsec-isakmp
crypto map Dukem-Map  20 match address 120
crypto map Dukem-Map  20 set peer 192.168.3.2
crypto map Dukem-Map 20 set transform-set myset

!--- Traffic to MN-PIX:
crypto map toMinneapolis 30 ipsec-isakmp
crypto map Dukem-Map  30 match address 130
crypto map Dukem-Map  30 set peer 192.168.2.2
crypto map Dukem-Map  30 set transform-set myset
crypto map Dukem-Map  interface outside

isakmp enable outside
isakmp key ******** address 192.168.3.2 netmask 255.255.255.255
isakmp key ******** address 192.168.2.2 netmask 255.255.255.255
isakmp identity address
isakmp policy 10 authentication pre-share
isakmp policy 10 encryption des
isakmp policy 10 hash md5
isakmp policy 10 group 1
isakmp policy 10 lifetime 1000
telnet timeout 5
ssh timeout 5
terminal width 80
Cryptochecksum:fb446986bcad922ec40de6346e9e2729
: end
```

Configuring the Houston PIX Firewall, HOU_PIX, for VPN Tunneling

Step 1   Configure an ISAKMP policy:

```
isakmp enable outside
isakmp policy 10 authentication pre-share
isakmp policy 10 encryption des
isakmp policy 10 hash md5
```

```
isakmp policy 10 group 1
isakmp policy 10 lifetime 1000
```

Step 2 Configure a preshared key and associate it with the peer (Houston and Minneapolis):

```
crypto isakmp key sept1302 address 192.168.1.2
```

Step 3 Configure the supported IPSec transforms:

```
crypto ipsec transform-set myset esp-des esp-md5-hmac
```

Step 4 Create an access list:

```
access-list 110 permit ip 10.30.10.0 255.255.255.0 10.10.10.0
    255.255.255.0
```

Step 5 Define a crypto map for both Houston and Minneapolis:

```
crypto map Dukem-Map 20 ipsec-isakmp
crypto map Dukem-Map 20 match address 110
crypto map Dukem-Map 20 set peer 192.168.1.2
crypto map Dukem-Map 20 set transform-set myset
```

Step 6 Apply the crypto map to the outside interface:

```
crypto map Dukem-Map interface outside
```

Step 7 Specify that IPSec traffic is implicitly trusted (permitted):

```
sysopt connection permit-ipsec
```

Step 8 Configure a NAT 0 policy so that traffic between the offices is excluded from NAT:

```
access-list VPN permit ip 10.30.10.0 255.255.255.0 10.10.10.0
    255.255.255.0
nat 0 access-list VPN
```

Example B-7 shows the Houston PIX configuration.

Example B-7 *Houston PIX Firewall Configuration*

```
nameif ethernet0 outside security0
nameif ethernet1 inside security100
enable password 8Ry2YjIyt7RRXU24 encrypted
passwd 2KFQnbNIdI.2KYOU encrypted
hostname HOU_PIX
fixup protocol ftp 21
fixup protocol http 80
fixup protocol h323 1720
fixup protocol rsh 514
fixup protocol smtp 25
fixup protocol sqlnet 1521
fixup protocol sip 5060
names
!--- Traffic to Reston HQ:
```

Example B-7   *Houston PIX Firewall Configuration (Continued)*

```
access-list 110 permit ip 10.30.10.0 255.255.255.0 10.10.10.0 255.255.255.0
!--- Do not NAT traffic to Reston HQ:
access-list VPN permit ip 10.30.10.0 255.255.255.0 10.10.10.0 255.255.255.0
pager lines 24
logging on
no logging timestamp
no logging standby
no logging console
no logging monitor
no logging buffered
logging trap 6
no logging history
logging facility 20
logging queue 512
interface ethernet0 100full
interface ethernet1 100full
mtu outside 1500
mtu inside 1500
ip address outside 192.168.3.2 255.255.255.0
ip address inside 10.30.10.1 255.255.255.0
ip audit info action alarm
ip audit attack action alarm
no failover
failover timeout 0:00:00
failover poll 15
failover ip address outside 0.0.0.0
failover ip address inside 0.0.0.0
arp timeout 14400

global (outside) 1 192.168.3.12-192.168.3.250 netmask 255.255.255.0
global (outside) 1 192.168.3.252 netmask 255.255.255.0
nat (inside) 1 10.30.10.0 255.255.255.0
!--- Do not NAT traffic to Reston HQ:
nat (inside) 0 access-list VPN
route outside 0.0.0.0 0.0.0.0 192.168.3.1 1

timeout xlate 3:00:00
timeout conn 1:00:00 half-closed 0:10:00 udp 0:02:00 rpc 0:10:00
h323 0:05:00 sip 0:30:00 sip_media 0:02:00
timeout uauth 0:05:00 absolute
aaa-server TACACS+ protocol tacacs+
aaa-server RADIUS protocol radius
no snmp-server location
no snmp-server contact
snmp-server community public
no snmp-server enable traps
floodguard enable
sysopt connection permit-ipsec
no sysopt route dnat
crypto ipsec transform-set myset esp-des esp-md5-hmac
!--- Traffic to Reston HQ:
crypto map Dukem-Map  10 ipsec-isakmp
```

continues

Example B-7 *Houston PIX Firewall Configuration (Continued)*

```
crypto map Dukem-Map  10 match address 110
crypto map Dukem-Map  10 set peer 192.168.1.2
crypto map Dukem-Map  10 set transform-set myset
crypto map Dukem-Map  interface outside
isakmp enable outside
isakmp key ******** address 192.168.1.2 netmask 255.255.255.255
  no-xauth no-config-mode
isakmp identity address
isakmp policy 10 authentication pre-share
isakmp policy 10 encryption des
isakmp policy 10 hash md5
isakmp policy 10 group 1
isakmp policy 10 lifetime 1000
telnet timeout 5
ssh timeout 5
terminal width 80
Cryptochecksum:b23cc9772a79ea76d711ea747f182a5f
```

Configuring the Minneapolis PIX Firewall, MN_PIX, for VPN Tunneling

Step 1 Configure an ISAKMP policy:

```
isakmp enable outside
isakmp policy 10 authentication pre-share
isakmp policy 10 encryption des
isakmp policy 10 hash md5
isakmp policy 10 group 1
isakmp policy 10 lifetime 1000
```

Step 2 Configure a preshared key and associate it with the peer (Houston and Minneapolis):

```
crypto isakmp key sept1302 address 192.168.1.2
```

Step 3 Configure the supported IPSec transforms:

```
crypto ipsec transform-set myset esp-des esp-md5-hmac
```

Step 4 Create an access list:

```
access-list 110 permit ip 10.20.10.0 255.255.255.0 10.10.10.0
  255.255.255.0
```

Step 5 Define a crypto map for both Houston and Minneapolis:

```
crypto map Dukem-Map 20 ipsec-isakmp
crypto map Dukem-Map 20 match address 110
crypto map Dukem-Map 20 set peer 192.168.1.2
crypto map Dukem-Map 20 set transform-set myset
```

Step 6 Apply the crypto map to the outside interface:

```
crypto map Dukem-Map interface outside
```

Step 7 Specify that IPSec traffic be implicitly trusted (permitted):

```
sysopt connection permit-ipsec
```

Step 8 Configure a NAT 0 policy so that traffic between the offices is excluded from NAT:

```
access-list VPN permit ip 10.20.10.0 255.255.255.0 10.30.10.0
   255.255.255.0
nat 0 access-list VPN
```

Example B-8 shows the configuration for the Minneapolis PIX Firewall.

Example B-8 *Minneapolis PIX Firewall Configuration*

```
nameif ethernet0 outside security0
nameif ethernet1 inside security100
enable password 8Ry2YjIyt7RRXU24 encrypted
passwd 2KFQnbNIdI.2KYOU encrypted
hostname MN_PIX
fixup protocol ftp 21
fixup protocol http 80
fixup protocol h323 1720
fixup protocol rsh 514
fixup protocol smtp 25
fixup protocol sqlnet 1521
fixup protocol sip 5060
names
!--- Traffic to Reston HQ:
access-list 110 permit ip 10.20.10.0 255.255.255.0 10.10.10.0 255.255.255.0
!--- Do not NAT traffic to Reston HQ:
access-list VPN permit ip 10.20.10.0 255.255.255.0 10.10.10.0 255.255.255.0
pager lines 24
logging on
no logging timestamp
no logging standby
no logging console
no logging monitor
no logging buffered
logging trap 6
no logging history
logging facility 20
logging queue 512
interface ethernet0 100full
interface ethernet1 100full
mtu outside 1500
mtu inside 1500
ip address outside 192.168.2.2 255.255.255.0
ip address inside 10.20.10.1 255.255.255.0
ip audit info action alarm
ip audit attack action alarm
no failover
failover timeout 0:00:00
failover poll 15
failover ip address outside 0.0.0.0
```

Example B-8 *Minneapolis PIX Firewall Configuration*

```
failover ip address inside 0.0.0.0
arp timeout 14400

global (outside) 1 192.168.2.12-192.168.2.250 netmask 255.255.255.0
global (outside) 1 192.168.2.252 netmask 255.255.255.0
nat (inside) 1 10.20.10.0 255.255.255.0
!--- Do not NAT traffic to Reston HQ:
nat (inside) 0 access-list VPN
route outside 0.0.0.0 0.0.0.0 192.168.2.1 1

timeout xlate 3:00:00
timeout conn 1:00:00 half-closed 0:10:00 udp 0:02:00 rpc 0:10:00
h323 0:05:00 sip 0:30:00 sip_media 0:02:00
timeout uauth 0:05:00 absolute
aaa-server TACACS+ protocol tacacs+
aaa-server RADIUS protocol radius
no snmp-server location
no snmp-server contact
snmp-server community public
no snmp-server enable traps
floodguard enable
sysopt connection permit-ipsec
no sysopt route dnat
crypto ipsec transform-set myset esp-des esp-md5-hmac
!--- Traffic to Reston HQ:
crypto map Dukem-Map 10 ipsec-isakmp
crypto map Dukem-Map 10 match address 110
crypto map Dukem-Map 10 set peer 192.168.1.2
crypto map Dukem-Map 10 set transform-set myset
crypto map Dukem-Map interface outside
isakmp enable outside
isakmp key ******** address 192.168.1.2 netmask 255.255.255.255 no-xauth
  no-config-mode
isakmp identity address
isakmp policy 10 authentication pre-share
isakmp policy 10 encryption des
isakmp policy 10 hash md5
isakmp policy 10 group 1
isakmp policy 10 lifetime 1000
telnet timeout 5
ssh timeout 5
terminal width 80
Cryptochecksum:d962d33d245ad89fb7c9b4f0db3c2dc0
```

Verifying and Troubleshooting

After you configure the PIX for VPN, the next step is to verify the configuration. The **show**, **clear**, and **debug** commands are used to verify and troubleshoot your configuration.

show Commands

- **show crypto ipsec sa**—Displays the current status of the IPSec security associations. This is useful in determining if traffic is being encrypted.

- **show crypto isakmp sa**—Displays the current state of the IKE security associations.

debug Commands

If you have problems establishing any of the VPN tunnels, use the following commands for troubleshooting:

Step 1   If you are connected to the PIX via the console port, enable debugging on the console using this command:

```
logging console debugging
```

If you are connected to the PIX via Telnet, enable debugging using this command:

```
logging monitor debugging
```

Step 2   To view debug information related to the VPN configuration, use the following commands:

- **debug crypto ipsec**—Used to debug IPSec processing.

- **debug crypto isakmp**—Used to debug ISAKMP processing.

- **debug crypto engine**—Displays debug messages about crypto engines, which perform encryption and decryption.

Step 3   To clear security associations (SAs), use the following commands in the PIX's configuration mode:

- **clear [crypto] ipsec sa**—Deletes the active IPSec security associations. The keyword **crypto** is optional.

- **clear [crypto] isakmp sa**—Deletes the active Internet Key Exchange (IKE) security associations. The keyword **crypto** is optional.

Task 6: Configuring Failover

Failover is configured on the PIX only at the Reston site.

Step 1   Make sure that failover is enabled:

```
failover on
```

Failover is enabled by default.

Step 2   Configure **failover ip address** for all interfaces that have an IP address
configured on them:

```
failover ip address inside 10.1.1.2
failover ip address outside 192.168.1.3
failover ip address dmz 172.16.31.2
failover ip address failover 1.1.1.2
```

Step 3   Check the status of your failover configuration:

```
show failover

Failover On
Cable status: Unknown
Reconnect timeout 0:00:00
Poll frequency 15 seconds
This host: primary - Active
Active time: 225 (sec)
Interface failover (1.1.1.1): Normal (Waiting)
Interface dmz (172.16.31.1):  Normal (Waiting)
Interface outside (192.168.1.2): Normal (Waiting)
Interface inside (10.1.1.1): Normal (Waiting)
Other host: secondary - Standby
Active time: 0 (sec)
Interface failover (1.1.1.2: Unknown (Waiting)
Interface dmz (172.16.31.2): Unknown (Waiting)
Interface outside (192.168.1.3): Unknown (Waiting)
Interface inside (10.1.1.2): Unknown (Waiting)
```

Step 4   Enable stateful failover:

```
failover link failover
```

Step 5   Power on the secondary unit.

Step 6   Check the status of your failover configuration:

```
HQ_PIX# show failover
Failover On
Cable status: Normal
Reconnect timeout 0:00:00
Poll frequency 15 seconds
        This host: Primary - Active
                Active time: 123(sec)
                Interface failover (1.1.1.1): Link Down (Waiting)
                Interface dmz (172.16.31.1): Normal
                Interface outside (192.168.1.2): Normal
                Interface inside (10.1.1.1): Normal
        Other host: Secondary - Standby
                Active time: 0 (sec)
                Interface failover (1.1.1.2):Normal
                Interface dmz (172.16.31.2): Normal
                Interface outside (192.168.1.3): Normal
                Interface inside (10.1.1.2): Normal


    Stateful Failover Logical Update Statistics
        Link : failover
        Stateful Obj    xmit        xerr        rcv         rerr
        General         435         0           0           0
        sys cmd         415         0           0           0
        up time         0           0           0           0
        xlate           27          0           0           0
        tcp conn        203         0           0           0
        udp conn        0           0           0           0
        ARP tbl         0           0           0           0
        RIP Tbl         0           0           0           0


    Logical Update Queue Information
                        Cur     Max     Total
        Recv Q:         0       0       0
        Xmit Q:         0       1       614
```

What's Wrong with This Picture?

Now that you have successfully gone through the configuration scenarios in the previous sections, this section focuses on problem solving after or during an implementation of the Cisco PIX Firewall. Examples B-9 through B-11 show the configuration of three PIX firewalls for this exercise.

Example B-9   *Atlanta PIX Firewall Configuration*

```
1.    : Saved
2.    :
3.    PIX Version 6.2(2)
4.    nameif ethernet0 outside security0
5.    nameif ethernet1 inside security100
6.    nameif ethernet2 DMZ security70
7.    enable password ksjfglkasglc encrypted
8.    passwd kjngczftglkacytiur encrypted
9.    hostname Atlanta
10.   domain-name www.BranchVPN.com
11.   fixup protocol ftp 21
12.   fixup protocol http 80
13.   fixup protocol smtp 25
14.   fixup protocol skinny 2000
15.   names
16.   access-list inbound permit icmp any host 192.168.3.10
17.   access-list inbound permit tcp any host 192.168.3.10   eq www
18.   access-list inbound permit tcp any host 192.168.3.10 eq 443
19.   access-list DMZ permit udp 172.16.3.0 255.255.255.0 host 10.10.3.240 eq ntp
20.   access-list VPN permit ip 10.10.3.0 255.255.255.0 10.10.2.0 255.255.255.0
21.   access-list VPN permit ip 10.10.3.0 255.255.255.0 10.10.10.0 255.255.255.0
22.   access-list LosAngeles permit ip 10.10.3.0 255.255.255.0 10.10.10.0
      255.255.255.0
23.   access-list Boston permit ip 10.10.3.0 255.255.255.0 10.10.2.0 255.255.255.0
24.   pager lines 24
25.   logging on
26.   logging timestamp
27.   interface ethernet0 auto
28.   interface ethernet1 auto
29.   interface ethernet2 auto
30.   mtu outside 1500
31.   mtu inside 1500
32.   ip address outside 192.168.3.1 255.255.255.0
33.   ip address inside 10.10.3.1 255.255.255.0
34.   ip address DMZ 172.16.3.1 255.255.255.0
35.   arp timeout 14400
36.   global (outside) 1 192.168.3.20-200
37.   nat (inside) 1 0.0.0.0 0.0.0.0 0 0
38.   nat (inside) 0 access-list VPN
39.   static (DMZ,outside) 192.168.3.10 172.16.3.10 netmask 255.255.255.255 0 0
40.   access-group inbound in interface outside
41.   access-group DMZ in interface DMZ
42.   route outside 0.0.0.0 0.0.0.0 192.168.3.254 1
43.   timeout xlate 3:00:00
```

Example B-9 *Atlanta PIX Firewall Configuration (Continued)*

```
44.  timeout conn 1:00:00 half-closed 0:10:00 udp 0:02:00
45.  timeout uauth 0:05:00 absolute
46.  aaa-server TACACS+ protocol tacacs+
47.  aaa-server RADIUS protocol radius
48.  no snmp-server location
49.  no snmp-server contact
50.  snmp-server community public
51.  no snmp-server enable traps
52.  floodguard enable
53.  sysopt connection permit-ipsec
54.  crypto ipsec transform-set BranchVPN esp-3des esp-md5-hmac
55.  crypto ipsec transform-set NothingNew esp-3des esp-sha-hmac
56.  crypto map BranchVPN 10 ipsec-isakmp
57.  crypto map BranchVPN 10 match address LosAngeles
58.  crypto map BranchVPN 10 set peer 192.168.1.1
59.  crypto map BranchVPN 10 set transform-set BranchVPN
60.  crypto map BranchVPN 20 ipsec-isakmp
61.  crypto map BranchVPN 20 match address Boston
62.  crypto map BranchVPN 20 set peer 192.168.2.1
63.  crypto map BranchVPN 20 set transform-set BranchVPN
64.  crypto map BranchVPN interface outside
65.  isakmp enable outside
66.  isakmp key ******** address 192.168.1.1 netmask 255.255.255.255
67.  isakmp key ******** address 192.168.2.1 netmask 255.255.255.255
68.  isakmp identity address
69.  isakmp policy 20 authentication pre-share
70.  isakmp policy 20 encryption 3des
71.  isakmp policy 20 hash md5
72.  isakmp policy 20 group 2
73.  isakmp policy 20 lifetime 86400
74.  terminal width 80
75.  Cryptochecksum:e0c04954fcabd239ae291d58fc618dd5
```

Example B-10 *Boston PIX Firewall Configuration*

```
1.   : Saved
2.   :
3.   PIX Version 6.2(2)
4.   nameif ethernet0 outside security0
5.   nameif ethernet1 inside security100
6.   nameif ethernet2 DMZ security70
7.   enable password ksjfglkasglc encrypted
8.   passwd kjngczftglkacytiur encrypted
9.   hostname Boston
10.  domain-name www.BranchVPN.com
11.  fixup protocol ftp 21
12.  fixup protocol http 80
13.  fixup protocol smtp 25
14.  fixup protocol skinny 2000
15.  names
16.  access-list inbound permit icmp any host 192.168.2.10
```

continues

Example B-10 *Boston PIX Firewall Configuration (Continued)*

```
17.  access-list inbound permit tcp any host 192.168.2.10  eq www
18.  access-list inbound permit tcp any host 192.168.2.10 eq 443
     access-list DMZ permit tcp 192.168.1.13 255.255.255.255 192.168.2.11 eq 1521
19.  access-list DMZ permit udp 172.16.2.0 255.255.255.0 host 10.10.2.240 eq ntp
20.  access-list VPN permit ip 10.10.2.0 255.255.255.0 10.10.10.0 255.255.255.0
21.  access-list VPN permit ip 10.10.2.0 255.255.255.0 10.10.3.0 255.255.255.0
22.  access-list LosAngeles permit ip 10.10.2.0 255.255.255.0 10.10.10.0
     255.255.255.0
23.  access-list Atlanta permit ip 10.10.2.0 255.255.255.0 10.10.3.0 255.255.255.0
24.  pager lines 24
25.  logging on
26.  logging timestamp
27.  interface ethernet0 auto
28.  interface ethernet1 auto
29.  interface ethernet2 auto
30.  mtu outside 1500
31.  mtu inside 1500
32.  ip address outside 192.168.2.1 255.255.255.0
33.  ip address inside 10.10.2.1 255.255.255.0
34.  ip address DMZ 172.16.2.1 255.255.255.0
35.  arp timeout 14400
36.  global (outside) 1 192.168.2.20-200
37.  nat (inside) 1 0.0.0.0 0.0.0.0 0 0
38.  nat (inside) 0 access-list VPN
39.  static (DMZ,outside) 192.168.2.10 172.16.2.10 netmask 255.255.255.255 0 0
     static (DMZ,outside) 192.168.2.11 172.16.2.11 netmask 255.255.255.255 0 0
40.  access-group inbound in interface outside
41.  access-group DMZ in interface DMZ
42.  route outside 0.0.0.0 0.0.0.0 192.168.2.254 1
43.  timeout xlate 3:00:00
44.  timeout conn 1:00:00 half-closed 0:10:00 udp 0:02:00
45.  timeout uauth 0:05:00 absolute
46.  aaa-server TACACS+ protocol tacacs+
47.  aaa-server RADIUS protocol radius
48.  no snmp-server location
49.  no snmp-server contact
50.  snmp-server community public
51.  no snmp-server enable traps
52.  floodguard enable
53.  sysopt connection permit-ipsec
54.  crypto ipsec transform-set BranchVPN esp-3des esp-md5-hmac
55.  crypto ipsec transform-set NothingNew esp-3des esp-sha-hmac
56.  crypto map BranchVPN 10 ipsec-isakmp
57.  crypto map BranchVPN 10 match address LosAngeles
58.  crypto map BranchVPN 10 set peer 192.168.1.1
59.  crypto map BranchVPN 10 set transform-set BranchVPN
60.  crypto map BranchVPN 20 ipsec-isakmp
61.  crypto map BranchVPN 20 match address Atlanta
62.  crypto map BranchVPN 20 set peer 192.168.3.1
63.  crypto map BranchVPN 20 set transform-set BranchVPN
64.  crypto map BranchVPN interface outside
65.  isakmp enable outside
```

Example B-10 *Boston PIX Firewall Configuration (Continued)*

```
66.  isakmp key ******** address 192.168.1.1 netmask 255.255.255.255
67.  isakmp key ******** address 192.168.3.1 netmask 255.255.255.255
68.  isakmp identity address
69.  isakmp policy 20 authentication pre-share
70.  isakmp policy 20 encryption 3des
71.  isakmp policy 20 hash md5
72.  isakmp policy 20 group 2
73.  isakmp policy 20 lifetime 86400
74.  terminal width 80
75.  Cryptochecksum:e0c04954fcabd239ae291d58fc618dd5
```

Example B-11 *Los Angeles PIX Firewall Configuration*

```
1.   : Saved
2.   :
3.   PIX Version 6.2(2)
4.   nameif ethernet0 outside security0
5.   nameif ethernet1 inside security100
6.   nameif ethernet2 DMZ security70
7.   enable password HtmvK15kjhtlyfvcl encrypted
8.   passwd Kkjhlkf1568Hke encrypted
9.   hostname LosAngeles
10.  domain-name www.BranchVPN.com
11.  fixup protocol ftp 21
12.  fixup protocol http 80
13.  fixup protocol h323 1720
14.  fixup protocol rsh 514
15.  fixup protocol smtp 25
16.  fixup protocol sqlnet 1521
17.  fixup protocol sip 5060
18.  fixup protocol skinny 2000
19.  names
     access-list inbound permit tcp any host 192.168.1.9 eq ftp
20.  access-list inbound permit icmp any host 192.168.1.10
21.  access-list inbound permit tcp any host 192.168.1.10  eq www
22.  access-list inbound permit tcp any host 192.168.1.10 eq 443
23.  access-list inbound permit tcp any host 192.168.1.11  eq www
24.  access-list inbound permit tcp any host 192.168.1.11 eq 443
25.  access-list inbound permit tcp any host 192.168.1.12  eq www
26.  access-list inbound permit tcp any host 192.168.1.12 eq 443
27.  access-list inbound permit tcp any host 192.168.1.13  eq ftp
28.  access-list Exchange permit tcp any host 192.168.1.14 eq 25
     access-list Exchange permit tcp any host 192.168.1.14 eq 443
     access-list DMZ permit tcp 172.16.1.13 255.255.255.255 10.10.11.221 eq 1521
29.  access-list DMZ permit udp 172.16.1.0 255.255.255.0 host 10.10.10.240 eq ntp
30.  access-list VPN permit ip 10.10.10.0 255.255.255.0 10.10.2.0 255.255.255.0
31.  access-list VPN permit ip 10.10.10.0 255.255.255.0 10.10.3.0 255.255.255.0
32.  access-list Boston permit ip 10.10.10.0 255.255.255.0 10.10.2.0 255.255.255.0
33.  access-list Atlanta permit ip 10.10.10.0 255.255.255.0 10.10.3.0 255.255.255.0
34.  pager lines 24
35.  logging on
```

continues

Example B-11 *Los Angeles PIX Firewall Configuration*

```
36.  logging timestamp
37.  interface ethernet0 auto
38.  interface ethernet1 auto
39.  interface ethernet2 auto
40.  mtu outside 1500
41.  mtu inside 1500
42.  ip address outside 192.168.1.1 255.255.255.0
43.  ip address inside 10.10.10.1 255.255.255.0
44.  ip address DMZ 172.16.1.1 255.255.255.0
45.  failover
46.  failover timeout 0:00:00
47.  failover poll 15
48.  failover ip address outside 192.168.1.2
49.  failover ip address inside 10.10.10.2
50.  failover ip address DMZ 172.16.1.2
51.  arp timeout 14400
52.  global (outside) 1 192.168.1.20-250
53.  nat (inside) 1 0.0.0.0 0.0.0.0 0 0
54.  nat (inside) 0 access-list VPN
55.  static (DMZ,outside) 192.168.1.10 172.16.1.10 netmask 255.255.255.255 0 0
56.  static (DMZ,outside) 192.168.1.11 172.16.1.11 netmask 255.255.255.255 0 0
57.  static (DMZ,outside) 192.168.1.12 172.16.1.12 netmask 255.255.255.255 0 0
58.  static (DMZ,outside) 192.168.1.13 172.16.1.13 netmask 255.255.255.255 0 0
     static (DMZ,outside) 192.168.1.14 172.16.1.14 netmask 255.255.255.255 0 0
59.  access-group inbound in interface outside
     access-group Exchange in interface outside
60.  access-group DMZ in interface DMZ
61.  route outside 0.0.0.0 0.0.0.0 192.168.1.254 1
62.  timeout xlate 3:00:00
63.  timeout conn 1:00:00 half-closed 0:10:00 udp 0:02:00 rpc 0:10:00 h323 0:05:00
     sip 0:30:00 sip_media 0:02:00
64.  timeout uauth 0:05:00 absolute
65.  aaa-server TACACS+ protocol tacacs+
66.  aaa-server RADIUS protocol radius
67.  no snmp-server location
68.  no snmp-server contact
69.  snmp-server community public
70.  no snmp-server enable traps
71.  floodguard enable
72.  sysopt connection permit-ipsec
73.  no sysopt route dnat
74.  crypto ipsec transform-set BranchVPN esp-3des esp-md5-hmac
75.  crypto ipsec transform-set NothingNew esp-3des esp-sha-hmac
76.  crypto map BranchVPN 10 ipsec-isakmp
77.  crypto map BranchVPN 10 match address Boston
78.  crypto map BranchVPN 10 set peer 192.168.2.1
79.  crypto map BranchVPN 10 set transform-set BranchVPN
80.  crypto map BranchVPN 20 ipsec-isakmp
81.  crypto map BranchVPN 20 match address Atlanta
82.  crypto map BranchVPN 20 set peer 192.168.3.1
83.  crypto map BranchVPN 20 set transform-set BranchVPN
84.  crypto map BranchVPN interface outside
```

Example B-11 *Los Angeles PIX Firewall Configuration*

```
85.  isakmp enable outside
86.  isakmp key ******** address 192.168.2.1 netmask 255.255.255.255
87.  isakmp key ******** address 192.168.3.1 netmask 255.255.255.255
88.  isakmp identity address
89.  isakmp policy 20 authentication pre-share
90.  isakmp policy 20 encryption 3des
91.  isakmp policy 20 hash md5
92.  isakmp policy 20 group 2
93.  isakmp policy 20 lifetime 86400
94.  terminal width 80
95.  Cryptochecksum:e0clmj3546549637cbsFds54132d5
```

After you have reviewed the configuration files for the three PIX firewalls, answer the following questions (the answers appear in Appendix A):

1 The VPN session is established, but no traffic, or just one-way traffic, is passing between the firewalls. Ellen starts enabled logging and starts a **debug icmp trace.** She pings the other end of the VPN node and gets the following results:

```
LOCAL_PIX(config)# 609001: Built local-host inside:192.168.4.1
106014: Deny inbound icmp src outside:192.168.2.6 dst inside:192.168.4.1
  (type 8, code 0)
106014: Deny inbound icmp src outside:192.168.2.6 dst inside:192.168.4.1
  (type 8, code 0)
106014: Deny inbound icmp src outside:192.168.2.6 dst inside:192.168.4.1
  (type 8, code 0)
106014: Deny inbound icmp src outside:192.168.2.6 dst inside:192.168.4.1
  (type 8, code 0)
106014: Deny inbound icmp src outside:192.168.2.6 dst inside:192.168.4.1
  (type 8, code 0)
609002: Teardown local-host inside:192.168.4.1 duration 0:00:15
```

What do these results indicate and what could be causing this problem? How would you help Ellen resolve this issue?

2 Eric cannot get the VPN tunnel to work from HQ to the Philadelphia branch office. He starts a debug and gets the following results:

```
crypto_isakmp_process_block: src 172.16.172.40, dest 172.16.172.34
VPN Peer: ISAKMP: Added new peer: ip:172.16.172.40 Total VPN Peers:1
VPN Peer: ISAKMP: Peer ip:172.16.172.40 Ref cnt incremented to:1
  Total VPN Peers:1
OAK_MM exchange
ISAKMP (0): processing SA payload. message ID = 0

ISAKMP (0): Checking ISAKMP transform 1 against priority 10 policy
ISAKMP:      encryption DES-CBC
```

```
ISAKMP:        hash MD5
ISAKMP:        default group 1
ISAKMP:        auth pre-share
ISAKMP:        life type in seconds
ISAKMP:        life duration (basic) of 2400
ISAKMP (0): atts are acceptable. Next payload is 0
ISAKMP (0): SA is doing pre-shared key authentication using id type
ID_IPV4
 _ADDR
return status is IKMP_NO_ERROR
crypto_isakmp_process_block: src 172.16.172.40, dest 172.16.172.34
OAK_MM exchange

ISAKMP (0): processing KE payload. message ID = 0
ISAKMP (0): processing NONCE payload. message ID = 0
ISAKMP (0): processing vendor id payload
ISAKMP (0): processing vendor id payload
ISAKMP (0): remote peer supports dead peer detection
ISAKMP (0): processing vendor id payload
ISAKMP (0): speaking to another IOS box!

return status is IKMP_NO_ERROR
crypto_isakmp_process_block: src 172.16.172.40, dest 172.16.172.34
OAK_MM exchange
ISAKMP (0): processing ID payload. message ID = 0
ISAKMP (0): processing HASH payload. message ID = 0
ISAKMP (0): SA has been authenticated

ISAKMP (0): ID payload
        next-payload : 8
        type         : 1
        protocol     : 17
        port         : 500
        length       : 8
ISAKMP (0): Total payload length: 12
return status is IKMP_NO_ERROR
crypto_isakmp_process_block: src 172.16.172.40, dest 172.16.172.34
ISAKMP (0): processing NOTIFY payload 24578 protocol 1
        spi 0, message ID = 2457631438
ISAKMP (0): processing notify INITIAL_CONTACTIPSEC(key_engine): got a
queue
  event...
IPSEC(key_engine_delete_sas): rec'd delete notify from ISAKMP
IPSEC(key_engine_delete_sas): delete all SAs shared with    172.16.172.40
```

```
return status is IKMP_NO_ERR_NO_TRANS
crypto_isakmp_process_block: src 172.16.172.40, dest 172.16.172.34
OAK_QM exchange
oakley_process_quick_mode:
OAK_QM_IDLE
ISAKMP (0): processing SA payload. message ID = 133935992


ISAKMP : Checking IPSec proposal 1
ISAKMP: transform 1, ESP_DES
ISAKMP:    attributes in transform:
ISAKMP:       encaps is 1
ISAKMP:       SA life type in seconds
ISAKMP:       SA life duration (basic) of 28800
ISAKMP:       SA life type in kilobytes
ISAKMP:       SA life duration (VPI) of  0x0 0x46 0x50 0x0
ISAKMP:       authenticator is HMAC-MD5
IPSEC(validate_proposal): invalid local address 172.16.172.34
ISAKMP (0): atts not acceptable. Next payload is 0
ISAKMP (0): SA not acceptable!
ISAKMP (0): sending NOTIFY message 14 protocol 0
return status is IKMP_ERR_NO_RETRANS
crypto_isakmp_process_block: src 172.16.172.40, dest 172.16.172.34
ISAKMP (0:0): phase 2 packet is a duplicate of a previous packet.
```

What could be the cause of this problem?

3 Bruce is having problems establishing a VPN session to the Seattle office. He gets the following debug results:

```
IPSEC(crypto_map_check): crypto map mymap 10 incomplete. No peer or
   access-list specified. Packet discarded
```

What is causing this problem, and how would you help Bruce successfully establish a VPN tunnel to the Seattle office?

4 The web administrator in Los Angeles needs to maintain the web servers in the DMZ from the internal network using terminal services (TCP Port 3389). Is the firewall in Los Angeles configured to allow this access? Explain your answer.

5 The web administrator in Los Angeles also needs to administer the web servers in Boston and Atlanta. Are the three firewalls configured to allow this access? Explain your answer.

6 The web server 172.16.1.13 needs to access an Oracle database server that sits on a segment connected to the internal network at 10.10.11.221. The web server initiates the connection on TCP port 1521 and retrieves inventory data. Can this connection be completed? Explain your answer.

7 The web server 172.16.1.13 needs to access an Oracle database server on the DMZ in Boston using the address 172.16.2.11. The web server initiates the connection on TCP port 1521 to retrieve financial data. Can this connection be completed? Explain your answer.

8 Is the configuration solution to Question 7 a good idea? Explain your answer.

9 The company has installed an FTP server on the DMZ segment in Los Angeles that customers can access to download updates. The FTP server's address is 172.16.1.9. Can all external users access this FTP server? Explain your answer.

10 The exchange server is installed on the DMZ segment in Los Angeles using the address 172.16.1.14. The firewall is configured to allow SMTP access for inbound mail and SSL access for users who want to connect using Outlook Web Access via an HTTPS connection. Will any users be able to receive their mail with this configuration? Explain your answer.

11 What needs to be done in Los Angeles to allow access to the mail server?

GLOSSARY

A

access list. A list kept by routers to control access to or from the router for a number of services (for example, to prevent packets with a certain IP address from leaving a particular interface on the router or firewall).

acknowledgment (ACK). A notification sent from one network device to another to acknowledge that an event occurred (such as the receipt of a message). See also *negative acknowledgment (NAK)*.

ActiveX. Microsoft's Windows-specific non-Java technique for writing applets. ActiveX applets take considerably longer to download than the equivalent Java applets; however, they more fully exploit the features of Windows 95. ActiveX sometimes is said to be a superset of Java. See also *applet* and *Java*.

address resolution. Generally, a method of resolving differences between computer addressing schemes. Address resolution usually specifies a method of mapping network layer (Layer 3) addresses to data link layer (Layer 2) addresses.

aggressive mode. The connection mode that eliminates several steps during IKE authentication negotiation (phase 1) between two or more IPSec peers. Aggressive mode is faster than main mode but not as secure.

AH. Authentication Header. A security protocol that provides data authentication and optional antireplay services. AH is embedded in the data to be protected (a full IP datagram).

algorithm. A well-defined rule or process for arriving at a solution to a problem. In networking, algorithms commonly are used to determine the best route for traffic from a particular source to a particular destination.

antireplay. A security service in which the receiver can reject old or duplicate packets to protect itself against replay attacks. IPSec provides this optional service by use of a sequence number combined with the use of data authentication. PIX Firewall IPSec provides this service whenever it provides the data authentication service, except when the service is unavailable for manually established security associations (that is, security associations established by manual configuration and not by IKE).

applet. A small program, often used in the context of a Java-based program, that is compiled and embedded in an HTML page. See also *ActiveX* and *Java*.

application layer. Layer 7 of the OSI reference model. This layer provides services to application processes (such as e-mail, file transfer, and terminal emulation) that are outside the OSI reference model. The application layer identifies and establishes the availability of intended communication partners (and the resources required to connect with them), synchronizes cooperating applications, and establishes agreement on the procedures for error recovery and control of data integrity. See also *data link layer, network layer, physical layer, presentation layer, session layer,* and *transport layer.*

authentication. In security, verifying the identity of a person or process.

B

bit. A binary digit used in the binary numbering system. Can be 0 or 1.

C

certificate. A digital representation of user or device attributes, including a public key, that is signed with an authoritative private key.

certification authority (CA). Responsible for managing digital certificate requests and issuing digital certificates to participating IPSec network peers. These services provide centralized key management for the participating peers.

Cisco IOS Software. Cisco system software that provides common functionality, scalability, and security for all products under the CiscoFusion architecture. Cisco IOS allows centralized, integrated, automated installation and management of internetworks while ensuring support for a wide variety of protocols, media, services, and platforms.

console. DTE through which commands are entered into a host.

cryptographic algorithm. An algorithm that employs the science of cryptography, including encryption algorithms, cryptographic hash algorithms, digital signature algorithms, and key agreement algorithms.

cryptographic key. Usually shortened to just "key." An input parameter that varies the transformation performed by a cryptographic algorithm.

D

Data Encryption Standard (DES). A standard cryptographic algorithm developed by the U.S. National Bureau of Standards.

data flow. A grouping of traffic, identified by a combination of source address/mask, destination address/mask, IP next protocol field, and source and destination ports, in which the protocol and port fields can have the values of any. In effect, all traffic matching a specific combination of these values is grouped logically into a data flow. A data flow can represent a single TCP connection between two hosts, or it can represent all the traffic between two subnets. IPSec protection is applied to data flows.

data link layer. Layer 2 of the OSI reference model. Provides reliable transit of data across a physical link. The data link layer is concerned with physical addressing, network topology, line discipline, error notification, ordered delivery of frames, and flow control. The IEEE divides this layer into two sublayers: the MAC sublayer and the LLC sublayer. Sometimes this is simply called the link layer. See also *application layer, network layer, physical layer, presentation layer, session layer,* and *transport layer.*

decrypt. Cryptographically restores ciphertext to the plaintext form it had before encryption.

decryption. Reverse application of an encryption algorithm to encrypted data, thereby restoring that data to its original, unencrypted state. See also *encryption.*

default route. A routing table entry that is used to direct frames for which a next hop is not explicitly listed in the routing table.

Diffie-Hellman algorithm. Introduced by Whitfield Diffie and Martin Hellman in 1976, this was the first system to use public keys, or asymmetric cryptographic keys. Today Diffie-Hellman is part of the IPSec standard. A protocol known as Oakley uses Diffie-Hellman, as described in RFC 2412. Oakley is used by the Internet Key Exchange (IKE) protocol (see RFC 2401), which is part of the overall framework called Internet Security Association and Key Management Protocol (ISAKMP; see RFC 2408).

Diffie-Hellman key exchange. A public key cryptography protocol that allows two parties to establish a shared secret over insecure communications channels. Diffie-Hellman is used within Internet Key Exchange (IKE) to establish session keys. Diffie-Hellman is a component of Oakley key exchange. Cisco IOS Software supports 768-bit and 1024-bit Diffie-Hellman groups.

digital certificate. A certificate document in the form of a digital data object (a data object used by a computer) to which is appended a computed digital signature value that depends on the data object.

digital signature. A value computed with a cryptographic algorithm and appended to a data object in such a way that any recipient of the data can use the signature to verify the data's origin and integrity.

DNS. Domain Name System. A system used on the Internet to translate names of network nodes into addresses.

dynamic address resolution. Using an address resolution protocol to determine and store address information on demand.

E

e-mail. Electronic mail. A widely used network application in which text messages are transmitted electronically between end users over various types of networks using various network protocols.

encapsulation. Wrapping data in a particular protocol header. For example, Ethernet data is wrapped in a specific Ethernet header before network transit. Also, when bridging dissimilar networks, the entire frame from one network is simply placed in the header used by the other network's data link layer protocol. See also *tunneling*.

encryption. Applying a specific algorithm to data to alter its appearance, making it incomprehensible to those who are not authorized to see the information. See also *decryption*.

end-to-end encryption. Continuous protection of data that flows between two points in a network. This is accomplished by encrypting data when it leaves its source, leaving it encrypted while it passes through any intermediate computers (such as routers), and decrypting it only when it arrives at its intended destination.

enterprise network. A large and diverse network connecting most major points in a company or other organization. It differs from a WAN in that it is privately owned and maintained.

ESP. Encapsulating Security Payload. A security protocol that provides data privacy services, optional data authentication, and antireplay services. ESP encapsulates the data to be protected.

Ethernet. A baseband LAN specification invented by Xerox Corporation and developed jointly by Xerox, Intel, and Digital Equipment Corporation. Ethernet networks use CSMA/CD and run over a variety of cable types at 10 Mbps. Ethernet is similar to the IEEE 802.3 series of standards.

F

Fast Ethernet. Any of a number of 100-Mbps Ethernet specifications. Fast Ethernet offers a speed increase that is ten times that of the 10BASE-T Ethernet specification while preserving such qualities as frame format, MAC mechanisms, and MTU. Such similarities allow the use of existing 10BASE-T applications and network management tools on Fast Ethernet networks. Based on an extension to the IEEE 802.3 specification.

firewall. A router or access server, or several routers or access servers, designated as a buffer between any connected public networks and a private network. A firewall router uses access lists and other methods to ensure the security of the private network.

flow. A stream of data traveling between two endpoints across a network (for example, from one LAN station to another). Multiple flows can be transmitted on a single circuit.

G

Gb. Gigabit. Approximately 1,000,000,000 bits.

Gbps. Gigabits per second.

Gigabit Ethernet. A standard for high-speed Ethernet approved by the IEEE (Institute of Electrical and Electronic Engineers) 802.3z standards committee in 1996.

GUI. Graphical user interface. A user environment that uses pictorial as well as textual representations of applications' input and output and the hierarchical or other data structure in which information is stored. Such conventions as buttons, icons, and windows are typical, and many actions are performed using a pointing device, such as a mouse. Microsoft Windows and the Apple Macintosh are prominent examples of platforms that use a GUI.

H

H.323. Allows dissimilar communication devices to communicate with each other using a standardized communication protocol. H.323 defines a common set of codecs, call setup and negotiating procedures, and basic data transport methods.

hijack attack. A form of active wiretapping in which the attacker seizes control of a previously established communication association.

HMAC. Hash-based Message Authentication Code. A mechanism for message authentication that uses cryptographic hash functions. HMAC can be used with any iterative cryptographic hash function, such as MD5 or SHA-1, in combination with a secret shared key. HMAC's cryptographic strength depends on the properties of the underlying hash function.

HMAC-MD5. Hashed Message Authentication Codes with MD5 (see RFC 2104). A keyed version of MD5 that lets two parties validate transmitted information using a shared secret.

HTML. Hypertext Markup Language. A simple hypertext document formatting language that uses tags to indicate how a given part of a document should be interpreted by a viewing application, such as a web browser.

HTTP. Hypertext Transfer Protocol. The protocol used by web browsers and web servers to transfer files, such as text and graphic files.

I

ICMP. Internet Control Message Protocol. A network layer Internet protocol that reports errors and provides other information relevant to IP packet processing. See RFC 792.

IKE. Internet Key Exchange. Establishes a shared security policy and authenticates keys for services that require keys, such as IPSec. Before any IPSec traffic can be passed, each router/firewall/host must verify its peer's identity. This can be done by manually entering preshared keys into both hosts or by using a CA service.

Internet. The largest global internetwork. It connects tens of thousands of networks worldwide and has a "culture" that focuses on research and standardization based on real-life use. Many leading-edge network technologies come from the Internet community. The Internet evolved in part from ARPANET. The Internet used to be called the DARPA Internet. Do not confuse it with the general term *internet*.

intrusion detection. A security service that monitors and analyzes system events for the purpose of finding (and providing real-time or near-real-time warnings about) unauthorized attempts to access system resources.

IP. Internet Protocol. A network layer protocol in the TCP/IP stack that offers a connectionless internetwork service. IP provides features for addressing, type-of-service specification, fragmentation and reassembly, and security. Defined in RFC 791.

IP address. A 32-bit address assigned to hosts using TCP/IP. An IP address belongs to one of five classes (A, B, C, D, or E) and is written as four octets separated by periods (called dotted-decimal format). Each address consists of a network number, an optional subnetwork number, and a host number. The network and subnetwork numbers together are used for routing, and the host number is used to address an individual host within the network or subnetwork. A subnet mask is used to extract network and subnetwork information from the IP address. CIDR provides a new way of representing IP addresses and subnet masks. Also called an *Internet address*.

IPSec. IP Security. A framework of open standards that provides data confidentiality, data integrity, and data authentication between participating peers. IPSec provides these security services at the IP layer. IPSec uses IKE to handle the negotiation of protocols and algorithms based on local policy and to generate the encryption and authentication keys it uses. IPSec can protect one or more data flows between a pair of hosts, between a pair of security gateways, or between a security gateway and a host.

IPSec client. An IPSec host that establishes IPSec tunnel(s) between itself and a security gateway/IPSec client to protect traffic for itself.

IP spoofing. An attack that occurs when an attacker outside your network pretends to be a trusted user either by using an IP address that is within the range of IP addresses for your network or by using an authorized external IP address that you trust and to which you want to provide access to specified resources on your network. If an attacker gets access to your IPSec security parameters, he or she can masquerade as the remote user authorized to connect to the corporate network.

ISAKMP. Internet Security Association and Key Management Protocol. The Internet IPSec protocol (see RFC 2408) that negotiates, establishes, modifies, and deletes security associations. It also exchanges key generation and authentication data (independent of the details of any specific key generation technique), key establishment protocols, encryption algorithms, or authentication mechanisms.

J

Java. An object-oriented programming language developed at Sun Microsystems to solve a number of problems in modern programming practice. The Java language is used extensively on the World Wide Web, particularly for applets.

K

Kb. Kilobit. Approximately 1000 bits.

kbps. Kilobits per second. A bit rate expressed in thousands of bits per second.

key pair. A set of mathematically related keys that consists of a public key and a private key. It is used for asymmetric cryptography and is generated in a way that makes it computationally infeasible to derive the private key from knowledge of the public key.

M

man-in-the-middle. A form of active wiretapping attack in which the attacker intercepts and selectively modifies communicated data to masquerade as one or more of the entities involved in a communication association.

Mb. Megabit. Approximately 1,000,000 bits.

MBps. Megabytes per second. A bit rate expressed in millions of binary bytes per second.

MD5. Message Digest 5. A one-way hashing algorithm that produces a 128-bit hash. Both MD5 and Secure Hash Algorithm (SHA) are variations on MD4 and are designed to strengthen the security of the MD4 hashing algorithm. Cisco uses hashes for authentication within the IPSec framework. Also used for message authentication in SNMP v.2. MD5 verifies the communication's integrity, authenticates the origin, and checks for timeliness.

N

negative acknowledgment (NAK). A response sent from a receiving device to a sending device indicating that the information received contained errors. See also *acknowledgment (ACK)*.

NetBIOS. Network Basic Input/Output System. An API used by applications on an IBM LAN to request services from lower-level network processes. These services might include session establishment and termination and information transfer.

network address translation (NAT). A mechanism for reducing the need for globally unique IP addresses. NAT allows an organization with addresses that are not globally unique to connect to the Internet by translating those addresses into globally routable address space. Also known as *Network Address Translator.*

network layer. Layer 3 of the OSI reference model. This layer provides connectivity and path selection between two end systems. The network layer is the layer at which routing occurs. It corresponds roughly to the path control layer of the SNA model. See also *application layer, data link layer, physical layer, presentation layer, session layer,* and *transport layer.*

NTP. Network Time Protocol. A protocol built on top of TCP that ensures accurate local timekeeping with reference to radio and atomic clocks located on the Internet. This protocol can synchronize distributed clocks within milliseconds over long time periods.

P

packet. A logical grouping of information that includes a header containing control information and (usually) user data. Packets most often are used to refer to network layer units of data. The terms *datagram, frame, message,* and *segment* also are used to describe logical information groupings at various layers of the OSI reference model and in various technology circles.

password. A secret data value, usually a character string, that is used as authentication information.

peer. A PIX Firewall or another device, such as a Cisco router, that participates in IPSec, IKE, and CA.

perfect forward secrecy (PFS). A cryptographic characteristic associated with a derived shared secret value. With PFS, if one key is compromised, previous and subsequent keys are not compromised, because subsequent keys are not derived from previous keys.

physical layer. Layer 1 of the OSI reference model. The physical layer defines the electrical, mechanical, procedural, and functional specifications for activating, maintaining, and deactivating the physical link between end systems. See also *application layer, data link layer, network layer, presentation layer, session layer,* and *transport layer.*

PKI. Public-key infrastructure. A system of certification authorities (CAs) (and, optionally, registration authorities [RAs] and other supporting servers and agents) that perform some set of certificate management, archive management, key management, and token management functions for a community of users in an application of asymmetric cryptography.

policy. Any defined rule that determines the use of resources within the network. A policy can be based on a user, device, subnetwork, network, or application.

port address translation (PAT). A translation method that lets the user conserve addresses in the global address pool by allowing source ports in TCP connections or UDP conversations to be translated. Different local addresses then map to the same global address, with port translation providing the necessary uniqueness. When translation is required, the new port number is chosen from the same range as the original following the convention of Berkeley Standard Distribution (SD). This prevents end stations from seeing connection requests with source ports apparently corresponding to the Telnet, HTTP, or FTP daemon, for example. As a result, Cisco IOS PAT supports about 4000 local addresses that can be mapped to the same global address.

port scan. An attack that sends client requests to a range of server port addresses on a host with the goal of finding an active port and exploiting a known vulnerability of that service.

presentation layer. Layer 6 of the OSI reference model. This layer ensures that information sent by a system's application layer can be read by another system's application layer. The presentation layer also is concerned with the data structures used by programs and therefore negotiates data transfer syntax for the application layer. See also *application layer, data link layer, network layer, physical layer, session layer,* and *transport layer.*

private key. A secret component of a pair of cryptographic keys used for asymmetric cryptography.

proprietary. Refers to information (or other property) that is owned by an individual or an organization and for which the use is restricted by that entity.

protocol. A formal description of a set of rules and conventions that governs how devices on a network exchange information.

proxy server. An intermediary program that acts as both a server and a client for the purpose of making requests on behalf of other clients. Requests are serviced internally or by passing them on, possibly after translation, to other servers. A proxy interprets and, if necessary, rewrites a request message before forwarding it.

public key. A publicly disclosable component of a pair of cryptographic keys used for asymmetric cryptography.

public-key certificate. A digital certificate that binds a system entity's identity to a public key value, and possibly to additional data items; a digitally signed data structure that attests to the ownership of a public key.

R

RADIUS. Remote Authentication Dial-In User Service. A database for authenticating modem and ISDN connections and for tracking connection time.

RFC. Request For Comments. A document series used as the primary means of communicating information about the Internet. Some RFCs are designated by the Internet Architecture Board (IAB) as Internet standards. Most RFCs document protocol specifications, such as Telnet and FTP, but some are humorous or historical. RFCs are available online from numerous sources.

risk assessment. A process that systematically identifies valuable system resources and threats to those resources, quantifies loss exposures (loss potential) based on estimated frequencies and costs of occurrence, and (optionally) recommends how to allocate resources to countermeasures to minimize total exposure.

risk management. The process of identifying, controlling, and eliminating or minimizing uncertain events that might affect system resources.

root CA. The ultimate CA that signs the certificates of the subordinate CAs. The root CA has a self-signed certificate that contains its own public key.

router. A network layer device that uses one or more metrics to determine the optimal path along which network traffic should be forwarded. Routers forward packets from one network to another based on network layer information. Occasionally called a gateway (although this definition of gateway is becoming increasingly outdated).

routing. The process of finding a path to a destination host. Routing is very complex in large networks because of the many potential intermediate destinations a packet might traverse before reaching its destination host.

RSA. A public-key cryptographic system that can be used for encryption and authentication. Rivest, Shamir, and Adelman invented this technique.

S

security association (SA). A description of how two or more entities use security services in the context of a particular security protocol (AH or ESP) to communicate securely on behalf of a particular data flow. It includes such things as the transform and the shared secret keys to be used to protect the traffic. The IPSec security association is established either by IKE or by manual user configuration. Security associations are unidirectional and are unique for each security protocol. So when security associations are established for IPSec, the security associations (for each protocol) for both directions are established at the same time. When you use IKE to establish the security associations for the data flow, the security associations are established when needed and expire after a period of time (or volume of traffic). If security associations are established manually, they are established as soon as the necessary configuration is completed, and they do not expire.

security gateway. An intermediate system that acts as the communications interface between two networks. The set of hosts (and networks) on the external side of the security gateway is viewed as untrusted (or less trusted), whereas the networks and hosts on the internal side are viewed as trusted (or more trusted). The internal subnets and hosts served by a security gateway are presumed to be trusted by virtue of sharing a common local security administration. In the IPSec context, a security gateway is the point at which AH and/or ESP are implemented to serve a set of internal hosts, providing security services for these hosts when they communicate with external hosts also employing IPSec (either directly or via another security gateway).

security management. One of five categories of network management defined by ISO to manage OSI networks. Security management subsystems are responsible for controlling access to network resources.

security parameter index (SPI). A number that, together with a destination IP address and security protocol, uniquely identifies a particular security association. When you use IKE to establish the security associations, the SPI for each security association is a pseudo-randomly derived number. Without IKE, the SPI is specified manually for each security association.

session layer. Layer 5 of the OSI reference model. This layer establishes, manages, and terminates sessions between applications and manages the data exchange between presentation layer entities. See also *application layer, data link layer, network layer, physical layer, presentation layer,* and *transport layer.*

SHA-1. Secure Hash Algorithm 1. An algorithm that takes a message of less than 264 bits and produces a 160-bit message digest. The large message digest provides security against brute-force collision and inversion attacks. SHA-1 (NIS94c) is a revision to SHA that was published in 1994.

Simple Mail Transfer Protocol (SMTP). An Internet protocol providing e-mail services.

spoofing. A packet illegally claims to be from an address from which it was not actually sent. Spoofing is designed to foil network security mechanisms, such as filters and access lists.

SSL. Secure Socket Layer. Encryption technology for the web used to provide secure transactions, such as the transmission of credit card numbers for e-commerce.

static route. A route that is explicitly configured and entered into the routing table. Static routes take precedence over routes chosen by dynamic routing protocols.

subnet address. The portion of an IP address that is specified as the subnetwork by the subnet mask. See also *IP address, subnet mask,* and *subnetwork.*

subnet mask. A 32-bit address mask used in IP to indicate the bits of an IP address that are used for the subnet address. Sometimes simply called a *mask.* See also *IP address.*

subnetwork. In IP networks, a network that shares a particular subnet address. Subnetworks are arbitrarily segmented by a network administrator to provide a multilevel, hierarchical routing structure while shielding the subnetwork from the addressing complexity of attached networks. Sometimes called a *subnet.* See also *IP address, subnet address,* and *subnet mask.*

symmetric cryptography. A branch of cryptography involving algorithms that use the same key for two different steps of the algorithm (such as encryption and decryption or signature creation and signature verification).

symmetric key. A cryptographic key that is used in a symmetric cryptographic algorithm.

T

TACACS+. Terminal Access Controller Access Control System Plus. A proprietary Cisco enhancement to Terminal Access Controller Access Control System (TACACS). Provides additional support for authentication, authorization, and accounting.

TCP. Transmission Control Protocol. A connection-oriented transport layer protocol that provides reliable full-duplex data transmission. TCP is part of the TCP/IP protocol stack. See also *TCP/IP.*

TCP/IP. Transmission Control Protocol/Internet Protocol. The common name for the suite of protocols developed by the U.S. Department of Defense in the 1970s to support the construction of worldwide internetworks. TCP and IP are the two best-known protocols in this suite.

Telnet. The standard terminal emulation protocol in the TCP/IP protocol stack. Telnet is used for remote terminal connection, allowing users to log in to remote systems and use resources as if they were connected to a local system. Telnet is defined in RFC 854.

TFTP. Trivial File Transfer Protocol. A simplified version of FTP that allows files to be transferred from one computer to another over a network, usually without the use of client authentication (for example, username and password).

timeout. An event that occurs when one network device expects to hear from another network device within a specified period of time but does not. The resulting timeout usually results in a retransmission of information or the dissolving of the session between the two devices.

transform. Lists a security protocol (AH or ESP) with its corresponding algorithms. For example, one transform is the AH protocol with the MD5-HMAC authentication algorithm. Another transform is the ESP protocol with the 56-bit DES encryption algorithm and the SHA-HMAC authentication algorithm.

transport layer. Layer 4 of the OSI reference model. This layer is responsible for reliable network communication between end nodes. The transport layer provides mechanisms for the establishment, maintenance, and termination of virtual circuits, transport fault detection and recovery, and information flow control. See also *application layer, data link layer, network layer, physical layer, presentation layer,* and *session layer.*

Trojan horse. A computer program that appears to have a useful function but also has a hidden and potentially malicious function that evades security mechanisms, sometimes by exploiting legitimate authorizations of a system entity that invokes the program.

tunnel. A secure communication path between two peers, such as two PIX Firewall units. It does not refer to using IPSec in tunnel mode.

tunneling. Architecture that is designed to provide the services necessary to implement any standard point-to-point encapsulation scheme. See also *encapsulation.*

U

UDP. User Datagram Protocol. A connectionless transport layer protocol in the TCP/IP protocol stack. UDP is a simple protocol that exchanges datagrams without acknowledgments or guaranteed delivery, requiring that error processing and retransmission be handled by other protocols. UDP is defined in RFC 768.

V

valid certificate. A digital certificate for which the binding of data items can be trusted; one that can be validated successfully.

Virtual Private Network (VPN). Allows IP traffic to travel securely over a public TCP/IP network by encrypting all traffic from one network to another. A VPN uses tunneling to encrypt all information at the IP level.

virus. A hidden, self-replicating section of computer software, usually malicious logic, that propagates by infecting another program. It does this by inserting a copy of itself into and becoming a part of that program. A virus cannot run by itself. The host program must run to make the virus active.

W

wildcard mask. A 32-bit quantity used in conjunction with an IP address to determine which bits in an IP address should be ignored when comparing that address with another IP address. A wildcard mask is specified when setting up access lists.

World Wide Web (WWW). A large network of Internet servers providing hypertext and other services to terminals running client applications, such as a browser.

worm. A computer program that can run independently, propagate a complete working version of itself onto other hosts on a network, and consume computer resources destructively.

INDEX

Symbols

^z command, 92

Numerics

3DES (Triple Data Encryption Standard), 164

A

AAA (authentication, authorization, and accounting), 8, 259–262
    configuration, 276–300
    Floodguard, 320
    servers
        identifying, 276–279
        specifying, 275
    support, 28
    troubleshooting, 303–306
aaa accounting command, 277
aaa authentication command, 277
aaa authentication console command, 282
aaa authorization command, 277
aaa-server command, 276–277
access
    AAA, 259–262
    attacks, 5
    authentication console, 282
    inbound configuration, 112–118
    lists, 115–118
    modes, 92
    NAS, 260
    networks
        security, 3
        threats, 4
        types of attacks, 4–6
        vulnerabilities, 3
    object grouping, 119–122
    PDM requirements, 212
    remote, 48–50
        SSH, 49–50
        Telnet, 48–49
    rules, 385
    VPN, 161
access control list. See ACL
Access Control Server (ACS), 28
access list entries (ACEs), 115
access-group command, 177, 385
access-list command, 173
accounting. See also AAA
    configuration, 295–299
    troubleshooting, 305
    viewing, 297
ACEs (access list entries), 115
ACL (access control list), 15
    downloading, 300–302
    TurboACL, 118–119

ACS (Access Control Server), 28
activation keys
    license, 163
    upgrading, 51–53
ActiveX, filtering, 248
Adaptive Security Algorithm (ASA), 17, 25–26
addresses
    command, 55
    IP
        global, 382, 384
        mapping, 381
        static port translation, 113–114
        translation, 29, 71–79
            bidirectional, 79
            commands, 73
            configuring multiple, 77–78
            NAT, 74
            PAT, 75
            static, 75–76
            troubleshooting, 79–82
advanced protocol handling, 123–124
aggressive mode (IKE), 164
AH (Authentication Header), 163
algorithms
    ASA, 17, 25–26
    SHA-1, 164
    transform sets, 175
alias command, 319
applets, filtering, 246–247
applications
    AVVID, 9–10
    multimedia
        H.323, 315–317
        RTSP, 315
        support, 314–317
    threats, 4
    types of attacks, 4–6
    vulnerabilities, 3
architecture
    AVVID, 9–10
    point-to-point architecture, 7, 26–27, 31–41, 68–76, 117,
    selecting, 7, 26–34, 36–41, 68–78, 84–85
Architecture for Voice, Video, and Integrated Data. See AVVID
arguments, crypto maps, 178
ASA (Adaptive Security Algorithm), 17, 25–26
assigning users to groups, 288
attacks
    guards, 317–321
    Syslog, 130–132
    threats, 4
    types of, 4–6
        access, 5–6
        DoS, 6
        reconnaissance, 5
    vulnerabilities, 3
authentication. See also AAA
    CAs, 167
    configuration, 279–287, 385
    cut-through proxy, 18, 26–27
    HMAC, 164
    IPSec, 162–164

CCSP Certification

Cisco Press

Get Prepared.   Get Experienced.   Get Certified.

Extend your CCSP™ self-study preparation to incorporate practical learning through KnowledgeNet interactive hands-on labs.

KnowledgeNet provides the Cisco knowledge and skills needed to gain—and retain— a competitive advantage. The KnowledgeNet suite of e-learning solutions is designed to fit every schedule, need, and learning preference. Cisco Press has partnered with KnowledgeNet to make it even easier to incorporate KnowledgeNet e-learning solutions into your CCSP exam preparation.

KnowledgeNet Interactive Hands-On 5-Pack LabWare Offer
6-Month Access—$49.00—normally $150.00

KnowledgeNet Cisco Secure PIX Firewall Advanced (CSPFA) LabWare 5-Pack

- Installing WebSENSE
- Configuring NAT, Statics, and Conduits
- Configuring the CSIS Feature Set
- Configuring Cisco Secure ACS NT
- Configure AAA and Authentication

KnowledgeNet Interactive Full LabWare Offer
6-Month Access—$249.00—a $500.00 value

Includes a complete KnowledgeNet LabWare offering that supports the Cisco Secure PIX Firewall Advanced course, including simulated exams to further retention and to help prepare for CCSP certification.

To take advantage of these special offers, please call 1-877-688-3717, ext: 4678.

Visit **www.ciscopress.com/knowledgenet** to learn more about these CCSP LabWare offers and register to win prizes from Cisco Press and KnowledgeNet (see reverse for details).

CISCO SYSTEMS

Cisco Press

Register to WIN

During April–June 2003 KnowledgeNet and Cisco Press partner to bring you a special promotion. Go to **ciscopress.com/knowledgenet** to learn how you can

- **Win FREE Cisco Press books!**
- **Register to WIN** a Dell AXIM handheld with KnowledgeNet's *Introduction to IP Subnetting* course loaded onto it!

Many network administrators are baffled by the use of IP subnetting and subnets. KnowledgeNet's *Introduction to IP Subnetting* course will introduce the concepts of IP subnetting and subnets as well as lay a foundation for further study at CCNP level courses.

At the completion of this course you will understand:

— Decimal to binary conversion

— Classful IP addresses and private IP address ranges

— How and why we use subnetworks

— Calculating the number of subnets and hosts available using a custom subnet mask

— Calculating the network number, broadcast address, and valid range of host addresses when given an IP address and custom subnet mask

Visit **www.ciscopress.com/knowledgenet** from April–June 2003 to register to win!

KNOWLEDGENET
the best of a new breed™

ciscopress.com

Q

R

S

T

☐ **YES!** I'm requesting a **free** subscription to *Packet*™ magazine.

☐ No. I'm not interested at this time.

☐ Mr.
☐ Ms.

First Name (Please Print)   Last Name

Title/Position (Required)

Company (Required)

Address

City   State/Province

Zip/Postal Code   Country

Telephone (Include country and area codes)   Fax

E-mail

Signature (Required)   Date

☐ I would like to receive additional information on Cisco's services and products by e-mail.

1. Do you or your company:
   A ☐ Use Cisco products   C ☐ Both
   B ☐ Resell Cisco products   D ☐ Neither

2. Your organization's relationship to Cisco Systems:
   A ☐ Customer/End User   E ☐ Integrator   J ☐ Consultant
   B ☐ Prospective Customer F ☐ Non-Authorized Reseller   K ☐ Other (specify):
   C ☐ Cisco Reseller   G ☐ Cisco Training Partner
   D ☐ Cisco Distributor   I ☐ Cisco OEM   _____

3. How many people does your entire company employ?
   A ☐ More than 10,000   D ☐ 500 to 999   G ☐ Fewer than 100
   B ☐ 5,000 to 9,999   E ☐ 250 to 499
   c ☐ 1,000 to 4,999   f ☐ 100 to 249

4. Is your company a Service Provider?
   A ☐ Yes   B ☐ No

5. Your involvement in network equipment purchases:
   A ☐ Recommend   B ☐ Approve   C ☐ Neither

6. Your personal involvement in networking:
   A ☐ Entire enterprise at all sites   F ☐ Public network
   B ☐ Departments or network segments at more than one site D ☐ No involvement
   C ☐ Single department or network segment   E ☐ Other (specify):
                                                           _____

7. Your Industry:
   A ☐ Aerospace   G ☐ Education (K–12)   K ☐ Health Care
   B ☐ Agriculture/Mining/Construction U ☐ Education (College/Univ.) L ☐ Telecommunications
   C ☐ Banking/Finance   H ☐ Government—Federal   M ☐ Utilities/Transportation
   D ☐ Chemical/Pharmaceutical   I ☐ Government—State   N ☐ Other (specify):
   E ☐ Consultant   J ☐ Government—Local   _____
   F ☐ Computer/Systems/Electronics

CPRESS

PACKET™

Packet magazine serves as the premier publication linking customers to Cisco Systems, Inc. Delivering complete coverage of cutting-edge networking trends and innovations, *Packet* is a magazine for technical, hands-on users. It delivers industry-specific information for enterprise, service provider, and small and midsized business market segments. A toolchest for planners and decision makers, *Packet* contains a vast array of practical information, boasting sample configurations, real-life customer examples, and tips on getting the most from your Cisco Systems' investments. Simply put, *Packet* magazine is straight talk straight from the worldwide leader in networking for the Internet, Cisco Systems, Inc.

We hope you'll take advantage of this useful resource. I look forward to hearing from you!

Cecelia Glover
Packet Circulation Manager
packet@external.cisco.com
www.cisco.com/go/packet

PACKET™